EMBRACING
NON-DIRECTIVITY

REASSESSING
PERSON-CENTERED THEORY AND PRACTICE
FOR THE 21ST CENTURY

Edited by
Brian E. Levitt

PCCS BOOKS
Monmouth

First published in 2005

PCCS Books Ltd
Wyastone Business Park
Wyastone Leys
Monmouth
NP25 3SR
UK
Tel +44 (0)1600 891 509
www.pccs-books.co.uk

**Embracing Non-directivity: Reassessing person-centered theory
and practice for the 21st century**

A CIP catalogue record for this book is available from the British Library

ISBN 978 1 898059 68 4

Cover design by Old Dog Graphics
Printed by ImprintDigital, Exeter, UK

for Noel,
mahal na mahal kita, always

CONTENTS

PREFACE

Non-directivity is the distinguishing feature of the revolutionary, anti-authoritarian approach to psychotherapy and human relations developed by Carl Rogers. At its most basic, non-directivity implies being responsive to the client's direction. It implies that individuals have the capacity and the right to direct their own therapy and lives. This book brings together an international collection of person-centered theorists and practitioners, each exploring an important facet of non-directivity as it relates to person-centered theory and practice. Their writings examine the history, theory, applications, and implications of the non-directive attitude. Non-directivity emerges in these pages as *a way of being* that remains vital, flexible and highly relevant to the practice of person-centered therapy and other person-centered applications.

Three broad themes underlie the organization of the chapters in this book: historical and theoretical perspectives on non-directivity, the non-directive attitude in individual psychotherapy, and an exploration of ethical issues and applications of the non-directive attitude beyond the realm of individual psychotherapy. Barbara Brodley's introductory chapter lays out the basic meanings of non-directivity, challenging common misunderstandings and setting the stage for the chapters that follow. The first section of chapters opens with Brian Levitt's exploration of non-directivity as foundational to client-centered practice. An essential historical backdrop is presented in Nathaniel Raskin's review of historic events in the development of client-centered therapy and the person-centered approaches. Garry Prouty provides a thread that connects the non-directive aspects in the work of Carl Rogers, Eugene Gendlin, and his own Pre-Therapy (a powerful approach to working with people with 'psychosis' and those with a severe, pervasive learning disability or dementia that is perhaps the most profound contemporary development in non-directive theory and practice). Marvin Frankel and Lisbeth Sommerbeck follow this with an examination of a philosophical error that occurred in the development and presentation of client-centered theory. Their discussion brings greater clarity to understanding non-directivity and person-centered theory and practice. Françoise Ducroux-Biass grounds non-directivity in the philosophical traditions of Europe with her exploration of non-directivity as an ontological concept. Peter Schmid rounds out the first section with an exploration of non-directivity from anthropological, epistemological and ethical perspectives.

The section on non-directivity in individual psychotherapy opens with a chapter that offers a transcript from one of Barbara Brodley's audio-recorded, client-centered therapy demonstration sessions, and a discussion by Brian Levitt and Barbara Brodley on the non-directive elements in that session. Beth Freire provides us with a chapter that adds to the body of client-centered research, with a qualitative analysis of a complete 12-session course of psychotherapy from the perspectives of the client and the therapist. This chapter includes transcripts drawn from selected sessions.

Marvin Frankel explores the Socratic method of inducing self-examination, which he sees as the progenitor of directive schools of psychotherapy. He contrasts Socratic dialogue with non-directive empathic understanding, shedding new light on the meaning of the non-directive attitude in psychotherapy. Along the way, he analyzes portions of transcripts from the well-known Rogers and Gloria filmed demonstration session (Rogers, 1965), as well as transcripts from his own non-directive work with a man just diagnosed with cancer, and later with that man's wife.

In the now famous Wisconsin studies (Rogers, Gendlin, Kiesler and Truax, 1967), Rogers and his colleagues found mixed results, leading many to the unfortunate and mistaken conclusion that non-directive psychotherapy could not be effective with psychotic clients. Garry Prouty's development of Pre-Therapy (Prouty, 1994; Prouty, Van Werde and Pörtner, 2002) has since proven this is not the case. Lisbeth Sommerbeck examines her own non-directive work with people diagnosed with severe mental illnesses, often informed by her understanding of Prouty's Pre-Therapy. She includes portions of transcripts that highlight her insights.

Sometimes commonly accepted treatment practices and guidelines go unexamined because they have the appearance of being correct and carry the authority of popular usage. This is true with regard to established, directive practices and guidelines in the field of alcohol and substance abuse treatment. Sue Wilders questions conventional wisdom and makes a strong case for the efficacy of non-directive work with alcohol and substance users.

Jerold Bozarth first published 'The Art of "Being" in Psychotherapy' in 2001 in *The Humanistic Psychologist*. It is updated and appears as Chapter 12 in this volume under the title: 'The Art of Non-directive "Being" in Psychotherapy'. It is Bozarth's definitive statement on the place of non-directivity in the being of the therapist and also offers an illuminating journey through Jerold's professional life as a non-directive psychologist.

Clients are vulnerable to therapist influence and situational influences in therapy. Marge Witty begins the last section by tackling this issue in the context of non-directivity and presents non-directivity as an essential 'antidote' to sources of social influence in psychotherapy. Barry Grant presents non-directive therapy as an ethically grounded therapy, and provides insight into the implications for empathic understanding. Kathy Moon examines congruence in terms of theory, ethics and practice. Her exploration helps to resolve the confusion that many have over the place of congruence in non-directive practice.

Non-directivity has numerous applications beyond the realm of individual psychotherapy, and the final chapters of the book explore four such areas. Jerold Bozarth examines the history and development of the non-directive group, and formulates postulates about its efficacy. John McPherrin provides us with a history of and guide to non-directive psychotherapy with couples and families. In their chapter, Jeffrey and

Cecily Cornelius-White provide a meta-analysis of research in education and examine the efficacy of non-directivity. The last chapter of this section is a reprint of a small gem written by C.H. (Pat) Patterson and C. Edward Watkins Jr, first published in 1982 in *Measurement and Evaluation in Guidance*. Although non-directivity and assessment are often seen as incompatible, their seminal essay shows how the non-directive attitude can have a place in an area of practice that is largely seen as directive.

We come full-circle and conclude with Nathaniel Raskin's 1947 paper, 'The Nondirective Attitude', a paper that has been widely referenced but unpublished until now. It is found in this book as an historical afterword. Nat Raskin has been kind enough to provide a copy that included Carl Rogers' comments to him in the margins in longhand. These comments are incorporated as footnotes. Though non-directive therapy was relatively new at the time, Nat was quick to realise its depth. Given societal norms, he also recognized the potential for this promising approach to be misunderstood:

> It has become clear that learning nondirective therapy is not a matter of acquiring technique, but of gradually gaining the conviction that people do not have to be guided into adjustment, but can do it themselves when accepted as they are ... It is not surprising that learning this method and philosophy is a slow process. For acceptance is one of the principles of human relationships which does not run very deep in our culture. (1947/2005: 346, this volume)

These words still ring true. Raskin first identified the non-directive attitude in client-centered psychotherapy almost six decades ago. It remains a rich, radical and often misunderstood concept, providing the impetus for the writings that follow.

Brian Levitt
Toronto
Summer 2005

REFERENCES

Prouty GF (1994) *Theoretical Evolutions in Person-Centered/Experiential Therapy: Applications to schizophrenic and retarded psychoses*. Westport: Praeger-Greenwood.

Prouty GF, Van Werde D & Pörtner M (2002) *Pre-Therapy: Reaching contact-impaired clients*. Ross-on-Wye: PCCS Books.

Raskin NJ (1947/2005) The nondirective attitude. In BE Levitt (Ed) *Embracing Non-directivity: Reassessing person-centered theory and practice in the 21st century*. Ross-on-Wye: PCCS Books, pp. 529–47.

Rogers CR (1965) Transcript of Rogers and Gloria. In EL Shostrom (producer) *Three approaches to psychotherapy. Part 1: Client-centered therapy* (Film and Transcript). Corona del Mar, CA: Psychological and Educational Films.

Rogers CR, Gendlin ET, Kiesler DJ & Truax C (1967) *The Therapeutic Relationship with Schizophrenics*. Madison: The University of Wisconsin Press.

ACKNOWLEDGEMENTS

Noel Nera, the man I love and my partner in life, knows more than anyone what this book and these ideas mean to me. As an artist and as a person, his integrity is always an inspiration to me. He has been there from the beginning of my professional journey, and his support has been total. No acknowledgement could ever be enough.

Many people have influenced my professional development over the years. I count two among them as my mentors: Barbara Brodley and Garry Prouty. When I first had the idea for this book, I thought surely Barbara should be the editor—she had another suggestion. She responded lovingly to my insecurities and concerns along the way, and shared in my joy as the process unfolded. Her contributions have been integral to this project. Her mentorship has been invaluable to me. Garry Prouty is simply the most humble genius I have ever met. Those who know him know what a joy it is to be around him. His enthusiasm and scholarship continue to inspire me. The faith he always has shown in me is a precious gift. When I ran my ideas for this book by him, and asked if he would contribute a chapter, he quickly sent me a manuscript that fit perfectly with the concept of the book. I knew then that something special had begun.

My gratitude goes to my publisher, Pete Sanders. I cannot imagine an easier person to work with. From the start, he was open to everything I wanted this book to be, and he has always been available with helpful advice and support when I needed it. Thanks also go to the other folk at PCCS Books: Maggie Taylor-Sanders, Sandy Green and Heather Allan.

My gratitude also goes to Barry Grant and Jeffrey Cornelius-White for unselfishly allowing Nat Raskin's unpublished 1947 paper on the non-directive attitude to be published here, as it was promised to them first and is slated for publication in *The Person-Centered Journal* this year.

There is not enough space to acknowledge individually each of the authors in this book, though each is extraordinary. I hope I have adequately conveyed my gratitude to them personally. It has been an honour to work with each of them—I am humbled by their contributions here. Because of them, this book is now a reality. Special acknowledgement must go to Kathy Moon, who gave extra time and effort to help with issues and tasks beyond her own chapter. Her help made it possible for several other chapters to appear in this book, strengthening the overall work. Bert Rice helped also in this regard, so my thanks go to him as well. Special acknowledgement must also go to Sue Wilders, my sister across the pond. I have great admiration for the strength and courage in her voice and the passion behind her ideas. Her support over the years, and particularly during my work on this project, has meant so much to me.

I must also mention three unique places: in Chicago, in cyberspace, and in Markham, Ontario. I was lucky enough to spend a number of years training and then working at the Chicago Counseling and Psychotherapy Center, surrounded by staff and students who were dedicated to understanding and embodying client-centered principles in therapy, consultation/supervision and organizational work. The Center will always feel like home to me. The CCTPCA network (http://texaslists.net/cctpca) has been a home away from home, giving me a person-centered place to argue and discuss ideas over the last ten years or so. I have learned so much from all of the listserve participants, and this book, in many ways, evolved from discussions and relationships that occurred on the network. I would be remiss if I did not also mention Assamiea Tea Shop in Metro Square, Markham, Ontario—the friendliest staff, the warmest atmosphere, and my favourite sweetened green tea. Much of this book was edited over long hours with a green tea at my side.

Finally, and most importantly, you, the reader—my gratitude to you for wanting to understand non-directivity more fully. I hope these pages will inform, challenge and inspire you.

ABOUT THE NON-DIRECTIVE ATTITUDE[1]

Barbara Temaner Brodley

The non-directivity of client-centered therapy has been viewed as impossible to practice and as rigid (Kahn, 1999); as a myth (Bowen, 1996); and as passé—an early phase of client-centered therapy that has been long discarded (Lietaer, 1998). These views are wrong and reflect significant misunderstandings of the concept. The following remarks are an attempt to address some of these misunderstandings and to frame some of the concepts that will be explored in this book.

First, client-centered non-directivity refers to an *attitude*—the non-directive *attitude* (Raskin, 1947)—*not* to specific behavior. Further, attitudes are not defined in terms of behavior, although they affect behavior. They are defined in terms of intentions, sensibilities, feelings and values. Attitudes are manifested in intentions that adapt to particular circumstances—thus they cannot be rigid. Non-directivity in client-centered therapy refers to an attitude that shapes the therapist's total presence and all of his expression and communication (Brodley, 1997). It structures the therapist's intentions in relation to his individual clients.

Second, all therapies *influence* their clients. The universal goal of therapy is to influence clients towards growth and healing. A therapy *must* influence in order to be effective. If it does not influence the client, any therapeutic change that occurs is *entirely* due to the client, not the therapy. The non-directive issue exists at a different level from the discourse on therapy as influencing clients. Beyond this discourse, non-directivity is most clearly understood at the level of the therapist's *concrete intentions* towards his client and at the level of *the therapist's awareness* of how his behavior may be perceived and experienced by clients.

Third, the non-directive attitude is intrinsic to Rogers' formulation of the therapeutic attitudes (1957, 1959) and the way they are embodied by therapists (Bozarth, 2002). It is part of their essential meaning. Empathic understanding, unconditional positive regard and congruence are all non-directive in respect to the client. The concept of non-directivity comes into existence *within the meaning* of these therapeutic attitudes—they are the source of the non-directive principle. The therapist's *immediate goal* in respect to the attitudes is to experience and maintain them in relation to the client—not to use them

---

1 Revision of a paper presented at the Second International Congress on Psychotherapy, Vienna, July 8, 1999, and published in 1999 in *Person-Centred Practice*, 7, 79–82. Reproduced by kind permission.

to direct the client.

Empathic understanding is an attitude. In interaction with clients, this attitude often leads the therapist to make empathic understanding responses that closely follow the client. These empathic responses are behavior, but they are not made with the intention to direct the client in any way. The therapist's *intention* in communicating his empathic understanding is to permit the therapist's inner understandings to be confirmed or corrected by the client (Rogers, 1986; Brodley, 1998a). This purpose, to check inner understandings, involves no goal to influence the client's narrative content in any specific way, nor any goal to influence his process. Empathic understanding, of course, does have *the effect* of influencing both the client's content and his process. These effects are important for therapeutic efficacy, but they are not part of the therapist's experienced intentions in the interaction.

Unconditional positive regard is also an attitude. The therapist's goal is to experience and maintain this attitude toward each client. Unconditional positive regard affects all of the therapist's communication—both what is expressed and what is deliberately excluded from expression to avoid misunderstanding. But there is no directivity towards the client involved in this attitude. Unconditional positive regard is rarely, if ever, deliberately and explicitly communicated in therapy interactions, although it *is there* and clients perceive it.

Congruence is fundamentally a state of integration within the therapist (Brodley, 1998b; Haugh, 1998). Like unconditional positive regard, it requires no deliberate communication to the client at all. The therapist does sometimes make *congruent communications from his own frame of reference*—self-disclosures and other comments. These behaviors, however, are not themselves congruence. Rather, they are products of congruence and they are not intended to direct the client. They are usually offered to permit the client an accurate perspective on, or an understanding of, the therapist or his ideas. They permit the client further choices in the relationship.

What is the role of the non-directive attitude? There are two general answers: (1) It expresses *values* in the therapy relationship; (2) It is *intended to protect* the client. The values expressed through holding the non-directive attitude are trust in and respect towards the client. Trust is held in the client's capacities for constructive self-determination. Respect is expressed for the client as an autonomous being with the right to self-determination. The non-directive attitude is intended *to protect* the client's safety, his freedom, his autonomy, his self-determination, his sense of self. It protects his sense of being an accepted and effective self. It is also intended to protect the client from the therapist's inherent structural power as an authority within the therapeutic context (Brink, 1987; Burstow, 1987).

The non-directive attitude infused throughout client-centered therapy is grounded in ethics (Grant, 1985). As in medical ethics, a primary value is to do no harm. An assumption underpinning the ethical grounds for the non-directive attitude is that persons are highly vulnerable to external controls and that personal autonomy, self-determination and an accepted sense of self are fragile characteristics.

The non-directive attitude was not *formalized* in Rogers' theory (Prouty, 1999); it is implicit in his writings and in his own therapy behavior. There are several reasons that some of us *formalize* the attitude. One reason is that some therapy approaches, partly influenced by Rogers' ideas, have incorporated directive intentions within the basic attitudes, thereby altering them. Gendlin's (1974) experiential therapy is a prominent example of this (Brodley, 1990). Consequently it has been necessary to elevate non-directivity from *the implicit and informal principle* that it was in Rogers' theory and therapy, to a *formal attitude.* This is necessary in order to clarify a major difference between client-centered therapy and other related therapies *and to preserve the existence of non-directive client-centered therapy.*

Another reason the non-directive attitude is needed as an explicit and formal principle is that client-centered therapists occasionally volunteer communications from their own frame of reference (Brodley, 1999). They may make a comment, ask a question or emit spontaneous and impulsive responses from their own frame (for example, an expression of pleasure at a client's self-defined success). All therapist-frame responses should be, of course, embedded in the basic therapeutic attitudes. They are also tempered and shaped by the non-directive attitude. Making the non-directive attitude an explicit and formal principle allows for a clearer understanding of therapist intent in these communications—hopefully avoiding confusion with directive communications that may appear on the surface to be similar, yet are clearly different in underlying intent.

Further, in therapy there are times when the client is not engaged in a self-exploring narrative. For example, the therapist and client are working out arrangements about appointments, or discussing the ending of therapy. Or, the client asks questions or requests accommodations from the therapist. In these situations awareness of the non-directive attitude—awareness of its values and awareness of the need to protect the client—guides the therapist's way of answering, accommodating or otherwise interacting with his client (Brodley, 1997). The non-directive attitude shapes the therapist's expression in these interactions such that he continues to express respect for the client's autonomy and self-determination, and protect the client's safety, freedom and constructive sense of self *as much as possible.*

The non-directive attitude is psychologically profound; it is not a technique. Early in a therapist's development it may be superficial and prescriptive—'Don't do this' or 'Don't do that.' But with time, self-examination and therapy experience, it becomes an aspect of the therapist's character. It represents a feeling of profound respect for the constructive potential in persons and great sensitivity to their vulnerability. Therapy is an art. As an art, it involves freedom within great discipline. The mature non-directive client-centered therapist functions freely, with certain values and intentions embedded in his character, and with internalized disciplines.

In 1975 Evans asked Rogers 'would you say today that you have perhaps qualified somewhat this notion of being non-directive?' (p. 26). Rogers replied:

> No. I think perhaps I enriched it, but not really qualified it. I still feel that the person who should guide the client's life is the client. My whole philosophy and whole approach is to try to strengthen him in that way of being, that he's in charge of his own life and nothing that I say is intended to take that capacity or that opportunity away from him. (p. 26)

It seems pretty clear that Rogers meant he remained committed to the non-directive attitude. It is in the bones of his theory and practice. It is not a myth.

REFERENCES

Bowen MV-B (1996) The myth of nondirectiveness: The case of Jill. In BA Farber, DC Brink & PM Raskin (Eds) *The Psychotherapy of Carl Rogers: Cases and commentary.* New York: Guilford Press, pp. 84–94.

Bozarth JD (2002) Nondirectivity in the Person-Centered Approach. *Journal of Humanistic Psychology, 42*(2), 78–83.

Brink DC (1987) The issues of equality and control in the Client-Centered or Person-Centered Approach. *Journal of Humanistic Psychology, 27*(1), 27–37.

Brodley BT (1990) Client-centered and experiential: Two different therapies. In G Lietaer, J Rombauts & R Van Balen (Eds) *Client-Centered and Experiential Psychotherapy in the Nineties.* Leuven: Leuven University Press, pp. 87–108.

Brodley BT (1997) The nondirective attitude in client-centered therapy. *Person-Centered Journal, 4*(1), 18–30.

Brodley BT (1998a) Congruence and its relation to communication in client-centered therapy. *Person-Centered Journal, 5*(2), 83–116.

Brodley BT (1998b) Criteria for making responses in client-centered therapy. *Person-Centered Journal, 5*(1), 20–8.

Brodley BT (1999) Reasons for expressing the therapist's frame of reference in client-centered therapy. *Person-Centered Journal, 6*(1), 4–27.

Burstow B (1987) Humanistic psychotherapy and the issue of equality. *Journal of Humanistic Psychology, 18*(2), 5–35.

Evans RI (1975) *Carl Rogers, The Man and His Ideas.* New York: EP Dutton.

Gendlin ET (1974) Client-centered and experiential psychotherapy. In DA Wexler & LN Rice (Eds) *Innovations in Client-Centered Therapy.* New York: Wiley, pp. 211–46.

Grant B (1985) The moral nature of psychotherapy. *Counseling and Values, 29*(2), 141–50.

Haugh S (1998) Congruence: A confusion of language. *Person-Centred Practice, 6*(1), 44–50.

Kahn E (1999) On the concept of non-directivity in the person-centered approach. Presented at the Second International Congress on Psychotherapy in Vienna, July.

Lietaer G (1998) From nondirective to experiential: A paradigm unfolding. In B Thorne & E Lambers (Eds) *Person-Centred Therapy.* London: Sage, pp. 62–73.

Prouty GF (1999) Carl Rogers and experiential therapies: A dissonance? *Person-Centred Practice, 7*(1), 4–11.

Raskin NJ (1947/2005) The non-directive attitude. In BE Levitt (Ed) *Embracing Non-directivity: Reassessing person-centered theory and practice in the 21st century.* Ross-on-Wye: PCCS Books, pp. 329–47.

Rogers CR (1957) The necessary and sufficient conditions of personality change. *Journal of Consulting Psychology, 21*(2), 95–103.

Rogers CR (1959) A theory of therapy, personality and interpersonal relationships, as developed in the client-centered framework. In S Koch (Ed) *Psychology: A study of a science, Volume 3, Formulations of the person and the social context.* New York: McGraw-Hill, pp. 184–256.

Rogers CR (1986) Reflection of feelings. *Person-Centered Review, 1*, 375–7.

Chapter 1

NON-DIRECTIVITY:
THE FOUNDATIONAL ATTITUDE

Brian E. Levitt

NON-DIRECTIVE BEGINNINGS

As an attitude or a way of being, non-directivity is the foundation of an approach to therapy and other endeavours in human relations that is uniquely values-based. Carl Rogers proposed this radical notion of non-directivity in relation to psychotherapy over 60 years ago. Rogers' approach was initially called 'Non-Directive Therapy', but as it was confused with other therapies also known as non-directive, Rogers renamed it 'Client-Centered Therapy'. As this approach to therapy was applied to realms of human relations outside of psychotherapy, yet another label emerged: the person-centered approach. Experiential (Gendlin, 1996) and process-experiential (Greenberg, 2002) approaches, which evolved from a client-centered base, were also identified as person-centered approaches. However, these approaches abandoned the core element of non-directivity.

Despite the name changes, and the added confusion of directive, humanistic forms of psychotherapy sharing the umbrella term 'person-centered approaches', Rogers' basic theory remained grounded in the non-directive stance. As late as 1977, Rogers wrote, 'The politics of the client-centered approach is a conscious renunciation and avoidance of all control over, or decision-making for the client' (p. 14). It is worth noting that when Carl Rogers published one of his most famous books exploring the body of his work in 1980, he titled it *A Way of Being*, not 'a set of techniques'.

Rogers asked a number of values-laden questions (1951), which bear repeating:

> Do we see each person as having worth and dignity in his own right? If we do hold this point of view at the verbal level, to what extent is it operationally evident at the behavioral level? Do we tend to treat individuals as persons of worth, or do we subtly devalue them by our own attitudes and behavior? Is our philosophy one in which respect for the individual is uppermost? Do we respect his capacity and right to self-direction, or do we basically believe that his life would be best guided by us? (p. 20)

A deep understanding of client-centered therapy as a non-directive therapy of values and attitudes can be arrived at by wrestling with these questions. Unfortunately, it is often lost sight of that client-centered therapy began with such basic questions regarding *values*, particularly the value of respect for individual freedom, as applied to therapy and human relations. The primary question that emerges is a challenge: 'How can I fully value my client's personhood, and not reduce him or her to an object?' Paolo Freire (1994) put it aptly when he stated:

> Any situation in which some individuals prevent others from engaging in the process of inquiry is one of violence. The means used are not important; to alienate human beings from their own decision-making is to change them into objects. (p. 66)

Client-centered theory is a theory that is self-consciously grounded in values. It is an ongoing meditation on what it would mean to put a set of values that fundamentally reflect the primacy of individual freedom and a respect for personhood into actual practice. A conscious relinquishing of power over the client by the therapist follows from this assumption of respect for the freedom of the client (Grant, 2004). This renunciation of therapist power over the client's process and goals is developed as a therapist attitude, or the non-directive attitude. Client-centered theory evolved from this central point of non-directivity, finding its first full expression in the core conditions as formulated by Rogers (1957).

ENTER THE NECESSARY AND SUFFICIENT CONDITIONS

The necessary and sufficient conditions for therapeutic personality change were formulated against a backdrop of the non-directive attitude. As Prouty (1994) made clear, 'Rogers, then, abstracts non-directiveness to a set of values held by the counsellor' (p. 4). Rogers (1957) presented six conditions, three of which are known to us as congruence, unconditional positive regard, and empathic understanding. This triad of values-based constructs (conditions 3, 4, and 5) has generally been referred to throughout the literature as the core attitudes or core conditions of client-centered therapy:

> 3. The second person, whom we shall term the therapist, is congruent or integrated in the relationship.
> 4. The therapist experiences unconditional positive regard for the client.
> 5. The therapist experiences empathic understanding of the client's internal frame of reference and endeavors to communicate this experience to the client. (p. 96)

Rogers (1957) provided additional detail concerning this set of attitudes. Regarding congruence, Rogers noted, 'It means that within the relationship he [the therapist] is freely and deeply himself, with his actual experience accurately represented by his awareness of himself' (p. 97). He further described unconditional positive regard by explaining, 'To the extent that the therapist finds himself experiencing a warm acceptance of each aspect of the client's experience as being a part of that client he is experiencing unconditional positive regard ... It means there are no conditions of acceptance' (p. 98). Empathic understanding is described as sensing 'the client's private world as if it were your own, but without ever losing the "as if" quality …' (p. 99). It is important to note that over the course of his career, Rogers continued to explore aspects and applications of these three conditions or attitudes, leaving behind the non-directive terminology, but never abandoning its spirit in his 'central hypothesis of respect for and reliance upon the capacity of the person' (Rogers, 1951: 36). The core conditions recognize the client as a subject with freedom and an innate capacity for growth and change, not as an object to be described and reduced by theory and acted upon by external forces.

INTRODUCTION OF DIRECTIVITY INTO THE MIX—MUDDYING THE WATERS

Carl Rogers encouraged his students to find their own paths. With continued exploration and research, new directions emerged in theory and practice that focused on the client's process in therapy, and how to *use* the personhood of the therapist and various other techniques in order to make the client's process more efficient. Exploring ways to make the client's process more efficient moved client-centered therapy, as Rogers formulated it, away from its non-directive core, and towards a process-centered or process-driven theory and approach, directed by the therapist. A shift occurs in this pursuit in which the therapist takes on the mantle of expert, no matter how seemingly benign. The therapist is seen as understanding the client's process from an expert stance, and directing it through various means, such as focusing (Gendlin, 1996) and empathically based techniques (Rice, 1974; Greenberg, 2002; Elliott, Watson, Goldman and Greenberg, 2004), to make the client's process more 'efficient'. Such a stance loses sight of the non-directive attitude that presupposes a set of values centered on client autonomy and freedom, forming the basis of Rogers' radical work. Prouty (2000) indicated that:

> It seems reasonable to describe one of the differences between Rogers and the experiential therapies as one of therapist intent. It is the purpose of experiential therapies to 'guide' the client towards experiencing. This is not the intent of Rogers' view of client-centered therapy, which facilitates client intent through a 'surrender' to *self-direction*. (p. 34, original emphasis)

Non-directivity in the experiential and process-experiential approaches was lost as the essential element informing the core conditions or attitudes. The core conditions, when discussed from these perspectives, are disembodied from their non-directive source.

AN ONGOING DEBATE—THE QUESTION OF NON-DIRECTIVITY IN THE PERSON-CENTERED APPROACHES

Patterson (2000) questioned the 'efficiency movement' that is seen to underlie many of the directive person-centered approaches. This focus on efficiency is key to an understanding of how an originally non-directive approach could become directive, and how the core conditions would necessarily be changed in the process. Grant (1990) explored the directive–non-directive split in the person-centered approaches, and distinguished between what he called 'instrumental' and 'principled' non-directiveness. Instrumental non-directiveness was seen as a method or tool for bringing about change, only to be used when it seemed to be doing so. In contrast, principled non-directiveness 'is an attitude that provides "space" for growth, not one that intends to cause it' (p. 81). Though he was elucidating an important distinction among person-centered approaches, the use of two different labels for non-directivity may also foster misunderstandings regarding what non-directivity actually is. Dividing non-directivity in terms of intent is not logical, as non-directivity implies only one kind of intent: a shedding of power over the client and his or her process, and a letting go of the expert stance or role. As Rogers (1951) indicated, 'Client-centered counseling, if it is to be effective, cannot be a trick or a tool. It is not a subtle way of guiding the client while pretending to let him guide himself' (p. 30). To be non-directive from an instrumental perspective, that is, to use non-directivity to effect change, is necessarily directive in intent, and should be acknowledged as such. Directivity can be understood on a continuum. Non-directivity cannot. Non-directivity is not a continuous concept. It is a discrete concept. Patterson (2000) rightly recognised this when he asserted that there is only one meaning to non-directivity. While the experiential and process-experiential approaches shifted away from client-centered therapy and its central and defining characteristic of non-directivity, others, including Brodley (1997), Bozarth (2000), Patterson (2000), Prouty (2000), and Raskin (2004), have continued to promote an awareness of the distinguishing non-directive feature of client-centered therapy.

A RETURN—NON-DIRECTIVITY AS A STARTING POINT

When non-directivity is taken explicitly as a starting point, as a foundational attitude or value, the core conditions emerge as expressions of non-directivity. They are values that flow from a non-directive stance. Though the non-directive terminology fell into disuse in Rogers' written work, it always remained implicit. It is the very fibre of the core conditions. The core conditions are inseparable from non-directivity (Brodley, 1995). It is argued here that the core conditions are not the same thing at all if they are not infused with, not supported by, or do not flow from a non-directive stance. They would not carry the same meaning as therapist attitudes or values. Without non-directivity, the commonly known core conditions are no longer accurately described by the labels of empathic understanding, unconditional positive regard and congruence. Or, as Brodley (1995) stated, 'realizing client-centered therapy is non-directive makes a difference in the way the therapy is practiced. And it makes a difference in what the client experiences'.

UNDERSTANDING THE CORE CONDITIONS AS EXPRESSIONS OF NON-DIRECTIVITY

A brief examination of each core condition in the context of non-directivity follows. A description of their essentially non-directive qualities is brought forth. How these core conditions are necessarily altered by the introduction of direction, or therapist efforts at increasing the efficiency of the client's process, is also explained.

EMPATHIC UNDERSTANDING: WHOSE MAP ARE WE FOLLOWING?

Lewis Carroll, in *Sylvie and Bruno Concluded* (1893), provided an instructive tale that helps to shed light on the difference between directive and non-directive empathy. At one point in the tale, the narrator speaks with Mein Herr:

'What a useful thing a pocket-map is!' I remarked.

'That's another thing we've learned from *your* Nation', said Mein Herr, 'map-making. But we've carried it much further than *you*. What do you consider the *largest* map that would be really useful?'

'About six inches to the mile.'

'Only *six inches*!' exclaimed Mein Herr. 'We very soon got to six yards to the mile. Then we tried a *hundred* yards to the mile. And then came the grandest idea of all! We actually made a map of the country on the scale of a *mile* to the mile!'

'Have you used it much?' I enquired.

'It has never been spread out, yet', said Mein Herr, 'the farmers objected: they said it would cover the whole country, and shut out the sunlight! So we now use the country itself, as its own map, and I assure you it does nearly as well.' (Ch. II, para. 41)

The most accurate map of something is the thing itself, or an exact duplicate of it. By extension, this concept can be applied to thinking about individual human experience. The question in relation to psychotherapy then arises: Whose map are we following? In other words, who is the expert? Non-directive empathy is an understanding that is entirely in the service of the client's own theory of him- or herself. From this perspective, the client is the map and the map-maker. The client is the expert. Non-directive empathy is an attempt at understanding the client's experience that comes as close as possible to wandering the actual terrain of the client's world. As a reflexive behavior produced by this non-directive attempt at empathic understanding, the therapist might check with the client from time to time to see whether he or she is reading/receiving the client's own map correctly, or as the client lives their own map. As Rogers (1986) explained, 'I am not trying to "reflect feelings". I am trying to determine whether my understanding of the client's inner world is correct—whether I am seeing it as he or she is experiencing it at this moment' (p. 376). Rogers went on to make clear that reflection of feelings in the context of empathic understanding was not meant to be a technique. In other words, reflection of feelings is a non-directive endeavor that flows naturally from attempts at empathic understanding.

To restate: with non-directive empathic understanding, the client's experience itself *is* the map. The therapist does not use his or her own personal theories or some other externally generated theory (that is, external to the client) as a map. Through non-directive empathic understanding, the therapist tries to understand the map in front of him or her from the client's worldview, as the client presents it. The only theory that is ever relevant is the client's own theory of him- or herself. From a non-directive stance, a unique kind of understanding is implied—it is not an understanding that is in any way an 'imposition of'. Rather, non-directive empathic understanding implies an attempt to understand as fully as possible the client's own frame of reference. Non-directive empathic understanding requires the therapist to surrender his or her own theories, external maps and biases in order to attempt to understand the world of another from that person's perspective. It becomes incumbent upon the therapist to follow the client as closely as possible and understand as accurately as possible from the perspective of the client, without a thought towards implementing techniques, placing client statements into external theory or deciding where therapy or the client's process should go. Attempting to understand the client from within his or her own lived experience of the world becomes a primary goal. Rogers (1951) quotes Nathaniel Raskin's 1947 (previously) unpublished paper (Raskin, 2005, Chapter 20 this volume) to explain that:

> there is simply no room for any other type of counsellor activity or attitude; if he is attempting to live the attitudes of the other, he cannot be diagnosing them, he cannot be thinking of making the process go faster. Because he is another and not the client, the understanding is not spontaneous and must be acquired, and this through the most intense, continuous, and active attention to the feelings of the other, to the exclusion of any other type of attention. (Rogers, 1951: 20)

Empathic understanding from a directive stance is an attempt to understand from an objective perspective, external to the client, or even from the therapist's own personal perspective. All theories of human personality that do not begin with the individual and his or her own unique reality are ways of neatly encapsulating the individual in order to direct our understanding, rather than letting the client direct our understanding by being their own map. Theories that are external to the client are necessarily reductionistic. However, clients are infinitely complex and constantly changing. Clients may, in fact, confound any possibility of constructing a useable, external map to describe them, as the terrain is always changing. As Whitman (1983: 72) wrote in *Song of Myself*: 'Do I contradict myself? Very well then, I contradict myself. (I am large, I contain multitudes.)'

Directive empathic understanding, at its extreme, would lead to understanding clients in terms of a map that broadly covers or describes behaviors, intents, drives, and complexes or aggregates of thoughts; in other words, an inch representing a mile.

Directive empathic understanding is in the service of a theory that is external to the client. Directive empathic understanding implies fitting the client into the therapist's map, or the implications of the therapist's map. The client is thereby reduced and his or her freedom is diminished. Raskin (1948) cautioned that when the non-directive attitude is not present as a part of empathic understanding:

> not only will 'reflection of feeling' tend to be inaccurate, but directive techniques will creep into the counselor responses, so that even when the goal of the counselor is to be non-directive, recordings of his interviews will show that he is making interpretations, giving support, and utilizing other directive techniques. ('Current Trends in Nondirective Therapy', para. 2, http://signs. portents.com/~matt/cct.development.html)

Non-directive empathic understanding requires comfort with a great deal of the not-knowing that comes with trying to empathically connect with the infinitely complex world of another human being. It is understanding without a safety net. From a non-directive perspective, if the client *is* the map, uncertainty will always be present for the therapist, as the therapist will never be able to see/experience the entire 'map'. The map followed with non-directive empathy is infinitely large and always subject to change. In fact, the therapist's ability to tolerate the infinite nature of the client's world may determine their ability to remain non-directive. As such, the titular character in Martel's (2002) *Life of Pi* might have easily levelled this accusation at those who prefer external theories to describe their client's experience:

> I know what you want. You want a story that won't surprise you. That will confirm what you already know. That won't make you see higher or further or differently. You want a flat story. An immobile story. You want dry, yeastless factuality. (p. 336)

Unconditional positive regard: How directive is your regard?

If unconditional positive regard, or being non-judgmental and caring, is non-directive, it is client-directed. What exactly does this mean? In other words, if the reader will forgive the necessary double negative, how do we make sense of the concept of non-directive non-judgment? If the process is to be fully directed by the client, then the therapist must let go of trying to decide upon what should or should not be explored, how a process should be furthered, or what is useful or good. A fundamental respect for the client's process, values and behaviors emerges. A fundamental respect for his or her very being is present. Judgments, in the sense of the regard in which we hold our clients, are not just about client traits, appearances, beliefs, thoughts or actions, but on a deeper level, about the client's process itself. Rogers (1951) offered this radical statement:

> To me it appears that only as the therapist is completely willing that *any* outcome, *any* direction may be chosen, only then does he realize the vital strength of the capacity and potentiality of the individual for constructive action. (p. 48, original emphasis)

From a non-directive stance, unconditional positive regard would mean that clients are inherently valuable and powerful (including their process), and that the therapist consciously renounces a need, interest or goal to actively change the client or their process, no matter how different, frightening or strange. The non-directive therapist does not have to change clients to value or understand them. Clients are embraced as they are. Further, and of the utmost importance from a non-directive perspective, the therapist trusts the *client's* process and goals as inherently valuable. The non-directive therapist can be with clients wherever they are and wherever they are going, or wherever they intend or choose to go. If unconditional positive regard is non-directive, or client-directed, the non-directive therapist does not wish to make a judgment about what should happen, how quickly it should happen, or what would be a more useful process. *The client's freedom is fully embraced.*

Once regard is directed *by the therapist*, it is conditional. In other words, the therapist places values and judgments on what should be discussed or what a client should feel, or in which direction their feelings should change. The following imperatives are likely to underlie a directive approach: 'you must not be depressed … you must not be suicidal … you must use therapy to grow, or to change something that harms you … you must process in a certain way or you will not make progress, or you will not make progress efficiently or quickly enough … feelings are the most important thing to focus on'. These are all judgments from the therapist about what should happen and who the client should be or become. Deciding to focus therapy on so-called positive emotions, or negative ones for that matter, is a therapist bias or direction, and not guided by the client or the client's process. Such direction influences the kind of regard a therapist can hold for a client, and it is no longer unconditional. The therapist in this case has placed conditions of worth on the client. When a certain kind of process becomes more valued than the client's own chosen process and direction (including the client's chosen pacing), the therapist is no longer holding an attitude of unconditional positive regard. This is true in experiential and process-experiential therapies. Regard for the client inevitably, even if subtly, becomes directive once a judgment is made about how a client should process and what a 'good' process would be. Or even simply that a client should process at all in therapy. Laing's (1967) comments provide us with an understanding of why embracing a non-directive stance might be so difficult:

> The history of heresies of all kinds testifies to more than the tendency to break off communication (excommunication) with those who hold different dogmas or opinions; it bears witness to our intolerance of different *fundamental structures of experience*. We seem to need to share a communal meaning to human existence, to give with others a common sense to the world, to maintain a *consensus*. (p. 77, original emphasis)

If regard is truly unconditional, then clients determine their goals in an atmosphere of acceptance. Clients do not have to need or desire change, and the therapist does not have to need change, or a certain or degree of change, for them. The therapist does not place an emphasis on the expression of feelings as a more valuable form of client expression. Non-directive therapy does not have to be about feelings at all. It is valid for a client to direct their use of therapy towards sorting out thoughts, for example, or to practice/ role-play anticipated situations at the client's request. The non-directive therapist would not be concerned where the process is leading. Indeed, expression of client feelings may never enter the picture. Schmid (2001) expressed the depth of unconditional positive regard when he wrote:

> it means the person as such is 'ap-preciat-ed' in his or her worth and dignity— esteemed as a 'precious' being. This means not to imagine what the Other actually might want to say ... but bona fide, in good faith and without hidden suspicion or evaluation to *take* ('ac-cept') the Other as he or she describes, exposes, discloses him- or herself, namely, 'at the face value'. (p. 51, original emphasis)

Congruence: What do I do with my self-awareness?

Congruence may be understood as the ability of the therapist to remain whole, integrated, and self-aware. Haugh (2001: 4) asserted that, 'For Rogers, congruence is not simply stating thoughts and ideas that come into the therapist's head. It involves an awareness of a lack of empathy and unconditional positive regard.' How does directivity impact upon congruence? How do we make sense of the difference between directivity and non-directivity in the context of congruence? Where does therapist self-awareness fit in? Non-directive congruence is framed as a disciplined therapist awareness of self, with no goal for the client tied to this awareness. To take this a step further, the non-directive therapist, working in the service of the client's direction, would manage his or her own self-awareness as much as possible so that it would not interfere with the client's process, and with the therapist's clear, empathic understanding of the client. A key focus as a non-directive therapist is upon the therapist's internal process as it affects his or her ability to attend to and make room for the client's process. If one is non-directive, a respect emerges in terms of not interfering with the client's process. Managing one's own self-awareness throughout the therapy process becomes a highly important goal for the therapist. A non-directive therapist might ask, 'How do my own issues and biases get in the way of maintaining empathic understanding, as well as being non-judgmental of and caring towards the client?' The non-directive therapist is concerned with how he or she might get in the way of the client's own process. A non-directive stance implies that the therapist recognizes the primacy of the client's process and right to self-direction. As Raskin (1948, para. 1, http://signs. portents.com/~matt/cct.development.html) stated, 'The nondirective point of view on this issue is that to the extent that some other frame of reference than the client's is introduced into the therapeutic situation, the therapy is not client-centered.' Therefore, therapist responses, if non-directive, are never meant to change the client's process because of a therapist decision that this change is what would be best for the client.

If congruence is explored from the standpoint of directivity, the therapist may decide to use expressions of his or her own self-awareness to influence therapy and the client's process. Directive congruence in this sense is a therapist tool or technique for making therapy more efficient, for creating movement, for creating change. There is less regard for the impact of imposing the therapist's frame of reference onto the client when congruence becomes an active tool to further or influence the therapeutic process. The process is no longer as fully client-guided, as the therapist's frame intrudes and inevitably interferes. Even if done with an air of experimentation this is still directive; a choice to intrude upon the client's frame of reference to have an impact. Congruence is being used as a technique to actively change the course of the client's process. Directive congruence is *used* to direct or impact upon the client's process by interjecting the therapist's own frame. Even if it is not consciously used, this directive expression of the therapist's congruence has the effect of interfering with the client's process, by giving more power in the moment to the therapist's process.

CONCLUSIONS REGARDING NON-DIRECTIVITY AS FOUNDATIONAL

Non-directivity is the source of attitudes at once distinct and unified that have come to typify client-centered therapy. As originally formulated, the core conditions take their very shape from the non-directive attitude. Each core condition flows from a deeply held understanding of, and strongly held belief in, non-directivity. Though this is not explicit in Rogers' writings, it is clearly implicit throughout. In every sense, the core conditions of client-centered therapy reflect a fundamental respect for the client's process, personal power and freedom. They are expressions of non-directivity.

As explained throughout this chapter, the core conditions, as described by Rogers, are no longer the same if any degree of directivity is insinuated, no matter how subtly. That is, if the conditions are in any way 'used', a therapist cannot be accurately described as non-directive. The labels used to name the core conditions may be the same, but the constructs or meanings behind them will be substantially different. Using the same labels for the core conditions when coming from varying degrees of directivity is a source of confusion, as the core conditions are invariably changed by directivity. Confusion is ultimately the only thing that is gained by grouping various orientations to therapy under the single term 'person-centered', when they differ on such a fundamental level in terms of whether they are directive or non-directive. Client-centered therapy is non-directive. Client-centered therapy is not experiential or process-experiential in focus. These therapies may have developed from a client-centered base, but they are distinct in terms of a shift in values away from client direction and towards therapist direction and the expert status of the therapist.

Any notion that the therapist knows what is best for the client results in a return to the therapist taking ownership of power and diminishing client freedom, and the values and attitudes that will flow from such a stance are necessarily and inexorably changed. Any *use* of the core conditions is no longer in keeping with the non-directive attitude; no longer in keeping with the radical notion of trusting the client to direct or guide therapy, their own processes and their own lives.

Directive empathic understanding is not the same as non-directive empathic understanding. Directive congruence is not the same as non-directive congruence. Directive unconditional positive regard is not the same as non-directive unconditional positive regard. In fact, directive unconditional positive regard cannot be said to be unconditional at all. Greater directivity results in being more empathically removed and being less able to truly understand the client. Without the non-directive attitude, therapist self-awareness, or congruence, may be used as a tool to actively influence, as opposed to a tool that helps to keep the therapist out of the client's way and from interfering in the client's freedom to direct him- or herself. As well, greater directivity leads to greater degrees of conditional regard. The non-directive attitude is essential to the nature of the therapeutic core conditions of empathic understanding, unconditional positive regard, and congruence. Non-directivity is a *foundational* stance, and the core conditions, as attitudes or values held by the therapist, are necessarily unique expressions of it.

REFERENCES

Bozarth JD (2000) Non-directiveness in client-centered therapy: A vexed concept. Paper presented at the Eastern Psychological Association, March 25, 2000, Baltimore, MD. Retrieved January 24, 2005, from http://www.personcentered.com/non-direct.html

Brodley BT (1995) Meanings and implications of the non-directive attitude in client-centered therapy. Unpublished manuscript of a lecture given in Portugal, October.

Brodley BT (1997) The attitude in client-centered therapy. *Person-Centered Journal, 4*(1), 18–30.

Carroll L (1893) *Sylvie and Bruno Concluded* (ch. 11). Retrieved January 24, 2005, from http://www.hoboes.com/html/FirebBlade/Carroll/Sylvie/Concluded/Chapter11.html

Elliott R, Watson JC, Goldman RN & Greenberg LS (2004) *Learning Emotion-Focused Therapy: The process-experiential approach to change.* Washington DC: American Psychological Association.

Freire P (1994) *Pedagogy of the Oppressed* (new revised 20th anniversary edition). New York: Continuum.

Gendlin ET (1996) *Focusing-Oriented Psychotherapy: A manual of the Experiential method.* New York: Guilford Press.

Grant B (1990) Principled and instrumental non-directiveness in person-centered and client-centered therapy. *Person-Centered Review, 5*(1), 77–88. Reprinted in DJ Cain (Ed)(2002) *Classics in the Person-Centered Approach.* Ross-on-Wye: PCCS Books, pp. 371–77.

Grant B (2004) The imperative of ethical justification in psychotherapy: The special case of client-centered therapy. *Person-Centered and Experiential Psychotherapies, 3*(3), 152–65.

Greenberg LS (2002) *Emotion-Focused Therapy: Coaching clients to work with their feelings.* Washington DC: American Psychological Association.

Haugh S (2001) A historical review of the concept of congruence. In G Wyatt (Ed) *Rogers' Therapeutic Conditions: Evolution, theory and practice. Vol. 1: Congruence.* Ross-on-Wye: PCCS Books, pp. 1–17.

Laing RD (1967) *The Politics of Experience.* New York: Ballantine Books.

Martel Y (2002) *Life of Pi.* Toronto: Vintage Canada.

Patterson CH (2000) On being non-directive. In CH Patterson *Understanding Psychotherapy: fifty years of client-centred theory and practice.* Ross-on-Wye: PCCS Books, pp. 181–4.

Prouty GF (1994) *Theoretical Evolutions in Person-Centered/Experiential Therapy: Applications to schizophrenic and retarded psychoses.* Westport: Praeger-Greenwood.

Prouty GF (2000) Carl Rogers and experiential therapies: A dissonance? In T Merry (Ed) *Person-Centred Practice: The BAPCA reader.* Ross-on-Wye: PCCS Books, pp. 30–7.

Raskin NJ (1947/2005) The nondirective attitude. In BE Levitt (Ed) *Embracing Non-directivity: Reassessing person-centered theory and practice in the 21st century.* Ross-on-Wye: PCCS Books, pp. 329–47.

Raskin NJ (1948) The development of nondirective therapy. *Journal of Consulting Psychology, 12,* 92–110. Retrieved January 24, 2005, from http://signs. portents.com/~matt/cct. development.html

Raskin NJ (2004) *Contributions to Client-Centered Therapy and the Person-Centered Approach.* Ross-on-Wye: PCCS Books.

Rice L (1974) The evocative function of the therapist. In DA Wexler and LN Rice (Eds) *Innovations in Client-Centered Therapy.* New York: Wiley, pp. 289–311. Reprinted in S Haugh & T Merry (Eds) *Rogers' Therapeutic Conditions: Evolution, theory and practice. Vol. 2: Empathy.* Ross-on-Wye: PCCS Books, pp. 112–30.

Rogers CR (1951) *Client-Centered Therapy: Its current practice, implications, and theory.* Boston: Houghton Mifflin.

Rogers CR (1957) The necessary and sufficient conditions of personality change. *Journal of Consulting Psychology, 21*(2), 95–103.

Rogers CR (1977) *On Personal Power.* New York: Delacourte Press.

Rogers CR (1980) *A Way of Being.* Boston: Houghton Mifflin.

Rogers CR (1986) Reflection of feelings. *Person-Centered Review, 4,* 375–7.

Schmid PF (2001) Acknowledgement: The art of responding. Dialogical and ethical perspectives on the challenge of unconditional relationships in therapy and beyond. In JD Bozarth & P Wilkins (Eds) *Rogers' Therapeutic Conditions: Evolution, theory and practice. Vol 3: Unconditional Positive Regard.* Ross-on-Wye: PCCS Books, pp. 49–64.

Whitman W (1983) *Leaves of Grass* (1892 edition). Toronto: Bantam Books.

Chapter 2

HISTORIC EVENTS IN CLIENT-CENTERED THERAPY AND THE PERSON-CENTERED APPROACH

Nathaniel J. Raskin

THE BIRTH OF CLIENT-CENTERED THERAPY, A 'NEWER THERAPY'

Carl Rogers arrived at Ohio State University in Columbus, Ohio, in December of 1939. Prior to this, he worked for twelve years in the Child Study Department of the Rochester (New York) Guidance Center, where he became its director. Rogers was offered a full professorship at Ohio State on the strength of his book, *The Clinical Treatment of the Problem Child* (Rogers, 1939). The book emphasized therapeutic methods. Rogers suggested that while a lot had been published on the causes of the behavior problems of children, there was a paucity of material on treatment, a ratio of something like twenty to one.

Rogers drew attention to a form of treatment called 'relationship therapy', which had some roots in the approach of analyst Otto Rank, and had been developed predominantly by social case workers. This method was primarily emotional rather than intellectual, and was applicable only to parents who believed *they* needed to be changed (as distinguished from those who saw their child as 'the problem').

In this form of therapy, the relationship between worker and parent was seen as core. The therapist tried to provide an atmosphere in which parents could become aware of their attitudes; it was an environment of acceptance, of non-criticism, and of encouraging the parents' initiative. The result was a clarification of the parents' thinking and feeling and a growth in their self-understanding. The parents determined independently how they wished to deal with their child. Rogers gave a detailed example of how one family in his Rochester center was helped. He also expressed the hope that his book would stimulate research.

Toward the end of the autumn quarter of 1940, Rogers received an invitation to address Psi Chi, the psychological honor society, at the University of Minnesota. His address occurred on December 11, 1940. This is often cited as the birth date of client-centered therapy. Rogers described a 'newer therapy', consonant with the 'relationship therapy' described in *The Clinical Treatment of the Problem Child* (Rogers, 1939), which had the aim of helping individuals not only to solve their present problems, but to grow in the ability to solve future problems in a more integrated way. He hypothesized that this capacity was part of a general drive toward growth. In this 'newer therapy', emotional elements were stressed more than intellectual aspects. There was also more emphasis on the immediate situation than on the past, and the therapeutic relationship itself was viewed as a growth experience.

PUBLICATION OF ROGERS' *COUNSELING AND PSYCHOTHERAPY* (1942), A GROUNDBREAKING WORK ON MANY LEVELS

Rogers' talk at University of Minnesota generated strong reactions, both favorable and unfavorable, and he decided to expand his thinking into the 1942 book, *Counseling and Psychotherapy*.

Almost two-fifths of the book was made up of 'The Case of Herbert Bryan', consisting of the typescripts of eight phonographically recorded verbatim interviews, a method worked out with the help of Bernard 'Bud' Covner, who had interned at the Rochester Guidance Center and became Rogers' first PhD at Ohio State. This kind of presentation was revolutionary, contrasting sharply with the subjective accounts of therapy being published at the time. It also provided data to study the therapeutic process objectively.

Rogers and his students developed methods of classifying client statements and counselor responses, and of measuring self-regarding attitudes. Great advances were made in the objective study of personality change and of therapist and client behavior.

Rogers' students at Ohio State included, in addition to Covner, Virginia Axline, Arthur Combs, Charles Curran, Thomas Gordon, Donald Grummon, Nicholas Hobbs, E.H. Porter, Jr., Victor Raimy, myself (Nathaniel Raskin), William U. Snyder and Bernard Steinzor. We sensed that we were part of a revolution in the field, both because of the objective and open character of our work and the trust in the self-determining capacities of individuals. Rogers also trusted his students, giving us important research and clinical responsibilities. Many of my fellow students went on to become outstanding authors, teachers, therapists, and professional leaders in their own right, for example, Snyder *et al.* edited *Casebook of Nondirective Counseling* (1947) and Charles A. Curran published *Personality Factors in Counseling* (1945).

ROGERS' STATEMENT OF HIS BASIC HYPOTHESIS

In *Counseling and Psychotherapy*, Rogers (1942) stated the basic hypothesis of his new method and theory:

> Effective counseling consists of a definitely structured, permissive relationship which allows the client to gain an understanding of himself to a degree which enables him to take positive steps in the light of his new orientation. (p. 18)

Rogers described this relationship as characterized by:

1. **The therapist's warmth and responsiveness** which gradually develops into a deeper emotional relationship, 'an affectional bond with defined limits'. The counselor

should be honest about being 'emotionally involved but this involvement must be strictly limited' for the good of the client (*ibid.*: 87).

2. **Permissiveness in regard to the expression of feeling.** '[T]he client comes to recognize that all feelings and attitudes may be expressed. No attitude is too aggressive, no feeling too guilty or shameful, to bring into the relationship ... In this respect the therapeutic relationship differs markedly from the other relationships of ordinary life' (*ibid.*: 88).

3. **Therapeutic limits.** These are seen as an important aspect of the counseling situation. Being strict about the time limits of the interview helps 'make the therapeutic situation a microcosm in which the client can meet all the basic aspects which characterize life as a whole, face them openly, and adapt himself to them' (*ibid.*: 89). In this belief, Rogers was undoubtedly influenced by Jessie Taft, psychologist at the Philadelphia Child Guidance Clinic, who saw therapy as 'a process in which the individual learns to utilize the therapeutic hour without undue fear, resistance, resentment or greediness, learns to take it and also leave it without denying its value and without trying to keep it forever because of its value'. Taft believed that the person accomplishing this had learned the secret of all hours. One of Taft's major contributions was to record very completely two treatment cases with children which appeared in her book, *The Dynamics of Therapy in a Controlled Relationship* (Taft, 1933).

Rogers advocated other limits in the interest of enhancing therapy. While children in play therapy may 'smash clay figures, break dolls, shout, spill water', they may not break windows or be destructive in the hallway or adjacent offices. (Rogers, 1942: 89)

4. **Freedom from pressure or coercion.** Rogers believed that it was important that counselors not impose their own biases into the therapeutic situation. 'The hour is the client's hour, not the counselor's' (*ibid.*: 89). With advice being removed from therapy, the stage was set for a process of self-directed growth and integration.

THE ESTABLISHMENT OF THE UNIVERSITY OF CHICAGO COUNSELING CENTER

During World War II, Rogers took leave from Ohio State and served as Director of Counseling Services for the USO (United Service Organizations). With John Wallen, one of his graduate students, he co-authored *Counseling with Returned Servicemen* (Rogers and Wallen, 1946). He accepted a position at the University of Chicago as Professor of Psychology and head of the Counseling Center, with the understanding that the work with students at the center would be completely confidential, with no reports to be made to officers of the University administration. He also organized the Center on the basis of empowering the staff, which was made up predominantly of graduate students, to assume the responsibility for the functioning of the Center (Grummon and Gordon, 1948).

A NEW CONCEPT OF TEACHING

In addition to his unusual approach to the organization of the Counseling Center, Rogers expressed a new concept of teaching. He wrote that he ceased to be a teacher, that he gradually began to trust students, and that in response they shared their feelings with him and raised questions he had not thought about. He told the students that what they did in any particular course was up to the students and himself jointly, that they could decide together what they wanted to do about examinations and grades. He described the change in his role as an educator as one of going from being a teacher and evaluator to being a facilitator of learning, which he saw as a very different occupation. Students were often chagrined at first but came to view Rogers' new approach as enhancing their learning as students and their growth as persons.

ADVANCES IN RESEARCH

There were also major advances in research after Rogers got to Chicago. A precedent-breaking entire issue of the *Journal of Consulting Psychology* in 1949 was devoted to a report of the 'parallel studies' project, comprising six investigations of the same group of ten completely recorded and transcribed cases, with pre- and post-tests (Raskin, 1949). The studies included measures of feelings regarding self and others, the pattern of client content (e.g., statement of problem, understanding or insight, discussion of plans), defensiveness, and maturity of behavior. There was an evaluation of outcome using the Rorschach test, and an analysis of the relationships among all these and counselor ratings of overall therapeutic progress on a 1 to 9 scale. Two of the key findings were that (1) the measures which had been applied to each interview provided an integrated and meaningful picture of the level of adjustment at which the client began therapy, the ending level, and the course of therapy in between, and (2) there was a significant relationship between the counselors' estimates of success and the degree of success based on the interview-analysis measures. Significant relationships were not found to exist between the Rorschach results and those of the five interview-analysis measures. It was also concluded that the research methodology was applicable to therapeutic approaches generally, and that such efforts would help put psychotherapy on a scientific basis.

'PSYCHOTHERAPY AND PERSONALITY CHANGE' RESEARCH PROJECT

The parallel studies project was succeeded five years later by a larger study carried out at the Counseling Center, which was supported by grants from private foundations and the federal government. The project was regarded as state-of-the-art for its time and was reported in a book edited by Rogers and Rosalind Dymond (later Cartwright), *Psychotherapy and Personality Change* (1954). It contained complete data on 29 clients seen by 16 therapists, as well as on a matched control group. Some clients served as their own controls, being tested at the beginning and at the end of a two-month period before therapy began, then at the end of therapy, and once more six to twelve months after termination. Like the parallel studies project, this study was interested in the concomitants of therapy, but it paid more attention to the outcome issue. It also measured changes in self differently, relying on the Q-technique of British psychologist William Stephenson. This was a sophisticated method of quantifying the way people viewed themselves at present and the 'ideal self', and facilitated the calculation of correlations, for example, between self-concept at the beginning of therapy and the end, and between self-concept and self-ideal at the start and the completion of treatment. Some of the results were that perceived self changes more during therapy, and to a degree significantly greater for clients than for control group subjects; that there is a significant increase in congruence between self and ideal during therapy; and that the direction of change in the perceived self is in a direction which expert judges view as positive.

Qualitative analysis revealed that clients, as a result of therapy, saw themselves grow in self-confidence, self-reliance, self-understanding, inner comfort and comfortable relationships with others, with a decrease in feeling guilty, resentful, driven and insecure and a need for self-concealment. Other results were that representations of ideal self were found to be much more stable than those of perceived self—that perceived self exhibited greater change than ideal self, but that ideal self became more discrepant from the 'adjustment score'. In other words the ideal self became less perfectly 'adjusted', or more attainable.

NECESSARY AND SUFFICIENT CONDITIONS

In 1957, Rogers wrote an article on 'the necessary and sufficient conditions of therapeutic personality change'. One of the contributions for which he is best known is the triad of therapist-offered conditions of empathy, congruence and unconditional positive regard. In keeping with his previous work, these concepts were carefully defined and could be quantified. They stimulated hundreds of articles, convention programs and research projects by theorists and practitioners of many different persuasions. G. T. Barrett-Lennard's Relationship Inventory, an instrument designed to measure these conditions, has also been used in hundreds of research projects, not only in psychotherapy, but in parent-child, student-teacher, worker-employer, and other human relations applications (Barrett-Lennard, 1988).

ARTICULATION OF THEORY IN KOCH'S *PSYCHOLOGY: A STUDY OF A SCIENCE*

The most rigorous exposition of Rogers' thinking, 'A theory of therapy, personality, and interpersonal relationships', appeared in 1959, after he had moved to the University of Wisconsin, in Sigmund Koch's *Psychology: A study of a science* (Rogers, 1959).

SCHIZOPHRENIA RESEARCH PROJECT AT THE UNIVERSITY OF WISCONSIN

In the spring of 1957, Rogers left Chicago to accept a Professorship in both Psychology and Psychiatry at the University of Wisconsin, his old alma mater. He was eager to test the hypothesis that, offered the 'necessary and sufficient conditions' of therapy, the process of change would be found to be the same in 'schizophrenic' persons as with 'normal' people.

With support from sources outside the University, Rogers and Eugene Gendlin, who had been his student at Chicago, formed a Psychotherapy Research Group to conduct and study therapy with hospitalized schizophrenic patients and normal, volunteer adults. The research plan called for the hospitalized subjects to be selected in matched pairs. By random choice, one would receive therapy, and the other serve as a control. There would be parallel testing and appraisal of all participants. Diagnostically, hospital clients were to be equally divided between a 'more acute' group hospitalized for less than eight months and a 'more chronic' group already in the hospital longer. They were to be assessed on a variety of change and process measures, including a seven-point scale developed by Rogers and his student, R. Rablen, depicting a low end of fixed and closed experiencing to a high end of an open and flowing process.

It proved impossible to carry out this ambitious plan fully. There were a number of methodological problems: the difficulty in matching pairs of patient subjects, the incompleteness of test and interview data, unexpected discharges and hospital transfers, and only partial success in replacing initial subjects.

The research results were mixed, some of the original hypotheses being supported by the data, others not. There were only small differences between the therapy and control groups in successful outcome. There were some positive findings: client-centered therapy was helpful with at least some of the 'chronic' or long-term schizophrenic patients; high therapist conditions of congruence and empathy did correlate with successful outcome; when these conditions were low, patients deteriorated. The results on the process or experiencing scale were also mixed: therapist conditions did not correlate with movement on the process scale; movement along the scale did correlate with successful therapy outcome; there was a correlation between therapist conditions and process level, rather than movement.

Unfortunately, Rogers' six years in Wisconsin turned out to be extremely difficult and disappointing, the most painful and anguished period, he said, in his whole professional life. A great deal of this had to do with Charles Truax, who organized the original data collection and analysis. The ratings on which his studies were based mysteriously disappeared. Different members of the research project claimed that Truax refused to give them access to the data on which they could do their studies. Someone discovered in his office a pile of manuscripts based on project data that contained Truax's individual copyright; apparently he intended to publish a work under his own name.

Most of the project staff clamored for Truax to be fired. Rogers, who had taken time out from the schizophrenia project to spend a year as a Fellow at the Center for Advanced Study in the Behavioral Sciences at Stanford University, arranged to meet in

California with Truax, who denied the allegations. He threatened to sue Wisconsin if the University tried to dismiss him.

In the end, it was agreed to include Truax as one of the editors of the book on the schizophrenia project, which was published in 1967. In many ways it was an important contribution. The findings added to the knowledge about research on and working with schizophrenic persons. There were chapters by Gendlin on techniques for working with this population, and verbatim transcripts of two interviews by Rogers with a hospitalized twenty-eight year old.

PROFESSIONAL RECOGNITION OF ROGERS DURING HIS WISCONSIN YEARS

While Rogers was at Wisconsin, he was elected the first President of the American Academy of Psychotherapists, the American Academy of Arts and Sciences made him a Fellow, the American Personnel and Guidance Association awarded him a certificate for outstanding research, and the Division of Clinical Psychology of the American Psychological Association recognized his Distinguished Contribution to the Science and Profession of Clinical Psychology. The Division credited him with initiating effective research on psychotherapy more than any other individual, with the first objective studies of the progress and effectiveness of psychotherapy, and for the first clear delineation of one way to do psychotherapy: client-centered therapy.

THE VALUING PROCESS IN THE MATURE PERSON

Rogers published an article in 1964 entitled 'Toward a Modern Approach to Values: The valuing process in the mature person'. He described a 'surprising commonality' in the value directions of maturing clients—they tend to move away from façades and from meeting the expectations of others; they value their own feelings, self-direction, being real, being open to new inner and outer experiences, being sensitive to others, and having deep relationships.

This description of mature persons received corroboration from the work of Julius Seeman, who had been a University of Chicago Counseling Center staff member in the 1940s and 1950s and research director of the study reported in *Psychotherapy and Personality Change*, the book edited by Rogers and Rosalind Dymond in 1954. He had gone from the University of Chicago to a distinguished career at George Peabody College of Vanderbilt University in Nashville, Tennessee. His book *Personality Integration* (Seeman, 1983), affirmed Rogers' formulation of the fully functioning person with his research. He found that high-functioning persons are healthier, more efficient in their perception of reality, have superior environmental contact, high self-esteem, confidence and trust in themselves, and possess a sense of autonomy that facilitates the development of caring and generative relationships.

INTERNATIONAL PERSON-CENTERED APPROACH COMMUNITY

A worldwide community of people interested in the person-centered approach has come into being. Oliver Bown, a member of the University of Chicago Counseling Center in the 1940s and 1950s, took a position at the University of Texas when he left Chicago. Charles Devonshire, a student of Bown's at Texas, was impressed by the more than 150,000 foreign students in educational institutions in the United States. He organized an Inter-Cultural Workshop, known as the Greenwood Workshop, in 1972 in San Mateo, California, which was designed to promote better interpersonal communication among foreign students and their American classmates, educators, counselors and communities. The workshop involved one hundred participants from 27 countries. They were led by two facilitators following the principles oulined by Rogers in his book on encounter groups (Rogers, 1970) and there were also sessions of the entire community with Rogers.

The evaluations of the student participants in the Greenwood Workshop were overwhelmingly positive. They felt that they had been understood, that they had developed greater skill in communicating, that they had developed an interest in trying to listen better to others, to be more sensitive to cultural differences when interacting with others, and to appreciate the beauty of cultural differences.

Of the fifteen American colleges and universities participating in the Greenwood Workshop, twelve decided to incorporate inter-cultural communication programs as a part of their student services programs. Devonshire set up inter-cultural communication projects up to two weeks long in the United States and Europe, resulting in even more significant changes in attitudes, feelings and behavior.

Devonshire, in a booklet co-authored by Jurgen W. Kremer (1980) wrote that since 1970 more than 1000 persons had been involved in person-centered workshops sponsored by his Center for Cross-Cultural Communication, in Germany, Holland, Italy, France, England, Scotland, Switzerland, Sweden and Spain, with 28 different nationalities represented. As a by-product, Facilitator Development Institutes had been established in Holland, Britain, Germany, France and Italy where several hundred persons had learned to serve as facilitators of intercultural communication groups. In January, 1980, the first person-centered learning program was started in Rome, described as having the purpose of developing skills and attitudes in client-centered therapy with individuals and of facilitating groups, using a person-centered approach. It was a part-time course lasting 18 months, including several 'intensives' which were week-long meetings blending cognitive and affective experiences, exploring various aspects of the person-centered approach and with opportunities for self-exploration. There were small group meetings and meetings of the entire community of approximately 50 students. In between these 'intensive' sessions the students, who came from all over Italy, met monthly in Milan, Rome or Naples, whichever was closest to them. Hundreds of students have been trained in this manner in Italy since 1978. At first, they were under the auspices of the Institute for Facilitator Development-Italy Center, co-directed by Devonshire and Alberto Zucconi. In the mid-eighties, Zucconi established the Institute for the Person-Centered Approach. At the turn of the century, about 50 people a year were completing a four-year training program, with a two-year Rogerian counseling program also being offered, and with larger numbers in shorter courses including teacher training, drug rehabilitation, health promotion, and community mental health.

ROGERS' WRITING AND WORKSHOPS IN CALIFORNIA

In addition to the two editions of *Freedom to Learn* (1969, 1983) and his book on encounter groups (1970), Rogers wrote three other books after moving to California, one on marriage and its alternatives (1972), another on personal power (1977), and finally *A Way of Being* (1980). Rogers' daughter Natalie, Alan Nelson, and Betty Meador and John K. Wood of the Center for Studies of the Person, offered three-week-long workshops in San Diego and Santa Cruz which were intended to explore the implications of the client-centered approach for therapy, education, intensive groups and other human relationships. There were regularly scheduled community meetings, in which the sixty-five or so participants dealt with very personal issues in a supportive environment characterized by the same principles of congruence, trust, and empathy offered in individual therapy.

Excited by the results, the group scheduled another workshop at Mills College in the summer of 1975, with an expanded staff, deciding to offer less structure and leave more of the decisions about the workshop to the entire group of 126 participants. Many of them found the lack of structure extremely frustrating and responded angrily, seeing the staff as irresponsible, but others took the initiative, suggesting needs, topics, and schedules. Without any formal announcement, the whole community assembled in the meeting room at pivotal times. While there were ups and downs, the participants were functioning as a supportive and egalitarian community midway into the sixteen days of the workshop.

INITIATION OF THE *PERSON-CENTERED REVIEW*

Rogers was wary of any institutionalization of client-centered therapy and the person-centered approach. In the first (February) issue of the *Person-Centered Review*, he explained,

I have always opposed the institutionalization of a client-centered 'school'— the founding of institutes, the granting of certificates of completion, the setting of standards for membership ... such institutionalization leads almost inevitably to an increasingly narrow, rigid, bureaucratic point of view. A second element to be considered is ... an aspect of the client-centered/person-centered approach that sets it apart. The approach is paradoxical. It emphasizes shared values, yet encourages uniqueness. It is rooted in a profound regard for the wisdom and constructive capacity inherent in the human organism ... At the same time, it encourages those who incorporate these values to develop their own special and unique ways of being ...

I see the exciting function of the new *Person-Centered Review* [that] ...

through its pages researchers in Germany can communicate with researchers in Texas and Massachusetts. Therapists in Poland can know the work of therapists in California. Educators in Israel and New York and Mexico can learn from each other ... The *Review* can be a vehicle for new ideas, innovative methods, thoughtful critiques, new models of research, and integrative philosophical and theoretical thinking ... I have high hopes for the *Review* and I wish it well. (1986: 3–5)

FIRST MEETING OF THE ASSOCIATION FOR THE DEVELOPMENT OF THE PERSON-CENTERED APPROACH (ADPCA)

The first meeting of the ADPCA was held in September of 1986 on the campus of the University of Chicago, at International House, a few blocks east of where the Counseling Center had been located and a few blocks west of the apartment building where Carl and Helen Rogers had lived from 1945 to 1957. The oldest person at the meeting, Carl was the most active, serving on a panel and holding an open session in which he was willing to respond to any questions or comments. He said that he was not afraid of death, only of being mentally incapacitated.

CARL ROGERS' DEATH

Carl was preparing for a return trip to South Africa with Ruth Sanford, when he died of a heart attack on February 4th, 1987, in La Jolla, at the age of 85, following surgery for a broken hip. He was surrounded in his last days by loving friends and colleagues. He was survived by his children, David and Natalie, and by six grandchildren. His wife, Helen, had died in 1979. Carl was mourned by thousands of admirers the world over.

FIRST WARM SPRINGS WORKSHOP

Jerold Bozarth of the University of Georgia wrote in the *Person-Centered Review*:
> A week after Carl Rogers' death, a four-day workshop was held in Warm Springs, Georgia. Jerold Bozarth and several graduate students organized the event. Formal presenters were Barbara Brodley, Jerold Bozarth, Chuck Devonshire, Nat Raskin, David Spahn, and Fred Zimring. The forty participants included graduate students, practitioners from Georgia, and others from Nevada, Kansas, Florida, and Illinois.
>
> The idea of the workshop developed in September, 1986 at the First Annual Meeting of the Association for the Development of the Person-Centered Approach. This initial spontaneous interest evolved into the Warm Springs workshop. (1987: 31–4).

Bozarth noted that Maria Bowen, Carl's close associate at the Center for Studies of the Person, had written of a fear of what would become of the person-centered approach in Carl's absence. A belief in the ability to carry on by those who were left without 'getting stuck by what Carl Rogers had said' was strongly expressed, a faith that there would be new formulations of thinking, organizing workshops and the perpetuation of the person-centered approach in other ways.

Bozarth concluded that perhaps Carl's greatest contribution was manifested at this workshop, the reminder of our unique personal power.

REFERENCES

Barrett-Lennard GT (1998) *Carl Rogers' Helping System. Journey and substance.* London: Sage.

Bozarth JD (1987) Person-centered workshop. *Person-Centered Review, 2*(3), 311–15.

Curran CA (1945) *Personality Factors in Counseling.* New York: Grune and Stratton.

Devonshire C & JW Kremer (1980) *Toward a person-centered resolution of interpersonal conflicts.* Dortmund, Germany: Padagogische Arbeitsstelle.

Grummon DL & Gordon T (1948) The counseling center at the University of Chicago. *The American Psychologist, 3,* 166–71.

Raskin NJ (1949) An analysis of six parallel studies of therapeutic process. *Journal of Consulting Psychology, 13*(3), 206–20.

Rogers CR (1939) *The Clinical Treatment of the Problem Child.* Boston: Houghton Mifflin.

Rogers CR (1942) *Counseling and Psychotherapy.* Boston: Houghton Mifflin.

Rogers CR (1957) The necessary and sufficient conditions of therapeutic personality change. *Journal of Consulting Psychology, 21*(2), 95–103.

Rogers CR (1959) A theory of therapy, personality, and interpersonal relationships, as developed in the client-centered framework. In S Koch (Ed) *Psychology: A study of a science, Vol. III. Formulations of the person and the social context.* New York: McGraw-Hill, pp. 184–256.

Rogers CR (1964) Toward a modern approach to values: The valuing process in the mature person. *Journal of Abnormal Social Psychology, 68*(2), 160–7.

Rogers CR (1969) *Freedom to Learn.* Columbus, Ohio: Charles E Merrill.

Rogers CR (1970) *Carl Rogers on Encounter Groups.* New York: Harper & Row.

Rogers CR (1972) *Becoming Partners: Marriage and its alternatives.* New York: Delacorte Press.

Rogers CR (1977) *Carl Rogers on Personal Power.* New York: Delacorte Press.

Rogers CR(1980) *A Way of Being. Boston*: Houghton Mifflin.

Rogers CR (1983) *Freedom to Learn in the 80s.* Columbus, Ohio: Charles E Merrill.

Rogers CR (1986) A comment from Carl Rogers. *Person-Centred Review 1*(1), 3–5.

Rogers CR & R Dymond (1954) *Psychotherapy and Personality Change.* Chicago: University of Chicago Press.

Rogers CR, Gendlin ET, Kiesler DJ & Truax CB (Eds) (1967) *The Therapeutic Relationship and its Impact: A study of psychotherapy with schizophrenics.* Madison: University of Wisconsin Press.

Rogers CR & Wallen JL (1946) *Counseling with Returned Servicemen.* New York: McGraw-Hill

Seeman J (1983) *Personality Integration.* New York: Human Sciences Press.

Snyder WU, Rogers CR & Carmichael, L (Eds)(1947) *Casebook of non-directive counseling.* Boston: Houghton Mifflin.

Taft J (1933) *The Dynamics of Therapy in a Controlled Relationship.* New York: Macmillan Company.

CHAPTER 3

FORMS[1] OF NON-DIRECTIVE PSYCHOTHERAPY: THE NON-DIRECTIVE TRADITION

GARRY PROUTY

Abstract

This chapter describes the non-directive principle in an integrative and historical context spanning roughly the last half-century through the sequential work of Carl Rogers, Eugene Gendlin and Garry Prouty.

THE NON-DIRECTIVE RELATIONSHIP

The client-centered relationship is characterized by empathy, unconditional positive regard, congruence and non-directivity (Rogers, 1957). Prouty (2000) provides a review of the non-directive principle as it appears in client-centered literature.

During the 1940s, the Zeitgeist of American psychology was highly directive. As an example, Thorne (1948) describes the therapist to be of superior experience and training, which thereby establishes a relationship of *dominance through prestige.*

A refreshing contrast was the new non-directive approach of Carl Rogers (1942: 115–26), who describes the quality of non-directivity in terms of *practice.* The client is described as taking responsibility for directing the interview. Second, the counselor responds in such a way as to indicate a recognition of the client's preceding message, and also responds to the client's immediate feelings and attitudes. The counselor indicates that decisions are up to the client and actually accepts them. Prouty (1994: 4) further adds to this practice description by suggesting that the counselor generally does not guide, direct, explain to or advise the client. Rogers next shifts his description of the non-directive principle to a set of *values* held by the therapist. The client has the right to select individual goals. The client has the right to be psychologically independent and to maintain psychological integrity. The client has the right to choose the right reality adaptation for himself or herself.

Raskin (1947/2005) further understands the non-directive principle as an *attitude.* He argues that the empathic attitude is inherently non-directive. Bozarth (1999) affirms and shares this view.

---

1. Merleau-Ponty (1983: 129–84) uses the philosophical concept of 'form' to describe emergent elements in nature that are both rooted and dialectic as well as evolving toward newer organization.

In a more *affect-oriented* statement, Bozarth (1999: 57) says: 'The essence of Rogerian therapy is non-directive empathy.' Finally, Van Belle (1980: 99) views non-directivity as *non-interference* with the actualizing process. *Reflections* themselves embody the non-directive principle because they are structurally designed to mirror client process. Thus we see that the non-directive principle has been defined in multiple ways: *practice, values, attitude, affect, non-interference and reflection.* One unifying thread is that the principle is *located in the therapist.*

NON-DIRECTIVE CONTACT

Rogers (1959) defines 'contact' as the first condition of a therapeutic relationship. Rogers (1957) defines this as the therapist and the client each making a perceived difference in the experiential field of the other. Prouty (1990) suggests that such a definition does not provide any opportunity for the development of therapeutic method or research operations. Consequently, Pre-Therapy is the theory and practice of 'psychological contact' as applied to clients with diagnoses of 'psychosis', dementia or those with severe learning disabilities. It is defined on philosophical, theoretical, practice and measurement levels. The theory of psychological contact is presented in three segments: contact reflections (method), contact functions (internal process) and contact behaviors (measurables). Complete and comprehensive reviews are available in Prouty (2002), Prouty, Van Werde and Pörtner (2002), and Prouty (2003).

CONTACT REFLECTIONS (CR)

The non-directivity of the contact reflection is first understood as the surrendered 'following' of the *concrete* process of the client. Such reflections are considered 'a pointing at the concrete' (Buber, 1964: 537). Contact reflections have the theoretical function of developing psychological contact between therapist and client. They are applied when there is not sufficient contact to initiate or maintain an empathic communication and the therapist lacks an understanding of the client's frame of reference (Sommerbeck, 2003). For a further discussion of technique, see Krietemeyer and Prouty (2003).

Situational reflections (SR)
Being embedded in a living concrete situation, environment or milieu constitutes our literal 'being in the world'. Accordingly, situational reflections facilitate reality contact for the client. An example would be 'Mary is playing with the cat' or 'John is at the door', concretely reflecting what is present in the client's environment.

Facial reflections (FR)
The human face, described as the 'expressive organ', embodies not-yet-formed 'pre-expressive' affect. Facial reflections facilitate the experiencing or expressing of affect. They develop or restore the client's affective contact. An example is 'You look sad' or

even more concretely, 'There are tears in your eyes'. Still another example could be, 'You look angry' or more literally, 'Your jaw is tight'.

Word-for-word reflections (WWR)

Many clients with diagnoses of 'schizophrenia', those with learning disabilities, or geriatric clients present verbal symptoms of incoherence. For example, many with diagnoses of schizophrenia present echolalia, neologisms, word-salads, etc. These are interspersed with social language. Such a flow of communication could be as follows: '(unintelligible), ring, (unintelligible), hat, (unintelligible) house'. Even though this makes no conventional sense, the Pre-Therapy approach would reflect the social language just as it occurs, word for word. These reflections give the experience of being *received as a human communicator*—a healing factor in itself. These reflections also facilitate communicative contact between client and therapist.

Body reflections (BR)

Many clients with diagnoses of schizophrenia express bizarre body symptoms such as echopraxia, catatonia, etc. Meddard Boss (1994) presents the concept of 'bodying forth'. This means that bodily symptoms (excluding medications) are a form of 'being-in-the-world' and, as such, express the person's existence. Body reflections, being empathic responses to such 'bodying forth', result in a shift toward more verbal communication, as illustrated in work reported by Prouty and Kubiak (1988) concerning the exploration of catatonia. There are two types of body reflection: (verbal) 'Your arm is in the air', or literal reflections through the body of the therapist.

Reiterative reflections (RR)

Not a specific technique, these reflections embody the principle of 're-contact'. If any specific reflection produces a response, the therapist should repeat it. There are two types of empathic reiterative reflection: short-term and long-term.

This exemplifies short-term reiteration: a patient remained silent and just touched her forehead, which the therapist kept reflecting with her own arm by touching her own forehead. The patient eventually said, 'Grandma'. Word-for-word reflections gradually moved her into some real feelings about her grandmother's death. An example of long-term reiteration occurred when a client kept pointing at her stomach. The therapist reiterated in a long-term mode by saying, 'Last week you said "Baby" and pointed at your belly'. Gradually, the process unfolded into a true story about a real pregnancy and an abortion.

This faithful reflection of pre-expressive process when the therapist *does not understand* the client's frame of reference is added to the non-directive principles that obtain when the therapist *does understand* the client's frame of reference. They all cluster together to form the non-directive principle, located in the therapist. This is perhaps summarized best by Rogers' (1980) famous phrase 'A Way of Being'.

Vignette

Van Werde and Morton (1999: 162) describe contact reflections and pre-expressive process in the interactions between a son and his mother dying from a brain tumor. The non-directive principle, as manifested in the son's contact reflections, is evident throughout this vignette:

[Please note that the apparent awkwardness of the mother's expression in this vignette is a function of her having a brain tumor, as well as English being her second language. These awkward expressions are marked with asterisks*, and are not typographical errors.]

Son:	(SR)	*Now I'm sitting on this side of the bed.*
	(SR)	*There is more light here.*
	(SR)	*I can read better here.*
...		
	(SR)	*I'm writing a bit.*
...		
	(BR)	*You hold your hands to your head.*
Mother:		*I was going to read.*
Son:	(WWR)	*You were going to read.*
Mother:		*Another paper.*
Son:	(WWR)	*Another paper.*
Mother:		*Kelloggs? Or what is the name?*
Son:		[Congruently] *Maalox?*
Mother:		*Yes. What?*
Son:	(WWR)	*What.*
Mother:		*What?*
Son:	(WWR)	*What.*
Mother:		*And which do you have to take then?*
Son:	(WWR)	*And which to take?*
	(BR)	*You keep your hands to your head.*
Mother:		*Yes.*
...		
Son:	(FR)	*... and you yawn.*
Mother:		*Yes. But I have to yawn.*
Son:	(WWR)	*Yes, I have to yawn.*
Mother:		*Yawn, yawn.*
Son:	(WWR)	*Yawn.*
Mother:		*Yes, Kelloggs.*
Son:	(WWR)	*Kelloggs.*
Mother:		*Yes. The Kelloggs Book. Yes.*
Son:	(WWR)	*Yes.*
	(RR)	*I came to sit on this side of the bed ... You were talking and your hand was on your head.*
Mother:		*And that was it.*

Son:	(WWR)	That was it.
Mother:		That was it, the deliberation.
Son:	(WWR)	The deliberation.

...

Son:	(FR)	... and you cough ...
Mother:		Yes, a bad cough ... I don't like it a bit.
Son:	(WWR)	You don't like it a bit.
	(RR)	You cough and say: I don't like it.
Mother:		I like it, I don't like it. Praying.
Son:	(WWR)	Praying.
Mother:		I like it, I don't like it.
Son:	(RR)	... and you say: praying.
Mother:		Now I am happy.
Son:	(WWR)	You're happy.
Mother:		Now I'm happy. Where I'm not happy, I am not happy ... And now I'm happy.
Son:	(WWR)	Now you are happy.
Mother:		Yes, that is fine isn't it?
Son:	(WWR)	That's fine.
Mother:		Voilà, that is the way it is. Am I happy, am I happy, am I not happy, am I not happy.* That's it.
Son:	(WWR)	That's it.

...

	(RR)	You cough and you said 'That's it'.
Mother:		And I cough and cough and cough.
Son:	(WWR)	And you say 'I cough'.
Son:	(FR, RR)	A big yawn and you say 'I cough'.

...

...

| Son: | (SR) | ... and you are silent now. |
| Mother: | | Yes. |

...

Mother:		Three times, I do good.
Son:	(WWR)	Three times, I do good.
Mother:		Mhm mhm ...

...

[Mother wipes her hand over the sheets.]

Son:	(BR)	You wipe your hand.
Mother:		My hand wipes the little chair.
Son:	(WWR)	Your hand wipes the little chair.
Mother:		I wiped the chair. Then I wipe loose. Then I don't wipe loose.
Son:	(RR)	You wiped the chair.
Mother:		Then I wipe it loose.

Son:	(SR)	Your hand is on the pillow.
Mother:		It looks like it, doesn't it …?
Son:	(WWR)	It looks like it, doesn't it …?
Mother:		Does somebody finally helps* me?
Son:	(WWR)	Does somebody finally helps me?
Mother:		Do I get help? Yes, don't I?
Son:	(WWR)	You ask if you are getting help.
Mother:		Yes … It is good isn't it?
Son	(WW):	You say it is good.
Mother:		It is [unclear…]
Son:	(WWR)	It is of the boys?
Mother:		Grandiose.
Son:	(RR, WWR)	I heard of the boys and you say grandiose.
Mother:		That's what I also heard in the beginning, and it isn't true.
Son:	(RR)	Grandiose.
Mother:		Why isn't that OK?
Son:	(WWR)	Why isn't that OK?
Mother:		It is good.
…		
Mother:		Yes. What is there left to do? What is there left to do?
Son:	(WWR, BR)	What is there left to do? And you hold your hand to your head.
Mother:		What is there still left over then? I want to do something about it though…
Son:	(WWR)	I do want to do something about it though.
Mother:		But what? Muscles. If all that is food for us … Goody goody good …
Son:	(WWR, RR)	Goody goody good … What there is still left over.
Mother:		If there still is something left over … You know what I mean, 'S'.
Son:	(WWR)	[surprised and very touched] You say my Christian name, 'S'.
Mother:		'S' I say, 'SQ'. [Forename and family name!]
Son:	(WWR)	'SQ', that's my name!
Mother:		That's your name. That's a beautiful name.

[S sits closer and caresses the hand of his mother.]

…

Son:	(SR)	And it turned a little bit darker outside …
Mother:		… and more quiet …
Son:	(WWR)	(agreeing and confirming) … more quiet …
Mother:		… and more quiet, that pleases me.
Son:	(WWR)	… and more quiet, that pleases you.

Quiet.

NON-DIRECTIVE EXPERIENCING

EXPERIENTIAL PROCESS

Gendlin (1964) describes his theory of experiencing as *concrete, bodily felt process*. *Concrete* means the person can directly refer to the experiencing. *Bodily felt* means it can be sensed in the organism. *Process* means there is a felt shift in experiential content A to experiential content B.

Reflection—the experiential response
Gendlin (1964) considers experiencing the essence of psychological change, irrespective of clinical technique. Rogers considers reflection the embodiment of empathy, unconditional positive regard and non-directivity. Although *historically* identified with the more directive focusing method, Gendlin (1968) considers reflection a response that facilitates the experiencing process. Reflection carries forth the concrete bodily felt process of the person. Reflection is always *at* the concrete, *at* the felt, and *at* process. *In this sense, reflection is still considered non-directive because it follows the experiencing process of the person.* Providing further emphasis on non-directive experiencing, Gendlin (1968) states that only the person knows his/her experiential track (process). A complete review of Gendlin's theory is available in Prouty (1994).

The problematic
Gendlin (1964) described hallucinations as 'structure-bound experiencing'. First, they are described by the client literally '*as such*' and as '*not his*'. Second, this particular structure-bound experience is *isolated,* meaning the experiencing is not included in the felt functioning of organism. Third, this implicitly felt functioning is *rigid,* not in experiential process. Finally, what is structure-bound is a static, repetitious and unmodifiable mode of experiencing. The problematic is how to turn this *non-process experiencing* into *process experiencing.* Stated another way, the problem concerns how to put hallucinations into an experiential therapeutic process, while still maintaining the non-directive attitude and approach.

PRE-SYMBOLIC PROCESS: A FURTHER EVOLUTION IN NON-DIRECTIVE EXPERIENTIAL PROCESS

The shift from non-process experiencing to process experiencing requires a philosophical shift from perceived immediate experience (Merleau-Ponty, 1962) to symbolized experience (Cassirer, 1955; Langer, 1961). Also, the semiotic explication of the concreteness of symbols themselves is another issue. This results in the *ultra-concrete* form of symbolization known as the 'Pre-Symbol' (Prouty, 1986). The Pre-Symbol is 'inseparable from what it symbolizes' and 'it cannot be clarified by something else' (Jaspers, 1971: 124). The Pre-Symbolic hallucination is an ultra-concrete symbolization of a psychologically traumatic experience—a complete description of the theory is available in Prouty (2004).

Vignette

Prouty and Pietrzak (1988) describe the non-directive application of the Pre-Therapy technique (contact reflections) to the hallucinatory experience. The following vignette describes a *non-directive* approach to Pre-Symbolic process—the shift from structure-bound, non-process experiencing to process experiencing. Contact reflections carry forth the concrete Pre-Symbolic hallucination towards an experiential therapeutic process, while maintaining the non-directive attitude and approach:

'Michael', a divorced man in his sixties, was referred as an outpatient. His original diagnosis was phobic-neurosis; however, the referring psychiatrist described the client as experiencing an acute depressive episode and was concerned over possible hospitalization for a developing schizophrenic psychosis. The client was not receiving medication. Presenting symptoms were intense, vivid images that the client periodically experienced as real. Corresponding physical problems were sweating, increased blood pressure, tremors, and other physical manifestations of anxiety. Frequently, these symptoms rendered the client non-functional. The symptoms occurred after the client married his 'common-law' wife of several years. The client reported no such symptoms during 30 years of previous marriage or during other intimate relationships.

Michael experienced images of being drowned and of persons without faces being hurt. He reported feelings of being in a dangerous situation that he could not explain.

Client:		*It's like I'm drowning.*
Therapist:	*(WWR)*	*You're drowning.*
Client:		*Yeah.*
Therapist:	*(RR)*	*It's like you're drowning.*
Client:		*Can't figure it—where I am.*
Therapist:	*(FR)*	*Where are you? Your face is twisted.*
Client:		*Where—it's horrible.*
Therapist:	*(BR)*	*It's horrible, you're moving all over.*
Client:		*It's like I'm drowning. Yes, it's me.*
Therapist:	*(WWR)*	*It's you.*
Client:		*It's me drowning. It's not big, it's a bathtub or something.*
Therapist:	*(WWR)*	*It's you—bathtub or something.*
Client:		*I can't breathe.* [Client, hands to throat]
Therapist:	*(BR)*	*It's choking you.* [Therapist, hands to throat]
Client:		*It's all over—faces, it's all over.*
Therapist:	*(WWR)*	*It's all over.*
Client:		*Black, clear people.*
Therapist:	*(WWR)*	*Black, clear people.*
Client:		*Cold. It's getting me.*
Therapist:	*(WWR)*	*Cold. It's getting me.*

	(RR)	*It's all over.*
Client:		*It's me in a bathtub. Faces. I'm in a bathtub.*
Therapist:	(WWR)	*You're in a bathtub.* [Long pause]
Client:		*I'm in a bathtub. I'm drowning. Faces, people, are they getting hurt?*
Therapist:	(WWR)	*It's you in a bathtub.*
Client:		*It's me—what's happening? It's getting me. I'm drowning. The faces are ugly.*
Therapist:	(BR)	*You turn away. You're drowning—ugly.*
Client:		*It's getting me.*
Therapist:	(WWR)	*It's getting me.*
Client:		*It's those faces.*
Therapist:	(WWR)	*It's those faces, ugly.*
Client:		*They're mad and black.*
Therapist:	(WWR)	*They're mad and black.*
Client:		*I'm drowning.* [Client cries.] *It's only one.*
Therapist:	(FR)	*You're crying. You're drowning. It's only one.*
Client:		*It's smothering me. There is no water in the tub.*
Therapist:	(WWR)	*It's smothering you. No water.*
Client:		*No water—the face is smothering me.* [Client cries more. Long pause]
Therapist:	(WWR)	*No water—the face is smothering you. You're crying.*
Client:		*It's my ex-wife. She is smothering me.* [Long pause] *Oh, I'm in the basement.*
Therapist:	(WWR)	*I'm in the basement.*
Client:		*Help me.* [Client sobs]
Therapist:	(WWR)	*It's your ex-wife.*
	(RR)	*You're in the basement.*
Client:		*Yeah, it's cold and dark.*
Therapist:	(WWR)	*It's cold and dark.*
Client:		*My bed is in the corner. It's small.*
Therapist:	(WWR)	*My bed is in the corner. It's small.*
Client:		*I sleep in the basement. My marriage smothered me.*
Therapist:	(WWR)	*My marriage smothered me.*
	(FR)	*You looked pained, eyes big.*
Client:		*Yeah, I hurt. My marriage smothered me. It's like I was drowning in the relationship.*
Therapist:	(WWR)	*You're hurting, the marriage was smothering. Your relationship was like drowning.*
Client:		*All those years I was suffocating because of our wedding vows. We couldn't get a divorce because we were Catholic. Being married again is being tied to those horrible memories of our marriage and religion.*
Therapist:	(WWR)	*Marriage is horrible because of vows.*
Client:		*I can't be married. I'm afraid of being suffocated and being lost at*

36

		sea.
Therapist:	*(WWR)*	*I can't be married. I'm afraid of being suffocated and being lost at sea.*
Client:		*It took forever for an annulment before. I can't live forever like that again.*
Therapist:	*(WWR)*	*It took forever for an annulment before. I can't live forever like that again.*
Therapist:	*(FR)*	*You stopped crying.*
Client:		*I don't know how to be married right. When I go to bed, I remember nights in the basement. Oh God, they were horrible.*

Later, Michael started dealing with issues relating to his past and current marriage. He had gained insight into how his past marriage affected his current marriage. The hallucinations ceased.

SUMMARY

This paper has traced the historical influence of the non-directive form through the theoretical work of Carl Rogers, Eugene Gendlin and Garry Prouty. The non-directive approach is manifested, as a form (see footnote, p. 28), in varying degrees in their work. Originating with Rogers (1942), non-directivity involves practice and values. Prouty (1994) further adds to this description by suggesting the therapist does not guide, direct, explain or advise. Raskin (1947/2005) suggests non-directivity is an attitude embedded in the therapist. Bozarth (1999) suggests that empathy is inherently non-directive. Van Belle (1980) suggests non-directivity is non-interference with the actualizing process. Reflection itself is considered non-directive since it mirrors client process.

Evolving from Rogers' suggestion of 'psychological contact' as the first condition of a therapeutic relationship, Prouty developed a treatment method (Pre-Therapy) for clients who are contact impaired. This includes persons diagnosed as 'psychotic', 'retarded' (those with learning disabilities) or suffering from dementia. The non-directive principle is focused there through the contact reflections which follow the very concrete pre-expressive aspects of client experiencing.

As the client-centered tradition evolved into the experiential phase (Hart, 1970), Gendlin (1964) defined experiencing as concrete bodily felt process. Reflection then became the facilitation of the experiencing process. However, his description of hallucinations resulted in a non-process understanding. The problem arose of how to develop a process conception of schizophrenic hallucinations. Shifting from an emphasis on experiencing to the concept of *symbolizing* experience, the semiotic understanding of the hallucination emerged as the Pre-Symbol. The use of contact reflection maintains a non-directive approach in carrying forth the Pre-Symbolic towards experiencing.

REFERENCES

Bozarth JD (1999) *Person-Centered Therapy: A revolutionary paradigm.* Ross-on-Wye: PCCS Books.

Boss M (1994) *Existential Foundations of Medicine and Psychology.* London: Jason Aronson.

Buber M (1964) Phenomenological analysis of existence versus pointing to the concrete. In M Freidman (Ed) *The Worlds of Existentialism.* New York: Random House.

Cassirer E (1955) Man—An animal symbolicum. In D Dunes (Ed) *Treasury of Philosophy.* New York: Philosophical Library, pp. 227–9.

Gendlin ET (1964) A theory of personality change. In P Worchel & D Burns (Eds) *Personality Change.* New York: Wiley, pp. 102–48.

Gendlin ET (1968) The experiential response. In E Hammer (Ed) *The Use of Interpretation in Treatment.* New York: Grune and Stratton, pp. 208–28.

Hart JT (1970) The development of client-centered therapy. In JT Hart & TM Tomlinson (Eds) *New Directions in Client-Centered Therapy.* Boston: Houghton-Mifflin, pp. 1–22.

Jaspers I (1971) *Philosophy,* Vol 3. Chicago: University of Chicago Press.

Krietemeyer B & Prouty GF (2003). The art of psychological contact: The psychotherapy of a retarded/psychotic client. *Person-Centered & Experiential Therapies, 2*(3), 160.

Langer S (1961) *Philosophy in a New Key.* New York: Mentor Books.

Merleau-Ponty M (1962) *The Phenomenology of Perception.* London: Routledge & Kegan Paul.

Merleau-Ponty M (1983) *The Structure of Behavior.* Pittsburgh, PA: Dusquenne University Press.

Prouty GF (1986) The pre-symbolic structure and therapeutic transformation of hallucinations. In M Wolpin, J Shorr & L Krueger (Eds) *Imagery: Recent practice and theory* (Vol. 4). New York: Plenum Press, pp. 99–106.

Prouty GF (1990) Pre-Therapy: A theoretical evolution in the person-centered/experiential psychotherapy of schizophrenia and retardation. In G Lietaer, J Rombauts & R Van Balen (Eds) *Client-Centered and Experiential Therapy in the Nineties.* Leuven, Belgium: Leuven University Press, pp. 645–58.

Prouty GF (1994) *Theoretical Evolutions in Person-Centered/Experiential Therapy: Applications to schizophrenic and retarded psychoses.* Westport, CT: Praeger-Greenwood.

Prouty GF (2000) A rejoinder to person-centered psychotherapy: One nation, many tribes. *Person Centered Journal, 7*(2), 125-8.

Prouty G (2002) Pre-therapy as a theoretical system. In G Wyatt and P Sanders (Eds) *Rogers' Therapeutic Conditions: Evolution, theory and practice. Vol. 4: Contact and Perception.* Ross-on-Wye: PCCS Books, pp. 54-62.

Prouty G (2003) Pre-therapy: A newer development in the psychotherapy of schizophrenia. *Journal of the American Academy of Psychoanalysis and Dynamic Psychiatry, 31*(1), 59–73.

Prouty G (2004, in press) The hallucination as the unconscious self. *The Journal of the American Academy of Psychoanalysis and Dynamic Psychiatry.*

Prouty G & Kubiak M (1988) The development of communicative contact with a catatonic schizophrenic. *Journal of Communication Therapy, 4*(1), 13–20.

Prouty G & Pietrzak S (1998) The pre-therapy method applied to persons experiencing hallucinatory images. *Person-Centered Review, 3*(4), 426-41.

Prouty G, Van Werde D & Pörtner M (2002) *Pre-Therapy: Reaching contact impaired clients.* Ross-on Wye: PCCS Books.

Raskin NJ (1947/2005) The Nondirective Attitude. In BE Levitt (Ed) *Embracing Non-directivity: Reassessing person-centered theory and practice in the 21st century.* Ross-on-Wye: PCCS Books, pp. 329–47.

Rogers CR (1942) *Counseling and Psychotherapy*. Boston: Houghton Mifflin.

Rogers CR (1957) The necessary and sufficient conditions of personality change. *Journal of Consulting Psychology, 21*(2), 95–103.

Rogers CR (1959) A theory of therapy, personality and interpersonal relationships as developed in the client-centered framework. In E Koch (Ed) *Psychology: A study of a science*. New York: McGraw-Hill, pp. 184–216.

Rogers CR (1980) *A Way of Being*. Boston: Houghton Mifflin.

Sommerbeck L (2003) *The Client-Centered Therapist in Psychiatric Contexts: A therapists' guide to the psychiatric landscape and its inhabitants*. Ross-on-Wye: PCCS Books.

Thorne FC (1948) Principles of directive counseling and psychotherapy. *American Psychologist, 3*, 160–5.

Van Belle HA (1980) *Basic Intent and Therapeutic Approach of Carl R Rogers*. Toronto: Wedge Publishing Foundation.

Van Werde D & Morton, I (1999) The relevance of Prouty's Pre-Therapy to dementia care. In I Morton (Ed) *Person-Centred Approaches to Dementia Care*. Bicester, Oxon: Winslow Press, pp. 139–66.

CHAPTER 4

TWO ROGERS AND CONGRUENCE: THE EMERGENCE OF THERAPIST-CENTERED THERAPY AND THE DEMISE OF CLIENT-CENTERED THERAPY

MARVIN FRANKEL AND LISBETH SOMMERBECK

Abstract

In this chapter we would like to demonstrate that person-centered therapists, as well as psychoanalysts, commit the category error and, in so doing, hopelessly confound the rules of their therapeutic discourse: the distinguishing features of psychoanalysis and person-centered therapy (PCT) cease to exist. In fact, such a confounding of the rules has been so extensive in the person-centered approach that it has resulted in the frequently asked question: 'What do we mean by PCT?' We will explain what the category error is and then show how it is committed, and the consequences of committing it, in psychoanalysis and PCT, respectively.

By discussing psychoanalysis as well as PCT, we will show that committing the category error is a very general phenomenon that blurs the distinction between different models of psychotherapy, as well as between therapeutic relationships and other kinds of relationship. Further, since other people's errors are often easier to acknowledge than our own, we hope that we, by starting with a demonstration of the category error in psychoanalysis, will make it easier for the reader to recognize it in PCT.

More specifically, we will argue that in committing the category error by introducing therapist congruence as an independent therapeutic agent, Rogers' theory of therapy changed radically from his pre-Wisconsin years to his post-Wisconsin years. This change meant, among other things, that the therapist's non-directive attitude was no longer implied in the theory. The term 'non-directive' is, however, used infrequently in the chapter. It is implied whenever we speak about empathic understanding, since empathic understanding is, by definition, post-dictive and not pre-dictive.

Finally, we will show that the reasons for this change in Rogers' thinking will be found in the therapists' difficulties with the client-population of the Wisconsin research.

THE CATEGORY ERROR

You would be making a category error, according to the philosopher, Gilbert Ryle (1949), if you treated the name of a class of things as if it were itself a member of that class. An obvious example of such an error would be to treat the category *dog* as if it existed on the same level as Collie, Cocker Spaniel, Bulldog, Beagle and Great Dane. A child who did not know what a dog was would be making a category error if, after being shown pictures of each of these five breeds, he or she were to then turn and ask: 'But where is the picture of the dog?' as if still another entity, the dog itself, existed alongside of particular kinds of dog.

Using the example above, the category error that concerns us here substitutes acting as a *genuine human being* for the category *dog*, and acting as a psychoanalyst, acting as a person-centered therapist, acting as a friend, acting as a spouse, acting as a son or daughter, for the particular breeds. When you have described all the ways in which a person relates to other people, you have described how a genuine person acts. It is thus a category error to consider *acting as a genuine human being* as a way of acting in addition, or opposed, to acting as a therapist. These are not different ways of relating or acting, two roles that a person might assume. Rather, each is a particular case of the other.

THE CATEGORY ERROR IN PSYCHOANALYSIS

AN EXAMPLE

In her book, *Psychoanalysis, The Impossible Profession*, Malcolm (1980) describes a seminar held at the New York Psychoanalytic Institute in which the following question was raised and heatedly discussed: 'Should the analyst express sympathy to a patient whose father just died?' Two prominent psychoanalysts disagreed. Leo Stone stated that he would certainly express his condolences. Such a statement would express his natural feelings of sympathy. Charles Brenner unhesitatingly acknowledged that he would remain silent and pursue the psychoanalytic hour in the usual fashion by maintaining neutrality. When Malcolm discussed this incident with a younger psychoanalyst, the latter argued in defense of Brenner: 'Charlie is a very kind man. He might not say anything to the patient, but I'm sure he would let him know somehow, probably with his eyes, how sorry he was.' Of course, this analyst has failed to grasp the significance of the issue. Undoubtedly Charlie would have been very unhappy to discover that his eyes betrayed his psychoanalytic mission. Malcolm (1980), however, presents, in her eyes, a presumably cogent defense of Stone's active expression of sympathy by quoting no less of an authority than Anna Freud:

> With due respect for the necessary strictest handling of the interpretation of transference, I still feel that we should leave room somewhere for the realization that the analyst and patient are also two real people, of equal adult status, in a real personal relationship to each other. I wonder whether our at-times-complete neglect of this side of the matter is not responsible for some of the hostile reactions which we get from our patients and which we are apt to ascribe to 'true transference' only. (p. 40)

Here we have the category error in full bloom. We are told not to forget that 'analyst and patient are also two real people', as if a psychoanalyst and patient are less real and human than two friends. Is Brenner less real and human when he conducts his psychoanalytic

41

session as he always does than Stone, who begins the session by expressing his sympathy? In light of the category error this issue of realness and genuineness is bogus. Both Brenner and Stone are being genuine or real whether sympathy is expressed or not expressed. Yet there is an important issue here, and that issue is nothing less than the meaning of the rules which guide the interaction between psychoanalyst and patient. Brenner understands these conceptual rules rather differently from Stone and we suspect that not only would he fail to express his sympathy for the death of the patient's father, but the thought may never occurr to him. Let us examine then, the concepts that guide the psychoanalytic relationship and note how Brenner's behavior is more consistent with these rules than is Stone's.

Analysis of the example

First, the psychoanalytic patient must be provided with maximum freedom to express his experiences, however idiosyncratic or anti-social. Second, within the context of the psychoanalytic model it is important for the patient to view all his feelings for the analyst, as well as his suppositions of the analyst's attitude and feelings, as his own inventions. In other words, whatever inhibitions the patient may have in narrating their experience must be viewed by the patient as self-induced, the product of *intra-personal defenses* rather than inter-personal defenses. In the present case, the analyst's expression of sympathy may make it difficult for a patient to convey his own possible feelings of ambivalence towards the death of his father for fear that the analyst would view him as a callous and uncaring human being. For example, should the patient say: 'I find it very difficult to talk about the death of my father', the analyst must have a basis for asking 'Why?' without feeling that he or she has in any way contributed to the patient's inhibition. If the patient then retorts: 'Well, I know how you think I ought to feel', Brenner could say with integrity: 'Can you point to anything I have said or done to indicate that I think there is a right way to feel about the death of your father?' Such a statement invites the patient to review his feelings in light of his own moral standards, rather than escape such self-analysis by transferring or attributing such feelings to the analyst. Brenner's neutrality does not allow the patient to escape critical self-analysis through transference. In stark contrast Leo Stone, by expressing his sympathy, would contribute to the client's inhibitions by having provided, with his expression of sympathy, his own judgment regarding what constitutes appropriate and inappropriate feelings on the death of one's father. Stone would have thus undermined the likelihood of the patient discussing his feelings within the context of the transference relationship which is the essence of psychoanalytic treatment. No less of an authority than Fenichel (1945) cogently argues on the importance of the psychoanalytic analysis of transference:

> While all therapies involve transference relationships it is only in psychoanalysis that the relationship is itself a subject for analysis. Unlike other therapies the analyst never gives advice for such advice if taken does not emanate from the strength of the patient but is instead a borrowed strength. (p. 564)

Thus transference, the inaccurate defensive attributions of the patient, contaminates all human relationships; but it is 'only' in the psychoanalytic relationship that these contaminants can be analyzed and this is possible, in major part, because of the opaque, neutral presence of the analyst. Brenner maintains this opaqueness and Stone undermines it. Moreover, if the expression of sympathy is necessary to sustain the relationship with the patient, then in Fenichel's terms, the relationship is too dependent on the 'borrowed strength' of the analyst's concern. In other words, the analyst's sympathy may permit the patient to have compassion for him/herself. Consequently the patient may not discover why he/she is unable to express legitimate compassion for him- or herself. Although Brenner does not commit the category error by acting as a person *in addition* to acting as a psychoanalyst, a person sympathetic to psychoanalysis would have considerable reason to be uneasy. The neutrality of the analyst may well have alienated too many patients. The Anna Freud quote does indeed point to a real problem when she speaks about 'some of the hostile reactions ... from patients ... which [are], ascribed to "true transference" only'. The analyst who spoke of Charlie's kind eyes was also acknowledging, by such a reference, that the transference model was less than optimal in creating an effective therapeutic relationship. Malcolm notes that applications for psychoanalytic training, as well as the number of patients prepared to enter psychoanalysis, had been dropping (Malcolm, 1980). Consequently, while Brenner's actions are more consistent with the rules of orthodox psychoanalytic discourse, he may be one of a vanishing breed owing to the diminished success of the transference model. In reply, Stone would argue that in addition to the transference relationship there is also a 'working relationship' or 'therapeutic alliance' between patient and analyst, and it is in the context of the 'working relationship' that he would express his sympathy (Greenson, 1967). Although the distinction between the transference relationship and working relationship or therapeutic alliance is commonplace, the rules for distinguishing the two in therapeutic discourse remain unclear. On the one hand, psychoanalysts regard transference as a ubiquitous phenomenon. All human relationships are, more or less, transference relationships. The notion of a working relationship or therapeutic alliance that is transference-free contradicts and nullifies the traditional understanding of transference. Consider the rules of the so-called working relationship such as the charging of fees, the forty-five minute session and the setting up of appointments on a strict timetable. These three aspects of the working relationship can be objectified, but the patient's feelings about fees, forty-five minute sessions and the setting up of appointments, are subjective transference reactions that are the result of the patient's developmental history. To question this fact is in effect a repudiation of the psychoanalytic model of therapy. Moreover, as Fenichel argued, it was only the psychoanalytic relationship that permitted the analysis of transference to take place, because psychoanalysts alone followed the rule of strict neutrality. Once strict neutrality is abandoned the psychoanalytic relationship resembles any other kind of therapeutic relationship. If the strict neutrality of the analyst confused and frustrated patients, consider how the distinction between the working relationship and the transference relationship may add to that confusion of the patient in analysis. Consider the following hypothetical possibility. If the psychoanalyst offers sympathy on the death of his father to the 'person', when he arrives, can we really expect the 'person' to offer their gratitude for the condolence, and then recline on the couch as a patient and express how disgusted he is at the false sentiments of sympathy offered by people, including the analyst? Can the analyst in question expect any patient to understand and accept the following reply: 'Oh, that was part of the working relationship. I wasn't your analyst then; I was simply a person offering sympathy to another person.' Of course this reply begs the question, for what is at issue here is the role the person in question is enacting. By committing the category error the analyst invites the patient on the couch to reply: 'As a person then, you offer false sympathy to a loss I do not feel, but as my analyst you have no thoughts on the matter. By the way, who is explaining this to me, my analyst or some person?!!'

THE CATEGORY ERROR IN MODERN PSYCHOANALYSIS

Despite the conceptual and clinical confusion of the 'working relationship', few analysts adhere to strict neutrality today. In fact, neutrality has ceased to be a primary goal. For example, Gaylin (2001) describes the therapist[1] as a 'person who will listen with an air of compassionate neutrality … beyond neutrality, a person who is supportive and reassuring, an ally.' Without even a reference to Fenichel, Gaylin encourages the patient to borrow from the analyst's strength. One half-century of psychoanalytic concern is thrown out the window, without even the trace of a footnote. The psychoanalyst has become the school counselor who cheers the students to optimism. But what of the analysis of transference with an analyst who is 'beyond neutrality' and reassuring? In a section on transference Gaylin writes: 'The importance of transference interpretations originally rested in part on the underlying assumption that they were independent of the ongoing relationship with the therapist. This does happen … but the projection is often contaminated by reality' (2001: 73). But Gaylin does not disclose the nature of that social reality. Instead, he commits the category error in asserting there is a social reality that is independent of the analyst–patient relationship, when in fact the latter defines the former. The psychoanalytic relationship in the hands of Gaylin does not contaminate transference so much as it renders it unanalyzable. In stark contrast, Brenner and those analysts who do not confuse the transference relationship with working relationships, therapeutic alliances, and who go 'beyond neutrality', can ask the patient what historical reality in their life may have led to their attribution that the analyst felt one way or another about the subject under consideration. Of course it could be argued that the 'neutrality' of Brenner was perceived by many patients as embodying too cold and too uncaring a physician and thus 'contaminated' the doctor–patient relationship. Why talk your heart out to a cold person? If such is the case, then 'neutrality' ceases to have the meaning Freud intended it to have. Freud intended his neutrality to convey

---

1. Though Gaylin employs the term 'psychotherapy' rather than 'psychoanalysis' he refers to psychoanalytic concepts like transference, neutrality and the unconscious in ways that are quite similar to contemporary psychoanalytic writings. It is in fact our argument that as a result of the category error, Gaylin himself would have difficulty in answering the question as to whether he was a psychoanalyst or a psychotherapist, and if the latter, what kind.

that he is not going to engage in value judgments. If you go to a dermatologist with a disfiguring ailment, you do not expect the dermatologist to exclaim how ugly you are. Similarly the neutrality of Freud was supposed to convey to the patient that the analyst would not suddenly exclaim how immoral he/she was. But if neutrality is understood as a sign of indifference and coldness, the patient may react by rejecting the relationship and seek a therapist who does not ascribe to the transference model and thus treats the patient in a more conventional way. Thus, Stone and Gaylin may be more effective therapists than Brenner and other orthodox psychoanalysts; but the problem here is defining what kind of therapy Stone and Gaylin are practicing. In compromising the transference model, Stone becomes his own man. He may express sympathy one day and another sentiment the next. Such personal expressions may ingratiate him to particular people he sees in treatment. Stone's enactment of humanness may be more therapeutic than Brenner's enactment of therapeutic concern, but the quality of Stone's humanity remains undefined and unteachable. It is not without some irony that we suspect that if Stone were alive and had read Gaylin's book he would have said that Gaylin has gone too far in abandoning neutrality and the transference model. Perhaps Stone would also realize that it was his scholarly work that led to the present muddle in psychoanalysis.

THE CATEGORY ERROR IN PERSON-CENTERED THERAPY (PCT)

The category error has also diluted the defining feature of PCT. Instead of a debate between Brenner and Stone we have only to refer to what we shall term 'Rogers-1', the author of *Client-Centered Therapy*, and 'Rogers-2', whose work with people diagnosed with schizophrenia altered his thinking in fundamental ways. Rogers-1 corresponds to Brenner in that just as Brenner remained true to the psychoanalytic model of transference, so Rogers-1 remained consistent to the philosophical and psychological model of client-centered theory; while Rogers-2, like Stone and Anna Freud, commits the category error which renders his therapeutic model eclectic at best and virtually undefinable at worst.

ROGERS-1

First, let us present Rogers-1. The subject index of *Client-Centered Therapy* (1951) refers neither to congruence or genuineness. This is not because congruence and genuineness are unimportant; quite the contrary. Rogers-1 devotes an entire chapter to the philosophical attitude of the client-centered counselor. Rogers-1 makes it abundantly clear that unless the therapist is comfortable (congruent) with the client-centered orientation, he/she would be best served by a more congenial philosophical and therapeutic outlook.

The client-centered approach of Rogers-1 can best be understood if we view Rogers within a historical setting. Prior to Rogers, psychotherapeutic approaches were dominated by a concern for unearthing particular content. Freud, Jung, Adler and others did not differ in their method of treatment. Free association, dream analysis, transference reactions were essential in every case. The difference between these theorists was that each believed that unless a particular content was examined, the patient could not be liberated from their past and therapeutic change would not occur. For Freud there were among other things, the Oedipus complex and the Electra complex; for Adler, sibling rivalry; and so on down the list. In contrast, Rogers offered a model of personality and psychopathology devoid of content but instead emphasizing process. Rogers argued that, regardless of content, psychopathological development occurs when a person becomes alienated from his or her own organismic valuing process in order to meet the perceived conditions of worth of significant others. Thus, a man with an Oedipus complex may renounce his sexuality in order to be regarded as wholesome. A woman suffering from sibling rivalry may project an affection for an unconsciously hated brother in order to be viewed as a fair and loving human being. Whatever the cause, clients who seek therapeutic help are past masters at compromising their own internal standards in order to meet the approval and love of significant others.[2] The client who enters therapy has, by so doing, acknowledged that in some ways, what he or she is, is not what he or she ought to be. The act of commencing psychotherapy is an act of self-criticism. But this initial self-critical act more often than not stalls once the person enters therapy. The implicit sense of 'responsibility', 'shame' or 'guilt' for being less than one could be is too heavy a weight to bear. To sustain self-criticism, self-love must exceed self-contempt. Consequently, the client must learn to engage in the sustained act of self-criticism through the non-judgmental attitude of the therapist. But Rogers goes much further. The therapist must convey much more than the absence of judgment to overcome the client's defenses. The therapist must convey an actual prizing or unconditional positive regard of the client. Rogers' unconditional positive regard for a particular client emanates from his view that it is in the nature of human beings to be creative and constructive members of a society that offers each individual the greatest scope for self-expression. In this view, when an individual such as Hitler emerges, it is because his innate pro-social nature has been corrupted, just as a once-friendly dog might become vicious on getting rabies. If young

---

2. However, in common with psychoanalysis, Rogers did believe in the dynamic unconscious and defense mechanisms. Rogers employed subception, distortion and denial as illustrations of unconscious defenses. Unlike Freud though, Rogers believed that a safe and encouraging therapeutic relationship could enable the client to release their unconscious defense strategies. Most importantly, the total acceptance experienced by the client would veridically reflect actual attitudes of the therapist's behavior and manner. In other words, the transference neurosis was not necessary to cure the neurosis that brought the client into therapy in the first place. Rogers-1 abhorred the concept of transference, because it suggested that the power of the therapist to demonstrate acceptance depended upon neurotic and infantile projections of the client, since an actual therapist–client relationship could never enable a client to overcome unconscious resistances. In contrast, Rogers-1 went further and attempted to show how such an actual relationship can be established. In addition, Rogers-1 argued that the authoritarian interpretative attitude of the psychoanalyst encouraged the infantile expressions of transference, whereas the more egalitarian client-centered therapeutic context discouraged such infantile dependency (Rogers, 1951, Chapter 5).

Adolf knew better he would not have *chosen* to be HITLER, the icon of evil, any more than a healthy dog would choose to become rabid.[3, 4] In either case Hitler, the destroyer of life, and the rabid dog may need to be put to death, but with the compassion that stems from a benign view of human nature, rather than revenge.

Unless the therapist accepts this benign view of human nature, the communication of therapeutic positive regard will always be conditional. In any case, Rogers devised a way of conveying unconditional positive regard without at the same time compromising the free flow of the client's experience. It was demonstrated by showing the client through unwavering empathic reflections that the therapist believed in the client's capacity to profoundly redirect their lives. If a client wanted advice, direction or reassurance then Rogers-1 would reflect the apprehensions of the client that leads him to discover from others the answers to difficult life questions.[5] Therapists of all persuasions would agree that clients must experience a freedom from the judgment of the therapist when narrating their experience. The Brenner–Stone debate was, in part, about the precariousness of such felt freedom. However, Rogers argued persuasively that the traditional therapeutic manner of relating to patients through the use of diagnostic tests, interpretations of the unconscious and concepts such as resistance and transference may rob clients of the validity of their experience. Could a patient deny the role of sexuality in their life and still feel prized by their Freudian analyst? Rogers thought not. Consequently Rogers developed a therapeutic method that hopefully democratized the patient–therapist relationship by minimizing the authoritarian role of the therapist. He hoped that consistent empathic understanding would virtually eliminate the client's perception of the therapist's conditions of worth. Empathic understanding places the client in the driver's seat. The client determines whether he or she is understood. Within the Rogerian framework the client is the ultimate arbiter as to the rightness or wrongness of the therapist's empathic understanding. When the client claims that the therapist is mistaken, it is assumed that the therapist has failed to catch some nuance in the patient's narrative.

---

3. In his book, *Explaining Hitler* author Ron Rosenbaum (1998) displayed a large photograph of Hitler as an innocent-looking infant. Rosenbaum received many letters of complaint for displaying the uncorrupted, innocent Adolf Hitler, as though the photograph belied Hitler's subsequent enactment of evil.

4. In Plato's terms Hitler *chose* to be evil because he was ignorant of the good life. Rogers simply offers a general bio-psychological model to account for this ignorance. The actualization drive is the hypothetical biological engine of the model, and the imposition of conditions of worth on the infant and child underlies the psychological events that undermine the full functioning of the inherently pro-social organismic valuing process.

5. Unconditional positive regard and empathy are independent variables. A client may feel very accepted by a therapist but only marginally understood, in which case the acceptance would not carry much weight for that client. Alternatively a client may feel very well understood, but quite rejected. For Rogers-1, unconditional positive regard and empathy, as independent therapeutic agents, were what was sufficient to instigate therapeutic change. Bozarth seems to disagree: 'I assert that the empathic and unconditional acceptance of the therapist is, in essence, the same experience' (1997: 89). Janet Malcolm, the noted journalist, has written a book discussing the questionable morality of the journalist who employs empathy without unconditional positive regard in order to exploit a person and get a story (Malcolm, 1990).

Indeed, for Rogers-1, the therapist is wrong[6] in his empathic response even if the client repeats precisely what the therapist stated moments before. The empathic response does not anticipate; it captures the cogent aspects of the client's narrative in the present. The concept of resistance is irrelevant in the context of client-centered therapy as described by Rogers-1. Unfortunately, as we shall see, for Rogers-2, resistance is not only relevant: it may often be provoked.

For Rogers-1 empathy has other functions besides maximally minimizing the risk of conveying conditions of worth.

First, clients would be in a position to actively relate to their own thoughts and feelings when they hear them vividly expressed by the therapist. Upon hearing their experience they may begin to elaborate their narrative more deeply and extensively. For example, imagine that you intend to write a letter to a close friend. If asked what you intended to write, you might offer a hazy outline of one or two sentences. However, upon writing the letter many pages might be written. What has happened? Upon writing the first sentence, the second and third follow more effortlessly. One *sees* what one wants to write. Similarly an empathic response allows one to *hear* what one wants to say. In this way clients would hopefully become tuned in to themselves; they would not speak, *and then* wait and wonder what profound meaning could be gained from the therapist's interpretation (psychoanalysis), philosophy (Ellis), behavioral exercises (behavioral therapy), or introspective strategy, or focusing (Gendlin). Remaining in the client's frame of reference through empathic reflections presumably facilitates independence and autonomy.

Second, by consistently being empathic, the therapist in effect informs the client that he or she will have to create their own insights, their own direction and if necessary live with their own mistakes. These two functions are quite different. In the first, empathy teaches the clients to listen critically to themselves. In the second, clients discover that the therapist profoundly believes such self-direction is possible. In effect, by expressing consistent empathy the therapist may succeed in demonstrating his unconditional positive regard for the client. Rogers-1 does not believe prods[7] are necessary. A prod could be an interpretation. A prod could be the simple offering of a novel way to construe experience. For example, a therapist could say to the client that, perhaps, if he saw the glass as half full rather than half empty, things wouldn't look so bad. If indeed the client was viewing the world as half empty, Rogers-1 would reply empathically, thereby underlining the bleakness of such a vision, and leave it up to the client to question the morbidity or richness or whatever of his outlook.

---

6. The therapist can be wrong in two senses in this framework. First, the therapist may not be attempting to understand the client in an empathic way. For example, a therapist may express his frustration. For Rogers-1 this is a grave error and inconsistent with the model of empathy in the context of unconditional positive regard. A second error is when the therapist offers an empathic response that does not dovetail with the client's experience. This error is less important. It is not unusual for a therapist to discover that their reflection failed to capture the essence of the client's experience. These errors can be very useful for the client insofar as the client may appreciate how their manner of expression could lead to a misunderstanding.

7. In this context a prod refers to any comment made from an external frame of reference (unempathic) that is made to enable the client to either gain insight or psychological support.

EMERGENCE OF ROGERS-2

In his celebrated tape with Gloria (1965) Rogers-2 emerged, and in the name of congruence, of genuineness, of being 'real', or of 'being himself' offers a number of prods to Gloria.

When Gloria speaks of her fears of taking a risk and talking to her daughter about her sex life without the support of an authority figure, Rogers responds by saying that one thing he feels very 'keenly' about is that 'it's an awfully risky thing to live'. In making such a statement Rogers is homogenizing Gloria's shame and anxiety, and trying to comfort her by showing her that her perception is congruent with his own. Indeed, that interview is so full of prods that Gloria winds up saying: 'I do feel you have been saying to me—you are not giving me advice, but I do feel like you are saying, "You know what pattern you want to follow, Gloria, and go ahead and follow it." I sort of feel a backing up from you.'

How much better if Gloria would have been given the opportunity to say: 'I do feel you understand me and it has become increasingly clear to me what pattern *I* ought to follow.'

Another prod includes the infamous or famous comment, depending on where you stand: 'You look to me like a pretty nice daughter.'

Such a prod provides Gloria with the kind of acceptance from an authority that she repetitively asks for. However, by informing Gloria that she looks like a pretty nice daughter, Rogers-2 is unwittingly also providing conditions of worth. Gloria has learned that by acting in a certain way with Rogers she will be viewed as a nice daughter. That is a far cry from consistent empathy and *un*conditional positive regard.

It is evident that Rogers-2 is somewhat uncomfortable when Gloria states what she hears from him, and so instead of empathizing with her sense of being *directed by him*, Rogers-2 offers his view: 'I guess the way I see it, you've been telling me that you know what you want to do, and yes, I do believe in backing up people in what they want to do. It's a little different slant than the way it seems to you.'

What led to this non-empathic give and take was a statement Rogers made much earlier in the tape. Confronted with Gloria's anxiety over taking chances, Rogers departs from empathy and prods Gloria with a question: 'What is it that you wish I might say to you?'

From that point on Gloria narrates her life, borrowing on the strength of Rogers' approval. It is not *her* talking out of *her* own organismic valuing, but instead she is leaning on Rogers. As she has stated earlier, unless she speaks through an authority figure, she remains uncomfortable expressing herself. Consequently, by the interview's end she is able to *accurately* say: 'I do feel you have been saying to me … '

Rogers' question, 'What is it that you wish I might say to you?' converted him into a ventriloquist … with Gloria playing the puppet.[8]

---

8. Just as the analyst undermines a transference interpretation by expressing condolences to a patient, thus abandoning neutrality, so does Rogers-2 undermine self-direction when he provides conditions of worth by employing prods.

The contrast between Rogers-1 and Rogers-2

Is consistent empathy possible? Can we be single-minded in putting ourselves in the shoes of another person? Rogers-1 certainly believes we can. In *Client-Centered Therapy*, Rogers-1 provides us with a lengthy quote from Raskin, who vividly describes the essence of therapeutic empathy:

> At this level, counselor participation becomes an active experiencing with the client of the feelings to which he gives expression, the counselor makes a maximum effort to get under the skin of the person to whom he is communicating, he tries to get within and to live the attitudes expressed ... to catch every nuance of their changing nature: in a word, to absorb himself completely in the attitude of the other. And in struggling to do this, *there is no room for any other type of counselor activity or attitude* ... (1951: 25; italics our own)[9]

For Rogers-1 empathy is, indeed, a full-time job. Even when confronted with a client who is contemplating suicide, Rogers-1 is able to reply empathically: 'You say that you may be afraid of yourself ... and are wondering why I don't seem to be afraid for you?'

Undoubtedly anticipating an attack from his critics for not taking a more direct approach that expresses the active concern of the therapist, Rogers writes:

> To me, it appears that only as the therapist is completely willing that any outcome, any direction may be chosen—only then does he realize the vital strength of the capacity and the potentiality of the individual for constructive action. It is as he is willing for death to be the choice, that life is chosen; for neuroticism to be the choice, that a healthy normality is chosen. The more completely he acts upon his central hypothesis, the more convincing is the evidence that the hypothesis is correct. (1951: 49)

Rogers-1 is not encouraging a dry, artificial, formal therapeutic relationship which denies the genuineness of the counselor. Of course a counselor may not understand or accept the client-centered framework, and may thus be empathic in a mechanical and inauthentic way. Rogers-1 profoundly believed that empathy and unconditional positive regard were all that was necessary to set in motion the client's capacity to realize all that was best in him or her. Critics of Rogers simply scoffed at such a notion. It was argued that unconditional positive regard and empathy would never release the forces of repression and enable a client to appreciate the full extent of their antisocial nature. Even so friendly a critic as Rollo May (1992) argued that empathy was powerless and even therapeutically irresponsible to employ with a client bent on destruction. Thus a counselor who is

---

9. We expect a brain surgeon to concentrate 100 percent on the surgery he/she is performing, though it may take ten to thirteen hours, and yet there are many psychologists including, as we shall see, Rogers-2, who have their own feelings spill over the therapeutic session; and this is assumed by many psychotherapists to be inevitable. The present authors, as well as Rogers-1 and Raskin, assumed consistent empathic responding within the client's frame of reference was quite possible if one was congruent with the 'attitude and orientation' of client-centered therapy. (Rogers, 1951, Chapter 2).

sympathetic to Freud or May would be incongruent in their effort to be consistently empathic, but such incongruence has nothing to do with the *humanistic model* of client-centered therapy (CCT); the philosophical and psychological foundation of client-centered therapy does not, *in and of itself*, promote such incongruence, any more than writing this article promotes incongruence.[10]

THE WISCONSIN PROJECT AND THE DEATH OF ROGERS-1

But then a change occurred; Rogers-1 and his co-workers decided to see whether empathy and unconditional positive regard would be effective with hospitalized patients diagnosed with schizophrenia. Rogers *et al.* (1967: 67–9) writes about the therapists' experience:

> The experience of most of the therapists on the project had been primarily with outpatient clients who came voluntarily for help. They were faced with many difficult problems in establishing a relationship with the hospitalized schizophrenics and likewise with the normals, *both of the groups being composed of individuals who were not seeking help.* The problems of the therapist and the solutions to these problems were manifold: sometimes pathetic, sometimes amusing. How is a male therapist to deal with a female ... client who dashes into the women's washroom when she sees him coming? ... The therapists came to realize that they were dealing with individuals who were unmotivated, often unreachable, largely without hope, lacking in any concept of therapy, and certainly lacking in any belief that a relationship could be helpful ... To be consistently rejected, over and over, to be unable to do anything helpful, to see no progress over long periods of time, to see no sign in the patient that he has any understanding of the relationship, to desire very much to be in touch with this person and to be unable to get through—these added together constituted a devastating experience. [italics our own][11]

Rogers (1967: 12) describes the changes in therapist behavior in this situation: ' ... the therapists in our group found themselves trying out and developing many new and different modes of response behavior. The variety of specific behaviors increased sharply'. (See pp. 56–8 of this chapter for examples of the variety.)

It should have been obvious that CCT as characterized in the foregoing pages

---

10. The point can perhaps be made clear if we imagine that Hobbes and Socrates were reading *Client-Centered Therapy* to see whether the underlying premise of the therapy appealed to them. Hobbes, who believed human beings were inherently selfish ('Life is nasty, brutish and short.') would be an incongruent client-centered therapist, but might find Freud quite congenial. Socrates, who argued that a person would never *knowingly* choose to be irrationally destructive, would find Rogers-1 quite congenial.

11. Rogers-2 writes as though it was inevitable that therapists would be frustrated and devastated by such an experience. Rogers-2 fails to note that frustration is a function of expectation and thus a sign that the expectations were in error. These authors see no reason why false expectations are inevitable when treating patients diagnosed as schizophrenic.

would not be effective with such a population. In fact, CCT with a *non-motivated* population is oxymoronic (Rogers, 1963). In the context of client-centered theory the actualization drive (motive) is always active and it ceases only when the organism dies. More concretely Rogers-1, who was prepared to allow a client to choose death in the hope he will choose life, is not the same as Rogers-2, who was quite willing to see *resistive* patients brought to him by hospital attendants. The sensible strategy would have been to restrict CCT, with its exclusive emphasis on unconditional positive regard and empathy as the therapeutic agents of the treatment, to motivated populations and to develop a new way of *relating* (as opposed to therapizing) for non-motivated populations.

Imagine that instead of therapy we were discussing penicillin, which is effective in combating certain forms of bacterial infection. Suppose further that because penicillin was ineffective against viruses, medical doctors ceased to prescribe it for bacterial infections! Such a preposterous turn of events did occur in the case of CCT.

Congruence: The masking of the category error

The failure of empathy as an effective therapeutic tool *with a non-motivated population* was rationalized and a new concept emerged, and Rogers-2 was born. The concept was congruence or genuineness or realness. Rogers-2 and his co-worker in Wisconsin, Eugene Gendlin, committed the category error just as Anna Freud, Stone and Greenson did among many others. Distinctions were made between the real person and the artificial therapist; between a real relationship and a therapeutic relationship. Within the blink of an eye, we are supposed to wonder whether Rogers-1 was genuine when he failed to tell his suicidal client how much that client's life meant to him—as he did, as Rogers-2, with Jim Brown in Wisconsin (Rogers *et al.*, 1967: 409). Here is how Gendlin characterizes the difference between Rogers-1 and -2, (though he would emphatically disagree on our characterization of the virtues of Rogers-1):

> Current developments in psychotherapy have obscured the lines between different orientations. For example, contrast psychoanalysis and CCT. What a sharp difference there once seemed to be! Today, looking back, we see the similarity; both were highly formal denials of a *real relationship* [italics our own]. One role-played a relationship of transference; the other role-played a perfectly neutral acceptance. We see two of a kind—artificial, formalistic avoidances of genuine interaction between two people ... Today client-centered therapists make 'genuineness' the first condition of therapy and therapist-expressivity and spontaneity main therapeutic factors. (Gendlin, cited in Hart and Tomlinson, 1970: 18)

These authors see no reason why false expectations are inevitable when treating patients diagnosed as schizophrenic. Gendlin fails to understand that a 'real' relationship is not a distinct entity from a therapeutic relationship. A therapeutic relationship's authenticity is determined only by the sincerity of the participants. Raskin is not unreal when he struggles to live the attitude of the other. Moreover, we have no reason to believe he is lying when he writes that empathic listening can be accomplished only to the 'exclusion of other types of attention' (Rogers, 1951: 29).

Rogers-2 commits the same category error as Gendlin in his description of genuineness:

> The more the therapist is himself or herself in the relationship, putting up no professional front or personal facade, the greater is the likelihood that the client will change and grow in a constructive manner.
>
> This means that the therapist is openly being the feelings and attitudes that are flowing within at the moment. The term 'transparent' catches the flavor of this condition: the clients can see right through that the therapist is in the relationship; the client experiences no holding back on the part of the therapist. As for the therapist, what he or she is experiencing is available to awareness and can be lived in the relationship and can be communicated *if appropriate*' (Rogers, 1980: 115; italics our own)[12]

Bozarth, a contemporary follower of Rogers-2, writes:

> How can the therapist experience the world of the client? The answer being proposed is that the therapist develop idiosyncratic empathy modes predicated upon the therapist as a *person*[13] [italics our own], the client as a person, and the therapist–client interactions. (1984: 64)

Rogers-2 and Bozarth imply that the 'person' of the therapist is somehow a distinct entity from the therapist, as if there was a natural antipathy between personalities and social settings (roles). But when speaking in public I would be no less a personality for sticking to my subject rather than suddenly exclaiming how nervous I was. Rogers-2 writes of communicating experiences 'if appropriate', but if he is following the dictates of Rogers-1 and Raskin his empathic attention and unconditional positive regard would always be appropriate! As for transparency, perhaps a better metaphor for the Rogers-1 type of CCT would be the original term employed by Rogers: reflectivity. When I am a person-centered therapist like Rogers-1—and I am successful—I am also reflective. I want my client not to see me *but to see himself or herself through me.*

One way to avoid the category error is to eliminate the bogus distinction between real, genuine and congruent in contrast to unreal, inauthentic and incongruent therapist behavior, and examine instead the timing and function of non-empathic behavior. By non-empathic behavior, we refer to all responses of the therapist that are not intended to reflect the immediate cognitive and emotional meaning of the client's *intended* narrative.

For example, it should be apparent that in Rogers-2's celebrated interview with Gloria, he made a number of non-empathic comments:

---

12. As we shall see, no criterion is given as to what constitutes appropriate and inappropriate unempathic therapeutic comments. This will be discussed further below.

13. How could a therapist act if not as a person? As a cow?

'You look to me like a pretty nice daughter';
'I guess one thing I feel very keenly about is that it's an awfully risky thing to live';
'I don't feel that's pretending' (an expression of care for Gloria);
'All I know is what I am feeling and that is, I feel close to you in this moment';
'The thing I might ask is—what is it—you wish I would say to you?'

How do Meador and Rogers (1984) characterize these non-empathic responses? 'Here Rogers presents himself as he really is, offering Gloria the experience of genuine caring from another, an experience she has felt deprived of in relation with her real father' (p. 188). We see once again the category error. Rogers 'as he really is' is non-empathic. What is the timing and function of non-empathic behavior? The question is of cardinal significance. Recall that Rogers-1 became famous and/or infamous precisely because he had gone to such lengths to avoid conveying conditions of worth by expressing non-empathic responses. He confesses how much he suffered when the reflection of feeling was so satirized by other schools of thought (Rogers, 1980). But Rogers-2 believes that we are able to know when and how to express feelings which emanate from our internal frame of reference without imposing themselves on our client.

THE TIMING AND FUNCTION OF NON-EMPATHIC BEHAVIOUR

When, then, is it appropriate for Rogers-2 and his co-workers to express their own thoughts and feelings, rather than empathically reflecting those of the client? We have scanned the writings and statements of Rogers-2 and have discovered two minimal clues. In the foregoing paragraph Rogers (1980: 115) writes that such statements can be made 'if appropriate'. Of course this begs the question. A second clue is offered in Rogers-2's introductory comments to the interview with Gloria when he states: 'When I am real in this fashion (genuine) I know that my own feelings will bubble up into awareness but be expressed in ways that won't impose themselves on my client.'[14] It would appear that therapists should express their own judgments when the impulse strikes. Bozarth (1984, 1997), goes one step further. Self-referential comments ought to be made because they bear an empathic connection to the person in question:

> As the supervisor of a student listened to the student's taped session with a client, he had strong consistent sexual feelings toward her. They had worked together as a student and teacher for two years in a relationship that had never involved sexual connotations. The supervisor turned the tape off and said, 'I'm having strong sexual feelings toward you.' (Bozarth, 1984: 70)

On the face of it such a comment would generally be regarded as inappropriate and out of context. Supervisors in their role of supervisors are not supposed to be regarding their

---

14. Once again Rogers-2 contradicts Rogers-1 and Raskin when he implies the inevitability of non-empathic responses, just as the psychoanalysts argue that counter-transference is inevitable. The difference is that because of counter-transference it is necessary that analysts themselves be analyzed to minimize the damage of their 'bubbling up' responses.

students in a sexual way. If the supervisor had said, 'Can I speak to you in a non-supervisory role and as a man to a woman he finds very attractive?' he would be asking for a new role relationship with the student. Many people might consider even this overture inappropriate and unethical, since the supervisor has considerable power over the student that could make it difficult for the student to decisively reject the erotic interest of her supervisor. However, Bozarth feels that such a comment of sexual attraction is quite appropriate. He writes that what appears to be utterly non-empathic may be profoundly empathic. He goes on to describe the positive consequences of the supervisor's 'bubbling up' expression:

> As they explored this experience of the supervisor, the student revealed that she had been having strong sexual feelings toward her client. She was disturbed and was quite embarrassed by having such feelings. The supervisor's expression of his feelings had captured the very essence of her strong sexual desire toward her client. It seemed that the supervisor's feelings represented an empathic understanding of the student's inner world rather than any separate feelings of the supervisor toward the student. This was more apparent when the supervisor's feeling disappeared after the student began to explore her dilemma. (Bozarth, 1984: 70)[15]

In any case, it is hard to imagine that Bozarth would argue that all such impulses are necessarily 'appropriate', and if not, he certainly does not provide the reader with a way to distinguish good impulsive self-referential responses from bad impulsive self-referential responses.

The function of non-empathic responses is self-evident, even if the timing isn't. Rogers-1 and his co-workers found in the Wisconsin hospital that their empathic responses failed to have the intended effect: (a) to convey unconditional positive regard; (b) to stimulate clients to explore their own feelings; and (c) to convey the genuineness of the therapist.

With regard to effect (a), to convey unconditional positive regard, Rogers-2 feels obliged to inform Gloria that she looks like a pretty nice daughter, because he must be uncertain that his reflections succeeded in conveying his deep regard for Gloria. The

---

15. Even though the supervisor was not intending to make an empathic response, Bozarth considers it is an empathic response because it resonates with the student's feelings for her client, and the supervisor's sexual feelings ceased once the subject was examined in greater detail. It does not occur to Bozarth that the supervisor's implied sexual overture was a failure of empathic understanding—because the student presumably never entertained either the supervisor's feelings for her, nor expressed any sexual feelings for him—and that the supervisor consequently feels rebuffed and loses his sexual desire. The loss of sexual desire on the part of the supervisor is thus not a consequence of empathic understanding that is catharted once expressed, but instead a function of rejection. Many a rapist would be comforted by this characterization of empathy since rapists often feel that despite the struggle and resistance put up by a woman, unconsciously the woman wants to be raped, just as this student wanted her unconscious desires for her client to come out in the open. We do not trivialize the horror of rape but it ought to be noted that once the rape is accomplished the rapist, like the supervisor, loses their desire. Would this prove the rapist was empathic with his victim?

consequence of his non-empathic comment results in Gloria's statement: 'Well, you're not really my father.' Ironically, their real therapeutic relationship had become muddied.

With regard to effect (b), to stimulate clients to explore their own feelings, after being asked a number of times by Gloria to provide her with an answer as to whether or not she should be honest about her sexual life with her daughter, Rogers-2 provides a prod:

> Rogers: 'I guess, I am sure this will sound evasive to you but it seems to me that perhaps the person you are not being fully honest with is you, because I was very much struck by the fact that you were saying: 'If I feel all right about what I have done, whether it's going to bed with a man or what, if I really feel alright about it, then I do not have any concern about what I would tell Pam or my relationship with her.[16]
>
> Gloria: 'Right. All right. Now I hear what you are saying. Then alright, then I want to work on, I want to work on accepting me then. I want to work on feeling alright about it. But that makes sense, that that'll come natural and then I won't have to worry about Pammie … '

Rogers and Meador (1980) feel that Gloria's statement indicates that 'Gloria has assimilated a real insight, an understanding that the solution to her problem is in herself rather than an authoritative opinion on how knowledge of her sex life will affect Pammie' (p. 188). But one can look at this excerpt in a different way. Indeed Rogers-2 has provided Gloria with an insight, but the insight is his own and not Gloria's. For the first time in the interview, Gloria listens to Rogers as we suspect most patients listen to Ellis: 'Right. Alright I hear you. Now I hear what you are saying …'. Exploration of Rogers-2 is taking place rather than self-exploration. Gloria hears, but she hasn't created the anatomy of her own vocabulary. Gloria's next sentence shows that the exploration of Rogers-2 has led nowhere: 'But when things do seem so wrong for me and I have an impulse to do them how can I accept that?'

In response, Rogers-2 reverts to Rogers-1: 'What you'd like to do is to feel more accepting toward yourself when you do things you feel are wrong. Is that right?'[17] This reflection does lead to self-exploration.

With regard to effect (c), to convey the genuineness of the therapist, Rogers-2 is obliged to tell Gloria: 'All I know is what I am feeling and that is that I feel close to you in this moment.'

Is Rogers-2 correct in believing that his empathic responses failed to provide Gloria with sufficient evidence of the sincerity of his closeness (caring)? Even if he is correct, would it not be better for her to be allowed to experience the isolation that results from

---

16. In claiming that Gloria was not being honest with herself, Rogers-2 is diagnosing Gloria's feelings in no less a way than Freud might. Certainly, Rogers-2 is presenting himself as an expert on reading authentic and inauthentic feelings and thoughts. This would be anathema to Rogers-1.

17. It is typical of Rogers throughout this interview with Gloria to revert to empathic reflections when his prods fail. There is one exception to this at the end of the interview, when Rogers *insists* that he feels close to Gloria even though she doesn't appear to comprehend such feeling on the part of a therapist whom she has known for only thirty minutes.

her vision of human relationships, rather than to be superficially assured? How often do parents say 'I love you', precisely because their actions failed to convey love? Do the words do more than camouflage the discord in the relationship? Furthermore, in questioning Gloria's skepticism regarding Rogers' feeling towards her, Rogers-2 is in effect denying Rogers-1's conviction that the client is always right and it is the task of the client-centered therapist to follow the feelings of the client rather than the reverse.

CONGRUENCE: THE EMERGENCE OF THERAPIST-CENTERED THERAPY AND THE DEMISE OF CLIENT-CENTERED THERAPY

In summary, in Rogers-2, non-empathic responses are to serve the same functions as empathic responses, but succeed only in increasing the likelihood of subverting the client's organismic valuing process by communicating coercive conditions of worth (however unwittingly, as in the case of 'loving' parents). Rogers' developmental model of psychopathology informs us that clients are particularly vulnerable to experiencing conditions of worth and succumbing in some way to them. Gloria was encouraged to be a nice client by Rogers when he told her that from where he stood 'she looked like a pretty nice daughter'. As stated before, can Gloria still feel that she can be a nice daughter if she gets angry at Rogers? Moreover, once the therapist begins to express his own judgments and feelings it becomes increasingly difficult to distinguish the clients' subjective idiosyncratic perception of coercion and objective coercion. Consider the following excerpts from therapists who regard themselves as either experiential or person-centered therapists and who worked with Rogers-2 in the Wisconsin project:

> Patient did not wish to be seen after first two contacts. I told him 'That's okay with me' only to find that 'It isn't okay with me.' I called him back and asked him to come in ten times, then decide. Since we had already decided to play cards, since he refused to sit in silence, he then provided a cribbage board. After five hours he indicated that he would like to come in as long as he is here. Now I have a cribbage partner who cheats, or tries to.
>
> I felt bored and angry with Mr SAF, with myself, and with the relationship. When I was finally able to partially express these feelings (about the thirtieth interview) the relationship seemed to improve. At present, I am not sure where it will go.
>
> Initially Mrs FIN was very resistant to therapy and, after four interviews, refused to come again. At this point the therapist *insisted* [italics our own] that Mrs FIN continue but gave her more freedom with the therapeutic hour by explaining that she could leave when overly uncomfortable. A turning point in the relationship occurred when, under the stress of moving to a new ward, Mrs FIN cried and expressed her feelings of aloneness and helplessness to the therapist. Possibly the most meaningful elements in the relationship with Mrs. FIN were my nonverbal expressions of concern and caring (seeing her on the ward, loaning my coat to her, etc.).
>
> He comes (I feel at my *implicit request* [italics our own], although I feel he

also wants, on some level to come); he talks constantly (I have to interrupt to make a response). For the first ten interviews or so, I felt that it made no difference to him whether it was me he talked to or anyone else. I feel now that he is beginning to be aware of me, and the relationship *begins* to develop. With this is coming slowly some show of embarrassment before me in regard to past and present extra-therapy feelings he discussed, as well as rare but meaningful spontaneous and felt interchanges between us.

The patient refused right from the start to meet with me. To every mention of 'next time' and to every invitation to enter a room with me, he reacted with explicit anger and demands that I leave him alone. Over some weeks I accepted his feeling, anger, dislike of me: I *let* [italics our own] him leave; I had him brought by attendants; I argued with him; I was both honest and dishonest: I could not help but react negatively to his rejection and I felt he cut the ground from under my *right* [italics our own] to be with him. Because of these feelings in me I decided that he should not be further *coerced* [italics our own], to see me, since he would only discover a threatened and threatening person in me.[18] How to make the contacts continue—and yet without the sort of coercion which brought this rejection and altered my inward climate? (Hart and Tomlinson, 1970: 16–17)

It is too obvious to belabor that the attitudes expressed by these therapists bear no relationship to the philosophical outlook of CCT as developed by Rogers-1. These descriptions exemplify coercion, manipulativeness, bullying and insincerity—and all rationalized by good intentions. These self-defined, person-centered therapists have now incorporated the psychoanalytic concept of resistance and the excerpts illustrate that Rogers-2, with the notion of congruence as an independent variable in the theory of therapy, encouraged exactly the kind of non-empathic authoritarian responses that he distanced himself from in his critique of the psychoanalytic concepts of resistance and transference in 1951 (see footnote 2, p. 45). Do these therapists sound any different from well-intended parents who helped shape these unfortunate patients in the first place? In effect, these therapists are best characterized as bad behavioral therapists. They behave as reinforcing machines, but they are defective machines because of their inconsistency and the inconsistency is the result of their hypocrisy. In attributing their boredom, anger and impatience to their genuineness they have given themselves license to be impulsive in doling out rewards and punishments. But such is not the judgment of Hart and Tomlinson, who write: 'Their style of approach varies, but their aims and touchstone of responsiveness are the same. The touchstone is experiencing the central phenomenon of experiential psychotherapy' (Hart and Tomlinson, 1970: 17). There are many today who no longer distinguish between experiential and PCT precisely

---

18. The therapist notes that the client's subjective experience of coercion reflects in part the objective coercive stance of therapeutic demands. In psychoanalytic terms the counter-transference of the therapist undermines the possibility of the client coming to grips with their own hostility.

because non-empathic 'congruent' responses permit therapists the widest possible latitude to express themselves from their own frame of reference. Furthermore, the rationalization that each of these approaches has the same 'touchstone of experiencing' hardly distinguishes therapeutic interaction from any other kind of social interaction. To be sure, these approaches vary, but the variability is a function of the personality of the therapist rather than the dictates of a psychotherapeutic model.

The therapy excerpts presented above are from a 1970 volume. The following quotations demonstrate that the category error is as alive among person-centered therapists today as it was more than thirty years ago. Under the heading 'How much of your "self" can you use therapeutically with your client?' Mearns (2000) states: 'One of the distinguishing features of the person-centered approach is the emphasis it places on the counselor's use of self' (p. 17). This is illustrated by a dialogue that contains several non-empathic counselor responses like the following:

> Andrea: (looks at counselor, expecting some response)
> (Silence)
> Counselor: (fidgeting and looking uncomfortable) I feel strange ... uncomfortable ... cold ... What you are saying makes perfect sense and yet I feel uncomfortable ... In fact, a little voice in me is saying 'That's a pity she needs to be so hard on herself'. (*ibid.*: 19)

Actually, empathic understanding is now the second-best choice. Referring to a therapist who has problems working with her clients' spirituality, Mearns writes:

> she developed the control that when coming to spiritual dimensions in her client she would maintain a very strict way of working, concentrating exclusively on partial or accurate empathy ... ' (*ibid.*: 38)

The contrast to Rogers-1, for whom unconditional positive regard and accurate empathy were defining characteristics of CCT, is striking.

The seeds for Rogers-2 were already present in Rogers-l. In *Client-Centered Therapy*, Rogers (1951) quotes at great length a memorandum from a staff therapist, Mr Oliver H. Bown, who states the importance of expressing personal feelings in the therapeutic context with Rogers' approbation (pp. 160–7): ' ... as a therapist I can allow a very strong feeling or emotion of my own to enter into the therapeutic relationship, and expect that the handling of this feeling from me by the client will be an important part of the process of therapy for him' (p. 160).

But if the therapist is intently engaged in the narrative of the client, one may ask whether the eruption of personal feelings suggests a lack of concentration. Certainly this is the impression Rogers-1 gives the reader when he states, through Raskin, that 'in struggling to do this (follow the internal frame of reference of the client), there is simply no room for any other counselor activity or attitude'. Rogers (1951: 160) seems to feel that there is room for another therapeutic activity that conveys the external frame of reference expressed by the therapist's feelings. In any case, it was not until the Wisconsin project that Mr Bown's memorandum became the most essential feature of PCT.

CONCLUSION

It is important to note that the authors are not suggesting that Rogers-1 was a better therapist than Rogers-2. But these authors are arguing that it is impossible to know what kind of therapy Rogers-2 was engaged in.

In summary then, the notion of genuineness as an independent therapeutic agent is not only operationally meaningless in psychotherapy, but also harmful in the sense that it makes a clear definition of a therapeutic model impossible. The central tenet of CCT, the maintenance of unconditional positive regard and the elimination of therapeutic conditions of worth, have been significantly compromised. The presumed success of Rogers-2 and his co-workers must be explained with reference to a non-Rogerian-1 theory of psychotherapy, i.e. to another theory of psychotherapy than the one Rogers presented in *Client-Centered Therapy* in 1951; and that theory must be documented by some other research than the research Rogers and his co-workers at the Chicago Counseling Center carried out in the early 1950s (Rogers and Dymond, 1954).

REFERENCES

Bozarth, JD (1984) Beyond reflection: Emergent modes of empathy. In RF Levant & JM Shlien (Eds) *Client-Centered Therapy and the Person-Centered Approach: New directions in theory, research and practice.* New York: Praeger, pp. 59–75.

Bozarth JD (1997) Empathy from the framework of client-centered theory and the Rogerian hypothesis. In AC Bohart & LS Greenberg (Eds) *Empathy Reconsidered.* Washington, DC: American Psychological Association, pp. 81–102.

Fenichel O (1945) *The Psychoanalytic Theory of Neurosis.* New York: Norton.

Gaylin W (2001) *Talk is Not Enough: How psychotherapy really works.* New York: Time-Warner.

Greenson R (1967) *The Technique and Practice of Psychoanalysis* (Vol. 1). New York: International Universities Press.

Hart JT & Tomlinson TM (Eds) (1970) *New Directions in Client-Centered Therapy.* Boston: Houghton Mifflin.

Malcolm J (1980) *Psychoanalysis: The impossible profession.* New York: A Knopf.

Malcolm J (1990) *The Journalist and the Murderer.* New York: Vintage Books.

May R (1992) The problem of evil: An open letter to Carl Rogers. In CRB Miller (Ed) *The Restoration of Dialogue.* Washington, DC: American Psychological Association, pp. 306–13.

Meador B & Rogers CR (1984) Person-centered therapy. In RJ Corsini (Ed) *Current Psychotherapies,* 3rd edn. New York: FE Peacock.

Mearns D (2000) *Developing Person-Centred Counselling.* London: Sage Publications.

Rogers CR (1951) *Client-Centered Therapy.* Boston: Houghton Mifflin.

Rogers CR (1963) The actualizing tendency in relation to 'motives' and to consciousness. In MM Jones (Ed) *Nebraska Symposium on Motivation.* Lincoln: University of Nebraska Press, pp. 1–24.

Rogers CR (1965) Transcript of Rogers and Gloria. In EL Shostrom (producer) *Three Approaches to Psychotherapy. Part 1: Client-centered therapy* (Film and Transcript). Corona del Mar, CA:

Psychological and Educational Films.

Rogers CR (1980) *A Way of Being*. Boston: Houghton Mifflin.

Rogers CR & Dymond R (Eds) (1954) *Psychotherapy and Personality Change*. Chicago: University of Chicago Press.

Rogers CR, Gendlin ET, Kiesler DJ & Truax C (1967) *The Therapeutic Relationship with Schizophrenics*. Wisconsin: The University of Wisconsin Press.

Rosenbaum R (1998) *Explaining Hitler*. New York: Random House.

Ryle G (1949) *The Concept of Mind*. London: Hutchinson.

CHAPTER 5

NON-DIRECTIVITY: AN ONTOLOGICAL CONCEPT

FRANÇOISE DUCROUX-BIASS

PROLOGUE

Three decades ago, among the faculty of the newly founded Person-Centered Institute International,[1] there was a man I did not yet know. Upon encountering him I was impressed quickly by the human and intellectual qualities he exuded. These qualities deeply influenced and furthered my understanding of Rogerian philosophy, as well as the concept of therapeutic time. As a result of my first contact with him, I quickly came to the conclusion that the freedom left to the client in non-directive therapy is not the product of therapist indifference or laissez-faire. Therapeutic time was also one of the first ideas that students at the Institute discussed with him. Because of this discussion it impressed me that it was possible for the client to manage the therapeutic hour, at least partially, provided he could have access to a 'visible clock'. Obviously there is far more to the concept of therapeutic time than a description of the clock, the report of which would be irrelevant here; however, the idea of the clock, irrespective of whether it is considered as an object or a time indicator, struck me and set my mind to the idea of time.

As hours passed a number of events occurred, still confused in my memory, with the exception of a very precise moment. It was surely very brief, but so intense that this moment seemed very long to me. It occurred during a demonstration interview, the video recording of which unfortunately was lost. The 'client' in this demonstration was one of our student colleagues who was fond of cows. The therapist happened to be Nat Raskin.[2] Suddenly, during the course of the demonstration, the client (who had been talking about a cow, of course) stopped, and a silence followed. During this silence the client and therapist stared intensely at each other. After a short time, which seemed hours to me, the dialogue resumed, and more feelings were expressed. At the end of the demonstration, I was shocked by the intrusion of a staff member who rather vehemently criticized the therapist for not interrupting the silence and for failing to make reference to the client's mother. He also told the therapist that he had been too passive. The video showed the opposite: the therapist's body language showed he was listening carefully to his client and was in no way passive—his shaking hand and the tense position of his arm

---

1. Person-Centered Institute International, founded by Carl Rogers, Chuck Devonshire and Alberto Zucchoni, located in Lugano, Switzerland.
2. Nat Raskin was the first person to identify the 'non-directive' attitude in psychotherapy.

alongside his body gave further evidence of an active stance. In addition, the client expressed his satisfaction with the result of the interview, and said that the silence was the consequence of an instant of sudden awareness—that had his mother been mentioned, he would have left immediately. This was my first experience of non-directivity and its facilitative action. From that day on I felt drawn to 'the non-directive attitude' (Raskin cited by Rogers, 1951: 29), and I developed great respect and affection for Nat Raskin.

Before my exposure to the non-directive attitude, I considered myself an animated object, laid open to events for which a solution had to be found. After some time, a very faint and confused idea started to develop in my mind: that I might not be that simple object, that something more, something I had not thought of before, was coming to life and rising in my awareness. At first I did not investigate this phenomenon much further. I was left with the vague feeling of incomplete exploration until I came upon the opportunity to resume this subtle survey. I then became intrigued and compelled by the concept of non-directivity.

NON-DIRECTIVITY

Non-directive is a term that describes an attitude of the therapist (or any person-centered practitioner, regardless of the application). I wondered: would the term 'non-directivity' imply a concept that has not yet been investigated? I skimmed the indexes of Rogers' major works without finding the word 'non-directivity'. I heard that Rogers did not like the term because, for quite a number of people who never tried to look deeply into the theory, it connoted an attitude of passivity and indifference in the therapist, an attitude labelled and dismissed as 'laissez-faire.' As a matter of fact, this interpretation was widespread in Continental European countries, to the point that talking about non-directivity, or even of the non-directive attitude, remains anathema in certain Rogerian training programmes. And yet Rogers' entire work expresses this concept, and it could be characterized well by this excerpt (Rogers, 1980: 115) from *A Way of Being*:

> Individuals have in themselves vast resources for self-understanding and for altering their self-concepts, basic attitudes, and self-directed behaviors. These resources can be tapped if a definable climate of facilitative attitudes can be provided.

We find here all the ingredients for a definition of the non-directive attitude: individuals have 'in *themselves* …', '*self*-concepts', '*basic* attitudes', '*self-directed* behaviors' (*ibid.*: 115, italics added). From their birth onwards, individuals possess capacities to develop themselves.

While this set of descriptors may define the non-directive attitude, it does not define the philosophical concept of non-directivity. The concept of non-directivity involves several other concepts that will be examined in turn.

Before proceeding to this examination, I shall first recall an experience that furthered my thinking on this topic. A few years ago, I worked diligently on the French translation of an English article written by Garry Prouty (1999) entitled 'Rogers and the Experiential Therapies: a Dissonance?' For me, the purpose of translating this work was twofold: to provide a simple translation into another language of what appeared to be most essential to the writer, and to facilitate as best I could the full import of his message. Every line of this article reminded me of those earlier moments following my observation of Nat Raskin's demonstration session during the workshop I described above. My experience and understanding of non-directivity was informed by a succession of instances leading to my becoming aware of something I knew inside but did not yet know 'in my head'. For the first time I was able to experience the 'existential as such' without any interfering preconceived notions, but still with the capacity to think and talk about it. My awareness of non-directivity as a concept gelled. And so it became natural for me to write as a postscript to this translation that non-directivity is an ontological concept.

WHAT IS ONTOLOGY?

Ontology is a word that comes from the Greek *ontos*, meaning 'it', 'being', or 'that which is', and *logos*, meaning 'speech'. It dates back to the end of the seventeenth century and describes the study of being: being alive. However, the study of being is much older than the name that refers to it. The philosophers of ancient Greece are among those who pondered the question of being. Parmenides, of the Eleatic school, 500 years before Christ, wrote 'Thinking and being are the same thing.' Plato affirmed Parmenides' assertion, but added that 'There is not [only] Being but many beings: Ideas.' (*Encyclopédie Universalis*, 1980: 95). Aristotle introduced the idea of metaphysics: a science that studies the Being as being, along with its essential attributes.

Across the centuries the question of being has remained an interest of philosophy, but discussion has varied according to the era. At present we are able to categorize the many ontological treatises into diverse fields that lead to areas of particular study. So, for example, we have titles like ontology and science, or ontology and language, or ontology and phenomenology. It is the last of these—ontology and phenomenology, which came to the fore in the middle of the nineteenth century—that is of interest here. In a chronology that is based on the history of their influence, I will focus on five philosophers who left their mark on what is called phenomenological ontology.

Husserl, a German philosopher (1859–1938), proposed abandoning the philosophical preconception of things in favour of 'returning to things in themselves'. He oriented his thinking toward the problem of subject and object as being correlated in the act of knowledge. He also introduced the idea of intentionality.

Heidegger, a German philosopher (1889–1976), was a student of Husserl's. He envisioned a revival of fundamental ontology: the problem of being necessitating a phenomenology of human existence—an analysis of *Dasein*, German for 'the being there'. The structure of Dasein and the ontological roots of its temporality—the basis for an historical sense of the self as being—is explicated by the description of ordinary life, one's relationship to the world, and one's relationship to others.

Three French philosophers followed who were influenced by the phenomenological streams of Husserl and Heidegger. They each made a strong impression upon contemporary philosophical thought.

Merleau-Ponty, (1908–1961) joined Husserl in his idea of 'returning to things in themselves'. For him phenomenology was the foundation for an existential philosophy that hinges on the lived experience of an intentional relationship with consciousness of the world and others.

Sartre (1905–1980) posited an atheistic existentialism:

> Being is isolated in its being. It does not relate with anything that is not itself. It has no knowledge of alterity [otherness] ... It is itself indefinitely itself and spends itself in being it. From that point of view it eludes temporality. (*L'être est isolé dans son être et il n'entretient aucun rapport avec ce qui n'est pas lui. Il ne connaît ... pas l'altérité ... Il est lui-même indéfiniment lui-même et il s'épuise à l'être. De ce point de vue ... il échappe à la temporalité.*) (1943: 32–3)

Lévinas (1906–1995) offers us, in contrast, a concept of phenomenology that moves toward alterity, not toward totality ... Lévinas connects the alterity of the Other, the 'otherness' of the Other, with temporality.

My intention is not to investigate the numerous theories written on the subject of phenomenological ontology. However, I am struck that notions of temporality are central to most of them: time that is, time that was, time that will be. Time, indeed, is important to the issue of non-directivity.

TIME

When speaking of time the idea of duration must be considered. Specifically or not, time is bound by two dates, or two hours, or two minutes. For example: last summer (between July and September) was unusually hot; I went out shopping for two hours (between 2 and 4 pm); the interview lasted five minutes (from 9.05 to 9.10). Time may also be open at the end, to allow for the concept of time without end. However, and extraordinarily enough, notions of time always have a starting point. It seems that human nature does not accept the idea of not knowing when 'it'—whatever it is—started. Finding out about the origin of the world is a major scientific preoccupation these days. What happens after death is also a source of preoccupation for many people. Between the beginning and the end, and maybe beyond, there is time. Time that passes by. Time that one has to account for in actions or inaction. Time that is energizing or boring.

INSTANT

The 'undividable' (*insécable*, [Sartre, 1943: 166]) instant is the dazzling timelessness of the indescribable (often chaotic) solitude that precedes awareness, before it becomes a recognized, existing feeling in awareness. Cohen (in Lévinas, 1987: 5) says that Lévinas 'describes the instant … in terms of existential "conquest"—the subject's escape from anonymous existence—an existential "fatigue"— the subject inescapably burdened with itself …'. Lévinas (1978: 77) added: 'What is absolute in the relationship between existence and an existent, in an instant, consists in the mastery the existent exercises on existence, but also in the weight of existence on the existent.' Pursuing his analysis of Lévinas' work Cohen (in Lévinas 1987: 6) states that 'The instant has no past or future, it is fragile, evanescent, worldless, and thus sees in the past and future, in the horizons of the world … an exit from itself'. Lévinas (cited by Cohen in Levinas, 1987: 6), extends his thinking by stating, 'If time is not the illusion of a movement, pawing the ground, then the absolute alterity of another instant cannot be found in the subject, who is definitively *himself.* This alterity comes to me only from the other.'

THE OTHER

At this stage of our consideration, and for the purpose of this chapter, the term other can be applied to the 'other' who lies within me, understanding that 'it' refers to 'me' in becoming. Thus the subject 'it' was anonymous and not considered yet an individual. Cohen (in Lévinas, 1987: 2) says that 'Lévinas' itinerary … takes us from anonymous existence to the emergence of subjectivity, to subjectivity's practice to its shattering relationship with alterity of the other person.' So it seems legitimate at this point to ask: Who is the other? Is it he[3] who is bored with a chaotic solitude? Is it he whose existence is void? Is it he who in a flaring instant gets in touch with himself, experiencing an exit from itself that might be recalled either in intimate solitude or in sharing with an other? Having exited from its past it enters the present in view of a future, itself called to become a past. Leaving itself, it is the existent in the process of mastering existence—It is in the process of becoming, becoming a he (or a she).

TEMPORAL DYNAMICS

The fulgurance, or lightning flash, of the instant gives light to the present and prepares the future. Jean-Paul Sartre (1943: 146) said:

> Without the succession of the 'after', I would *at once* be what I want to be, there would no longer be a distance between me and me. (*Sans la succession des 'après', je serais tout de suite ce que je veux être, il n'y aurait plus de distance entre moi et moi.*)

Instead, there would be a 'void'. Without 'temporal dynamics', as Sartre (1943: 165) calls the succession of the after becoming the before and the present becoming the

---

3. Author's note: the masculine is intended as a general gender.

future, the existing me prevented from becoming would never be me, remaining forever an anonymous it. What boredom! Boredom is a non-living entity, the negation of the after. Therefore, as a non-living entity, it cannot be the present and prepare the future. Etienne Klein (2003: 6) says,

> Boredom is like a coin ... it has a double face ... On tails ... it indicates an absence of being, an existential void ... [On heads] it offers the possibility to get in touch with oneself.

How are temporal dynamics created? Khersonsky (1935, translated by Lévinas, cited by Cohen in Lévinas, 1987: 11–12) proposed that, 'Concrete living time flows from one instant to another *without delaying* (emphasis added) with any one of them'. The fulgurance of the instant, which was preceded by the present before, the now past, gives light to the here-and-now present. And to 'something that is':

> Consciousness ... is already hypostasis;[4] it refers to a situation where an existent is *put in touch* [my italics] with its existing ... The appearance of a 'something that is' constitutes a veritable inversion at the heart of anonymous being ... *Existing is its own* [emphasis added] ... In order for there to be an existent in this anonymous existing, it is necessary that a departure from self and a return to self—that is, that the very work of identity—become possible ... The present ... is a rip in the infinite beginningless and endless fabric of existing ... The present ... has a past, but in the form of remembrance. It has a history, but it is not history.
>
> Positing hypostasis as a present is ... a matter of the ... function of the present ... It is like an *ontological* [emphasis added] schema. (Lévinas, 1987: 51–2)

EXPERIENCING

The idea of the instant shall now be related to the idea of experiencing. I intend to limit the use of the term 'experiencing' to the inner experience of the existing human being who becomes aware of its being and that of the other—the inner experience of the existent in the process of mastering existence. It is an outsider's view of an internal process.

If we consider that an *experience* is the apprehension of reality that coalesces towards an improvement of knowledge (be it mental, physical, psychological or of any kind), we see that from the beginning Rogers (1942: 207) used this term to express

> the perception of the related nature of previously known facts ... We are familiar with this type of phenomenon ... It often occurs in the solution of a puzzle. Various elements have been observed. *Suddenly* [emphasis added], they are perceived in a new relationship which provides the solution.

---

4. As from Webster's New Collegiate Dictionary : the substance or essential nature of an individual, p. 110, 3a.

Sometimes this experience is called an 'Aha!' experience, because of the sudden *flash* [emphasis added] of understanding which accompanies it.

Nat Raskin (cited in Rogers, 1951: 29) talks of 'an active experiencing with the client of the feelings to which he gives expression …' Although we find the term 'experiencing' used here and there in a substantive manner e.g., in the phrase 'the experiencing of the potential self', (Rogers, 1961: 76), to my knowledge, it does not seem to have been considered in itself as an important concept in Rogers' works until 1961:

> Gendlin has called my attention to this significant quality of *experiencing* as a *referent* [emphasis added] … New feelings are experienced with *immediacy* [emphasis added] and richness of detail, both in the therapeutic relationship and outside. The experiencing of such feelings is used as a clear referent.' (Rogers, 1961: 150–1)

Finally, Rogers' (1980: 141) description of experiencing is drawn from the

> concept of 'experiencing' as formulated by Gendlin (1962) … Briefly, it is his view that at all times there is going on in the human organism a *flow of experiencings* [emphasis added] to which the individual can turn and turn again and again as a referent in order to discover the meaning of those experiences.

Revisiting what has been explored to this point regarding the instant and experiencing, we find in both the same notions of suddenness *(flash, immediacy)*, body reaction, fluidity and continuity *(flow, succession, movement)*, getting in touch with, awareness and consciousness, departure of self and return to self again and again, referent, and ownership.

It can be said that experiencing is primarily an affair of the instant; its occurrence is immediate and often implicit. Although most of the time it is unclear and fuzzy, it is as sudden as a flash. Then, like time, 'It flows from one instant to another without delaying' (Khersonsky, 1935, translated by Lévinas, cited by Cohen in Lévinas, 1987: 12). As Rogers (1961: 140 and 149–50) said:

> feelings … 'bubble up', 'seep through' … and the client is often not clearly aware of what has 'hit' him … Yet, this does not seem too important because the event is an entity, a referent, which can be returned to, again and again if necessary, to discover more about it.

When something emotionally important happens to an individual, it is immediately felt inside like a hit—a kind of 'gut' feeling for Gendlin (1996: 12), and a kind of 'visceral' feeling for Rogers (1951: 97).

Experiencing may seem to loosen, only then to persist with a different flavour. The ongoing instant-after-instant experience, being simultaneously absorbed into a mental process followed by clear or unclear symbolization, is enriched with new sensations and expanded into awareness until meaning finally takes place. Rogers (1951: 97) says:

> I came also to appreciate what I think of as 'moments of movement'. Feelings are explored until the precise word which for him describes the feeling he has

... [Then] change actually occurs ... [with its] rather obvious physiological concomitants ...

Borrowing from Van Belle (1980: 45), it can be said that the individual finally 'incorporates his experience [and] owns it'.

AN ILLUSTRATIVE VIGNETTE

The following transcript of a therapy session, provided by a friend of mine, illuminates the concepts explored thus far: being in a void, time, the instant, awareness, temporal dynamics, experiencing and the other within. The characteristics of experiencing are earmarked in italics within the transcript. Background information is provided here as a context to aid in understanding the transcript of the therapy session provided below. Thirty years ago, Maria[5] went to see a therapist for what she thought was a most trivial problem. Having moved to England from a distant town in a foreign country, she was referred to this therapist because he spoke her native language. He knew nothing of her past situation and did not enquire about it. Maria was a mother of three, a girl aged five and twin boys aged two who were to go to kindergarten. The twins needed new shoes, but when Maria was in the shoe shop she could not decide which ones to buy. This was the problem she brought to therapy. The therapist reported that during the first interview he tried to remain open to the nature of the material she was describing; she seemed to be seeking advice that he felt in no position to give her. The second interview resembled the first one. When she came with the same problem to the third interview, the therapist found that he felt stuck; there was no hint of a feeling, thought or self-representation that he was able to discern in the material she presented. Maria appeared to be emotionless, her only preoccupation was choosing a pair of shoes, and her only criteria were such things as the quality of the leather and the colour. The therapist felt it was his responsibility to tell her that he could not help her with this choice that seemed to cause her so much trouble. However, he was touched by Maria's emotionless demeanour and attempted instead to find a way to stay in contact with her, as he was struggling to connect empathically. It is at this point, when the therapist said to Maria, tentatively and with a soft and warm voice.

    'Could you tell me how you felt, when you were in the shop?'

    The answer set her off like a shot. She looked livid and said: 'I feel sick; where is the bathroom?'

    He showed her the way. When she came back a few minutes later, her face was less pale. She sat down more calmly and in an exhausted voice said: 'Well, I knew it all the time but couldn't believe it ... You know, I have been working on it in therapy before, but stopped therapy when my father was arrested. I thought that everything

---

5. All identifying information in the vignette and transcript was altered to protect the client's anonymity.

was over, that now I could live normally ... But no ... Now, only now ... I realize it wasn't over ...'

A long pause, and then with a hurried and gasping voice she said: 'It was horrible ... I have just been vomiting bits of fresh flesh, bits of my flesh ... It's horrible ... I must have been seven ... he used to take me on his knees ... His hands under my skirt, his finger deep down there ... and kissed me there ... At first I was a bit frightened ... It was odd. Then I thought: "That's my dad," it must be OK for a dad to be like this with his little kid ... and I would let myself go ... and even come to enjoy it ... But there was something in me that said that it was not normal, so all of a sudden I would stop enjoying ... Until next time ... It went on for years until I got the curse for the first time. I was very young ... ten only. Because of me being so young, my mother took me to the doctor who explained the facts of life to me ... I did not say anything but was stunned, hit. I suddenly realized how bad my father was, how bad I was to have enjoyed it ... and ... I stopped eating. I became ill, and my parents thought it was because I was too young for the curse ... But inside, the feeling that I had been made to choose the wrong when told it was the good was boring holes like an acid in my gut ... My dad did that ... But he was my dad, could he be that wrong? ... I could not tell him, and I could not tell my mum either ... nor my sisters and brothers or friends ... You know, we were a "good" family ... There was no room for questioning ... It went on for years.'

A long pause ... Her eyes vaguely staring at the floor. She seemed to go deep inside herself looking for something ... After a while her hands, which right from the beginning she had kept tightly clasped on her knees, seemed to loosen and she went on with a sigh and a slightly more relaxed voice: 'A time came when I had to decide for my future. My mum said that to work with children would be good for me. So I chose to be trained as a children's nurse ... The training included courses on social psychology. During one of them, I suddenly discovered what is called sexual harassment and abuse and ... realized that I had been abused ... The blow was so bad that I had to go and see a counsellor in emergency ... Time passed by. I met the man who was to become my husband. I stopped therapy when I got married ... Livia was born ... Then ... then I discovered that my brothers and sisters had also been abused ... What a blow again ... Had to see a counsellor again. With his help I was able to tell my mother ... And with a legal helper I told the police. My father was arrested, convicted of incest and jailed ...'

Tears were now running down her face: 'Again, once more I thought it was all over ... My husband's job was transferred to England. Things were new, I had less time to think about the past. I gave birth to the twins, Marco and Luca ... They are two years old now, they are going to kindergarten and must get adequate shoes, you see ...'

Sobs: 'And now, only now I know ... That's my father ... That's the little voice that was telling me it was wrong ... But how could it be wrong since it was my father? ... Only now, do I realize that I always had a hard time deciding what to do ... Hard time deciding about my future ... Did Silvio, my husband, love me, and did I really love him were never-ending questions. ... How difficult it had been for me when it came to choose the place we are living in ... How hesitant I have been ... Without help (meaning people telling me what to do) I could not make a decision ... And now it's the shoes ... The shoes tell me ... Oh, it's terrible ... (with raging tears) no, it's not the shoes ... it's the bits of flesh ... it's my flesh ... it's me ...'

Taking a deep breath and with a faint smile on her face: 'I'll buy those shoes now, you know ... but I've to get clear from that horrible feeling inside ...'

In this vignette a flow of instantaneous experiencings is apparent, each one followed by some strand of awareness. Characteristics of experiencing can be seen throughout. Words such as 'stunned', 'hit', 'blow', and 'suddenly' show immediacy and suddenness. Visceral feelings are conveyed by the words 'I am sick' and 'enjoying'. 'Something' and 'the little voice' express referents to which the client comes back after a while. Fluidity and continuity are apparent in the many 'thens' and 'agains' that are spread through the whole narrative. Departure from self and return to self are evident in the repeated words: 'I thought it was over,' followed by 'but', 'no' ... 'then' ... Consciousness comes out clearly with the expressions, 'I knew it all the time' and 'I realized'. However, it is not until the words 'It's bits of my flesh, it's my flesh, it's me' were finally uttered that consciousness and ownership really took place.

'The present has a past,' said Lévinas 'but in the form of remembrance. It has a history, but it is not history' (1987: 52). When she came to therapy Maria was like the 'tails' side of Klein's coin, an existential void—she had a history she could not connect with. Maria's history really started the moment she owned her present experience, her experiencing. By then she was becoming ... She came to therapy with factual issues—a seemingly emotionless preoccupation with choosing a pair of shoes, a history not yet alive in her present. But she perhaps discovered, as Mrs Oak discovered in her session with Carl Rogers, that 'I came here to solve problems, and now I find myself just experiencing myself' (Rogers, 1961: 80). There could not be a more phenomenological existential conclusion.

By its nature, fruitful experiencing belongs to the person alone. It is nonetheless true that experiencing can flower best under the conditions found in non-directive relationships. When two persons interrelate, in therapy or otherwise, to create an in-depth relationship they will both experience a fruitful outcome. For Schmid (2003: 110):

the theory of therapy understands therapy as *both* personality development *and* encounter person to person, and the practice is characterized by *presence*—which means a principled non-directivity and empathic positive regard as a way of being 'with' the client, *together with* a position 'counter' the client, i.e. a committed 'en-counter' as a person meeting the Other face to face ... The relationship moves from a mere contact to presence, from attention to co-experiencing.

The vignette allows us to enter and explore this field of person-to-person relationships.

When the therapist asked Maria how she felt inside the shop, Maria was hit in the gut. As previously mentioned, when something emotionally important happens to an individual, it is immediately felt inside like a hit, a kind of visceral feeling. And that visceral feeling, which was her own, directed her way through, at her own pace. At the end of the session, Maria said that the therapist's presence had been important to her. Although there were pauses in her narrative that seemed to be long, the therapist felt that Maria was having a deep inner dialogue with herself. It was clear that Maria knew her way, and the silent presence of the therapist helped her to go ahead. Any intervention from the therapist, no matter how seemingly empathic, would have either interrupted or diverted this process.

DEFINITION OF THE CONCEPT OF NON-DIRECTIVITY

The principle of non-directivity permeates the whole of Rogers' work, though as already noted, the concept as such was never defined explicitly. Nevertheless, the non-directive attitude, mapped out by Raskin (1947/2005), is still used to describe what pervades the therapist's being and initiates and guides his non-directive behaviour. The core conditions within the therapist enable him to offer his presence to his client. He does not apply the conditions. He is the conditions, and in so being them, he offers them to the client. The therapist responds to a call from the client, with himself as the 'only tool'. (Schmid, 2003: 114). Tentatively, I might suggest that non-directivity is the ability of the client-centred therapist to be with an other in such a way that he empowers that other with the directivity he gave up when he became client-centred. Non-directivity stems from the therapist's way of being, a natural shift that transforms the directivity of the therapist into the client's own directivity. A positive stance.

Client and therapist spring from a same 'We' (Schmid, 2003: 114), an idea that was announced by Rogers (1961: 82) when he said, 'There is … within the therapist, a profound experience of the underlying commonality—should we say brotherhood—of man.' It could be said that this assertion is echoed in Rogers' (1959: 213) first condition for therapeutic change, which stipulates 'that for therapy to occur it is necessary that two persons are in contact'. The therapist in our vignette was experiencing that kind of brotherhood—in 'stuckness'—with Maria. He also felt, without knowing what it was about, that something was simmering beneath Maria's seeming emotionlessness—he struggled to connect with and understand the other before him. To do so, he dared to ask her a question. The question was not intended to change or direct her. Rather, it showed his empathic responsiveness in the course of being so thoroughly with Maria in the moment. His intent, after all, was only to establish contact with her, but the question also happened to hit viscerally in a way that led her to establish contact with her real feelings, which she had 'covered up'.

For this therapist the client came first. Once the stuckness was over, the therapist's silent listening allowed Maria to speak and to lead the way: the client became the expert. The question asked by the therapist was not inquisitive as such. It was just a question of interest in order to establish contact from a non-directive therapist, which shifted directivity over to the client.

CONCLUSIONS

As Schmid (2003: 113) notes, 'An approach is phenomenological if the direction, the movement *goes* from the client to the therapist.' In therapy and in any other situation where a relationship is involved, non-directivity is a way of facilitative responsiveness that exactly meets the needs of a phenomenological approach. Non-directivity requires from the therapist, (or educator, etc.) a way of being that enables the other to discover and own his potentialities, to become directive of his existence, to be his way of being. In therapy, the presence of the therapist for the client is an invitation for the client's presence. The ontological nature of the relationship is clear: 'the relationship moves from mere contact to presence, from attention to co-experiencing and "being with"' (Schmid, 2003: 112).

Furthermore, non-directivity is a matter of time. Non-directivity is the ontological concept of being with, as a person in the presence of an-Other, on the here-and-now raft of time:

> Concrete 'living time ... flows from one instant to another without delaying with any one of them' ... It is ... [the] insertion of the Other's time into mine, that establishes the alterity of veritable time, which is neither the Other's time nor mine (Khersonsky, 1935, translated by Lévinas, cited by Cohen in Lévinas, 1987: 11–12).

> It is a function of the present. It is like an ontological schema (Lévinas, 1987: 52).

From an existential phenomenological perspective it could be said that non-directivity is the non-directional property of a human being to be, to be aware of his own being and of that of the other, in the same instant, in a unique place. Consequently, a reorganization begins to occur simultaneously, the instant being followed by another instant. This reorganization belongs to the individual at his own pace and within his own ability of the moment. This occurred within Maria in the lightning flash of her visceral reaction to the therapist's question, and in the instants that followed. The respectful silence of the therapist in our vignette comes back into focus. His silent presence proved to be the right way to answer Maria's call. Interference or intervention would have driven her away from her feelings. In general, such interference would act as a foreign body diverting the flow of change. It would be disrespectful of the person, of the other, as it is obvious that the person who is 'experiencing' such a process would be harmfully dispossessed of his own process. As Bozarth (2004) states, 'Non-directivity means directivity from the client ... even *only* from the client.'

REFERENCES

Bozarth JD (September, 2004) personal communication.

Encyclopédie Universalis France SA, (1980) Vol. XII: 95.

Gendlin ET (1996) *Focusing Oriented Psychotherapy*. New York: Guilford Press.

Khersonsky N (1935) *The Notion of Time*. (translated from Russian by Lévinas, cited by Cohen). In Lévinas (1987) (Tr. R Cohen) *Time and the Other*. Pittsburgh: Duquesne University Press.

Klein E (2003) *Les Tactiques de Chronos*. Paris: Flammarion.

Lévinas E (1978) *Existence and Existents*. The Hague: Nijhoff.

Lévinas E (1987) (Tr. Cohen R) *Time and the Other*. Pittsburgh: Duquesne University Press.

Prouty GF (1999) Carl Rogers and experiential therapies: A dissonance? *Person-Centred Practice, 4* (1), 4–11. Reprinted in T Merry (Ed)(2000) *Person-Centred Practice: The BAPCA reader*. Ross-on-Wye: PCCS Books, pp. 30–7.

Raskin NJ (1947/2005) The nondirective attitude. In BE Levitt (Ed) *Embracing Non-directivity: Reassessing person-centered theory and practice in the 21st century*. Ross-on-Wye: PCCS Books, pp. 329–47.

Rogers CR (1942) *Counselling and Psychotherapy*. Boston: Houghton Mifflin.

Rogers CR (1951) *Client-Centered Therapy*. London: Constable.

Rogers CR (1959) A theory of therapy, personality and interpersonal relationships, as developed in the client-centered framework. In S Koch (Ed) *Psychology: A study of a science. Vol. 3, Formulations of the person and the social context*. New York: McGraw-Hill, pp. 184–256.

Rogers CR (1961) *On Becoming a Person*. London: Constable.

Rogers CR (1980) *A Way of Being*. Boston: Houghton Mifflin.

Sartre J-P (1943) *L'Etre et le Néant*. Paris: Gallimard.

Schmid PF (2003) The characteristics of a person-centered approach. *Person-Centered and Experiential Psychotherapies, 2*(2), 111–14.

Van Belle HA (1980) *Basic Intent and Therapeutic Approach of Carl Rogers*. Toronto: Wedge Publishing Foundation.

Webster's Seventh New Collegiate Dictionary (1967) Springfield, MA: Merriam.

CHAPTER 6

FACILITATIVE RESPONSIVENESS: NON-DIRECTIVENESS FROM ANTHROPOLOGICAL, EPISTEMOLOGICAL AND ETHICAL PERSPECTIVES

PETER F. SCHMID

Abstract

To be non-directive does not only mean to do therapy without directing, guiding or controlling the client. Rather, it is an expression of an image of the human being that rests on a fundamental respect for the client's autonomy and sovereignty on the one hand, and on presence as a distinctive way of being in the therapeutic relationship on the other. Both respect and presence spring from a basic trust in the client's personhood. Therefore, the essence of non-directiveness proves to be a genuine consequence of person-centred anthropology and epistemology, and cannot be removed from the person-centred approach to which it is essentially connected. Non-directiveness is an expression of the 'art of not-knowing'. Regarding the human being as a person, and thus understanding the person-centred relationship as an encounter person to person, requires acknowledging the other as truly an Other in the sense of encounter (dialogical) philosophy. It requires facilitating client self-directedness by existentially responding to the client's opening up and call in the relationship. Ultimately, as a response to being addressed by the client out of responsibility, the essence of non-directiveness is an ethical issue with political consequences.

John Shlien (2003: 219), eloquent defender of a client-centred therapy according to the principles elaborated by Carl Rogers, frankly stated that non-directivity is 'certainly an awkward term' because of the image it creates as having no direction.

Historically, the concept of non-directivity was often misunderstood as describing a passive (non-)behaviour or as lacking a sense of direction in the process of therapy. It was confused with laissez-faire, and even lack of interest. Others interpreted it as a method or technique in the sense of guidelines or rules for therapist behaviour, and concluded 'do's and don'ts' for therapist interventions. It was perverted into a technique of mechanistic and wooden mirroring. It was mixed up with structuring, and misinterpreted as ignorance of influence and expertise and as denial of power. It was used by therapists preferring to remain in hiding, and as an excuse to deny the therapist's openness as a person in the encounter with the client. It was re-interpreted over and over, and twisted in its meaning, until it was no longer recognizable. Many abolished it completely. Few concepts were so profoundly misunderstood or so widely used to make fun of and discredit the person-centred approach.

THE CONCEPT OF NON-DIRECTIVITY AS DISCUSSED IN THE PERSON-CENTRED APPROACH

Quite early in the history of the person-centred approach, the concept of non-directivity marked a crucial point in the understanding of its principles; it might even be seen as *the* expression of the paradigmatic shift from problem-, solution- and therapist-centred to client- and person-centred therapy. Even some 60 years later, it only recently became *the* password for those who claim to adhere to truly 'Rogerian' therapy. In recent years theoreticians and practitioners who understand themselves as 'non-directive client-centred therapists'—thus making 'non-directivity' the shibboleth of being genuine to Rogers' intentions—claim that there is a fundamental distinction between those who follow Rogers' original approach and other orientations, developed out of (and away from) Rogers' concepts. Barbara T. Brodley (2002, 2003), for example, enumerates Bozarth, Brodley, Brody, Patterson, Raskin, Shlien, Witty, Zimring and others as being within the first category; and lists focusing-oriented therapy (Gendlin, 1996; Hendricks, 2002), experiential therapy (Lietaer, 1998) and process-experiential therapy (Elliott and Greenberg, 2002) among the other approaches. As a matter of fact, in these experiential traditions, the concept of non-directivity was widely given up and replaced by an experiencing-oriented and process-focused stance, together with a distinction between contents and process. The debate about the nature and importance of non-directivity, often fought in internet postings (e.g. the CCT/PCA e-mail network, http://texaslists.net/cctpca), came up anew and very strongly after controversies at the Person-Centered and Experiential World Conference 2003 in Egmond aan Zee in The Netherlands (PCEP, 2004).

Trying to understand carefully the original meaning of the concept as elaborated by Carl Rogers, it can be found that non-directiveness is an expression of a basic anthropological and epistemological stance; that is, a philosophical conviction, not a matter of method or technique (if method and technique are understood in their usual contemporary meaning, and not in their original sense, in which they mean 'way' and 'art and science' respectively).

In order to understand how the focus shifted in the comprehension of 'being non-directive', from the early days to contemporary discussion, we need to take a look into the history of the concept.

CARL ROGERS: 'THE PERSON WHO SHOULD GUIDE IS THE CLIENT'

In the beginning, Rogers' emphasis on non-directivity was a counter-position to the traditional medical model and the more directive forms of psychotherapy that were in vogue at that time: classical psychiatry, psychoanalysis and behaviour therapy (see Schmid 1996: 268–70, 1999, 2002b). In order to separate his way of approaching a client from manipulative or guiding therapeutic behaviour he called it 'non-directive,' as opposed to the traditional 'directive' approach (Rogers, 1942; Raskin, 1947/2005). Although in the beginning the emphasis was on the way of proceeding and on the counsellor skills (i.e., which intervention brings about which change?), the underlying intention was clear: creating a non-judgemental atmosphere, a relationship free from anxiety, and fostering verbalisation of the client's emotions and experiencing, as well as their self-exploration. Thus, from the very beginning of his 'newer therapy', at a time when the main task for the therapist was to be an alter ego for the client, Rogers opposed control over the client, or therapist-centred attitudes and behaviours, and wanted to stress the responsibility of the client. Most important of all, he wanted to emphasize trust in the client and his or her capabilities. He stated clearly: 'Nondirective counseling is based on the assumption that the client has the right to select his own life goals, even though these may be at variance with the goals his counselor might choose for him' (Rogers, 1942: 126–7).

As early as 1942, Rogers wrote that the difference between a 'directive versus non-directive approach' (pp. 108–28), is a difference in philosophy of counselling and values. Therefore, the question for him was whether there is a right of the experienced and more capable to guide the inexperienced and less capable or, conversely, a right to independence for every person. This difference between problem-centred and client-centred is, according to Rogers, an issue of social and political philosophy (see Schmid, 2004a: 37–8).

Non-directivity was the term for the shift of the focus of attention of both therapist and client from therapist interpretation and guidance to client awareness of and attentiveness to his or her inner world of experiencing. The term 'client-centred' (Rogers, 1951) expressed in a positive way what the term 'non-directive' conveyed in an exclusionary one. From the very beginning, non-directiveness must be seen in the context of the philosophy of experience-centredness, and of the therapist's unconditional positive regard for and empathic listening to the client (see Barrett-Lennard 1998: 59–60; Schmid, 1996: 268–70, 1999).

Further developments in Rogers' experience, understanding and theory of therapy, stressing the encounter quality of the person-to-person relationship of psychotherapy (Rogers, 1962), did not abolish the concept of non-directivity. Seen from the relational, inter-subjective perspective, non-directivity still was seen as a core aspect of the expression of trust in the client's self-healing capacities—that is, their actualizing tendency. But it got an additional importance as an expression of the 'way of being with' the client (see below).

Rogers (1975: 26), interviewed by Evans, responded to the question of whether he would say that he had qualified somewhat the notion of being non-directive during the later periods of his work:

> No. I think perhaps I enriched it, but not really qualified it. I still feel that the person who should guide the client's life is the client. My whole philosophy and whole approach is to try to strengthen him in that way of being, that he's in charge of his own life and nothing I say is intended to take that capacity or that opportunity away from him.

Recent and current debate: Non-directivity as realization of the core conditions …

In the last two decades the controversial issue of non-directivity has usually been discussed in combination with the understanding of the core conditions and their sufficiency;

that is, in terms of attitudes (see Schmid, 1996: 268–70, 2001b: 66–8).

Keith Tudor and Tony Merry (Tudor and Merry, 2002: 89; Tudor *et al.*, 2004), among others, state that non-directivity is a matter of attitude not of behaviour. Merry (1999: 75) points to the non-authoritarian nature of person-centred therapy: 'The counsellor does not choose the "agenda" for the client or attempt to control or determine the processes that occur within the client.'

Jerold Bozarth (1998: 51 and 86, 2002) regards non-directivity as a practice application of the therapist's unconditional positive regard, and as an essential component of Rogerian empathy. For him the non-directive attitude generally is a logical deduction from the central theoretical hypothesis. 'There is, in essence, no room for directivity in Rogers' conceptions of therapy and the therapist's role' (1998: 56).

Barbara Temaner Brodley (1999a: 79) asserts that 'the concept of non-directivity comes into existence within the meaning of these therapeutic attitudes', namely the core conditions. According to Brodley (1997, 1999b, 2003; Merry and Brodley, 2002) the non-directive attitude is inherent in the term 'client-centred' and inherent in the therapeutic attitudes. She argues that it is a part of their essential meaning, because it guarantees the protection of the client's autonomy. Thus, living the basic attitudes is inherently non-directive and respectful of the client's self-determination. She maintains that the attitudes are expressed by empathic following responses, a willingness to answer questions and accommodate requests from clients and unsystematic responses from the therapist's frame of reference—behaviours that do not violate the client's fundamental right to self-determination. Brodley (1990, 1999a) further emphasizes that 'client-centred' and 'experiential' are two different therapies that turn on the issue of directivity and influence. Garry Prouty (1999) argues similarly.

Lisbeth Sommerbeck (2004) views the non-directive attitude of the client-centred therapist as a logical consequence of the uniqueness of each individual client and the unconditional positive regard towards him and of the assumption that the human organism's continuous interaction with its environment is a non-linear dynamic system. Therefore, the client-centred therapist not only *should not* be an expert, but *cannot* be an expert on what is best for the client.

Expertism is also an issue for Cecil H. Patterson (2000: 181–4). He claims that the matter of being non-directive is to free a process of self-discovery and self-actualization, to foster autonomy, responsibility and self-determination. Patterson argues against the idea it that could make sense within a 'principled non-directivity' (see below) that the therapist may offer activities, exercises, techniques, directions, advice, interpretations, etc. in order to please the client and his or her wishes. He underlines that it is naïve to believe that clients are really completely free to reject such offerings from one who is perceived, to some extent at least, as an expert. 'Moreover, these offerings are inconsistent with respect and with the end of client-centered therapy—a responsible, independent, self-actualizing client' (*ibid.*: 182). He also remarks that the definition of 'placebo' is 'to please the client'.

Paul Wilkins' (2003: 85–98) asserts that it is the therapist's intention that matters. He reinforces that Rogers' point was to contrast his approach to approaches with a 'knowing better' stance of therapists, to place emphasis on the client's right to select the goals in therapy. So he sees non-directivity as a relative concept, contrasting with the idea that therapists, not clients, are the experts. Though non-directive therapists do influence their clients (by their own experiences, cultural biases, their way of behaving and talking, their office, dressing, etc.), their basic intention communicates the message that the client is capable of deciding on his or her own about the process and contents of therapy. In opposition to the criticism that therapists should not deny but should deliberately use their expertism (i.e., the therapist must not be non-directive), Wilkins argues that no such stance is needed. He points to the theory that different psychopathologies do not require different treatments (opposing what experiential therapists argue—that it is important to bring about specific processes in order to more efficiently support change). As Rogers (1957) put it—therapist expertise is only a need of insecure therapists (see Schmid 2004a, 2005a, 2005b).

Dave Mearns and Brian Thorne (2000: 191) shift the focus of interest in the debate about non-directivity from the therapist's behaviour to the client's experience. They assert: 'The importance of directivity is not in what the counsellor *does* but in what the client *experiences*. [...] The question which should be asked is not "is the therapist behaving directively?" but "is the client being directed?"' In doing so, they decisively stress the importance of the relationship for the understanding of the importance of non-directiveness.

... OR AS AN OUTDATED CONCEPT TO BE REINTERPRETED OR REPLACED

Others think that certain kinds of directivity are not incompatible or irreconcilable with a person-centred stance: David Cain (1989, 1990) does not regard non-directivity as a basic characteristic of the person-centred approach. He thinks that to impose non-directivity on the client may hinder or restrict him or her. Of course, an imposition of non-directivity would be entirely inconsistent with the intention that comes from holding a non-directive attitude. In Cain's eyes the task is to learn with the client how he or she is learning best; otherwise the therapist would hinder themselves in offering their personal and professional resources and will not be able to adjust to the individuality of each client.

Barry Grant (1990, 2004) positions himself against Cain who, in his view, seems to have an 'in order to' attitude and an orientation towards effectiveness. Coming from an ethical point of view, Grant considers non-directiveness to be 'the hallmark of client-centered therapy, the characteristic that distinguishes it from all other therapies' (2004: 158). He also states that 'Non-directiveness, the absence of intention to cause specific effects or bring about specific changes in clients, is consistent with respecting the right to self-determination' (*ibid.*). He goes on to make a distinction—on the basis of the image of the human being and the motive of acting that the therapist holds—between instrumental 'non-directiveness' as a means for growth and 'principled non-directiveness'. According to Grant, the latter is to be understood as a fundamental expression of respect, regarding the other as a mystery. Principled non-directiveness is an absence of the intention to make anything in particular happen. It is an expression of an attitude towards the world of facing it as a miracle, as an object of love, not will.

David Coghlan and Edward McIlduff (1990), not unlike gestalt therapists, discriminate between process and content. They discriminate between giving a structure concerning the means of processing and being directive concerning the content.

Germain Lietaer (1992; 1998), an influential advocate of the experiential wing in humanistic therapies, favours the shift from non-directivity to experience-orientation. He distinguishes between directivity and manipulation and believes that directivity 'in its positive aspects refers to the therapist's task-oriented responses and interventions' (1998: 63). In his opinion, to be non-directive simply means that there is no therapy plan. He emphasizes that directivity has nothing to do with manipulation, control or pressure and warns of a 'directivity phobia' (Lietaer 1992b: 11–12, 16, Lietaer and Dierick 1996: 15).

The advocates of focusing-oriented (Gendlin, 1996), process-experiential or process-guiding (Elliott and Greenberg 2002), emotion-focused (Greenberg, 2002) and goal- or clarification-oriented therapy (Sachse, 2003, 2004) distinguish between directivity regarding the content of the client's communications and directivity regarding the therapeutic process. Experiential and process-directive writers assert that their directive intentions are focused on clients' process, not their content (e.g. Greenberg, Rice and Elliott, 1993; Gendlin, 1974). They do not intend to direct clients' content in the sense of directing the client to talk about certain topics. But they see it as the therapist's task to steer the client's process according to their knowledge about the importance and nature of it. In return, Brodley (2003) and others criticise that they overlook the fact that any process-directive procedure changes the content of their client's thoughts, feelings and communications and that process-directive therapists ignore that their directive procedures require the client to surrender to the therapist's expertise.

Finally, there are authors who simply view 'nondirectiveness' as a 'myth' (Bowen, 1996) and try to use transcripts of Rogers' therapy or demonstration sessions to prove their assertion. In doing so they provide a classic example of understanding and discussing the concept of non-directivity on the level of intervention techniques.

Some misunderstandings: What non-directivity is not

Following from this short survey, some classic misunderstandings of the concept of non-directivity can be cleared up easily (see Schmid 1996: 268–270).

Non-directivity is not inactive

Non-directivity has nothing do with passivity or inactivity, nor is it something like abstinence. It has nothing to do with non-involvement. Also, the caricature of a wishy-washy behaviour ('non-direct'), never taking a stand, squirming with embarrassment, always hesitating to ask questions (see Pörtner 1994: 74), has nothing at all to do with person-centredness. The same goes for simple restatements or a wooden technique of reflecting of feelings (Rogers, 1986a). The peak of misinterpretation was definitely reached

80

when non-directivity was contorted into the technique of simply mirroring the client's words. Non-directivity is in actuality an active and proactive way of interaction in the encounter process of therapist and client, as will be shown below.

Non-directivity is not (necessarily) unstructured

Structure refers to a specific order. A group or a dialogue can be structured or unstructured in terms of the various issues of setting in therapy, including its time frame, the order of speakers in a group and other elements of structure. Brainstorming, to examine another example, is structured if there is the rule that all ideas are collected without comment or assessment. Directivity refers to the intention as to why such an order is set or denied. It has to do with the way somebody tries to reach his goals (see Schmid, 1996: 175–6; Coghlan and McIlduff, 1990). This leads to the question of influence.

Non-directivity is not non-influential

The notion of 'directive versus non-directive' has nothing to do with whether therapy is an influencing process. Of course, there is therapist intent to influence the client. Otherwise, why would therapists do therapy with clients? In relationships there is no way not to influence; one cannot not influence. The relevant issue is the nature of the influence (see also Patterson, 2000: 182). It is the nature of therapist influence that should be questioned when the issue of 'directive versus non-directive' is examined. In being empathic, the person-centred therapist and facilitator avoids directivity in terms of selecting the topics, interpreting the meaning of the client's feelings and cognitions and steering the process of therapy. Non-directive empathic understanding is an influencing attitude and behaviour. It most likely influences clients to treat themselves and their processes in a similar way. Active listening of this type influences.

   The misunderstanding of non-directivity as non-influencing highlights an often neglected difference: what a therapist does (or fails to do) always has an effect or impact, but this must not be confused with an intention to have a *certain* effect. Therapists are always paying more attention to certain things and less to others—intention makes the difference as to what impact or influence this has on the client. Concerning his work in groups, Rogers stated (1971: 276), 'there is no doubt that I am selective in my listening and hence "directive", if people wish to accuse me of this.' He stresses that he is unquestionably much more interested in the meaning the experiences have for a client in the moment and the feelings which they arouse in the client, than the stories they tell. 'It is these meanings and the feelings to which I try to respond' (*ibid.*). Thus, even active listening may be seen as directive in terms of influencing. But the crucial point is how it is done, and whether one aims at a specific goal.

Non-directivity is not a denial of power

As there is influence, there is power. The claim for non-directivity is not a denial of power, as is often insinuated. On the contrary, the non-directive therapist is very aware of his power and therefore uses it particularly carefully; that is, in a way that brings about empowerment of clients by trust in their resources. In other words: the goal of person-centred influence is to foster the process of actualization. The 'means' to do so is by being present—a way of being and behaving that is explicated in the description of the core conditions (see below). Everything else, including any kind of directivity, is incompatible with these 'means' (see Patterson, 2000).

Non-directivity is not a technique

It is definitely inadequate to deal with all of these questions in a discussion on the level of techniques. Non-directivity is nothing that is used 'in order to'; it is not an instrument. It is true that non-directive therapists do not direct, control, guide, steer, put something into somebody's mind or manipulate. It is true that they do not give advice, interpret, diagnose, question, interrogate, instruct, rate, evaluate, judge. And it is also true that these 'don'ts' are consequences of a fundamental non-directive attitude.

But there is much more. It is important to emphasize that discussing non-directivity on the level of behaviour is wrong. It is necessary to view non-directivity in the context of the attitude(s). But even this does not necessarily strike at its core (as the ongoing discussion proves). Non-directivity is a matter of the underlying image of the human being, a matter of the theory of knowledge that is held and a matter of the respective ethical stance.

Non-directivity is thus a matter of basic beliefs. People who think that directivity is necessary in therapy and counselling have a different image of the human being, a different concept of how to deal with knowledge and a different ethical stance from those who work with their clients on the basis of non-directiveness. Since it is of no use to argue over beliefs (they precede acting, thinking and science), there is no way to say who, ultimately, is right. There is no way to convince each other (Schmid, 1999: 178–9). Different convictions lead to different consequences. The only thing one really can record is that there *is* a difference; and to have an honest look at the consequences.

THE NATURE OF THE THERAPEUTIC RELATIONSHIP ACCORDING TO A PERSON-CENTRED IMAGE OF THE HUMAN BEING

PERSON-CENTRED ANTHROPOLOGY: THERAPY AS PERSONALISATION AND AS ENCOUNTER PERSON TO PERSON

The name of the person-centred approach was not chosen by coincidence. Whatever else the reasons were to coin the term '*person*-centred,' it was also meant from the very beginning to express a certain anthropological stance, based on a specific image of the human being, developed in the occidental philosophical tradition. Rogers' thinking was deeply rooted in this tradition. As the name suggests, the underlying key concept of person-centred therapy is the understanding of the human being as a person, and the understanding of the therapeutic relationship as an encounter (or meeting) person to person.

What it means to be a *person*, and the consequences that follow for a person-centred approach to psychotherapy, has been described previously in detail (Schmid, 1991, 1994, 1998a, 1998c, 2002c: 58–65, 2004b, 2005c). What follows is only a brief summary.

The person-centred image of the human being is based on the view of men and women as persons. According to two different yet dialectically linked traditional strands of meaning in the history of theology, philosophy and psychology, the human being is characterized as a person if he or she is denoted in his or her unique individuality, worth and dignity, as well as in his or her interconnectedness. Both the substantial notion of being a person (i.e., being from oneself) and the relational conception of becoming a person (i.e., being from and towards others), belong to the meaning of this person-centred image of the human being. They are dialectically and inseparably connected. To be a person describes autonomy *and* interconnectedness, individuality *and* solidarity, sovereignty *and* commitment. Carl Rogers combined both views in a unique way for psychotherapy when he built his theory and practice upon the actualizing tendency as the motivational force constructively working on behalf of the client (substantial dimension), which is maximized in a facilitative relationship of a certain kind (relational dimension). This facilitative relationship is an encounter provided by a person who is really present; that is, living the core conditions described by Rogers (1957) as fully as possible in this relationship (see below).

Person-centred personality and relationship theory understands personalisation as a process of becoming independent *and* of developing authentic relationships. Therefore, the respective theory of therapy understands therapy as both personality development and encounter person to person. At the same time it is important to be aware that both client and therapist are understood as persons. Both therapist and client develop together in this relationship. Thus, both notions of being a person are also important for the therapist: unconditional acknowledgement and empathic positive regard as a way of being 'with' the client, together with a position 'counter' to the client; that is, a committed 'en-counter'.

According to dialogic (or encounter) philosophy the relationship to somebody as a person is called an *encounter*. To encounter means to meet the unexpected. Between persons, it means to meet face to face. One of the consequences of viewing the human being as a person is the realization that accepting another person means truly acknowledging him or her as an *Other* in the sense of dialogical thinking. He or she is no alter ego, no close friend a priori, no identifiable person. He or she is an entirely different person. Etymologically, the word 'encounter' comes from the Latin 'contra', which means 'against', To en-counter another person, first of all, means recognizing that the Other really 'stands counter', because he or she is essentially different from me. Therefore encounter is an amazing meeting with the reality of the Other. It means that one is touched by the essence of the opposite (Guardini, 1955). In order for this to happen, there must be a non-purpose-oriented openness and a distance which leads to amazement. 'Being counter', according to Martin Buber (1923), is the foundation for meeting face to face, an event in which one becomes present to the Other.

This 'position' appreciates the Other as somebody independent, as an autonomous individual, different and separated from me, worthy of being dealt with. In being counter the otherness of the Other is appreciated. To stand counter also means to give room to each other and to express respect. In facing the Other I can see him or her and acknowledge the Other's uniqueness and qualities. (More on encounter as a basic category for the person-centred approach: Schmid, 1991, 1994, 1998b, 2002a, 2002c, 2002f).

Moreover, if a person is constituted through their relationship to another person, to be a person means to be a *response*. The movement always originates from the Thou: it is the call, the addressing of another human being, which evokes a response—a response from which I cannot escape, because nobody can respond in my place. We are obliged and responsible to the Other and owe him or her an answer—making the 'priority' of the Other. This is particularly important for the understanding of the nature of a therapeutic relationship: the client is the call, the therapist as a person is the response to this call, whence, out of his response-ability, his responsibility derives (see below). What happens in psychotherapy, if it is understood as an encounter relationship, is that the client is opening up and revealing him- or herself and the therapist is responding as a person.

PERSON-CENTRED EPISTEMOLOGY: THE PHENOMENOLOGICAL PARADIGM SHIFT FROM I–THOU TO THOU–I

In facing Others I do not think what I could know about them, but I am ready to accept what they are going to disclose. The challenge of encounter is 'to be kept awake by an enigma' (Lévinas, 1983: 120). The Other is different. Thus, in order to do justice to him, he must not be seen from my perspective. He or she is the one coming towards me, approaching me. The movement goes from the Thou to the I, not the other way round—an epistemological paradigm shift of tremendous importance and consequence.

It follows that the person-centred approach is a *phenomenological* approach. The word 'phenomenon' comes from a verb in the Greek language, which in its active form (φαίνειν) means 'show, bring to light, make appear, announce'; in passive voice (φαίνεσθαι) it means 'be shown, come to light, appear, come into being'. A therapeutic approach is phenomenological if the direction, the movement, goes from the client to the therapist: the client 'shows and announces'. The therapist tries to 'perceive and understand'. This denotes a Thou-I relationship, as opposed to the 'egology'—as Emmanuel Lévinas (1983: 189) called the traditional occidental thinking—of the conventional humanistic approaches. Therefore, the person-centred approach goes radically beyond these 'humanistic' approaches.

Person-centred therapy turns the established understanding of psychotherapy completely on its head. The conventional model rests on the idea that it is the therapist who has to gain knowledge about the client in order to treat them, paralleling the traditional medical model Carl Rogers so strongly opposed. In the traditional (objectifying) approach the questions are: What do I (the therapist) see? What can I observe? What is over there? What can I do? How can I help? Rogers' approach proceeds just the other way round: What does the client show, disclose, reveal; what does he or she want to be understood? The task of the therapist then is not to try to get knowledge about the client but to ac-knowledge the person who is showing him- or herself (Schmid, 2002c).

From the understanding of 'person', it follows that being a person means: to disclose, to reveal oneself to oneself and to the Other. This is the special notion of 'person' inherent to the person-centred approach. It is far different from what many people, including therapists of various orientations, mean when they say 'I see you as a person.' The word may be the same; the meaning is not. The meaning definitely goes beyond what is considered to be the common ground of all humanistic approaches in psychology, namely that the human being comes into the view as a human (hence the name), and not only according to the criteria of natural science—a development undoubtedly important in overcoming an objectifying understanding of therapy (Schmid, 2003). Many still refer to this conception, if they regard the human being as a person, including authors from within the 'Rogerian family of therapies' (see Lietaer, 2002).

However, as just mentioned above, the notion of being a person, as it is the underlying ground of the person-centred approach, is much more specific and radical. He or she is the expert on his or her life, not the therapist. This epistemological paradigm change also implies that the expert in the therapeutic endeavour, in any respect, is the client. The therapist's task is to be present and ask the question: 'What is the client's call?' Thus, the respective task is to keep one's ability to be surprised and touched.

There are three possible positions on expertism in psychotherapy. The first claims that the therapist is the expert for the content and the process (the methods, the means, the procedure, the skills). This is a principle held, for example, in cognitive behaviour therapy. A second position sees the client as the expert on the content and the therapist (at least partially) as the expert on the process—the expert on the way therapy proceeds. This position can be found in gestalt and experiential therapies. The third possibility asserts that the client is expert for both problems and methods, content and process, and the therapist is a facilitator—a stance only to be found in genuine person-centred therapy. According to its personal anthropology it is the client who is the expert on his or her life, because he or she is the experienced; he or she is the one opening up and directing the way of the process. In the view of a genuinely personal anthropology it is of no use to separate the process from the person, and it is impossible to separate content and process—in a very significant sense the process is the content is the meaning. Therefore, it also seems to be artificial to separate between relationship-, content- and process-experts. As a matter of fact, from a person-centred perspective, both are experts, yet in a different sense. One might say: the therapist is the expert on not being an expert on the life of another person (Schmid, 2001c, 2003, 2004a).

PERSON-CENTRED THEORY OF THERAPY: THE THERAPIST'S PRESENCE AS THE RESPONSE TO THE CALL OF THE CLIENT

The existential response, the respective stance to enable a person to open up, is *presence*. 'Presence' derives from the Latin words *esse*, which means 'to be', and *prae* ('in front of') which is an intensifier. Thus, *prae-esse* is not just 'being', but 'really being'. Presence means to be authentic as a person; fully myself and fully open; whole; fully living the individual 'I am'; fully living the relationship 'I am'. The challenge is, at one and the same time, to be oneself and in relationship. Being able to be touched, impressed, surprised, changed, altered, growing and also being able to stick to one's own experiences and symbolizations (instead of taking the experiences, interpretations and stances of the others), to value from within (without judging the person of the other), to have one's own point of view.

What Rogers described as core conditions corresponds with presence, as understood on a deeper, dialogical-personal level. Presence, in the sense of encounter philosophy, is the existential core of these attitudes. It is further explained by the description of the conditions, which Rogers always understood holistically as interrelated; intrinsically connected, a 'triad variable'. That is, each one of the conditions makes no therapeutic sense without the others. Rogers' (1986b) description of the therapeutic relationship as being present to the Other seems to be, more than he himself noticed, a basic and comprehensive depiction of a therapeutic encounter relationship. Together, congruence, unconditional positive regard and empathy constitute one human attitude, one fundamental way of being, relating and acting, truly characterized as psychophysical presence, a way of being, a way of 'being with', a way of 'being in encounter'. The necessary and sufficient conditions for therapeutic change, in their intrinsic connectedness, constitute a way of being with the client that is crucial for the therapeutic endeavour. They are not three separate qualities. They are one fundamental way of understanding oneself and the Other as a person (see Schmid 2001a, 2001b, 2001c, 2002a). Hence, presence is an expression of authenticity, as it is related to the immediately present flow of experiencing. It reflects congruence, as well as the difference between a person's experiencing and symbolization, and between his or her symbolization and communication. Presence is an expression of empathy, because, in existential wonderment, it is related to what the Other is experiencing. And presence is an expression of positive regard without conditions, as acceptance of myself and personal acknowledgement of the Other, of whatever immediately present feelings he or she is experiencing.

When the therapist is present to the client, there is no hidden therapeutic agenda. Presence in this meaning is always *im-media-te*; that is, without media, without preconceived means. The therapist accepts the client in his or her moment-by-moment process—including what brought him or her to this moment and the possibilities of further development in the future. This excludes diagnosing and pathologising the client and precludes the therapist having any predetermined method. Such lack of categorisation invites the therapist to experience the client as a unique individual, embracing their entire personhood without favour or discrimination. (For more on the notion of presence, see Schmid, 1994, 1996, 2002a, 2003; see the interesting piece of research by Geller and Greenberg, 2002.)

NON-DIRECTIVENESS AS REALISATION OF AN ANTHROPOLOGICAL, EPISTEMOLOGICAL AND ETHICAL CONVICTION

NON-DIRECTIVENESS IS AN EXPRESSION OF *PERSON*-CENTREDNESS

From the discussion above, it is clear that approaching a human being as a person is necessarily a non-directive enterprise; that is, a way of becoming aware of and relating to the other person that does not follow any preconceived direction, because the direction originates from the other person. If one fails to become aware of and relate to the Other in this way, the Other is immediately changed from a person to be encountered to an object to be treated. So, if one wants to adhere to an image of the human being as a person, and approach Others in a person-centred way, non-directivity is unavoidable as the only way to become aware of the other as a person. Otherwise, he or she will be dealt with necessarily in an objectifying manner.

It is as simple as this: non-directiveness means that the client is seen as a person who is able to find his own answer, and therefore it is not the therapist's task to direct the client towards a specific answer, or even towards an answer at all. Non-directiveness means that the therapist enters into an encounter relationship in which both client and therapist do not know where the relationship will lead.

Being non-directive, responding in a facilitative way, unfolds the notion of 'person' as a response to another person's call. Non-directiveness must be understood as a consequence of the personhood of the client (and also of the therapist). Like 'person', non-directivity has both a substantial and a relational dimension, and must be seen as a realization of the Other's autonomy. It must be comprehended through the person-to-person relationship.

As to the substantial notion of 'person', non-directiveness radically stresses the uniqueness, dignity and freedom of the person. It is an expression of the substantiality of the other person; that is, of the right of self-determination and responsibility, and the capacity of the self-healing potential. It is an expression of the conviction that the process of change is unpredictable in its specificity, because it is idiosyncratic for each client (Merry and Brodley, 2002). This stance is characterised by the fundamental and unequivocal respect held by the therapist. A fundamental and principled non-directiveness is the logical consequence of an image of the human being which favours the uniqueness of the Other over standardising diagnosis, and prioritises acknowledgement to knowledge. Consequently, directive means are inconsistent with the goal of autonomy, responsibility and self-determination, and they are incompatible with unconditional positive regard and acknowledgement.

As to the relational notion, and from an encounter perspective—becoming aware of the Other as a mystery and an enigma—there is no doubt that realizing the 'way of being with' others called 'presence' is non-directive in principle. Non-directiveness denotes the ability to be surprised by the Other and to be open to what the Other is willing to reveal as a person. To be present principally implies not to make something happen, but to be open to a unique process between two (or more) persons. If the therapist does not see himself in the position of the expert for the other person's life, but as a person meeting another person, then guiding, steering or directing would be completely incompatible with this self-understanding. Directive means are inconsistent with impartial and unbiased listening, and inconsistent with being empathic.

Both notions of person, the substantial and the relational, belong together and cannot be separated.

Non-directiveness is an expression of the therapist's authenticity. Authenticity means that authors encounter authors and not copies. Authenticity is non-directive, because inherent in it is the notion that only the author of a life can change it. Thus authenticity strictly opposes any expert behaviour, be it in terms of content and decisions, in terms of how to get there; that is, means, methods and techniques. If authenticity is what therapy is about, the only legitimate 'techné' (the original Greek word which means 'art') is im-media-cy, or im-media-te presence (presence without media), in other words, the encounter person to person. To be precise, non-directive therapy is a process to overcome preconceived techniques and methods (which always come in between humans) by making them superfluous.

Therapies, theories and practices that concentrate on the experience (therefore calling themselves 'experiential'), reduce the person as a whole to the experience as a part. Thus they are no longer person-centred, but focus instead on only one aspect of the person ('focusing-oriented therapy' or 'focusing therapy'). They not only pay less attention to the relationship in a dialogical way, and thus miss the essence of an encounter relationship, but also re-introduce the therapist as an expert in terms of directing the process ('process-directional' or 'process-guiding'). They do so even if they limit themselves to process-guiding activities and do not intend to influence the content (see Prouty, 1999; Schmid, 2002d). Consequently, they no longer need the concept of non-directiveness.

Non-directivity cannot be split in terms of being non-directive on one level and directive on another at the same time. Therefore, non-directivity can mean only that there is no goal set by the therapist regarding the content and no method regarding the process; no intention to aim at something specific. Non-directiveness means that the respect for, and thus the trust in, the person is the overall principle, as is openness in the process of the relationship. Consequently, non-directivity is an expression of not using preconceived means to influence the therapeutic process in a way chosen by the therapist.

In other words: presence, as the way of being with a person, is non-directive per se.

NON-DIRECTIVENESS IS AN EXPRESSION OF THE 'ART OF NOT-KNOWING'

Non-directiveness is a fundamental consequence of the epistemological insight that the movement in therapy, its direction, comes from the client. If it is the client who 'knows best', the therapist's task is to be present and follow. The therapist does not see any need to control the direction the client takes. As already mentioned, Merry (1999: 44 and 75) emphasizes that non-directivity is 'a general non-authoritarian attitude maintained by a counsellor whose intention is empathically to understand a client's subjective experience.' Merry also writes that 'the particular characteristic of the actualising tendency, whilst its direction is regarded as constructive and creative, cannot be predicted and should not be controlled or directed' (*ibid*.: 76). Taking this one step further, I rather like to think this is because of creativity and spontaneity evolving in a person who is neither directed nor controlled.

Non-directiveness is a non-purpose-oriented openness towards the Other. It is the only way to genuinely encounter a client as a person, and as a consequence it is the therapist's contribution to an encounter relationship. Thus, first of all, the task is to let go of one's ideas of the client, even if these ideas are well-intentioned. Sidney Jourard (1968) points out that disregarding one's prejudices is an invitation to the Other to also let go—let go of yesterday's ideas, interests and goals and explore new ones. Both therapist and client transcend their ideas about the client and provide the chance for new, creative possibilities.

So, non-directiveness is ultimately an expression of the 'art of not-knowing' (Schmid, 2001b, 2002c); the art of being curious, open to being surprised. It is a kind of sophisticated naïvety (see Husserl, 1950) towards the client, where the challenging part is the unknown and not-yet-understood. It is an openness to wonderment, surprise and what the client has to disclose. The underlying phenomenological idea is that 'each experience, which deserves this name, thwarts an expectation' (Gadamer, 1999: 362). Following a term by Wittgenstein (1969) this might also be called 'creative ignorance'.

NON-DIRECTIVENESS IS THE RECOGNITION OF THE CLIENT'S SELF-DIRECTIVENESS

As early as 1942 Rogers (p. 87) writes that what is non-directive for the therapist is self-directed for the client (centred on the directions of the client) and thus, 'client-centred'. 'Self-directivity' of the client is the goal of person-centred therapy and counselling. This stresses the understanding of Mearns and Thorne (see above) that the important thing about non-directivity is what it means for the client. Person-centred therapy is not about the therapist being non-directive; it is about the client being self-directive.

Art Bohart (2004) further develops the concept of self-directedness. He emphasizes that it is the client, as an active, intelligent and thinking being and agent, who makes empathy and the core conditions work. The client is an active self-healer. Bohart's central observation and theory is most profound, and has far-reaching consequences. Building upon it, it follows that the concept of non-directiveness means that the process is client-centred: not only in the traditional meaning that the attention is centred in the client, but also that it is the client who—as an active self-healer—directs the process. Therefore, it might make sense to think of the process in terms of 'client-directiveness'; which might not only be an adequate term, but also one less open to potential misunderstanding than non-directiveness.

Thus, non-directiveness is neither a principle as such, nor a statement about every single behaviour or action of the therapist. It is not a set of behaviours or a technique. It is an active expression of being impressed by the Other (and not by one's own ideas,

89

combinations and solution proposals) and being interested in him or her. To be non-directive is a 'way of being with', and a consequence of the trust in the client's actualizing tendency. To be non-directive means valuing the otherness and uniqueness of the Other. It is a precondition for encounter as well as the basic realization of a genuine encounter relationship. Non-directiveness is an epistemological issue. In non-directiveness, the values of the therapist are expressed not to gain external control over the client, but to respect his or her organismic self-directedness and personal autonomy. Non-directiveness denotes the ability to be surprised by the Other and to be open to what the Other is willing to reveal as a person. The therapists' task is to respond to the innate capabilities to lead his or her own life; to do everything that is facilitative to this end. The most facilitative thing one can do is to respect and acknowledge the client as a person, with all their abilities mentioned. Presence is the incarnation of such *facilitative responsiveness*.

To summarise: non-directiveness is a dimension of presence, an expression of presence. Presence means that the therapist is responding existentially; that is, as a person, to the call of the client. Thus, non-directiveness is a way of facilitative responsiveness. The client, as his or her own expert in terms of the content (the client is the one who 'knows' what it is all about) and in terms of the process (i.e., the way of communication, the 'languages', the means of therapy) directs the process of therapy and the process of his or her life.

NON-DIRECTIVENESS IS AN EXPRESSION OF PERSON-CENTRED ETHICS

By doing psychotherapy, a decision is made to respond to the misery, to the grief, to the life of another person; to share his or her joys and sorrows. As stated above, it derives from being addressed by the Other, from being touched, being asked, called; from being appealed to. In every personal encounter there lies the response to a call. And the response grows out of responsibility, that is, out of 'response ability', the ability to respond. The Other is an appeal and a provocation; the person in need represents a demand. This means that the need of the Other is there first and that psychotherapy is responding, answering to a demand. In short: psychotherapy from a person-centred perspective has its origin in the Other.

The epistemological paradigm change for psychotherapy achieved by Carl Rogers, from knowledge to ac-knowledge-ment on the part of the therapist, leads us to understand the therapist as somebody who is called to respond. This makes psychotherapy an ethical challenge. Starting especially from a phenomenological consideration, as Rogers did, psychotherapy must be regarded as an ethical phenomenon. If the personal perception of the Other is the basis of the relationship, an ethical relation is created. Whatever else psychotherapy might be (art, science, practical philosophy of life, spiritual discipline, etc.), it is an ethical enterprise, as described earlier (Schmid 2002d, 2002e, 2003).

The Other is never an object to perceive or to know about. The Other cannot be understood by a refinement of the methods of perception. The Other must be understood by increasing empathic sensitivity and by increasing openness to being touched by clients through their opening-up—by what they show and disclose. It is this reverse of the usual order of communication which makes the person-centred way of communicating unique among the therapeutic orientations and justifies the designation 'non-directive'. In the process of therapy the client's response-ability grows and the therapist's 'responses' more and more become *co-responses* of the client and the therapist to the experiences in the relationship (see Schmid, 2003).

Taking a closer look at the core of person-centred theory, as expressed in Rogers' 1957 statement, we find that its ethical foundation is already included: psychotherapy means responding to the client's incongruence, responding to a vulnerable or anxious person (the second, and often ignored, necessary condition!) Even more: if the six conditions (Rogers, 1957) are necessary and sufficient for a constructive development of the person by means of psychotherapy, then it is the therapist's obligation to take them into account (contact, client incongruence, communication of therapist's attitudes) or to offer them respectively (congruence, unconditional positive regard, empathy). After all, it is a matter of the image of the human being that is held.

Thus, non-directiveness also 'is a principled and ethical stance' (Merry, 2004: 42), 'an essentially ethical commitment' (Worsley, 2004: 130; see also Grant, 1990). As such, it comes 'before' theory and practice, which are influenced by it. The art of not-knowing is a consequence of this ethical stance. It is a way of relating towards each other in which we are obliged to provide for each other as persons, and to provide for ourselves. It is a humble attitude towards the unknown (Grant, 1990), a humble attitude at the sight of the uniqueness of the Other. In the interpersonal encounter which we call therapy, we are addressed and asked to respond, thus assuming a deep responsibility; an obligation in which our fellow human expects us to render the service we owe to each other. In the end, what we owe each other is nothing else but love. Non-directiveness is an expression of this ethical stance. Non-directiveness is an expression of love.

NON-DIRECTIVENESS IS A POLITICAL ISSUE: THE EXPRESSION OF A BASIC COMMITMENT TO EMANCIPATION

Finally, it becomes clear that non-directiveness is the expression of a basic belief in the self-directive capacities of the person—it is a philosophy, a commitment to emancipation. The 'facilitative responsiveness' of the non-directive therapist, in the language of dialogic or encounter philosophy, carries these meanings. It is the self-understanding of the therapist as a person who is present to respond as a person to a person in need. Thus non-directivity is much more than an attitude or a posture, let alone a rule or a technique. When taken simply as a rule or technique, non-directivity becomes perverted to the opposite of what it is meant to be. Today, non-directivity might not be an up-to-date term that unambiguously expresses what the matter is about. The term itself states only what person-centred therapy is not about. But the issue at stake—emancipatory psychotherapy versus alienating control—is perfectly up to date, perhaps more than ever.

What John Shlien (2000) said regarding person-centred therapy, is true for non-directiveness: 'It is not good manners. It is in the character.'

91

REFERENCES

Barrett-Lennard GT (1998) *Carl Rogers' Helping System: Journey and substance.* London: Sage.

Bohart AC (2004) How do clients make empathy work? *Person-Centered and Experiential Psychotherapies, 3*(2), 102–16.

Bowen MV-B (1996) The myth of nondirectiveness: The case of Jill. In: BA Farber, DC Brink,& PM Raskin (Eds) *The Psychotherapy of Carl Rogers: Cases and commentary.* New York: Guilford, pp. 84–94.

Bozarth JD (1998) *Person-Centered Therapy: A revolutionary paradigm.* Ross-on-Wye: PCCS Books.

Bozarth JD (2002) Nondirectivity in the person-centered approach: Critique of Kahn's critique. *Journal of Humanistic Psychology, 42*(2), 78–83.

Brodley BT (1990) Client-centered and experiential: Two different therapies. In G Lietaer, J Rombauts & R Van Balen (Eds) *Client-Centered and Experiential Therapy in the Nineties.* Leuven: Leuven University Press, pp. 87–107.

Brodley BT (1997) The nondirective attitude in client-centered therapy. *The Person-Centered Journal, 4*(1), 61–74.

Brodley BT (1999a) About the nondirective attitude. *Person-Centred Practice, 7*(2), 79–82.

Brodley BT (1999b) On the concept of non-directivity in the person-centered approach. Paper given at the 2nd World Council for Psychotherapy. Vienna, July 8, 1999.

Brodley BT (2002) Research and values. Paper at the Carl Rogers Centennial Conference, La Jolla.

Brodley BT (2003) Directive and non-directive therapies in the person-centered community. Unpublished paper.

Buber M (1923) *Ich und Du.* Heidelberg: Lambert Schneider, 8th ed. 1974.

Cain DJ (1989) The paradox of nondirectiveness in the person-centered approach. *Person-Centered Review, 4*(2), 123–31.

Cain DJ (1990) Further thoughts about nondirectiveness and client-centered therapy. *Person-Centered Review, 5*(1), 89–99.

Coghlan D & McIlduff E (1990) Structuring and nondirectiveness in group facilitation. *Person-Centered Review, 5*(1), 13–29.

Elliott R & Greenberg LS (2002) Process-experiential psychotherapy. In DJ Cain & J Seeman (Eds) *Humanistic Psychotherapies: Handbook of research and practice.* Washington: APA, pp. 279–306.

Gadamer H-G (1999) *Wahrheit und Methode: Grundzüge einer philosophischen Hermeneutik, Vol. 1.* Tübingen: Mohr.

Geller SM & Greenberg LS (2002) Therapeutic presence: Therapists' experience of presence in the psychotherapy encounter. *Person-Centered and Experiential Psychotherapies. 1*(1&2), 71–86.

Gendlin ET (1974) Client-centered and experiential psychotherapy. In DA Wexler & LN Rice (Eds) *Innovations in Client-Centered Therapy.* New York: Wiley, pp. 211–46.

Gendlin ET (1996) *Focusing-Oriented Psychotherapy: A manual of the experiential method.* New York: Guilford.

Grant B (1990) Principled and instrumental nondirectiveness in person-centered and client-centered therapy. *Person-Centered Review, 5*(1), 77–88. Reprinted in DJ Cain (Ed)(2002) *Classics in the Person-Centered Approach.* Ross-on-Wye: PCCS Books, pp. 371–7.

Grant B (2004) The imperative of ethical justification in psychotherapy: The special case of client-centered therapy. *Person-Centered and Experiential Psychotherapies, 3*(3), 152–65.

Greenberg LS (2002) *Emotion-Focused Therapy: Coaching clients to work through their feelings.* Washington, DC: APA.

Greenberg LS, Rice LN & Elliott R (1993) *Facilitating Emotional Change: The moment-by-moment process*. New York: Guilford Press.

Guardini R (1955) Die Begegnung: Ein Beitrag zur Struktur des Daseins. *Hochland 47*(3), 224–34.

Hendricks MN (2002) Focusing-oriented/experiential psychotherapy. In DJ Cain & J Seeman (Eds) *Humanistic Psychotherapies: Handbook of research and practice*. Washington: APA, pp. 221–51.

Husserl E (1950) *Cartesianische Meditationen und Pariser Vorträge: Gesammelte Werke, Vol. I*. Den Haag: Martinus-Nijhoff.

Jourard SM (1968) *Disclosing Man to Himself*. New York: Van Nostrand.

Lévinas E (1983) *Die Spur des Anderen: Untersuchungen zur Phänomenologie und Sozialphilosophie*. Freiburg i. Br.: Alber.

Lietaer G (1992) Von 'nicht-direktiv' zu „erfahrungsorietiert": Über die zentrale Bedeutung eines Kernkonzepts. In R Sachse, G Lietaer & WB Stiles, (Eds) *Neue Handlungskonzepte der Klientenzentrierten Psychotherapie: Eine grundlegende Neuorientierung*. Heidelberg: Asanger, pp. 11–21.

Lietaer G (1998) From non-directive to experiential: A paradigm unfolding. In B Thorne & E Lambers (Eds) *Person-Centred Therapy*. London: Sage, pp. 62–73.

Lietaer G (2002) The client-centered/experiential paradigm in psychotherapy: Development and identity. In JC Watson, RN Goldman & MS Warner (Eds) *Client-Centered and Experiential Psychotherapy in the 21st Century*. Ross-on-Wye: PCCS Books, pp. 1–15.

Lietaer G & Dierick P (1996) Client-centered group psychotherapy in dialogue with other orientations: Commonality and specificity. In R Hutterer, G Pawlowsky, PF Schmid & R Stipsits (Eds) *Client-Centered and Experiential Psychotherapy: A paradigm in motion*. Frankfurt/M: Peter Lang, pp. 563–83.

Mearns D & Thorne B (2000) *Person-Centered Therapy Today: New frontiers in theory and practice*. London: Sage.

Merry T (1999) *Learning and Being in Person-Centred Counselling*. Ross-on-Wye: PCCS Books.

Merry T (2004) Classical client-centred therapy. In P Sanders (Ed) *The Tribes of the Person-Centred Nation: An introduction to the schools of therapy related to the person-centred approach*. Ross-on-Wye: PCCS Books, pp. 21–44.

Merry T & Brodley BT (2002) The nondirective attitude in client-centered therapy. *Journal of Humanistic Psychology, 42*(2), 66–77.

Patterson CH (2000) *Understanding Psychotherapy: Fifty years of client-centred theory and practice*. Ross-on-Wye: PCCS Books.

PCEP (2004) *Person-Centered and Experiential Psychotherapies. Journal of the World Association for Person-Centered and Experiential Psychotherapy and Counseling* (R Elliott, D Mearns & PF Schmid, Eds) Vol 3: Papers from the 6th World Conference for Person-Centered and Experiential Psychotherapy and Counseling. Ross-on-Wye: PCCS Books.

Pörtner M (1994) (Ed) *Praxis der Gesprächspsychotherapie: Interviews mit Therapeuten*. Stuttgart: Klett-Cotta.

Prouty GF (1999) Carl Rogers and experiential therapies: a dissonance? *Person-Centred Practice, 7*(1), 4–11.

Raskin NJ (1947/2005) The non-directive attitude. In BE Levitt (Ed) *Embracing Non-directivity: Reassessing person-centered theory and practice in the 21st century*. Ross-on-Wye: PCCS Books, pp. 329–47.

Rogers CR (1942) *Counseling and Psychotherapy*. Boston: Houghton Mifflin.

Rogers CR (1951) *Client-Centered Therapy. Its current practice, implications, and theory*. Boston: Houghton Mifflin.

Rogers CR (1957) The necessary and sufficient conditions of therapeutic personality change. *Journal of Consulting Psychology, 21*(2), 95–103.

Rogers CR (1962) The interpersonal relationship: The core of guidance. *Harvard Educational Review 4*(32), 416–29.

Rogers CR (1971) On facilitating encounter groups. *The American Journal of Nursing, 71*(2), 275–9.

Rogers CR (1975) A dialogue with Carl Rogers. In RI Evans *Carl Rogers: The man and his ideas*. New York: EP Dutton, pp. 1–118.

Rogers CR (1986a) Reflection of feelings. *Person-Centered Review 1*(4), 375–7.

Rogers CR (1986b) A client-centered/person-centered approach to therapy. In IL Kutash & A Wolf (Eds) *Psychotherapist's Casebook: Theory and technique in the practice of modern times*. San Francisco: Jossey-Bass, pp. 197–208.

Sachse R (2003) *Klärungsorientierte Psychotherapie*. Göttingen: Hogrefe.

Sachse R (2004) From client-centered to clarification-oriented psychotherapy. *Person-Centered and Experiential Psychotherapies, 3*(1), 19–35.

Schmid PF (1991) Souveränität und Engagement: Zu einem personzentrierten Verständnis von 'Person'. In CR Rogers & PF Schmid, *Person-zentriert: Grundlagen von Theorie und Praxis*. Mainz: Grünewald; 5th edn. 2004, pp. 15–164.

Schmid PF (1994) *Personzentrierte Gruppenpsychotherapie: Ein Handbuch. Vol. I: Solidarität und Autonomie*. Cologne: EHP.

Schmid PF (1996) *Personzentrierte Gruppenpsychotherapie in der Praxis: Ein Handbuch. Vol. II: Die Kunst der Begegnung*. Paderborn: Junfermann.

Schmid PF (1998a) 'On becoming a person-centered approach': A person-centred understanding of the person. In B Thorne & E Lambers (Eds) *Person-Centred Therapy: A European Perspective*. London: Sage, pp. 38–52.

Schmid PF (1998b) 'Face to face': The art of encounter, in B Thorne & E Lambers (Eds) *Person-Centred Therapy: A European perspective*. London: Sage, pp. 74–90.

Schmid PF (1998c) *Im Anfang ist Gemeinschaft: Personzentrierte Gruppenarbeit in Seelsorge und Praktischer Theologie*. Stuttgart: Kohlhammer.

Schmid PF (1999) Personzentrierte Psychotherapie. In G Sonneck, T Slunecko (Eds) *Einführung in die Psychotherapie*. Stuttgart: UTB für Wissenschaft—Facultas, pp. 168–211.

Schmid PF (2001a) Authenticity: the person as his or her own author. Dialogical and ethical perspectives on therapy as an encounter relationship. And beyond. In G Wyatt (Ed) *Rogers' Therapeutic Conditions: Evolution, theory and practice. Vol 1: Congruence*. Ross-on-Wye: PCCS Books, pp. 217–32.

Schmid PF (2001b) Comprehension: the art of not-knowing. Dialogical and ethical perspectives on empathy as dialogue in personal and person-centred relationships. In S Haugh & T Merry (Eds) *Rogers' Therapeutic Conditions: Evolution, theory and practice. Vol 2: Empathy*. Ross-on-Wye: PCCS Books, pp. 53–71.

Schmid PF (2001c) Acknowledgement: the art of responding. Dialogical and ethical perspectives on the challenge of unconditional personal relationships in therapy and beyond. In JD Bozarth & P Wilkins (Eds) *Rogers' Therapeutic Conditions: Evolution, theory and practice. Vol 3: Unconditional Positive Regard*. Ross-on-Wye: PCCS Books, pp. 49–64.

Schmid PF (2002a) Presence: Im-media-te co-experiencing and co-responding Phenomenological, dialogical and ethical perspectives on contact and perception in person-centred therapy and beyond. In G Wyatt, & P Sanders (Eds) *Rogers' Therapeutic Conditions: Evolution, theory and practice. Vol 4: Contact and Perception*. Ross-on-Wye: PCCS Books, pp. 182–203.

Schmid PF (2002b) Person-Centered Psychotherapy, In A Pritz (Ed) *Globalized Psychotherapy*. Vienna: Facultas, pp. 701–13.

Schmid PF (2002c) Knowledge or acknowledgement? Psychotherapy as 'the art of not-knowing'—Prospects on further developments of a radical paradigm. *Person-Centered and Experiential Psychotherapies, 1*(1&2), 56–70.

Schmid PF (2002d) The necessary and sufficient conditions of being person-centered: On identity, integrity, integration and differentiation of the paradigm. In J Watson, RN Goldman & MS Warner (Eds) *Client-Centered and Experiential Psychotherapy in the 21st Century: Advances in theory, research and practice*. Ross-on-Wye: PCCS Books, pp. 36–51.

Schmid PF (2002e) Anspruch und Antwort: Personzentrierte Psychotherapie als Begegnung von Person zu Person. In WW Keil & G Stumm (Eds) *Die vielen Gesichter der Personzentrierten Psychotherapie*. Vienna: Springer, pp. 75–105.

Schmid PF (2002f) Encountering a human being means being kept alive by an enigma (E Lévinas), Prospects on further developments in the person-centered approach. In J Marques-Teixeira & S Antunes (Eds) *Client-Centered and Experiential Psychotherapy*. Linda a Velha: Vale & Vale, pp. 11–33.

Schmid PF (2003) The characteristics of a person-centered approach to therapy and counseling: Criteria for identity and coherence. *Person-Centered and Experiential Psychotherapies, 2*(2), 104–20.

Schmid PF (2004a) Back to the client. A phenomenological approach to the process of understanding and diagnosis. *Person-Centered and Experiential Psychotherapies, 3*(1), 36–51.

Schmid PF (2004b) New men?—A new image of man? Person-centred challenges to gender dialogue. In G Proctor & MB Napier (Eds) *Encountering Feminism: Intersections between feminism and the person-centred approach*. Ross-on-Wye: PCCS Books, pp. 179–90.

Schmid PF (2005a) Anmerkungen zu einer Personzentrierten Psychopathologie. *PERSON 8*(1) in press.

Schmid PF (2005b) Authenticity and alienation: Towards an understanding of the person beyond the categories of order and disorder. In S Joseph & R Worsley (Eds) *Person-Centred Psychopathology: A positive psychology of mental health*. Ross-on-Wye: PCCS Books, pp. 75–90.

Schmid PF (2005c) In the beginning there is community: Implications and challenges of the belief in a triune God and a person-centred approach. In J Moore & C Purton (Eds) *Counselling and Spirituality: Experiential and theoretical perspectives*. Ross-on-Wye: PCCS Books, in press.

Shlien JM (2000) Response to Edwin Kahn, to be considered as an open letter, June 2000. Quoted in an email by Lisbeth Sommerbeck, posted on cctpca network, July 17, 2003.

Shlien JM (2003) *To Lead an Honorable Life: Invitations to think about client-centered therapy and the person-centered approach. A collection of the work of John M Shlien*. [P Sanders (Ed)] Ross-on-Wye: PCCS Books.

Sommerbeck L (2004) Non-linear dynamic systems and the non-directive attitude in client-centered therapy. *Person-Centered and Experiential Psychotherapies 3*(4), 291–9.

Tudor K & Merry T (2002) *Dictionary of Person-Centred Psychology*. New York/London: Routledge.

Tudor LE, Keemar K, Tudor K, Valentine J & Worrall M (2004) *The Person-Centred Approach: A contemporary introduction*. Houndsmills: Palgrave Macmillan.

Wilkins P (2003) *Person-Centred Therapy in Focus*. London: Sage.

Wittgenstein L (1969) *Philosophische Untersuchungen: Schriften 1*, Frankfurt/M: Suhrkamp.

Worsley R (2004) Integrating with integrity. In P Sanders (Ed) *The Tribes of the Person-Centred Nation: An introduction to the schools of therapy related to the person-centred approach*. Ross-on-Wye: PCCS Books, pp. 125–47.

CHAPTER 7

'IT ENLIGHTENS EVERYTHING YOU DO': OBSERVING NON-DIRECTIVITY IN A CLIENT-CENTERED THERAPY DEMONSTRATION SESSION

BRIAN E. LEVITT AND BARBARA TEMANER BRODLEY

Outside of the person-centered community, it is not commonly known that Carl Rogers introduced the practice of audio-recording psychotherapy sessions for research analysis and was the first researcher to publish a complete psychotherapy transcript (Rogers, 1942). The practice of recording actual sessions has since become a common element in therapy research. It has also become an important part of training in many theoretical orientations beyond client-centered, and many professionals use it in order to critique their own work as a part of their ongoing development. Recording therapy demonstrations for teaching purposes has also been a logical extension of Rogers' pioneering use of research recordings.

Students and psychotherapists interested in learning about client-centered therapy report that they find it helpful to see what non-directive therapy looks like in practice, especially after having some exposure to the basic elements of Rogers' theory. Live demonstrations, transcripts, audiotapes, and videotapes of therapy sessions have become invaluable learning resources. Rogers' participation in the now famous Gloria demonstration session (Rogers, 1965), captured on film, is seen as a landmark in this regard. With this in mind, we offer a transcript of a demonstration therapy session in this chapter.

What follows is a transcript of a demonstration session audiotaped in a graduate psychology class in client-centered therapy. The therapist is Barbara Brodley and the volunteer 'client', Jean (a code name), is a student from the class. Barbara has 50 years of experience as a client-centered therapist, and has written extensively on non-directive theory and practice (e.g., Brodley, 1990, 1994, 1997a, 1999a, 1999b, 2000a, 2000b, 2001, 2002, 2004). In her typical 11–12-week classes in client-centered therapy, Barbara exposes her students to several of Carl Rogers' interviews (both on tape and in transcript form), in addition, she always does a demonstration session with a volunteer from the class, usually in the second or third week of the course. We chose this particular transcript as it is a representative example of what can be expected in a non-directive demonstration session, and also because it includes a portion of the classroom discussion that followed the demonstration. Barbara's comments during this discussion illuminate the approach, and the students, newcomers to client-centered theory and practice, also offer observations that shed light on non-directive practice. Following the transcript we provide a brief analysis of the demonstration session and classroom discussion, focusing specifically on non-directive elements.

TRANSCRIPT OF A DEMONSTRATION THERAPY SESSION AND CLASSROOM DISCUSSION

T: Well, I'm interested in whatever you'd like to share with me.

C1: I really need to talk to you about a recent relationship that I've started. It's been about a little bit over a month. And I've absolutely fallen for this person and am smitten. And, and ...

T1: You're in love?

C2: Yes. (T: Uhm-hmm.) And, and it's very premature to say that, but I feel that I go along with all the clichés that, you know, when you know, you know. (T: Uhm-hmm.) And everything about this person is what I've always wanted and more. (T: Uhm-hmm.) And I couldn't be happier, but at this point I'm almost—I've had thoughts that almost seem to start to sabotage the relationship, thoughts of loss. I have something that's so important to me, now I'm just thinking about like, what if I lose it?

T2: Uh-huh. Anticipating loss.

C3: Right. (T: Uhm-hmm.) And, and just thoughts like, 'Maybe I should leave before he leaves so I don't have to get hurt.' (T: Uhm-hmm.) Silly thoughts like that and sometimes I share it with him because we're both very honest with each other. And he brought up the fact that I have this continuing, uhm, you know, thoughts of like loss or, or needing to know how he feels, uhm, (T: Uhm-hmm.) because I'm always honest with him. And, I mean, we do both express to each that we both very much like each other and we are at the same place, but it's almost as if I need to hear it all the time, (T: Uhm-hmm.) be reassured, (T: Uhm-hmm.) uhm, because if I don't I get that feeling of, you know, this isn't going to work out, it's going to fall apart in the end just like everything else.

T3: A scared feeling.

C4: Right.

T4: Doomed, too. A doomed kind of feeling.

C5: Yeah. (T: Uhm-hmm.) Yeah. And I think that has a lot to do with my previous relationship because it was very destructive. (T: Oh.) And I don't know how to tie in but I just, I guess it's just that whole central theme of being hurt and loss that (T: Uhm-hmmm.) eventually I'm going to get hurt.

T5: Uh-huh. I see. You're speculating that because you were very hurt (C: Yeah.) from this former relationship that somehow that will happen again. (C: Right.) And you have thoughts about it. Even thoughts about maybe you should break up before, (C: Right.) before you're hit. Uhm-hmm.

C6: Right. And I know those are silly and they're very illogical but they're just silly thoughts that quickly come into my head, and then of course I combat them with, within my head again and say, 'That's (T: Uhm hmm.) a silly way to live.'

T6: You know or believe they're silly but they, they express your fearfulness and (C: Exactly.) anxiety that you will lose this person and lose this love.

C7: Right. (T: Uhm-hmm.) Right. So I guess I'm just trying to—(T: Uhm-hmm.) I don't know—I'm trying to grow from it. And I'm trying to stay within the present and just be, be happy with what's in the now and not get (T: Uhm-hmm.) caught up with the future, because I think that if I continue to think about the what-ifs and the future that I will ultimately sabotage the relationship.

T7: Uh-huh. Uh-huh. (C: So.) The tendency you're describing is to anticipate the future and it's a bleak one or (C: Right.) one of loss and so you're trying to combat that by reminding yourself now, 'It's good now and so I'm (C: Right.) focusing on the present.' (C: Right.) But these thoughts keep coming up.

C8: Yeah. (T: Yeah.) Yeah. (T: Uhm-hmm.) I don't know if it's important to try to understand why they are, but part of me thinks that, maybe that I should try to figure out where they're coming from and why I'm having them and why this intense feeling still remains of being guarded and … and somebody said to me that it's a feeling of being vulnerable (T: Uhm-hmmm.) that …

T8: That word works; I mean, you *feel* vulnerable.

C9: Right. Because I, there's something I truly want (T: Uh-huh.) and want to work out and I want to give myself to, but then there's that guardedness like I've been hurt before, I've been hurt a lot before and I don't, don't want to do it again.

T9: Uhm-hmmm. One thing you were saying was that you're not sure how much trying to figure it out will help, will free you of these feelings; (C: Right.) that's one direction. Uhm, the other is just trying to, so to speak, correct your thoughts abruptly, thinking of the future and just focusing on the present.

C10: Right. (T: Uhm-hmm.) It's like …

T10: Uhm-hmm. So you don't know what to do about it. (C: *Laughs.*) Or you don't know what's best to do about (C: Right.) this.

C11: Right. Or maybe it's a combination of them all. (T: Uhm-hmm.) But …

T11: But you're suffering.

C12: Yeah.

T12: Yeah. (C: Yeah.) Because you have love and you feel at least now it's reciprocated but you're really frightened that you're going to lose it. (C: Yeah.) You find yourself reacting out of that fear in various ways both interactively and just in your mind. (C: Right.) And then you try to correct for that.

C13: Uhm-hmm. And he and the relationship are suffering, too. It's not just me because of these thoughts or these feelings. (T: Uhm-hmmm.) Because sometimes when I express these strange thoughts it upsets him and then it upsets him to the fact of telling me, 'Why don't you understand that I feel the same way about you? Why do you think about these things?' Like one thought I had was, and I said it to him: I said, 'What if I just left? Would you miss me?' And it's just the most ridiculous (T: Uhm-hmm.) thing ever and it sounds so immature. And he was very turned off and then pushed away by that because he said, 'Why would you ever …?'

T13: 'Why would you think of that?'

C14: ' … think that? (T: Uhm-hmm.) And why would …?' you know. And he very nicely said, 'I'm here to stay.' Which is reassuring (T: Uhm-hmm.) but at the same time it kind of pushed us away from each other too (T: Uhm-hmm.) a little bit.

T14: Just momentarily, huh.

C15: Right.

T15: So you're aware that, that this apprehension, this almost expectation is affecting some of your interaction with your partner and creating at least moments that aren't so good (C: Right.) between you.

C16: And the moments as they build up feel like it (T: More.) becomes a bigger part of the relationship.

T16: Uh-huh. As there are more of them.

C17: Right. So I think I try to live by being honest and open and saying what I feel just to have an open line of communication between us both. (T: Uhm-hmm.) But I think now I'm realizing there's times where I just should shut up and keep it to myself (T: Uhm-hmm.) because they're silly thoughts and they're not what I—they are what I'm feeling, but not a lot of them are logical or truly what I'm feeling. They're just quick thoughts that enter my mind. (T: Uhm-hmm.) And I think sometimes we'd be better off if I just kept them to myself.

T17: Uh-huh. It's kind of a dilemma that sort of a basic or historic inclination is to be very outward and open and expressive and honest in a relationship. Then you look at some of these incidents, and the way in which they feel like they're adding up to a kind of negative element in the relationship is by being honest by telling him. So you don't know what to do but you're thinking maybe you should inhibit some of these thoughts. (C: Right.) Uhm-hmm. (C: Right.) Inhibit them as far as saying them to him.

C18: Right. (T: Uhm-hmm.) And, as I said before, trying to understand where they come from maybe I can alleviate some of the thoughts (T: Uh-huh.) in total because they are, they are harmful to me and they, and they do put a lot of stress on me and (T: Uh-huh.) sometimes they just go in and out but sometimes I really ponder on them …

T18: Dwell.

C19: And dwell, yeah, (T: Uhm-hmm.) dwell is a great (T: Uhm-hmm.) word. Dwell on them.

T19: Sometimes they're just sort of flitting through you (C: Right.) and not staying. But sometimes you really get caught up (C: Right.) in them and then those are bad times (C: Right.) emotionally.

C20: And, what I realize with those little things … we just spent, we went to dinner last night and just tiny little comments that he would say that meant nothing, and this is gonna sound really silly to everybody. I like leaned over to kiss him a very passionate kiss. And he said, 'Not every time has to be a passionate kiss, it can just be a little kiss.' (T: Uhm-hmm.) And that small little comment for whatever reason hurt me a lot. (T: Uhm-hmm.) And I don't know if it's just because now I feel like those little comments are building up so there's already some destruction in the relationship, (T: Uhm-hmm.) so any little comment adds to the destruction. (T: Uhm-hmm.) Do you understand? Does that make sense?

T20: Yeah. On his part?

C21: Uhm, well yeah. Well that's what I think. I think that I'm thinking on his part (T: Uhm-hmm.) because it's. . .

T21: When he reacted that way it hurt you and upset you. And what you're explaining,

I think, is that you're fearful that he kind of put away that stronger expression from you, (C: Right.) that was coming from you, because he's already being affected by some of your need for reassurance and your expression and worry and so on. (C: Exactly.) Is that it?

C22: Exactly. (T: Uhm-hmm.) So I feel like there's already, yeah, that's exactly what it is: like a hole, a hole starting or (T: Uh-huh.) a destructive pattern starting in our relationship and it's so early, it's so … not that it shouldn't be that way, but I wouldn't want it to be that way.

T22: Uhm-hmm. (C: But.) I didn't understand what you just said.

C23: I …

T23: It shouldn't …

C24: These feelings I have of worry. If things are already going wrong and I'm already pushing him away. And I'm saying that it's okay to have issues in relationships no matter what part of the relationship, the beginning, middle (T: Oh.) or what have you. I'm saying it's not wrong, but I wouldn't want, I don't want it to happen because it is so early. You hear those things that it's a swinging-from-a-chandelier period or a (T: Uhm-hmm.) really happy-go-lucky time in the relationship. But it is that way, so I have to accept that's …

T24: Uhm-hmm. You're worrying because it's so early in this relationship and at this early stage to impart feelings and then interactions that then worry you in terms of what effect they're having on the relationship. You have a bigger picture which is that, yeah, relationships whether they're early, middle, later, eternally, they can have problems (C: Right.) and there can be conflicts. So that rationally you say, 'Okay', but emotionally you're worried because these feelings have sprung up so early, and also that you've expressed them and it appears to you that he's reacted to them or there's some evidence that he's reacted to them (C: Right.) so it's worrying you.

C25: Right. Then I have to remind myself that it's all my reality, (T: It's all.) all my perception, (T: Uhm-hmm.) not his. (T: Uhm-hmm.) But part of me that really wants to know what his perception is … (T: Uhm-hmm.) But then again when I think about it, if I ask him again it's only gonna irritate him more (T: Uhm-hmm.) because I'm always asking these questions.

T25: Uhm-hmm. You do ask him and he reassures you that he cares about you. And what you're saying is that somehow it doesn't work or if it works for the moment it doesn't help the next day or whatever. (C: Right.) Something's happening in you that makes you fear that you're going to have a terrible loss.

C26: Yeah. When I think about it, when I usually ask him, he responds in a manner, 'Why do you need to know? Do you really need me to tell you how I feel?' (T: Uhm-hmm.) But when the reassuring has to do just on his own,[1] like he'll just look at me and tell me, 'You're, you're beautiful'. And, (T: Uhm-hmm.) we're not at the point where we say, 'I love you' but he just looks at me (T: Uh-huh.) and he says, 'I like you.' And I know what he, I think I know what he means.

---

1. An accurate transcription of the client's actual wording.

T26: Cause that's very strong.

C27: Right. (T: Uhm-hmm.) 'Cause I look at him the same way and say it. (T: Uh-huh.) So I think it's that reaction when I …

T27: When you're asking …

C28: It's …

T28: When you're asking for reassurance you don't get much reassurance.

C29: Right.

T29: He's, apparently, put off or somehow that situation doesn't work for him as opposed to when he's spontaneously feeling (C: Right.) and he'll say something. (C: Right.) So that there are reassuring experiences with him, but you can't elicit them very well. (C: Right.) In fact, it seems or you feel like it has the opposite effect; it's off-putting or something. Is that it?

C30: Yeah. That's exactly right. When he's talking about past relationships: we just talked about this the other day. The last relationship he was in, it was only very brief, like a month and a half and the woman would ask him the same question, 'How do you feel?' And he wouldn't want to answer because he said he knew what she wanted to hear from him, but what he had to say wasn't what she wanted to hear. And he said, 'Every time … this', and this gave me some insight—he said, 'Every time a woman asks that, I feel like she ultimately wants to know "You're the one, you're the person I want to spend the rest of my life with."' (T: Ah. Uh-huh.) So that question to him (T: Uh-huh.) has a lot of meaning. (T: Uh-huh.) And a lot of pressure I think to it. (T: Uhm-hmm. Uhm-hmm.) So I guess I understood, but it still doesn't make it better because that's what I do want to hear from him.

T30: Uh-huh. In fact, you'd like to hear him (C: Sure.) express his feeling.

C31: But I know that he wouldn't because it's only been a month and that's, (T: Uh-huh.) that's a pretty intense …

T31: He wants to be more prudent, (C: Right.) even if he had the feelings he wouldn't want to put himself behind them by, by saying …

C32: Right. That's a very vulnerable place.

T32: His character.

C33: Right. I wouldn't even say it because it is so (T: Uhm-hmm.) vulnerable, just putting yourself that much out there.

T33: Uhm-hmm. (pauses 6 seconds.) So you … (pause 4 seconds) What I'm thinking is that you were saying before that you were getting some better understanding while you're having these very insecure feelings. You're fearful you're being destructive of the relationship and (T: Yeah.) that's clear that you feel that. But the more basic feeling is (pause 3 seconds) just an anxiety or fearfulness that this beautiful feeling and sense of rightness about this person (C: Right.) is going to result in loss. (C: Yeah.) And, uhm, and I guess you don't feel you understand (C: Yeah. No I.) why it's so strong or why it's so …

C34: It's funny because he said—he thought I was being quite comical—he said, 'It has to do with your father, right?' 'Cause he obviously knows …

T34: Something about your background?

C35: Well, no. That I'm in psychology and he just, (T: Oh. Uh-huh.) thinks in a Freudian way. How, (T: Uhm-hmm.) everybody—not everybody, but most people who don't know that much about psychology—(T: Uhm-hmm.) say it has to do with your father. But it did make me think about my father and he was asking, 'Have you ever lost somebody?' But I think it's just a combination of going through relationships and dealing with hurt and loss and that's the only thing I can really come to, or with my father the feeling of never being good enough or … I don't know, I try to go through everything in my life (T: Uhm-hmm.) to figure it out, (T: Uhm-hmm.) but I think it's gonna take a lot longer than a few hours (T: Uhm-hmm.) to figure it out.

T35: To figure it out.

C36: Yeah.

T36: Mhm. There's a lot to it. So looking at it historically you have had a sense of not being fully accepted by your father, (C: Uhm-hmm.) that's true. But then what you seem to be saying is that you've gone through a number of experiences of suffering loss. And you're speculating, I guess, or thinking, surmising that maybe that was why, given the intensity of your feelings for this particular man, (C: Uhm-hmm.) that you're having these fears at this level. (C: Right.) Is that right?

C37: Yeah.

T37: Kind of like you got sensitized to a loss through other relationships—something like that.

C38: Right. (T: Uhm-hmm.) Right. I notice as you say that I was thinking that with my father the feeling that I was never good enough maybe ties into the, the insecure feeling I have that I'm not good enough for this person. (T: Uh-huh.) And then comes in the feeling of 'if I'm not good enough, he's not …'

T38: Gonna stay.

C39: Yeah. 'He's not gonna stay.'

T39: Uh-huh. So there is some line of thought there that feels like it makes some sense. That is the feeling that you don't have full acceptance from your father or it was erratic or whatever, you're saying maybe engendered in you something about you, about yourself, (C: Right.) making you doubt yourself or your lovableness or your validity in some way. (C: Right.) And that that might be more of the root of this situation (C: Right.) of how insecure you find yourself feeling even though this man does seem to really care about you. (C: Right.) But you're not sure. (C: Right.) You're really working on trying to figure this out because you're in love.

C40: Uhm-hmm. I'd like to be past it and (T: Uh-huh.) leave it in the past.

T40: Be free. Be free (C: Right.) of it (C: Right.) and just more comfortable in the relationship (C: Yeah.) and not need, not feel that need for reassurance or …

C41: Right. Right. So … yeah, I think it is a combination of my own self-image, my own perception of myself, and of past loss. (T: Uhm-hmm.) I hate to tie my father into it (*chuckles*), (T: Uh-huh.) but it could be. (T: Uhm-hmm.) And I think even talking with you it makes me think … 'cause I didn't even think about my own self-image before, but talking about it more I think helps me, (T: Uhm-hmm.) logically, think about different, different reasons.

T41: Uhm-hmm. That what you're suggesting, I think, that there may be, uh, sort of a complex of reasons or set of reasons (C: Uhm-hmm.) or maybe some early, historical relation to your father's impact on your other experiences with people where you felt or had a loss.

C42: Yeah. Yeah. And I think I'm realizing, too, that I really benefit from talking to somebody, (T: Oh.) therapy ...

T42: (*inaudible*) (C: Yeah.) talking reminds you that or brings that (C: Right.) (*inaudible*).

C43: Because now I think of it, my past relationship, it was so destructive. I think there's still a lot of issues that I need (T: Uhm-hmm.) to work through.

T43: Uh-huh. Because of what happened with that particular person.

C44: Right. (T: Uhm-hmm.) Right. And I would hate for those issues to also enter into this one.

T44: It could hurt this relationship.

C45: Right.

T45: You think that.

C46: Right.

T46: I think we probably should stop. Is there anything else you'd like to say?

C47: No, thank you very much.

(*end of session*)

COMMENTS—CLASSROOM DISCUSSION

T: Oh, you're very welcome. Uh, before ... Please stay here. Is that okay?

C: Okay. Uhm-hmm.

T: Uhm, would you be able to make some comments to us all about how it felt to interact with me?

C: Sure.

T: Pros and cons.

C: Sure.

T: Whether or not it was helpful or any problems

C: No, it was very helpful. It was very easy to step away from the classroom probably because I felt ... feel very passionate about this and it's very present. (T: Uh-huh.) And I was also not surprised but, because I'm very new to client-centered, I liked that there was a lot of interaction. I find in my, my sessions, uhm, my comments are very, very brief, I think, and I really enjoyed that yours were (T: More.) detailed and there's more substance (T: Uhm-hmm.) to your comments with me. And it was very mutual, (T: Uh-huh.) back and forth.

T: I guess because I was responsive and trying to articulate.

C: Right. And they weren't just brief comments, it was (T: Uh-huh.) very detailed.

T: You liked that they were more complicated, (C: Right.) sometimes.

C: Right. And you pulled in things from, you know, moments before.

T: That was useful?

C: Yeah. I think so. (T: Uhm-hmm.) 'Cause it helped me also kind of connect things (T: Uhm-hmm.) as well. So I felt very comfortable which is unusual (*chuckles*). When there's a group of people like here.

T: You were speaking very, uh, personally and honestly about your situation in front of the group and (C: Yeah.) it's surprising to you how you could feel as comfortable as you did. And you felt pretty comfortable with me.

C: Yes, I felt very comfortable.

T: Well, I felt the same way. I enjoyed our interaction. It was just a starting interaction so I don't feel, as usual, I don't feel highly competent in my understanding for awhile. I certainly have to get used to interacting with a person. But I felt pretty much like I would feel with a new client, (C: Right.) I would say. Even though we had the group here. (C: Right.) Any flaws in the way I was were not due to the group situation, because I wasn't distracted at all and that felt good. So it was good for me.

C: I had a fear though, towards the end I had a fear that you were getting, uhm, very bored with my (T: Oh.) topic just because I think, the anxiety with it all. And, and I haven't really talked with other people about it, but I know in talking about relationships I often feel like I obsess about it and bore people to death. So I felt like all these, the nit-picking and the over and over again with you, it's like, 'Oh, god.'

T: You felt that. (*inaudible*).

C: Yeah, I feared that I'm boring you.

T: You didn't bore me, (C: *giggles.*) not for a second. (C: Good.) Yeah, but I understand that feeling. (C: Right.) When I listen to people, therapeutically, even if they've gone over the same topic, in a certain sense, many times, I rarely feel that they have. It's because my listening is very particular. (C: Right.) And that makes it less likely that I would get bored. (C: Right.) Also I do think I'm a relatively interactive therapist. It isn't necessarily that way. And I'm glad that that was good for you. Someone else might be bothered because my responses are a little more complicated. I do adjust that with the client. Either they let me know or they become confused, you know, because I make a response a little too complex for them to take in so then there's all that adjustment. And we don't have much time to make an adjustment in a demonstration, (C: Right.) But I'm glad that it was all right with you and a good thing that you felt I was responsive. I do feel that it's important to be responsive, but that doesn't necessarily mean to be verbal. Uhm, it means to me to be present and really attending to the person and reacting to the person and sometimes that is more verbal and sometimes it's not verbal at all. I've done sessions where I said nothing or hardly anything, maybe. But if you were to watch me you'd say 'She's pretty active', with my face and so on. I wouldn't want to set a standard or level of verbalness or level of activity. I think that's very individual. And, if I'd been less verbal it might have been all right with you. But if we worked together for several weeks, at some point you might say, 'You know, I wish you'd say more.' If that was something that you really needed or wanted. Everything doesn't come out in the first session, so you learn how to adjust to your client. Your client to a certain extent adjusts to you also. And you don't have to make yourself into something different for any other person but it's a back and forth. Are there any observations or comments the class would like to make?

Student: I'd like to make a comment. I thought it was great the way you checked in and said, you said something like, uhm, 'I didn't understand what you meant'. (T: Uhm-hmm.) You were checking in with her subjective world, not imposing your own objective views, (T: Uhm-hmm.) trying to find what she really, really meant in that. (T: Uh-huh.) And we talked about that earlier. Uhm, so I found that very interesting.

T: Yeah. It was a direct inquiry to …

Student: Because (*inaudible*) therefore I understood it more after she explained it again. (T: Uh-huh.) And I thought that was very interesting because I was going down a different road also. Then when she explained it, 'Oh.'

T: Although things like that do not have a directive intent, they so often, we influence the client through the interaction. Client-centered therapy influences the client. It better, otherwise it's not a therapy, by definition. But there's influence and there's influence. You can say we're directive because we're responsive and we're trying to understand empathically as opposed to some other thing. Yes, all that's true, but there's still a profound attitude in non-directivity and it enlightens everything you do. You really have no goal or goals or expectations of the client. And you're just trying to maintain your own wholeness and integration and be present and understand as best you can and then check that as best you can. And sometimes that's awkward and sometimes it's fluid.

Student: (*to Jean*) I really like the point that you made about connecting the dots because I really saw that as well. Earlier comments that you were making referring to the fact that you felt the relationship to be doomed. And the fact that you (*to Barbara*) kept going back to the previous thought that she had shared (T: Uhm-hmm.) in connection. It was like a dance. It really was like a dance in terms of really connecting the dots and it was interesting to actually see it. (T: Uhm-hmm.) I guess this is the way I'm interpreting it. I think to the client it demonstrates that you understand, you are actively listening to her in terms of the anguish that was going on with her. (T: Uhm-hmm.) And that it wasn't a fleeting thought in terms of a regurgitation (T: Right.) of what she was saying but it was actually connected. (T: Yes.)

T: Yeah. I appreciate what you're saying very much. To be empathic, to understand anything that somebody else is presenting to you, involves an internal process that is necessarily interpretive and inferential. In other words, you're not just repeating words. And if you're a client-centered therapist there are instances where we repeat what the client says. I mean, it's just a spontaneous response; it is not just a repeating of words and it shows often in the way the voice is and the expressiveness of the therapist. You see this in Rogers. This particular something that the client's really saying and Rogers just repeats those words. Well, he's not just repeating the words. He's processed something. And I think you were really picking that up. And in one way that my conception of empathic understanding showed in this interaction is in what is the immediate attempt to communicate. There's immediate and immediate.

I think that therapists can vary somewhat in sort of the range of the material that leads to the response. If you look at Rogers' work, and I'm pretty sure my own, although I haven't studied it systematically, you'll see responses that are based on elements in what the client has expressed a page earlier on. What it is, is trying to understand now; but now isn't just the utterances of right now. And that's a matter of judgment or intuition. The client will verify for you. They'll look puzzled if it's out of range of what they mean. If they've left it behind, they're gonna probably give some reaction or they'll ignore it or they'll say, 'No, I was really emphasizing …' They'll just correct you.

Student: But isn't that still quite different from if you had deliberately instructed yourself to synthesize or to make connections?

T: Oh, yeah. Very different. It's a spontaneous process that isn't because you've given yourself the instruction to do it, which I think results in a much different process. It has to do with the nature of understanding what a person is getting at, and what we're trying to understand is what they're trying to express and then we're unique people listening to that, so there will be differences in the elements that we pull into that expression. And that can have an influence on the client, too. For example, I might, in formulating my empathic response, refer to something that the client said a minute or two ago that really isn't right now on his mind and so because I included it in checking my understanding it sort of gears him in that direction. Well, why not? My intention is not to direct him. My intention is to really capture understanding of what the client is getting at, and it's not perfect. It's an interactive and very spontaneous process, so there will be influences depending upon my mentality and my sensitivity that are different than some other therapist's mentality and sensitivity listening to the same material. Even though there will tend to be overall a similarity in different therapists' responses. So I really appreciate you seeing that and commenting on it. Is there any other reaction? Any problems? (*pause 4 seconds*). (*To client*) Do you have any afterthoughts?

C18: I really enjoyed it. It was, it was very helpful, not only just for my own individual growth but also in understanding client-centered therapy better.

T1: Good. Good. Well, thank you so much.

C: Thank you.

DISCUSSION

The empathic understanding response process is the most frequently scrutinized feature of client-centered therapy transcripts. It is an interaction between therapist and client in which the therapeutic attitudes towards the client—empathic understanding, unconditional positive regard and congruence (Rogers, 1957, 1959)—are expressed by the therapist as she is listening to the client in order to experience the client's intended communications of feelings and personal meanings. It is *following* the client as he narrates, and from time to time checking with the client (Rogers, 1986; Brodley, 1997b) to provide an opportunity to validate or modify the therapist's understandings. However, in research by psychologists outside the client-centered theoretical orientation (e.g., Mathieu-Coughlan, and Klein, 1984), there is an unfortunate tendency to analyze empathic understanding responses in such a way as to suggest a technique, a form for the therapist to follow to deepen or further the client's 'process' (e.g., Rice and Greenberg, 1984).

It would certainly be a fairly straightforward process to break down Barbara's responses in the transcript above in order to suggest a 'how to' approach to non-directive therapy, a map for others to follow. Nevertheless, breaking down empathic responses into a technique would not yield an accurate representation of what a non-directive therapist does. It would effectively remove the heart from client-centered therapy, which is the non-directive attitude (Raskin, 1947/2005, Chapter 20 this volume; Brodley, 1997a; Levitt, 2005, Chapter 1 this volume). As Barbara relates in the class discussion that follows the demonstration session, 'It enlightens everything you do.' With this awareness, we will show non-directivity's footprints in the transcribed demonstration session, finding those signs that point beyond behaviors and words to an underlying non-directive attitude. In providing examples of where we believe non-directivity can be seen, the danger of concretizing non-directivity as a set of techniques remains. It must be emphasized that it is the attitude that underlies these examples that is essential to non-directivity. It is 'a way of being', to borrow Rogers' phrase (Rogers, 1980), and this can be subtle.

THE CLIENT DIRECTS THERAPY

Barbara states from the beginning of the session that she is open to whatever Jean brings— 'I'm interested in whatever you'd like to share with me.' Not only is this statement an expression of unconditional positive regard for the client and the client's own narrative process, it is also a clear expression of non-directive intent—the client directs therapy. It is evident throughout the demonstration that the client is always the source and substance of therapy and its direction. The material is always what the client brings, and she dictates the pace. Barbara follows Jean's lead, never introduces new ideas, and never offers interpretations. Nowhere in the transcript do her responses suggest otherwise.

When a therapist holds the non-directive attitude, her responses to client questions tend to carry this attitude. The therapist does not take client questions as an opportunity to direct or intervene. They are not an opening for the non-directive therapist to take the lead. For example, Jean asks Barbara (C20), 'Does that make sense?' Barbara's response (T20) is empathic to the request, and she answers tentatively, 'Yeah. On his part?' Without holding a non-directive attitude, she might have responded by turning Jean's question into material to be processed, not by following Jean's direction and answering it. In response to questions, if the therapist has a directive attitude, she takes on the role of expert on the client and the client's needs.

The therapist is not the expert on the client and the client's needs

Statements from the therapist's own frame of reference are a spontaneous expression of her non-directive attitude (Brodley, 1999a). The tentative quality of Barbara's responses is a natural consequence of this attitude, as seen throughout the transcript ('I think …', 'Is that it?', 'I guess …', '… something like that'.). The non-directive therapist knows that she does not know the client's world with certainty. A comfort with not knowing is therefore a common characteristic of non-directive therapists, who recognize that the client is the true expert on himself and his needs. This is typically seen in the tone and wording of empathic understanding responses, which are always tentative. It is also seen in non-defensive therapist remarks, such as sharing that she has not understood the client. When Barbara says to Jean (T22), 'I didn't understand what you just said', she is expressing a number of things. First, she shows an interest in understanding Jean. Such an expression also points to her not needing to be seen as an expert, as she is able to comfortably share her ignorance in the moment. Her intent is not to direct the client with her expression of not understanding, but to remain empathically connected to what the client is presenting, to continue following the client's direction.

A non-directive therapist will also not feel the need to hide her own thought processes, and empathic responses may sometimes have a 'thinking out loud' quality to them. Such a response transparently includes her thought process, but not in order to direct the client in any way. It is genuine and devoid of technique or format—'so you … (*pause 4 seconds*) What I am thinking is that you were saying before that …' (T33).

The therapist's only goal is to understand the client's meanings

Empathic understanding responses are seen throughout the transcript. Though it is possible to categorize or classify them further, we avoid doing so here, beyond noting that they can be verbal or nonverbal, of varying lengths, word-for-word repetitions of the client's words or the therapist's own wordings. At their core, they are all spontaneous products of an attempt to understand—'It's a spontaneous process that isn't because you've given yourself the instruction to do it …' (Brodley, from the class discussion).

What matters most is that the client-centered therapist's intention is a non-directive one—'My intention is not to direct him. My intention is to really capture understanding of what the client is getting at, and it's not perfect' (Brodley, from the class discussion). Empathic understanding responses are not a technique. They flow spontaneously from a deeply held non-directive attitude and intention. Following the client's meanings accurately is the therapist's intent. Jean's comments often show that she recognizes Barbara's comments as accurately giving back what she expressed ('Yes', 'Right', 'Yeah', 'Exactly', 'That's exactly right').

When Barbara brings in material previously given by Jean in dialogue from a few minutes earlier, it is an empathic response to the aliveness of what Jean brings in the present moment. It is not because Barbara is trying to change the direction, add new material, or suggest connections for Jean. As Barbara shares with the class, 'Now isn't just the utterances of right now.' Empathic understanding responses are not limited to the content of the words immediately expressed by the client, but are informed by the client's ongoing meanings and the individual context. It is important to note that the client's meanings evolve and change. As clients change, the context of their meanings changes with them. The non-directive therapist is sensitive to this, and does not maintain a static theory of the client. In fact, the non-directive therapist does not hold any theory of the client at all.

Directive interpretation always flows from a theory or framework held by the therapist about the client. It is external to the client—it is a sort of mold, regardless of how flexible or detailed, that the client is fit into. Interpretation, when it occurs in a *non-directive*, client-centered interaction, is a process of trying to understand the client's meanings in the context of what the client expresses, in the context of the client's ongoing theory of herself that she unfolds and presents in therapy. Non-directive interpretation is never from a theory held by the therapist—it is never a process of understanding the client by placing him into an external context. This leads to another central notion in non-directive theory and practice: recognizing that each client is unique.

EACH CLIENT IS UNIQUE

In the sense that each client is seen as a unique individual, non-directive therapy is truly client-centered. Therapy is not centered on what a general client would or should be. It is not centered on a theory external to the client. It is not centered on the therapist using his self-awareness as a technique to have an impact on the client. The focus of the therapist is entirely on understanding the client as an individual, in all of his uniqueness, from moment to moment.

For the non-directive therapist, the focus is always on what the client offers, never on the therapist's theories in relation to what the client offers. This focus on the client's unique frame of reference is central to non-directive empathy (Levitt, 2005, Chapter 1 this volume). For example, Jean brings in a reference to her father when she repeats something her boyfriend has asked her (C34: 'It has to do with your father, right?'). Barbara responds directly to what Jean gave her (T35: 'Something about your background?'), and it is clear that she was not holding a theory (e.g., psychodynamic) in the way she received this information from Jean. External theorizing (seeing Jean within a psychodynamic framework) did not enter the picture for Barbara in trying to understand what Jean was expressing. It is also not simply that Barbara is unaware of such theories, as she quickly grasps the meaning Jean intended when Jean corrects her empathic response (C35: 'Well, no. That I'm in psychology, and he just (T: Oh. Uh-huh.) thinks in a Freudian way.'). Jean's intended meaning, though grounded in psychodynamic thinking, comes from her. Barbara is seen here again taking only what was given (see Grant, 2005, Chapter 14 this volume).

Barbara discusses another aspect of non-directivity in relation to the uniqueness of each client when she explains to the class that it takes time to get used to interacting with each client. There is an adjustment that the non-directive therapist makes to being with each client, attempting to meet that client where he is, not directing the client to meet the therapist where she is at. From a non-directive stance, none of this is ever at the expense of congruence. Further, empathic contact should improve as the therapist continues to understand the uniqueness that the client brings.

Another facet of client uniqueness relates to the issue of boredom. Clients fear boring their therapists, and therapists of all orientations do sometimes report being bored by their clients. What occurs during the discussion portion between Barbara and Jean is an important interaction in this regard. First, Jean apparently feels safe enough to share with Barbara that she fears she may have bored her. Barbara does not use Jean's concern as material to create an intervention to instruct Jean or that will further her processing in some way. She takes it as it is given. She does not analyze it or redirect it, but responds to the heart of what Jean is expressing, a desire to know if she has bored Barbara. Barbara responds in a manner that is fully non-directive—she recognizes the request for an honest answer, and lets Jean know that she never felt bored. This is also not the comment of a therapist who simply wants her client to feel good, and offers the client a platitude. Barbara's further explanation tells us that there is something deeper, and this something is informed by the non-directive attitude. She tells Jean, 'When I listen to people, therapeutically, even if they've gone over the same topic, in a certain sense, many times, I rarely feel that they have. It's because my listening is very particular … And that makes it less likely that I would get bored.' Barbara is alluding to empathic understanding and unconditional positive regard as they are informed by a non-directive attitude. As Nat Raskin (1947/2005) explains, when the non-directive therapist is empathically engaged, it is such an all-consuming process that there is room for nothing else. When a therapist is sincere in her attempt to non-directively and empathically understand her client, boredom is unlikely. However, boredom still may occur. Boredom in the context of non-directivity would imply that the therapist has somehow become alienated from her client and has lost empathic understanding or contact. Somehow, the therapist's regard for what the client is presenting has become conditional. When non-directive, the therapist is always interested in connecting with and understanding whatever the client brings, not just those things the therapist would prefer to connect with. This is where congruence is essential. Therapist self-awareness is essential in enabling the therapist to recognize when her own issues are getting in the way of being empathic towards and unconditionally acceptant of a client—boredom is a red flag that this is occurring.

THE NON-DIRECTIVE ATTITUDE CAN SPILL OVER

Barbara's non-directive attitude is not only present during the demonstration. The transcript of the class discussion shows that her attitude remains within her. The non-directive attitude is very much a part of who Barbara is, and we can see how it is expressed spontaneously in several instances beyond the therapy demonstration. For example, as described above, we can see Barbara's non-directivity when Jean expresses a concern that she bored her, and Barbara lets her know that she did not. It is not a rule that the non-directive attitude always spills over into other areas beyond therapy, but for therapists who have nurtured this attitude in themselves, it often does.

REFERENCES

Brodley BT (1990) Client-centered and experiential—Two different therapies. In G Lietaer, J Rombauts & R Van Balen (Eds) *Client-Centered and Experiential Psychotherapy in the Nineties.* Leuven: Leuven University Press, pp. 87–108.

Brodley BT (1994) Some observations of Carl Rogers' behavior in therapy interviews. *Person-Centered Journal, 1*(2), 37–48.

Brodley BT (1997a) The non-directive attitude in client-centered therapy. *Person-Centered Journal, 4*(1), 18–30.

Brodley BT (1997b) Criteria for making empathic responses in client-centered therapy. *Person-Centered Journal, 5*(1), 20–8.

Brodley BT (1999a) Reasons for responses expressing the therapist's frame of reference in client-centered therapy. *Person-Centered Journal 6*(1), 4–27.

Brodley BT (1999b) The actualizing tendency concept in client-centered theory. *Person-Centered Journal, 6*(2), 108–20.

Brodley BT (2000a) The therapeutic clinical interview—Guidelines for beginning practice. In T Merry (Ed) *Person-Centred Practice: The BAPCA reader.* Ross-on-Wye: PCCS Books, pp. 103–9.

Brodley BT (2000b) Personal presence in client-centered therapy. *Person-Centered Journal, 7*(2), 139–49.

Brodley BT (2001) Congruence and its relation to communication in client-centered therapy. In G Wyatt (Ed) *Rogers' Therapeutic Conditions: Evolution, theory and practice. Vol. 1: Congruence.* Ross-on-Wye: PCCS Books, pp. 55–78.

Brodley BT (2002) Client-centered: An expressive therapy. *Person-Centered Journal, 9*(1), 59–70.

Brodley BT (2004) Uncharacteristic directiveness: Rogers and the 'On anger and hurt' client. In R Moodley, C Lago & A Talahite (Eds) *Carl Rogers Counsels a Black Client: Race and culture in person-centred counselling.* Ross-on-Wye: PCCS Books, Ltd, pp. 36–47.

Grant B (2005) Taking only what is given: Self-determination and empathy in non-directive client-centered therapy. In BE Levitt (Ed) *Embracing Non-directivity: Reassessing person-centered theory and practice in the 21st century.* Ross-on-Wye: PCCS Books, pp. 248–60.

Levitt BE (2005) Non-directivity: The foundational attitude. In BE Levitt (Ed) *Embracing Non-directivity: Reassessing person-centered theory and practice in the 21st century.* Ross-on-Wye: PCCS Books, pp. 5–16.

Mathieu-Coughlan P & Klein MH (1984) Experiential Psychotherapy: Key events in the client-therapist interaction. In LN Rice and LS Greenberg (Eds) *Patterns of Change.* New York: Guilford Press, pp. 213–48.

Raskin NJ (1947/2005) The nondirective attitude. In BE Levitt (Ed) *Embracing Non-directivity: Reassessing person-centered theory and practice in the 21st century.* Ross-on-Wye: PCCS Books, pp. 329–47.

Rice LN & Greenberg LS (1984) *Patterns of Change.* New York: Guilford Press.

Rogers CR (1942) *Counseling and Psychotherapy.* Cambridge, MA: Riverside Press.

Rogers CR (1957) The necessary and sufficient conditions of personality change. *Journal of Consulting Psychology, 21*(2), 95–103.

Rogers CR (1959) A theory of therapy, personality and interpersonal relationships, as developed in the client-centered framework. In S Koch (Ed) *Psychology: A study of a science, Vol. 3, Formulations of the person and the social context.* New York: McGraw-Hill, pp. 184–256.

Rogers CR (1965) Client-centered therapy, Film No. 1. In EL Shostrom (Producer) *Three Approaches to Psychotherapy.* Three 16mm color motion pictures. Orange, CA: Psychological Films, Inc.

Rogers CR (1980) *A Way of Being.* Boston: Houghton Mifflin.

Rogers CR (1986) Reflection of feelings. *Person-Centered Review, 1*(4), 375–7. Reprinted in DJ Cain (Ed)(2002) *Classics in the Person-Centered Approach.* Ross-on-Wye: PCCS Books, pp. 13–15.

Chapter 8

THE EXPERIENCE OF NON-DIRECTIVITY IN CLIENT-CENTERED THERAPY: A CASE STUDY

Elizabeth S. Freire

Non-directivity is a core issue in the ongoing debate around the definition and identity of client-centered therapy (see Shlien 1986; Merry, 1990; Hutterer, 1993; Prouty, 1999; Sanders, 2004). The principle of non-directivity, according to the 'classical' view, is one of the distinctive features of client-centered therapy, which 'highlights many of the differences between person-centered therapy and most (if not all) approaches' (Merry, 2004: 42). Others, however, argue either that non-directivity is impossible to attain (Bowen, 1996; Lietaer, 1998; Kahn, 1999) or that it can be ineffective. Cain (1990), for instance, states that for some clients, 'The therapist's nondirectiveness is experienced … as frustrating, constraining, counterproductive, annoying, and possibly indicative of passivity, lack of involvement, caring, or willingness to help' (p. 91). Moreover, Sachse and Elliott (2002) assert that additional therapeutic strategies need to be added to the attitudes of empathy, acceptance and genuineness in order to influence outcome favorably.

Considering Cain's (1990) position that 'Without knowing the client's experience, one can only speculate about the effect of the therapist's nondirectiveness' (p. 91), the research team[1] of the Delphos Institute[2] in Brazil, undertook an empirical inquiry into the client's experience of the therapeutic process and outcome in client-centered therapy. A qualitative form of empirical inquiry was chosen because this was thought to be better suited to providing insight into the complex experiential phenomenon of the therapeutic process. As Rennie (1995) points out, the qualitative methods of inquiry are capable of answering questions about the meaning and value of psychotherapy in the lives of individual human beings in a way 'that is difficult if not impossible to achieve within the mode of natural science' (p. 323).

Our inquiry included seven clients and six client-centered therapists of the Delphos Institute. One week before the clients started therapy they completed an initial written questionnaire (IWQ), with the following questions:

1. Why are you coming for therapy?

---

1. The participants of the Delphos research team were Aline Piason, Cláudia Silveira Martins, Elizabeth Freire, Luciene Geiger and Renata Beatriz da Silva.
2. The Delphos Institute is a person-centered institution located in Porto Alegre, in the south of Brazil, which offers both internships for undergraduate academic students of psychology, and a training program for already licensed psychologists.

2. What are your expectations about the therapy?
3. What would you like to change in yourself and in your life?

Each client's first twelve therapeutic sessions were audio-recorded. Then, 48 hours after the completion of the twelfth session, clients participated in a research interview in which the audiotape of the twelfth therapy session was played back to them. Clients were then asked by the researcher to stop the tape at any point of significance or interest they recalled, and to report what they recollected of their thoughts and feelings during those moments. This inquiry procedure was an adaptation of the technique of Interpersonal Process Recall (IPR) developed by Elliott (1986) and Rennie (1990, 1992, 1994, 2001).

A few days after the IPR interview, clients were interviewed again by the researcher in order to evaluate the therapeutic outcomes up to that point (evaluation interview). This interview had the following guided questions:

1. How has the experience of therapy been for you?
2. How do you feel about your therapist?
3. What do you consider has changed in you since this therapy experience began?

After these questions, the researcher showed the client her previous answers to the Initial Written Questionnaire and asked:

4. Were these expectations accomplished?
5. What would you like to change in yourself and in your life now?
6. Do you think something is lacking or has lacked in your therapy experience? What?

At the time of this writing, the data collected are being analysed through grounded-theory methodology[3] (Rennie, Phillips and Quartaro, 1988; Rennie, 2001). As this analysis is not yet completed, I decided to pick only one of the research project cases to illustrate the nature of the results that we have been finding. This case can be seen as a paradigmatic instance, which reveals some general features of the client's experience of client-centered therapy. Of course, the conclusions drawn from the analysis of this particular case are not intended as claims of foundational knowledge; rather they are intended to represent a tentative understanding, which ought to be supported by further analysis of other cases.

The client in the case I selected is Julia,[4] a 23-year-old woman. I was her therapist. I chose to present the case of one of my own clients, as this afforded me the opportunity to provide some relevant data related to therapist intention during the therapeutic

---

3. Grounded-theory methodology emphasizes the generation of theory through the inductive examination of data. It is developed from data that are collected and analyzed systematically and recursively, generating a blend of descriptive and constructed categories with the former often subsumable under the latter. Through grounded-theory methodology, the researcher constructs categories that help to explain the descriptive categories and the relationships among them.
4. All names presented in this case are fictitious in order to preserve confidentiality.

interaction that otherwise would not be accessible. The presentation of this case is divided into two parts. The first part is an analysis of the therapeutic relationship, based on the transcriptions of all twelve sessions of therapy and on my experience as the therapist in these sessions. Since the amount of data analyzed is huge, only selected excerpts of the first and fifth sessions, clustered in four units, are presented in this chapter. The second part is an analysis of the client's experience of the therapeutic process and outcome based on the IPR and evaluation interview.

THE THERAPEUTIC RELATIONSHIP

Unit 1

Beginning of the first session

I had no previous knowledge about Julia before our first meeting. I also had not read her answers to the IWQ. As soon as we sat in the consulting room and I turned on the tape recorder, she began talking:

C1: Well, I don't know what to do, like, how it is done ... (laugh)
T1: You don't know how to start ...

Therapist's account of her experience
Julia's first statement sounded like an indirect way of asking me to instruct her as to how she should, or was expected to, behave in the therapeutic interaction. But instead of explaining to her how she should behave or how client-centered therapy works, I made an empathic understanding response[5] of the immediate experience I perceived her to be expressing in her request. Through this response, I intended to communicate to Julia that I was receptive to listening unconditionally to whatever she wanted to talk about. Instead of saying explicitly to her that she might talk about whatever she wanted, I chose to communicate this concretely and implicitly through my attitude and behavior. I did not want to respond to Julia with explanations and instructions, because I did not want to take a position of expertise and power in the relationship

C2: Yes, that's it ... (laugh) ... well, it's that I ... spoke to Marcia [a member of the research team], I was needing to, but that was even before, I was needing to start therapy, I don't know, someone to listen, I don't know ... (T: Uhm, hmm ...) ah ... and because I was having some problems at home, and all ... so she told me about you, that there was this research, right ... so I ... well, I'm going to make the

---

5. Empathic understanding response is a therapist's attempt to articulate the client's point of view, an attempt to accurately articulate the experience the client has expressed or has been striving to express (Brodley, 1998).

most of it … (laugh) … because I really don't know how it's done; is it me who begins to talk or do you ask?

T2: When you spoke to Marcia you were having problems in the family?

Therapist's account of her experience

Julia insisted on her request for instructions. It seemed to me that she was rather insecure regarding whether she was really allowed to talk about whatever she wished. Her request for instructions sounded somewhat like a request for confirmation and approval, as if she was expecting me to respond: 'yes, it is ok for me if you start to talk'. But I did not want to assume this role of expert who judges and decides what she can or cannot do. I did not want to be the person in the relationship who has the power to approve or disapprove of anything, or who has the expertise to decide what she should do or how she should behave. So, in order to refuse the assumption of this role of expert in the relationship, I answered Julia's question with an empathic understanding response, which simply repeated the statement immediately prior to her request for instruction.

Comments

The critics of non-directivity might argue here that this empathic understanding response was in fact a suggestion to the client to talk about her problems in the family, and therefore the therapist would be actually instructing or directing the client. But since the therapist had just repeated the client's statement, it is more accurate to say that the therapist simply reflected back to the client one possible direction that the client had already considered by herself. Moreover, the therapist's response apparently did not influence the client's direction, since she did not choose to talk further about her problems at home after the therapist's response. It is only much later in the session that the client chooses this direction.

C3: Yes, problems … no, it's various things … one is … in relation to my chosen career … I study administration at university and I realized that it isn't exactly what I want, right … so, this is one fact … another fact is … ah … let's say … ah, the relationship with my father, we had an argument, now, the last time we had a serious argument … he broke off all relations with me … then I realized … gee! I need to do some therapy, or something like that …

T3: You felt bad when this happened …

Therapist's account of her experience

I made an empathic understanding response, reflecting back to Julia the feeling I perceived she was expressing in her narrative about the argument with her father. When Julia said, 'I realized that I need to do some therapy,' I perceived empathically that she was also expressing that she felt really bad when her father broke off relations with her.

Comments

Julia introduced in C3 the two main issues that she will unfold over the rest of the session: her career choice and the argument with her father.

116

C4: Well, I don't know if I felt bad, because everything happened like a kind of revolution; what happened was the last straw of many things that have happened over the years. I think it all started when I was fifteen, sixteen years old: I think it was at this age ... it's just that I don't know where to start (laugh) ...

T4: You don't know if you want to talk about this or if you want to talk about something else ...

Therapist's account of her experience

As in T1, I did not accommodate Julia's request for suggesting a direction that she should take. Instead, I made an empathic understanding response to her immediate experience expressed in the request, in an attempt to allow the locus of decision making to remain with her.

Comments

Julia interrupted her narrative about the painful feelings she experienced in the relationship with her father and made another request for instruction, as if she was asking for the therapist's permission to go further along this pathway. Perhaps she was not feeling safe enough at that moment to explore these painful experiences because she was subceiving them as threatening to her self-concept.

C5: Yes ... well ... it's difficult like this, of us talking like this, of us to ... normally I talk like this with people who I have more ... with Marcia, who I have known for a long time, like ...

T5: As if you feel ashamed?

C6: Yes, also (laugh) ... it is complicated ... (laugh) ... on my way over on the bus I was thinking: 'Oh! My God, what am I going to talk about? Is she going to ask me something?' Because asking questions is easier than me starting to talk!

T6: Like having to talk about yourself, it is not so easy ...

C7: Yeah ... (laugh)

(silence: 10 seconds)

C8: Well ... then, then, as I was saying before ... in relation to university, right ...

T8: Uhm, hmm ...

C9: (She talks for four minutes about her situation in the university and her doubts about remaining in the administration course—she has been studying there for three and a half years—or leaving it and starting the accountancy course.)

Comments

In C5 and C6 Julia asked again for therapist direction (although rather indirectly), and again the therapist responded to these requests (in T5 and T6) with empathic understanding responses. After the T6 response, Julia stayed silent for 10 seconds. This brief pause seems like a turning point in the session. After that silence she went forward, dwelling on her self-experiences in relation to the university and her wish to change the course, and then she made no more requests for direction. It can be inferred from this shift in Julia's behavior

117

that, in these seconds of silence, she realized that the therapist would not ever accommodate her requests to direct her process, and that it was really up to her to decide what to talk about or which direction to choose. Julia eventually decided to talk about her doubt in regard to staying in the administration course or changing to accountancy.

Therapist's account of her experience

From the very first moments of our interaction, I strove to show to Julia, through my empathic understanding responses, that I had no private agenda for her; that she was allowed to proceed in whatever way was comfortable for her; that I was there with her to listen to whatever she chose to talk about. I tried to show this not as an expert, through theoretical explanations of how therapy works, but concretely through my own behavior.

Comments

This is radically opposed to most therapeutic approaches, which require the therapist to assess the client's current psychological functioning prior to the initiation of therapy itself. The first interviews are generally used to take the client's history and to arrive at a diagnosis in order to determine the therapeutic strategies and techniques to be applied in the client's 'treatment'. But in client-centered therapy, on the contrary, therapy begins immediately, with the therapist trying to understand the client's world in whatever way the client wishes to share it. Also, as Raskin and Rogers (2004: 264) point out, 'The first hour may be the first of hundreds or it may be the only one; this is for the client to determine.'

Therapist's account of her experience

I chose not to take the responsibility for instructing or indicating issues that Julia should talk about because I believed that she was the best expert about herself, and that she knew better than I which issue was important to talk about and when and how it would be appropriate to delve into it. That is, it was ultimately my deep trust in Julia's internal processes and capacity for personal change that supported my attitude of refusing to lead her by making suggestions to her. Indeed, I trusted that if I refused to take the lead in the therapeutic process, Julia would eventually take the lead herself. Even Julia's insistent requests did not shake my trust in her capacity for choosing the best direction for the therapeutic process.

Comments

According to Bozarth (1998: 111), 'It is essential that therapists have nearly unfaltering "faith" that individuals given the opportunity will engage in optimal mode of experiencing. … it is this unfaltering belief that provides the structure and direction for all therapeutic behavior.' In other words, it is the therapist's ultimate trust in the client's actualizing tendency[6] that leads to the non-directive attitude (see also Brodley, 1997; Freire and

---

6. According to Rogers' theory of therapy (1959), the actualizing tendency is 'the inherent tendency of the organism to develop all its capacities in ways which serve to maintain or enhance the organism' (p. 196). It is a tendency toward growth, development and fulfillment of potentialities (Bozarth and Brodley, 1991).

Tambara, 2000). Merry (2004) points out that there is always a temptation for the therapist to provide direction or to assume responsibility for the client's process, but a 'classical' client-centered therapist acknowledges that she cannot 'know what direction the therapy should take, or what "issues" may or may not prove to have significance for the client' (p. 41). The therapist acknowledges that the client is the only expert on her life, and therefore the client is the only person who really knows which is the best direction to take in the therapeutic process.

Moreover, the therapist's conscious renunciation of setting the agenda for the therapeutic process also expresses a deep commitment to avoid disempowering the client. In fact, insofar as a therapist sets the agenda for the client, she takes this responsibility away from the client and therefore exercises power over her. By contrast, client-centered therapy, according to Rogers (1977: 14), is characterized by the therapist's 'conscious renunciation and avoidance of all control over, or decision making for the client'. Therefore, 'It is not that this approach gives power to the person; it never takes it away' (Rogers, 1977: xii). The therapist's non-directive attitude leads to a complete disruption of the therapist's personal control in the therapeutic relationship and the reversal of the traditional dynamic of power in therapy (see Natiello, 2001; Proctor, 2002).

Therapist's account of her experience

My persistent refusal to suggest a direction to Julia was driven by my continuing attempt to communicate unconditional positive regard for her. Any issue that I might suggest could be understood by her as being worthier than the issue that she might have chosen by herself. Through my empathic understanding responses, on the contrary, any judgment that I might have about what would be best for Julia to talk about or to experience at the moment was put aside.

Comments

Empathic understanding responses make it possible for the therapist to communicate to the client that her immediate experience is being received unconditionally; that is, with no conditions of worth. As Sommerbeck (2004) points out, empathic reflection

> entails the least risk of conveying conditional regard to the client and the least risk of imposing on the client's feeling of freedom to express whatever is on his or her mind and the least risk of tempting the client to act according to perceived conditions of worth rather than according to his or her own sense of what is reasonable. (email)

Bozarth (1998) and Merry (2004) also conclude that the therapist's empathic and non-judgmental following of the client's experiencing is the purest way to communicate unconditional positive regard.

Unit 2

Middle of the first session

In the overall analysis of this session, it was found that the therapist responded to Julia exclusively with empathic understanding responses. The excerpts below illustrate some of these responses:

C: ... so, then, everyone, my boyfriend, my mother, everyone says : 'Oh! No, you must graduate, and then you go and study accountancy' ... oh! Well, I think I will do what they say, even though I go to university I am not willing ... I cannot stand going to that university anymore ... I go because I have to, because I have to finish ...

T: You are forced to go ...

C: Yes ... I do not have the spirit to go to class ...

T: You are unmotivated ...

C: Yes ...

T: To go to classes ...

C: Yes, I'm reluctant ...

...

C: ... but what now? If I give up they will call me crazy, right? 'What! You are about to graduate!' and I don't know what else ... then you go by what people say ... at the same time you try and see ... gee, and now ... I'm going to change to accounting and all this time that I studied administration I'll ... at the same time I think of quitting and changing to accounting, I am reluctant, thinking about all this time that I wasted, you know, how am I going to change like that ...

T: And to feel that you have wasted all that time ...

C: That I wasted it ... like a fear that it creates a reaction, like ... that later I will take responsibility for it, myself ...

T: That you'll blame yourself for throwing away all those years ...

C: (interrupting) Yes, all these years and more ... but ... (pause: 7 seconds)

T: You do not want this sensation that you have lost all these years, but you are feeling that you are wasting time ...

C: Yes, that I am only going just to go, you know ... I'm just going because I have to finish the course, then, I think: gee! There is still a year and a half to go ...

T: 'Will I be able to bear another year and a half?'

C: (together with therapist) Another year and a half ... I think that a year and a half is an enormous distance ...

T: It will be a long time ...

C: (together with therapist) A long time ... although sometimes it is not, right, it flies past ... but in agony it is a long time (laugh) ...

T: It discourages you to think that there is still a long time to go ...

C: A long time ...

Therapist's account of her experience

My empathic understanding responses were attempts to represent Julia's internal frame of reference in the immediate interaction, and to communicate as deep an understanding of her experience as possible.

Comments

These empathic understanding responses were, as Bozarth (1998) depicts them, a 'kind of as-close-as-possible-following of the client as she narrates and expresses herself' (p. 62). In many moments Julia and the therapist spoke the same words at the same time. This phenomenon seems to indicate that the therapist was following the client's track so closely that the client could guess what the therapist was going to say and could even complete the sentence for her. This strong attunement between therapist and client can be understood as an expression of the phenomenon of empathic resonation (see Barrett-Lennard, 1993; Rud, 2004).

UNIT 3

THIRD PART OF THE SESSION

In the excerpt below Julia shifted smoothly and spontaneously from the issue of the career choice to the issue of the relationship with her father:

C: ... I said a lot of stuff (laugh) I thought I would not be able to say anything (laugh) ... well, that's it then! It is just this that I have to see ... if I want to continue at university or not ...

T: You feel that you need to decide ...

C: I don't know, because at the same time I'm afraid to decide (laugh) ... understand? If I have to decide, I get scared ... I see that I am delaying things, delaying ... at the same time I think: 'Am I not wasting this time', you know? Then, I am letting it pass, at the same time I think ... you know ... I do not have the courage to ... to ...

T: You feel you are putting it off ...

C: (together with therapist) putting it off ...

T: You are not wanting to see the problem ... but you know that it is there ...

C: Yes, exactly ...

T: Deceiving yourself, like that ...

C: Exactly ... my life is so mixed up, it is that ... gee! I am 23, I will be 24 next month ... I don't know, I have not got anything of substance for myself yet, you know? I imagined that at this age I would already have a career, that I would be fine, you know, all that ... to have made plans before, that is the problem, I think ... we fall short ... we do all that planning, planning, and when you look at it, it is nothing like that ... this is so much more frustrating ...

T: The plans that you made for yourself, not ...

C: Yes, I think it is very frustrating ... Oh! I don't know! It is very complicated! I think

121

that everyone must go through this crisis when ... thinking about life ...

T: Like you reached a moment when you started to question: 'where am I going in life?'

C: Yes, where am I going? ... I know it only depends on me ... ok, I have my family, but there is a moment when pride is more important ... I like to pay for all my own stuff because I know that later I will not have my parents there to pay ... so I like doing this now already ...

T: It is a personal demand to be able to have this independence as soon as possible ...

C: Yes ... like, an apartment for me, my own house, a place where I can ... that I leave my parents' house and have total independence ...

T: You are in a hurry for this ...

C: I am, I am in a big hurry for this ... and ... this was one of the arguments that I had with my father, for me, if I could leave their house, not because of my mother, or my brothers, but because of my independence that I want and because of him, because he has the wrong idea about me ... my father thinks I am, the last time he said this, that I am manipulative, then I told him: 'Well, if you think I am manipulative, it is because you are, because you are seeing this in me, but you are not accepting this about me, and because this is what you are' ... so, it was a confrontation like that ... horrible, isn't it ... We had a serious argument about this, then I said: 'Well, if you do not trust your daughter, if you do not trust your family, then you do not trust anybody in this world ... and I am sad for you because of this, you do not trust anyone, not even your own daughter, so I want, for me, if I could, to leave this house today' (with a choking voice), that is how I spoke to him: 'I would leave your house as soon as possible, because you do not trust me, because you do not know, because you have hurt me with this', that is how I spoke to him; then he said: ' Oh! You want to leave my house?' Then I said: 'Because of you'; then he said: 'Oh, ok then, as from today I'm breaking all relations with you' ... of course it was much bigger than this, it was an argument that lasted about two hours, but, this willingness that I have to leave home is because of this also ...

T: Because you felt very hurt by him ...

C: (crying) This ... has hurt me very deeply ...

T: It is difficult to live with him after what has happened ...

C: Yes, we do not even speak ... he keeps to himself and I keep to myself ... a few days ago he even said 'Hi' to me, but I do not want a 'hi' from him, I want him to apologize to me, that is what I want ... just that he will never apologize ... He left his wife, left his children, fifteen years ago, to be part of an association, a syndicate, and ... it is a rebellion I have because of this ... this is what I am starting to realize now, you know?

Comments

Responding to Julia exclusively with empathic understanding responses, the therapist neither pushed her nor hurried her towards any direction. Julia's pace and choice were so respected that she started to explore the painful experiences with her father only in the very moment that she found it was right for her to do so. She decided exclusively by herself when and how to dive into these experiences. Although Julia had glanced at these feelings in the very beginning of the session, it was only at this moment that she chose to immerse herself in experiencing them, probably because it was only at this moment that she felt safe enough to do so. It is likely that the therapist's non-judgmental and empathic attitude towards her promoted a climate of safety in the relationship that helped her to eventually break her defenses up and to openly experience her painful feelings of 'rebellion' and 'hurt' towards her father.

The analysis of this session contradicts Sachse and Elliott's (2002) assertions that clients do not know how to deal with their own problems in a constructive way because they 'become aware that deepening the process means "facing up" to unpleasant or painful experiences' and that 'little progress seems to occur without deepening therapist interventions' (p. 96). On the contrary, what was found in this case was that the client 'deepened' her process, facing up to painful experiences without any intentional or directive 'deepening therapist intervention'.

T: You feel extremely rebellious because your father has been absent ...

C: Gee! Totally absent ... totally ... and now he wants to start participating with life at home ... after this argument I had with him I said: 'No, you failed as a father; if I do not respect you, it is because you do not respect me, and if I do not have respect for you it is because you failed as a father' [...] so, it is this that is revolting to me also ... it is because of this that I want to leave home, like, I want to have if I can, I want to have my family the way I want it, not like this, I do not want to live in a family like this, you know ...

T: Your revulsion over him is really huge ...

C: Oh! It is huge! ... he ran away from his obligation to be a father, because even on the weekends he brought work home ... after he entered into politics, he was not even home on the weekends, and now he wants to return again ... he wants to talk about stuff with me ... he wants to come back, after we had this argument ... but as from now I do not know if it matters anymore, everyone is grown up ... I used to be very close to my father, before, I think he suffered more in relation to this ... with this argument ...

T: It has created an abyss between you and him ... you do not know, you do not believe that now it is possible to re-establish that relationship ...

C: This ... I don't know, it can even be what it is, but not how it used to be, before he went into public life, like ...

T: This grief will always be there ...

C: Because that is how it is, if it were ... ok, fine, it is one thing if he wants to value his ego, his self-esteem and all, but that is one thing that does not benefit the family, so, he chose his life, how he wanted his life to be, he did not think about the family ... so then why get married, why have children? This is what I keep on thinking: why leave his wife abandoned in the house?

T: You felt like he was rejecting the family ...

C: Yes, because I think he was not mature enough to see that he is a father, and that he also is a husband, I do not think he had the maturity to see this ... the moment that he got married, that he started a family, he should have accepted that family, he does not have that maturity …

T: And this is what you demand from him …

C: Yes, this is what I demand … It is just that he does not see this … the only conversation that he has is about this association that he administers, that is all he talks about … he does not ask you how it is going at university, where it is that you work … so, gee, it is a rebellion like that, it is a … not exactly a rebellion, I don't know, it is something like that … now I have resolved to nullify this person, I do not get on with him anymore, because he chose something else for his life, so I do not need to have this person in my life …

T: You have decided to ignore him …

C: Yes, I will ignore him, he is not part of my life, since the moment that he actually said: 'I am breaking all relations of father and daughter, do not ask me for anything, you will not get anything from me', so … oh, so, ok, it is you who says this, I am making it clear that it is you who is talking like this, it is you who is breaking relations with me … so, ok …

T: It was he …

C: (interrupting) Yes, I made it clear that he is the one who is saying this: 'If you want something from me, you will have to come looking for me, because I will not'… then he came and said 'Hi' to me one day when I arrived home; I was making dinner for him, and just like that, he came and said 'Hi', but I do not want a 'hi' from him …

T: You are waiting for him to …

C: (interrupting) I want him to apologize, apologize for everything that he said to me, you know, I do not know if it will change anything, at this stage now, he could even apologize, but I do not know if it will change anything … because my idea that I have of him, is an idea that is already formulated …

T: That this hurt you feel is so old, that you do not know if apologizing will be sufficient …

C: Yes … (together with therapist) will be sufficient …

T: But can we stop here?

C: Yes, we can …

Therapist's account of her experience

Although my empathic understanding responses helped Julia express her painful feelings of resentment and anger towards her father as if she were releasing them in a catharsis, it was not my intention to produce such an effect in her. Actually, there was no particular process or behavior that I was intending to produce in her. I only had the intention of communicating my experience of unconditional positive regard for her.

Comments

During these last fourteen minutes of the session, with the help of the therapist's empathic acceptance, Julia was able to listen to herself and to experience what was going on within her. Then, she was able to fully experience the feelings of resentment and anger towards her father, which heretofore she has not been not totally aware of. Barrett-Lennard (1993) uses a metaphor of the midwife assisting a birth to depict this phenomenon:

> Hearing from another the essence of our personal feeling and meaning which we have been struggling to articulate and express, which perhaps is like a chameleon that keeps changing and disappearing as we pursue it, and which may evoke sickening anxiety in us, to hear in this context a listener who is devoting his/her whole attention to what we are going through speak back to us that which we ourselves are strenuously and barely grasping can have the impact of a skilful midwife assisting in a literal birth. (p. 8)

The client's movement within this session shows the power and wisdom of the organismic actualizing tendency. Insofar as Julia felt safe enough in the therapeutic relationship, she chose to fully experience her painful feelings regarding the relationship with her father in an attempt to integrate them into her self-concept. It was not necessary that the therapist instruct her to go in that direction, since it was not the therapist's expertise but the client's organismic actualizing tendency, promoted by the climate of freedom and safety within the therapeutic relationship, which ultimately drove her to explore and integrate these experiences. As Rogers (1946: 420) pointed out: 'If we can provide understanding of the way the client seems to himself at this moment, he can do the rest.' Merry (2004) also comments upon the role of the therapist's empathic understanding in the client's process:

> Empathic understanding is not employed in order to achieve any particular effect or outcome, including encouraging clients to focus on selected aspects of experience, to bring issues or problems to the client's attention, or help a client towards an insight or 'personal growth'. Paradoxically, however, any of these (and others) may be outcomes of the client's experience of being understood with empathy and without judgement. (pp. 34–5)

UNIT 4

EXCERPTS FROM THE FIFTH SESSION

The qualitative analysis of the entire twelve sessions of this therapeutic process showed that the therapist responded to Julia exclusively with empathic understanding response throughout each session. Therefore, the excerpts of the first session presented in Units 1, 2 and 3 of this chapter, and the excerpts of the fifth session presented below in this unit, can be understood as paradigmatic instances, which represent the pattern of interaction between client and therapist throughout the therapeutic process.

C: One thing that I have realized about me, that I do not know why, is that I always think that people will be judging me, looking at me and then having an idea about me that ... that is not pleasant ... so, at university, I always keep my distance, I never approach people, I wait for them to come and speak to me ... I always leave home thinking: 'My clothes are ok, aren't they? What will they think,' you know? I can never leave feeling tranquil, like, without thinking: 'Oh! Tough luck to other people!' ... a guy looks at me and I immediately think that there is something wrong ...

T: You have a sensation that there is something wrong with you ...

C: Yes, I don't know, it is strange ... (silence: 10 seconds) Because ... it is like I feel that they are judging me all the time ... maybe in the same way that I sometimes judge some people, maybe that is why I think that they will judge me too, but they are not even bothered, it is just one more person in the middle of others ... they do not even know I exist, or something like that, but as I have this habit of observing many people, I observe a lot, then I think that they could be observing me too ...

...

C: I think that ... , when they look at me I think that they are already criticizing me ... I keep on looking at university, everybody is neat, and me all ... When I arrive at university, I think: why did I wear these pants? Why did I put on these shoes? Why did I come dressed like this? I should have gotten dressed better! ... it is always the same deal: what are they going to think of me? I should not be so worried all the time ... [...] Why should I be bothered, it is my way of being, why does it bother me so much? (pause: 5 seconds)

T: You get angry with yourself for worrying so much ...

C: (together with the therapist) Yes ... yes ... for worrying so much about what other people think of me ...

Therapist's account of her experience

Although Julia asked the question, 'Why does it bother me so much?' in a strong tone of voice, I did not take responsibility for answering it. I believed that she was the only person who truthfully knew the answer. But if I had explicitly said to her, 'You know better than me the answer to your question'. Julia would not have felt accepted and understood, since her experience at that moment was that she did not really know the answer. So, instead of expressing verbally my trust in her organismic wisdom, I attempted to express it concretely, through an empathic understanding response. With my response—'You get angry with yourself for worrying so much'—I intended to communicate to Julia that her immediate experience relating to her question was understood and accepted unconditionally by me and, moreover, it was accepted unconditionally because I trusted her capacity to deal with this experience in a constructive way and to find a constructive response to it. By not responding directly to her question I also avoided assuming a position of expertise in the relationship, that is, I avoided being the person in the relationship 'who knows'.

Comments

In other therapeutic approaches where the therapist assumes a position of power and expertise in the relationship, it would be expected that the therapist would try to answer or to help the client to answer this kind of anguished question. In fact, it is a strong

126

temptation for any therapist to give interpretations, explanations, advice or suggestions; all the more so when the client asks for them. But in client-centered therapy, the therapist's trust in the client's ability to find the best answers for her own questions prevents the therapist from offering responses from her frame of reference which might hinder the client's process of finding out truly her own responses.

C: It is something that makes me angry that, when I have to get dressed a bit better, like for an interview, and then people notice that I got dressed a bit better ... and when they say: 'Oh! You got dressed up today, where are you going?' Even my boyfriend has said: 'Oh! Where are you going like that? You look beautiful.' and I want to ask: 'Oh, ok, then on other days I'm ugly, right?' [...] I become furious, why say that? ... [it means that] on other days I am ugly, untidy ...

T: You feel like you were being criticized with these comments ...

C: Yes, I do not consider these comments as a compliment: 'Oh, you are so beautiful' ... I do not consider ...

T: You consider that they are criticizing you because before you were not ...

C: (interrupting) Yes ... why can't I consider it a compliment? (pause: 5 seconds) ... I don't know!

T: You cannot see it as a compliment, you only see it as a criticism ...

Therapist's account of her experience

Again I avoided giving responses from my own frame of reference to Julia's question, 'Why can't I consider it a compliment?' and answered her with an empathic understanding response.

C: (together with therapist) No, I only see it as a criticism ... I think that I am very negative, usually I see everything as a criticism ... (laugh) everything is criticism ...

T: It is difficult to hear a compliment, to recognize a compliment as a compliment, you only hear the criticism ...

C: Yes ... I only hear the criticisms ... (silence: 10 seconds) I don't know, maybe this has got to do with my childhood, I don't know ... maybe for having gone through all that ...

T: For having heard a lot of criticism during your childhood ... [7]

C: And being used to only hearing that kind of mocking from others ... and not opening my mind ...

Comments

The therapist's trust in Julia's capacity to find constructive answers proved to be correct, since she eventually found a significant answer to her questions about why she worries

---

7. In a previous session, Julia related that during her childhood she suffered mocking from her schoolmates. In this current session, I understood that Julia was making reference to this experience when she said 'for having gone through all that'.

so much about what other people think of her and why she only hears criticism from others. Julia realized that it is something that comes from her childhood, for being used to hearing only mocking from others. Also, it is worth noting that she achieved this response spontaneously, without any external guidance.

T: Like you really believed you were those things that they said ...
C: Yes ... I think that is it ... and then what to do to change this? To become better? I must! How am I going to ... how do I transform this?
T: You really want to be able to transform this ...

Therapist's account of her experience
Again, I refused to answer Julia's question: 'How do I transform this?' with any suggestion or advice, because it would put me in a position of technical expertise in the relationship. I trusted that the real source of change resided within her, and that any suggestion or advice would be counter-productive in locating and activating her self-healing resources.

C: For example, there is something that until today is like this ... this has marked me a lot, it was ... [she tells about her father building a fence, that he nailed down all the wood for the fence all at once, and then he had to cut it in half. She told him how to resolve the problem and her brother said: 'At last you finally had an idea, your head is not useful for anything'] it was something like that, that marked me ... at the time I was furious with him, and it is something that has stayed with me till today ...
...
C: I never felt like I was part of the family, I think that I have never felt like I was from somewhere, truthfully ... as if I belonged somewhere ...
T: You feel different ...
C: Yes, I feel very different from many people, at university, I do not feel as if I am part of the university, at home I do not feel as if I am part of the family, at my boyfriend's house I also do not, I do not feel like I am part of it ... I don't know, maybe I am looking for a place where I can feel: 'Oh! I am a part of this place', you know?
...
C: Gee! I think there are people who do not care about half the stuff that I do, I keep thinking, you know ... that I give great value to this, of the feelings that people think about, or that they do not think about ... or that I do not like to annoy anybody, to hurt anybody, so I hold myself back so as not to do this ...
T: You feel you stress yourself out, unnecessarily, in order to not hurt others ...
C: This is why I cannot wait to get my own space just for me, because then who wants to go to my house can go, I will not have to go to anybody's house!

Comments
Before the end of the session, Julia achieved some significant answers to her questions: the realization that a statement her brother made to her many years ago, that her 'head is not useful for anything', stayed with her until this day, and that it was something that

marked her; and the realization that she never felt like she was part of the family, and that she was looking for a place where she could feel she belonged. These understandings, or insights, seem to have arisen spontaneously from Julia's inner organismic wisdom. The therapist did not influence or suggest any of these answers; her only role in the client's process of finding these responses was to create a climate where the client felt deeply understood and unconditionally accepted in the relationship.

CONCLUSION

The analysis of the therapeutic interaction, illustrated in the excerpts above, shows that throughout the therapeutic process the therapist strove to keep her frame of reference, including her judgments and evaluations, out of the client's path. The therapist consistently followed the client's individual process as it emerged, without attempting to control the course of therapy. Also, the client's process was not guided by the therapist's evaluations of which direction would be the most appropriate to take—the directions the client actually chose to take were totally driven by her inner appraisal of the experience. The conclusion that arises from this analysis is that the therapist's attitude in this therapeutic relationship was consistently non-directive (see Bozarth, 2000, 2002; Merry and Brodley, 2002; Sommerbeck, 2002).

THE CLIENT'S EXPERIENCE OF PROCESS AND OUTCOME

Through the analysis of Julia's responses to the IPR and evaluation interview, the following categories emerged:

I—THE CLIENT'S EXPERIENCE OF THE THERAPEUTIC PROCESS

• *I was not being judged*
Julia experienced the therapist's non-directiveness essentially as a non-judgmental attitude that supported her internal locus of evaluation.

'I did not feel like I was being judged. She would make comments about how I was feeling, but never said if I was right or wrong. She didn't say, it was me who thought: am I right, and then: no, I was wrong […] it was me who evaluated myself.'
'[I] liked it, because we keep on talking and the person is not judging you or anything. I have a problem with this business about thinking that someone is judging me, the color of my clothes, the way I walk, I don't know […] so then I enjoyed talking. I even got in to it, and did not see the time go by.'

• *I found it a bit funny at the beginning*
At first Julia perceived the therapist's non-directive attitude as strange, and she wanted the therapist to speak more.

'I thought it strange that, I always thought that in therapy a person talks, right, the therapist says something, like, explain, that says like: "Oh, this is a characteristic of you, because you are more like this ... " you know, the therapist speaks, but it is the person who keeps talking and she just makes comments ... That is what I found a bit funny at the beginning.'

'At the beginning I thought that she could have spoken more; I wanted her to speak more, but then I saw how it was, that I would speak and she would comment on a few things. Afterwards I got used to this way of therapy. I even liked it, because we keep on talking and the person is not judging you or anything.'

• *The therapist understood a lot of what I said*

Julia had the experience of being empathically understood by the therapist. She also perceived the therapist's efforts to understand her.

'I think that Beth was able to understand a lot of what I said. She was able to capture what I was saying, that sometimes not even I could. I could not express myself, and she paid sufficient attention to say a word, something to help ...'

• *The therapist was really present*

Julia made reference to the presence of the therapist, indicating that she experienced the therapist as being in 'total' attunement to her. The therapist's efforts to understand the client's internal frame of reference had also sometimes reached the perception of feelings and meanings of which the client was still scarcely aware: 'I was not even getting there and she had already got there before me.' However, as was pointed out in the previous analysis of the therapeutic relationship, the therapist had not intended to uncover 'unconscious' meanings and feelings. It is likely that the therapist sought such an active experiencing of the client's internal frame of reference that she somehow ended up communicating some meanings that were just on the edge of the client's awareness.

'I felt that she was there, really present. Sometimes even beyond that, sometimes I was not even getting there and she had already got there before me, she cleared it up a bit more.'

• *It was good to talk about everything I was going through*

Julia found the experience of 'talking' within the therapeutic relationship as being positive and quite helpful. The experience of talking had helped her to 'become more conscious', 'to see the situation better', and 'to confront it', She also indicated the presence of a climate of freedom in the relationship which allowed her to talk at ease with no external disturbances.

'It was good for me to talk about everything I was going through ... At least, when we talk about something, we become more conscious about it ... Sometimes we swallow a lot of stuff, or we do not think about all this stuff and all that tension just accumulates.'

'At times I thought I would not be able to say anything, but then I arrived here, sat down and started to talk, talk, talk, then I realized that I still had stuff to talk about. So ... I felt good when I left here.'

'It is good, you talk, after you express yourself, that you talk, then you think: ok, so then this is a problem, right? Where is it? What is this? ... then I get to see the situation better. Because sometimes you think about it, but when you talk about it is when you really confront it, that is when you are confronting it.'

Comments

It is noteworthy in Julia's report that she did not acknowledge the therapist's expertise, or the therapist's influence in expanding her understanding. She said that she was able 'to see the situation better' just because she talked about it. This fact corresponds to Rogers' (1946) discovery that the client is able to achieve insights truly and spontaneously without the therapist's guidance.

Furthermore, the experience reported by Julia does not fit with the findings reported by Rennie (1990, 1994, 2001) in his research on the client's experience of the therapeutic hour. Using IPR interviews, Rennie found that the client's experience is often covert: 'Clients often do not disclose to the therapist all that they are experiencing and some of what they do not disclose has to do with their sense of the therapist' (Rennie, 2001: 126).

It is readily apparent that neither Julia, nor any other client who participated in our research, made reference to any kind of covert experience during their IPR interviews. The key to understanding this absence of 'covert experiences' in our study can be found in Rennie's study itself. Rennie (2001: 124) explains that when the client was following a path or track of thought and feeling, she was 'just doing it', and 'In this state, the presence and contributions of the therapist, if in line with the track, were hardly noticed.' This fits with Julia's experience—she did not notice the therapist's influence on her talking. But, according to Rennie, when the therapist's activity is not in line with the client's track, the client feels disturbed by the therapist. When this happens, 'The clients defer to the therapist's authority ... clients may rail inwardly ... without letting the therapist know about their discontent because of the power dynamics entailed in the relationship with the therapist' (Rennie, 2001: 136).

It is reasonable to conclude that it is the absence of 'power dynamics' in client-centered therapy and the therapist's determination to follow the client's path (through empathic understanding responses) which ultimately explain the differences between the experience of the therapeutic hour reported by clients in our research and the experience reported by clients in Rennie's study.[8] Client deference was one of the major categories derived from Rennie's (1994) analysis. The author reported a number of ways

---

8. It is puzzling that among the eleven therapists who participated in Rennie's study, five were described as 'person-centered'. Certainly they were not 'classical', or non-directive client-centered therapists. This fact reinforces the importance of clear definitions regarding the identity of client-centered therapy (see Sanders, 2004).

in which the client's deference was expressed:

> They respected the therapist's judgment even when not agreeing with it. They made allowances. They followed the therapist's lead. They attempted to understand the therapist's frame of reference to make the therapist's work easier. They resisted criticizing or challenging the therapist. And so on. (p. 126)

Rennie (1994, 2001) found that the client senses a pressure from the therapist's demands or apparent expectations, and complies because she wishes to please the therapist—to be a good client:

> The client has fear of criticizing the therapist. Clients may feel that it is not their place to question their therapist's approach because they view themselves as naïve laypersons and the therapist as an expert who probably knows what he or she is doing, even though it is not immediately obvious. (Rennie, 1994: 430-1)

It is not surprising that the phenomenon of client deference did not appear in our study, since the client-centered therapist, as Bozarth (1998: 6) pointed out, 'eschews knowledge "about" the client, relates as an equal to the client, and trusts and respects the client's perceptions as the authority about him/herself.' In client-centered therapy there is no room for client deference, since 'clients are viewed as going in their own ways, allowed to go at their own pace, and to pursue their growth in their unique way' (Bozarth, 1998: 6). In fact, in client-centered therapy, it is the therapist who defers to the client. Bower (cited in Bozarth, 1998: 9) made a qualitative study of six notable client-centered therapists doing therapy, and he found that the therapists were experienced as being a 'shadow to the client', disappearing in deference to their clients: 'There was neither intervention nor intrusion of the personality of the therapist.'

II—THE CLIENT'S EXPERIENCE OF THE THERAPEUTIC OUTCOMES

Before starting therapy, Julia had written in the initial written questionnaire that she came to therapy because she was 'in search of a better understanding of attitudes and emotional problems' and 'in search of an inner force'. She wrote that she would like to change her 'concern with the perfection of her attitudes and the other person's too' and her 'relationship with some persons'. In the evaluation interview, after the twelfth session, Julia made an appraisal of the outcomes of therapy and talked about the goals and expectations that she had written in the IQW. In the analysis of this interview, the following categories emerged.

• *There has been a huge change*
Julia experienced a huge change in her way of being after therapy and she concluded that therapy was quite helpful for her.

'Well ... there has been a huge change.'

'I think that the therapy has helped me a lot.'

'I think it helped me, it helped all those times that I came and spoke.'

• *I'm doing my stuff*

Julia reported a shift in her locus of evaluation from 'others' to 'self'. She realized how much she used to be dependent on the evaluations of others and how much of her life used to be guided by the demands of others. Then she ceased to look to others for approval or disapproval, and she came to accept the locus of choices, decisions and evaluative judgments as being within herself.

'Before [therapy] I was very much like: "What are other people going to think?" you
    know? … Maybe therapy has helped me with this, because before I left doing many
    things because of others, and now I'm not, I'm doing my things … Sometimes I did
    not go somewhere because someone could not go with me, or I did things that I did
    not really want to … I used to help my mother, doing things that my brothers did
    not do and stopped doing my stuff … Now I'm doing my stuff … I'm valuing
    myself, I'm valuing my own stuff …'

'I am managing to think better about my stuff, and I'm managing to decide. I'm no
    longer so indecisive. I know what I have to do. I have a better knowledge about
    myself, about my capacity.'

This shift in the locus of evaluation has also been related to successful therapeutic processes in client-centered therapy by Rogers (1951, 1961) and Raskin (1952/2004).

• *I'm valuing myself*

Julia reported achieving a feeling of self-worth and a better understanding of her own capacities.

'I'm valuing myself, I'm valuing my own stuff …'

'I know what I have to do. I have a better knowledge about myself, about my capacity..'

• *I feel much stronger*

Julia found the 'inner force' that she was looking for when she started therapy. She also reported achieving greater self-confidence and self-expressiveness: 'Now I feel I have the courage to say', 'I am able to talk about what is on my mind, say what I am feeling', 'I can place myself more', which improved her ability to accomplish her plans for life and to cope with conflicts in relationships.

'I think that therapy has also helped me in relation to what I wrote down [in the initial
    questionnaire]: "in search of an inner force", because I feel much stronger … I have
    never had a moment this difficult in my life as this year has been … I was feeling
    weak … I was very sensitive in any type of situation …'

'I'm beginning to achieve my plans, without being afraid to have to take a step. I think

that before I was afraid to face … I even went to interviews, but I think that I did not conduct myself as a person decided, and this time I was able to show that this is what I want. I think that I achieved a better posture since I decided to fight for that vacancy, to have a stronger attitude, and I think I am a bit like that now. I can even see it in my relationship with my family. Before, everything that my sister said affected me … before, I accepted everything, and now I question: "Why? Why?" Now I see that not everything she said was right. Before I always thought that everything she said was right, even though she is younger than me. Now I question everything a little, I do not think that everything is right. And before, maybe I did not think so, but I did not have the courage. Now I feel I have the courage to say: "No, that is not correct …" It seems that I feel stronger to talk to my mother also. Before then I was not able to, and now I am able to tell her that I do not agree with some attitudes; I can place myself more. Before I could not. Sometimes I had arguments that I was not able to say in words, I could only cry. Now I can cry, and at the same time I am able to talk about what is on my mind, say what I am feeling.'
'I think that I was able to become disinhibited …'

• I'm more flexible with myself and with other people

Julia reported the achievement of greater self-acceptance, which brought forth a more positive and realistic self-concept: 'I used to demand too much from myself.' Moreover, her greater self-acceptance gave rise to greater acceptance of others as well: 'I am able now to have more patience with other people.' This phenomenon is explained in proposition XVIII of Rogers' theory of personality (1951: 532): 'When the individual perceives and accepts into one consistent and integrated system all his sensory and visceral experiences, then he is necessarily more understanding of others and more accepting of others as separate individuals.' Furthermore, Julia showed a shift from a rigid mode of experiencing self and others to an attitude of openness and flexibility: 'I'm more flexible with myself and with other people.'

'I saw in therapy that I always try to do my best possible, always, just that there is stuff that gets in the middle of the way that sometimes you will not make that thing better, and it happens with other people also. I am able now to have more patience with other people and try to stop and listen first to what happened and then to scold (laugh) or not even scold, but try and listen to the other person. It was something that before I did not even stop to listen … […] I am able to relax more, understand other people: man, if you tried, did everything possible and still were not able to … […] I'm more flexible with myself and with other people. It is something that I used to demand too much from myself: "Why did I do it like that? Why did I not do it another way? It could have been better!" Then I saw that it is not quite like that, and if it is not quite like that for me, it is also not like that for other people, so I noticed that I demanded a lot of myself, and therefore, of other people too, but every person has a characteristic. I think that I have become more tranquil in this respect.'

• *I started looking for who I am*

Julia started therapy with a specific problem in mind and afterwards she started to look for her self, or 'way of being'.

'Truthfully, when I spoke to Marcia I needed to do therapy, it was because I had fought with my father, it was more because of my family, because I did not feel well at home, I did not feel as if I was part of the family. When I started, it was more because of this, but after it was becoming more like for my way of being ... I ended up realizing that they have a way of being and that I am not the same! Then I started looking for who I am ...'

This phenomenon was depicted by Rogers (1961) as a common experience in client-centered therapy:

The problem as stated in the first interview will not be the problem as seen in the second or third hour, and by the tenth interview it will be a still different problem or series of problems ... As I follow the experience of many clients in the therapeutic relationship which we endeavor to create for them, it seems to me that each one is raising the same question. Below the level of the problem situation about which the individual is complaining lies one central search. It seems to me that at bottom each person is asking, 'Who am I, really? How can I get in touch with this real self, underlying all my surface behavior? How can I become myself?' (Rogers, 1961: 109)

• *I enjoyed having therapy*

Julia considered the experience of therapy as being 'good', pleasant and quite valuable.

'I enjoyed having therapy, it was a very good experience. Beth was also very nice. I valued it quite a lot. ... I think that each person, in truth, that everybody should have therapy, everyone has their problems, that they have had since childhood, or something that has happened to them. I enjoyed doing it, something different. I was really needing it; it was good.'

CONCLUSION

The analysis of the Evaluation Interview draws an overall picture of the client's experience of the therapeutic outcomes after 12 sessions. In short, the client experienced:

• a shift in her locus of evaluation from others to self
• a feeling of self-worth, with a better understanding of her own capacities
• greater self-confidence and self-expressiveness
• an inner strength
• improved ability to accomplish her plans for life and to cope with conflicts in relationships

- greater self-acceptance, which brought forth a more positive and realistic self-concept
- greater acceptance and understanding of others
- more openness and flexibility in her mode of experiencing self and others.

These outcomes, achieved through a client-centered therapeutic relationship where the therapist was consistently non-directive, strongly contradict Sachse and Elliott's (2002) assertion that 'clients without specifically targeted help from therapists usually do not process their problems effectively' (p. 100). On the contrary, the outcomes found in this study indicate that clients can be truly and spontaneously capable of clarifying, checking and modifying their motives, goals and convictions towards a more positive and better integrated adjustment to living. According to client-centered theory, this capacity of the client emerges from the basic motivating force for growth and change operating in the human organism: the actualizing tendency. As Rogers (1986) expressed it:

> in person-centered therapy the person is free to choose any direction, but actually selects positive and constructive pathways. I can only explain this in terms of a directional tendency inherent in the human organism—a tendency to grow, to develop, to realize its full potential. (p. 127)

The therapeutic outcomes found in this present study support a non-directive therapeutic stance, and directly contradict Sachse and Elliott's (2002) conclusion that 'additional therapeutic strategies appear to be needed to influence outcome favorably' (p. 100). In fact, the analysis of Julia's case supports the assertion that a psychological environment free of threat and rich in unconditional positive regard and empathic understanding, promoted by a non-directive client-centered therapeutic relationship, is sufficient to tap the client's vast inner resources for growth and development.

Author's note: I want to thank Chantel Lawler very much for translating the therapeutic sessions and interviews from Portuguese to English. Her work was of inestimable help in the completion of this chapter.

REFERENCES

Barrett-Lennard GT (1993) The phases and focus of empathy. *British Journal of Medical Psychology,* 66, 3–14.

Bowen MV-B (1996) The myth of non-directiveness. In BA Farber, DC Brink & PM Raskin (Eds) *The psychotherapy of Carl Rogers: Cases and commentary.* New York: Guilford Press, pp. 84–94.

Bozarth JD (1998) *Person-Centered Therapy: A revolutionary paradigm.* Ross-on-Wye: PCCS Books.

Bozarth JD (2000) Non-directiveness in client-centered therapy: A vexed concept. Paper presented at the Eastern Psychological Association Conference, Baltimore, MD.

Bozarth JD (2002) Non-directivity in the person-centered approach: Critique of Kahn's critique. *Journal of Humanistic Psychology, 42,* 78–83.

Bozarth JD & Brodley, BT (1991) Actualization: A functional concept in client-centered psychotherapy. *Journal of Social Behavior and Personality, 6*, 45–59.

Brodley BT (1997) The non-directive attitude in client-centered therapy. *The Person-Centered Journal, 6*, 4–27.

Brodley BT (1998) Criteria for making empathic responses in client-centered therapy. *The Person-Centered Journal, 5*, 20–8

Cain DJ (1990) Further thoughts about non-directiveness and client-centered therapy. *Person-Centered Review, 5*, 89–99.

Elliott R (1986) Interpersonal process recall (IPR) as a psychotherapy process research method. In L Greenberg & W Pinsof (Eds) *The Psychotherapeutic Process: A research handbook.* New York: Guilford Press, pp. 503–29.

Freire E & Tambara N (2000) Client-centered therapy: The challenges of clinical practice. *The Person-Centered Journal, 7*, 129–38.

Hutterer R (1993) Eclecticism: An identity crisis for person-centred therapists. In D Brazier (Ed) *Beyond Carl Rogers.* London: Constable.

Kahn E (1999) A critique of non-directivity in the person-centered approach. *Journal of Humanistic Psychology, 39*, 94–110.

Lietaer G (1998) From non-directive to experiential: A paradigm unfolding. In B Thorne & E Lambers (Eds) *Person-Centered Therapy: A European perspective.* London: Sage, pp. 62–73.

Merry T (1990) Client-centred therapy: Some trends and some troubles. *Counselling, 1*, 17–18.

Merry T (2004) Classical client-centred therapy. In P Sanders (Ed) *The Tribes of the Person-Centred Nation: An introduction to the schools of therapy related to the person-centred approach.* Ross-on-Wye: PCCS Books, pp. 21–44.

Merry T & Brodley BT (2002) The non-directive attitude in client-centered therapy: A response to Kahn. *Journal of Humanistic Psychology, 42*, 66–77.

Natiello P (2001) *The Person-Centered Approach: A passionate presence.* Ross-on-Wye: PCCS Books.

Proctor G (2002) *The Dynamics of Power in Counselling and Psychotherapy: Ethics, politics and practice.* Ross-on-Wye: PCCS Books.

Prouty GF (1999) Carl Rogers and experiential therapies: A dissonance? *Person-Centred Practice, 7*, 4–11.

Raskin NJ (2004) An objective study of the locus-of-evaluation factor in psychotherapy. In NJ Raskin, *Contributions to Client-Centered Therapy and the Person-Centered Approach.* Ross-on-Wye: PCCS Books, pp. 54–71.

Raskin NJ & Rogers CR (2004) Person-centered therapy. In NJ Raskin *Contributions to Client-Centered Therapy and the Person-Centered Approach.* Ross-on-Wye: PCCS Books, pp. 245–89.

Rennie DL (1990) Toward a representation of the client's experience of the psychotherapy hour. In G Lietaer, J Rombauts & R Van Balen (Eds) *Client-Centered and Experiential Psychotherapy in the Nineties.* Leuven: Leuven University Press, pp. 155–72.

Rennie DL (1992) Qualitative analysis of the client's experience of psychotherapy: The unfolding of reflexivity. In S Toukmanian & D Rennie (Eds) *Psychotherapy Process Research: Paradigmatic and narrative approaches.* Newbury Park, CA: Sage, pp. 211–33.

Rennie DL (1994) Client's deference in psychotherapy. *Journal of Counseling Psychology, 41*, 427–37.

Rennie DL (1995) On the rhetorics of social science: Let's not conflate natural science and human science. *The Humanistic Psychologist, 23*, 321–32.

Rennie DL (2001) Experiencing psychotherapy: Grounded theory studies. In DJ Cain & J Seeman (Eds) *Humanistic Psychotherapies: Handbook of research and practice.* Washington DC: American Psychological Association, pp. 117–44.

Rennie DL, Phillips JF & Quartaro GK (1988) Grounded theory: A promising approach to conceptualization in psychology. *Canadian Psychology, 29*, 139–50.

Rogers CR (1946) Significant aspects of client-centered therapy. *The American Psychologist, 1*, 415–22.

Rogers CR (1951) *Client-Centered Therapy.* Boston: Houghton Mifflin.

Rogers CR (1959) A theory of therapy, personality, and interpersonal relationships as developed in the client-centered framework. In S Koch (Ed) *Psychology: A study of science: Formulation of the person and the social context, vol. 3.* New York: McGraw-Hill, pp. 184–256.

Rogers CR (1961) What it means to become a person. In CR Rogers, *On Becoming a Person.* Boston: Houghton Mifflin, pp. 107–24.

Rogers CR (1977) *Carl Rogers on Personal Power.* New York: Delacorte Press.

Rogers CR (1986) Rogers, Kohut and Erickson. *Person-Centered Review, 1*, 125–40.

Rud CR (2004) *Entre metáforas y caos: De la intervención pasiva a la contemplación activa en psicoterapia.* Buenos Aires: Nueva Generación.

Sachse R & Elliott R (2002) Process-outcome research on humanistic therapy variables. In DJ Cain & J Seeman (Eds) *Humanistic Psychotherapies: Handbook of research and practice.* Washington DC: American Psychological Association, pp. 83–115.

Sanders P (2004) (Ed) *The Tribes of the Person-Centred Nation: An introduction to the schools of therapy related to the person-centred approach.* Ross-on-Wye: PCCS Books.

Shlien JM (1986) Roundtable discussion: What is most essential to the continued development of the theory and application of the person-centered approach? *Person-Centered Review, 1*, 334–52.

Sommerbeck L (2002) Person-centered or ecletic? A response to Kahn. *Journal of Humanistic Psychology, 42*, 84–7.

Sommerbeck L (2004) E-mail sent to pcintl@listserv.uga.edu on 10/06/2004.

CHAPTER 9

SOCRATIC SELF-EXAMINATION BY MEANS OF NON-DIRECTIVE EMPATHY: THE ANATOMY OF EMPATHIC REFLECTIONS

MARVIN FRANKEL

Abstract

In this chapter directive schools of psychotherapy, exemplified by the approaches of Freud, Perls, Ellis and Gendlin, are viewed as descendants of the directive Socratic method of inducing self-examination: in contrast to Rogers, who broke new ground in facilitating self-critical examination through non-directive empathic reflections. The chapter will also discuss the anatomy of the empathic attitude. Finally, the essay shows that deviations from empathic reflections are disruptions of the non-directive attitude, and represent a return to the directive view that the client requires more than his/her own voice to find an optimal direction for his/her life.

SOCRATIC SELF-EXAMINATION

Socrates argues that the unexamined life is not worth living. What constitutes the unexamined life? The unexamined life is reflexively authorized by historical convention, habit and current intellectual fashion. It is not so much the absence of judgment that characterizes the unexamined life, so much as it is the absence of judiciousness.

It is important to note that Socrates does not recommend self-examination as an intrinsically pleasurable pursuit, though it may be. Instead, he reminds his readers that self-examination is directly relevant to how one should conduct one's life. In other words, self-examination is therapeutic, a means to an end.[1]

We learn further that self-examination is enacted through conversation; self-examination does not resemble the isolated activity of Rodin's *Thinker*. Instead, it is a public social activity. Self-examination is behavior: behavior that occurs between no fewer than two people.

A typical example goes like this: Socrates encounters a famous general on the streets

---

1. A key difference between self-examination in a Socratic conversation and self-examination in a psychotherapeutic session is that in the latter it is the client's relationship to the concept, for example, courage, under consideration that is the subject of analysis, rather than the meaning of the concepts themselves. Of course, it is highly problematic as to whether one can discuss the former without an understanding of the latter. It prompts one to wonder why philosophic discourses on the defining nature of virtues and vices are not required readings for psychotherapists.

of Athens and a conversation ensues on the subject of courage (de Botton, 2000). The general is rather confident of this intellectual terrain; after all, 'courage' is critical to the conduct of the soldier. He is convinced that he will explain the nature of courage to Socrates. For his part, Socrates understands that the subject of courage is profoundly important for anyone in conducting his or her life. Is there any serious venture that does not require courage? Even the asking of a question may require courage; insofar as it confesses one's ignorance. Although Socrates is aware of the practical everyday relevance of courage in every walk of life, he claims to be uncertain about the defining feature of courage, and so he takes advantage of this chance encounter to see what he can learn from the general.

Socrates might ask a direct question: 'What is courage?' The general responds with the weighty confidence of his status and common sense: 'Courage is when a soldier stands firm in the face of attack.' Much to the general's chagrin, the answer does not resolve the issue but prompts another question: 'Is the soldier lacking in courage when making a strategic retreat?'[2]

The inquiry exposes an inconsistency in the general's thinking. If we are familiar with these conversations, we know the inconsistency is of the malignant kind, and we know the outcome: the general discovers he is a general who does not know what courage is, but unfortunately, as we shall see, this insight is dwarfed by his defeat in conversation. How does one get defeated in conversation? It is when the conversation takes a turn and the subject matter becomes subordinated to the egos of the participants. Right and wrong become less relevant than winning and losing. The general loses the argument and, because he is more interested in the issue of winning and saving face, he learns nothing. As for Socrates, unlike the general, he does learn something. He learns that the knowledge of his ignorance (in this case his ignorance about the precise nature of courage) is well founded, and that realization remains a beacon to this day: knowledge of ignorance is an achievement. But it is more than that—it is an active point of departure for conducting one's life. Socrates can confess ignorance and yet live an active life. Doubt and uncertainty are not antithetical to living with a sense of conviction.[3]

In these dialogues, Socrates enacts an adversarial role. He is the gadfly. We are led to believe that without the searching questions of Socrates, the general would never discover his ignorance. In other words, Socrates is not non-directive in his probing of the general. But does the general profit from the direction offered by Socrates? Does the general discover his ignorance? Has he learned anything from the conversation? It does not take much insight to know that the general fails to discover that he does not know the nature of courage. We, the readers, know that the general is not about to go the Athenian library and pore over the literature to see what the sages have written about the nature of courage, or go about making inquiries of his learned friends. No, the

---

2. Not to belabor the obvious, but every client in psychotherapy often realizes that a strategic retreat may be necessary in the giving up of immediate gratification in order to win the war and gain long-term satisfaction.

3. Is it any different for the client who must make decisions under the penumbra of doubt, and yet sustain a vital life?

general feels defeated, humiliated; and we can be sure that when he speaks to his friends he will make further claim to the knowledge of courage that he does not have, and refer to Socrates as that nihilist who plays rhetorical games because he enjoys controversy for its own sake. In other words, Socrates certainly failed to teach the general anything about the nature of courage—or anything else for that matter.

Of course we must bear in mind that the general did not leave his home and take his walk that day wondering whether he possessed an understanding of courage. How could he, since he assumed that indeed he had that understanding? On being asked, he was willing to pass this knowledge on to Socrates and in so doing earn his respect, as well as the approbation of the gathering crowd. Consequently, the general felt he had all to gain and nothing to lose.

Unfortunately, in facing Socrates, the general was on a collision course. His need to demonstrate how wise he was rendered him incapable of becoming wiser.[4] Of course, Socrates is in part responsible for the failure of the general to learn anything at all. Socrates evidently feels that unless he poses questions upon hearing inadequate answers, little light would ever be shed on the subject. In effect, Socrates is saying: 'Look, general, you may not like it but you need me. I am necessary if we are going to penetrate your smugness and I am necessary if we are going to understand the complexity of the subject at hand. You must face the inadequacy of your answers to my rather simple questions.'

Socratic self-examination thus requires not simply a conversation of equals, but instead requires the student to humbly accept the superiority of the teacher. Of course, the irony does not escape us that the superiority of the teacher in this case is his appreciation of his ignorance, while the humility of the student is his appreciation of his arrogance.

As we can see, Socrates is hardly non-directive. He considers, and the reader agrees, that his questions are necessary if the general is going to realize the inadequacy of his knowledge.[5] This is primarily because the general does not question his conclusions, and the reader realizes that Socrates' questions are the questions the general ought to have asked of himself. What actually happens, however, is that Socrates forces him to defend his conclusions. In contrast to the general, the reader learns a great deal. Somehow the dialogue between Socrates and the general enables him/her to discover how little he/she knows about courage. Self-examination and enlightenment do take place for the reader. The reader is in a position to learn from Socrates for two reasons. First, and most significantly for the subject at hand (non-directive psychotherapy) the reader, unlike the

---

4. In psychoanalytic terms we can say that the general resists the cure (knowledge). Is not all so-called resistance anything more than the person's decision to maintain self-respect, rather than the respect that would be his/her due from the therapist if the latter's view was accepted? After all, the interpretation is deemed necessary precisely because it is assumed that the client is defending him/herself against the unflattering implications. Of course the directive therapist assumes that their view is the correct view of the matter and so in their terms the client is resisting the truth, be it the Oedipus complex or an erroneous generalization (Ellis and Harper, 1975).

5. This is essentially a repetition of the socialization during which the child must come to accept the greater authority of the parent. After all, few children would digest more than candy and ice cream if given the choice.

general, appreciates the strong possibility that he/she suffers from ignorance. Indeed, this is why he is reading Plato. In reading Plato, the reader expects Socrates to teach him/her something vital, something that will enable him to live a better and richer life, by allowing him/her to distinguish between a superficial and profound understanding of the issues under consideration. He accepts the fact that Socrates has superior knowledge to him, the reader. What allows him to do that? This brings us to the second major difference between the reader and the general. The reader is not struggling to maintain self-esteem in the face of Socrates' inquiries. The reader's effort to learn is not on a collision course with his effort to maintain self-respect. Socrates does not stand in judgment before him. He does not hear Socrates saying, in effect: 'So even a general, who has probably bestowed many medals on the chests of soldiers for showing courage, has little knowledge as to what constitutes courage.' Instead, the reader is alone with the dialogue before him. No one sees his/her confusion. Confusion is thus not a sign of stupidity, and therefore a source of humiliation; liberated from the prison of conceit the reader can reflect upon the dialogue and the meaning of courage in his own life.

The client who enters the office of a psychotherapist is much like the reader in one vital respect. The client realizes that he/she suffers from certain ignorance. There is a discrepancy between the way he/she ought to be conducting his/her life and the way he/she *is* conducting his/her life. Consequently, the decision to see a therapist is in effect a decision to be self-critical, to enter into a relationship that may require a protracted period of self-examination.[6]

However, unlike the reader of Plato, the client, while being self-critical, is also struggling to maintain self-respect in a face-to-face encounter with an expert: the therapist who, like perhaps every other individual he has encountered, may judge his inadequacies as critical character flaws rather than unfortunate learned behaviors. Despite the seeming non-judgmental quality of the therapist's manner, the client may imagine the therapist's judgment that he/she deserves his/her fate as a proper punishment. Nevertheless, despite these fears the client hopes that the following narrative will be acceptable to the therapist: 'I am not conducting my life as it ought to be conducted, but I want to appreciate myself for having this very concern. It is my understanding that you (the therapist) can help me without judging me as everyone else might or has.'

In the abstract, this may not seem to be so difficult a feat, but when the client describes in considerable detail his decisions, his goals and the consequences of his actions, it is difficult to comfortably maintain self-respect when the consequences ultimately involve the sufferings of significant others. The man who confesses that he no longer loves his wife has others to answer to besides himself. There are his wife, his children, his in-laws and his own parents, not to speak of friends. And there is now one more person who may be perceived as sitting in judgment, and that is the therapist. Of course, all therapists deny making moral judgments or judgments regarding the

---

6. I am here speaking only of clients who label themselves as such, rather than those individuals who are named and treated as clients by psychologists and psychiatrists. The latter were much more like the general than the reader.

intellectual shallowness of their clients. In fact, aside from the moral therapeutic movement championed by Mowrer (London, 1982), I don't know of any therapeutic school of thought that encourages the client to see him- or herself in moral terms. Quite the reverse was the case in psychoanalysis; for Freud it was an overly zealous conscience that is often responsible for many personality disorders. In this context, the client is repressed and neurotic because of their moral concerns.[7]

Aside from *being perceived* as a moral and intellectual judge, most therapists resemble Socrates in another important sense. Most therapists feel that they are necessary to direct and question the client so that he/she is able realize the full nature of their ignorance. The psychoanalytically oriented therapist certainly feels that he/she has realms of knowledge that the client will have to acknowledge and internalize. Unconscious defense mechanisms and complexes will have to be illuminated by the analyst, and it is inevitable that the patient will unconsciously employ strategies to evade learning. Consequently, like Socrates, the analyst feels it necessary to penetrate the defenses of the client, and he does so by making inquiries and interpretations. The behavioral therapist, the experiential therapist, the cognitive-behavioral therapist, differ from the psychoanalytically oriented therapist and from each other only in the kind of direction and instruction they offer. Directive psychotherapeutic schools of thought require that the client realize that the therapist has a definite piece of knowledge to convey, which is required to live the life that he/she wishes to live. Rollo May (1992) goes further in stating that a failure to direct the client to confront his moral life may encourage the immoral drift of the patient's life. However, therapists from all persuasions insist that they do not sit in judgment on the client.[8] Therapists will not even regard the client as ignorant, since the word has pejorative implications, but will speak of 'dysfunctional thinking'—as if the latter means much more than the former. Instead the therapist regards the client as mentally ill, or at the mercy of his unconscious or of his dysfunctional thinking, and no more responsible for ceasing to love his wife than having high blood pressure. The directive therapist wishes clients to view their life in terms of cause and effect. After all,

---

7. Socrates does not openly insult the people he shows to be intellectually misguided or vapid. The general is not ignorant by choice, but instead trapped by his conceit. But what reader can deny the pleasure in viewing the general's distress when his smugness and pomposity is revealed to the public?

8. In the famous documentary films three famous psychotherapists, Rogers, Perls and Ellis, do a therapeutic interview with Gloria. Perls aggressively asks Gloria a series of questions such as why she places her hands on her chest when speaking, or why she twists her ankle at particular moments, or where she would like to be when suffering from insecurity during her narrative. Perls evidently feels that such inquiries are necessary to provoke Gloria to reconsider her strategies for living. Despite his protestations of 'neutrality', Gloria feels attacked and humiliated as she attempts to fight back and recapture the moral ground that she feels she may have lost. Perls goes further and confesses that in the course of the interview he does not hesitate to manipulate the client so that she can gain 'his' insights. Ellis offers his explanation for Gloria's self-defeating strategies. Like Perls, he also feels that without his explanations Gloria would remain in the dark. In contrast Rogers, for 99 percent of the interview, simply offers a 'non-directive' empathic understanding of Gloria's concerns. Gloria repeatedly asks for advice but Rogers, for the most part, replies that he cannot provide the kind of answers she is looking for, but instead can possibly facilitate her finding her own answers.

by definition the neurotic is presumably not free to choose.[9] Rather inconsistently, these same therapists do not hesitate to applaud and congratulate their patient's actions that result in more socially acceptable behavior. It would appear that by definition mentally healthy people are responsible agents, and mentally unhealthy people are not responsible agents. Diagnostic categories are employed to illustrate the mechanical rather than moral nature of the neurotic's life, and this is the case even when the symptoms are amoral conduct, as in the case of the sociopath.[10] It makes no more sense to get angry at the amoral conduct of a sociopath than to hit your watch because it has stopped.

We can see, then, that despite their protestations to the contrary, therapists are likely to be perceived as critical judges, and so clients like the general may take flight from self-examination. In effect, the client may reject the messenger in rejecting the threatening message. When this happens it has been called negative transference. 'Is not a soldier still courageous when making a strategic defeat to fight another day?' was the question that sent the general into a hasty retreat and a rejection of the messenger, Socrates. Why was this question so threatening? There are two reasons. First, the consideration of the question ought to have been obvious to the general. How humiliating that it wasn't! Second, the general cannot answer the question. He is lost. Socrates is at fault. In effect, in offering direction, Socrates displays, however unwittingly, the shortcomings of the general. Is it any different in the psychotherapeutic context? In offering direction, is the client confronted with a reflection of his/her inadequacy? Indeed this happens so often that concepts like resistance and transference are terms that are understood and accepted as inevitable by-products of any protracted psychotherapeutic exchange.

It may well be that people like the general, who have no reason for questioning the nature of their convictions, do require direction of a sort to realize the problematic nature of the premises that guide their lives. But the client who enters therapy is unlike the general. In the act of seeing a therapist the client is behaviorally expressing: (a) some dissatisfaction with the conditions of his/her life; (b) some measure of hope that the conditions can be modified to permit a more preferred way of life; (c) a belief in their ability to make decisions and execute a plan of action, since after all the person did in fact decide to enter therapy; (d) a sense of responsibility, insofar as he/she decided to seek aid rather than stand pat. This sense of responsibility is also indicated by the fact that the client is seeking personal help in the hope that he/she could do something which can make a significant and positive difference; (e) a belief that there exists a body of knowledge that has some empirical and/or experimental foundation that can help him/her to realize a better way of life; (f) a willingness to be self-critical in examining what acts of commission

---

9. Nevertheless in posing questions, interpretations and suggestive advice the directive therapist certainly resembles judgmental authority figures from the past, and thus unwittingly encourages 'resistance' and other forms of defense.

10. It is hoped it will become apparent that for the non-directive therapist the client is held as a responsible agent only insofar as the client narrates a sense of responsibility. The non-directive therapist rejects the use of diagnostic categories, but instead devotes his entire understanding to the context that the client places him/herself in. A client may in fact employ a diagnostic category to describe their behavior, in which case the non-directive therapist will reflect the 'reality' of that category. A more detailed examination of the non-directive approach follows below.

or omission have resulted in a less than satisfactory way of life; (g) a hope that the therapist will be able to offer benevolent help rather than harsh judgments. However, since the client has a history of capitulating to the 'conditions of worth' of significant others, there is always the wavering fear that such hope may be unrealistic. In effect the client is a bit like Hamlet, with 'To be' illustrating a hope in a non-judgmental and rewarding therapist and the 'Not to be' illustrating the fear that the price of self-examination is the punishing judgments of authority. In these critical ways the client bears no relation to the general. If the general were to be like the client, it would be as though the general approached Socrates and said: 'I am in a quandary. I am a general and I sense that courage is an important element in military life, but I have little understanding of courage; can you help me?'

In any case, the client entering therapy is indeed confessing a certain ignorance in the way his/her life is being conducted. Perhaps, then, self-examination between a therapist and a client can proceed without the directive probes of the therapist. Perhaps the self-protective defenses of the client need not be mobilized to counter the threat of such directions. Perhaps the self-critical attitude that the client brings to the relationship can be encouraged simply through empathic understanding.

NON-DIRECTIVE THERAPY: CARL ROGERS

The first psychotherapist to depart from the Socratic model of inducing self-examination was Carl Rogers. However, Rogers had practiced as a directive psychotherapist and was in the habit of offering interpretations to his patients. Evidently during this early phase of his career he felt that such directive interpretations were necessary to induce therapeutic change. Rather serendipitously, he discovered that a coincidental empathic reflection just after a therapeutic session engaged the patient in a much more meaningful way than the many interpretations he had offered during the session. The idea was born that patients can redirect their lives under certain therapeutic conditions simply by listening to themselves through empathic reflections. It is important to note that Rogers did not change his approach because he felt his interpretations as a directive therapist had been wrong; instead, he felt that the directive way of offering such interpretations failed to produce therapeutic change.[11]

Freud encountered a similar problem when he offered interpretations. Often the patients rejected these efforts. Indeed, Freud coined the concept of resistance to explain the patent's rejection of the therapist's interpretations. Resistance was not an obstacle to

---

11. An interpretation offers the client a novel understanding of their narrative that is viewed by the therapist as necessary for subsequent therapeutic change. It is assumed that the client would be unable to realize this understanding unless it is provided by the therapist. In psychoanalytic therapy the interpretations are generally of three kinds. The analyst may point to similarities in the patient's narratives such as a patient's relationship to women in general; the analyst might suggest a symbolic meaning to a dream or fantasy; and finally the analyst may provide a historical interpretation of the patient's narrative. An empathic reflection, as we shall see below, is simply an effort to communicate an understanding of the client's intended narrative.

therapeutic change in Freud's view, but instead a palpable symptom of the illness. In contrast to Freud, Rogers argued that resistance was a consequence of directive counseling, rather than the patient's flight from health. Rogers went further and argued that the transference neurosis, another form of resistance, was also a consequence of directive counseling in that it established an authoritarian relationship between therapist and patient that closely paralleled the parent–child relationship (Rogers, 1951). It could be argued that Freud and other therapists fail, in part, when being directive because in fact their analyses or interpretations are simply wrong. For example, were women who rejected the penis-envy interpretation in flight from health or in fight to health? It also could be argued that Rogers, when being directive, failed to offer his interpretations at the proper time, when the patient was ready to accept an interpretation that was not immediately flattering. Ideally, psychoanalysts (Rogers was a Rankian) are trained to offer such interpretations only when they sense that the client is available to accept the 'truth' value of such interpretations. Ironically, the concept of resistance testifies to the failure of directive analysts to master this intuitive art. In stark contrast, Rogers realized upon giving his empathic reflection that the client was immediately in a state of readiness to entertain the relevance of her own narrative. Suddenly the concept of resistance became utterly irrelevant. This may be so because on hearing an empathic reflection the client is being asked to consider whether he/she is being understood, whereas on hearing an analytic interpretation the client is being asked to determine whether their own view is wrong and the proffered view correct.

At first, Rogers referred to his psychotherapeutic method as non-directive counseling, then as client-centered therapy and finally as person-centered therapy. Rogers preferred the term 'client' to 'patient' since he felt that it implied a greater sense of equality in the psychotherapeutic relationship. Finally, Rogers preferred 'person' to 'client' to underline the person-to-person or I–Thou relationship that pointed to the unique quality of intimacy, as well as equality that characterized the ideal psychotherapeutic relationship.

The essential feature of non-directive therapy or therapeutic self-examination was the exclusive empathic reflections of the client's narrative. The empathic reflections of the therapist are then reflected upon by the client and induce a clarification of and/or an addition to the story he/she wishes to tell. In effect, the client is attempting to make substantial changes in his/her narrative, in order to tell a more optimal story.

THE ANATOMY OF EMPATHIC REFLECTIONS

The client's story or narrative has four principal elements (Duncker, 1939). The empathic therapist attends to each of these elements, as well as their relationship to each other. First there is a *situation* that is being either described or implied. Gloria, in her filmed interview with Rogers (1965), presents four situations to Rogers with her opening statement. First, she expresses her concern over what to tell her nine-year-old daughter about her sex life with men she dates but does not love. Second, she wants to have an 'open' relationship with her daughter. Third, she refers to her daughter's former emotional instability. Fourth, she expresses a request for Rogers' judgment as to what she ought to do. These situations are all related to one another. Unlike the Freudian psychoanalyst, the non-directive Rogerian does not have a theory that can direct him/her as to which of the four situations is the most critical. For example, a psychoanalyst might regard the request for an answer as a sign of transference that symbolizes Gloria's need for paternal or parental approval, and thus the analyst might highlight that point or note it on a scratch pad. In contrast, the non-directive therapist works more intuitively in what may be called the art of this therapeutic approach and simply judges, however tentatively, which critical situation of the four is the most important for Gloria in her own terms. In the interview Rogers chooses to empathically address Gloria's concern over the loss of honesty with her daughter:

> Rogers: And it's this concern about her and the fact that you really aren't, that this open relationship that has existed between you now you feel that it's kind of (Gloria: Yes, I feel like), damaged.

This reflection essentially relates to the interrelatedness of the first three situations, but not the fourth. In being empathic the therapist never questions the 'reality' status of the situation, but instead offers an empathic understanding. If a client claimed to be Napoleon and was concerned about not receiving sufficient respect, Rogers might reply:

> Here you are an emperor, a man of extraordinary accomplishment, but the public doesn't give you your due.

The second principal element of a narrative is the *meaning* or meanings it has for the narrator or client. After presenting Rogers with the situation regarding her concern about telling her daughter about her sex life, she proceeds to explain why the situation is so meaningful to her:

> Gloria: I feel that in time she'll distrust me, yes. And also I thought, well gee, what about when she gets a little older, and she finds herself in touchy situations, she probably wouldn't want to admit it to me, because she thinks I'm so good and so sweet (um-hum). And yet I'm afraid she could think I'm really a devil. And I want so bad for her to accept me. And I don't know how much a nine-year-old can take.

Here Gloria is touching on five critical themes that are central to living an optimal life: honesty, trust, authenticity, reciprocity, and the limits of mutual understanding (without benefit of a Socratic question). Honesty can beget trust, as well as encouraging the subsequent honesty of the other, if only the 'authentic' real person is allowed to be seen; and yet the authentic person may be a source of revulsion to the other. Rogers empathically reflects:

> And really both alternatives concern you, that she might think you're too good or better than you really are, (Gloria: Yes), and she might think you are worse than you are.

Rogers is mistaken here. Gloria is afraid that her daughter might simply think that she is a bad person because of who she actually is, and not worse than she is. However, by now Gloria understands that Rogers is trying to communicate his understanding rather than a diagnostic interpretation, and so she knows that he is easily corrected.

Gloria: Not worse than I am. I don't know that she can accept me the way I am …

Perhaps a majority of empathic reflections attempt to capture the meaning of the narrative for the client. In the final moments of the interview Gloria discusses the unfortunate relationship she has had with her father and what it has meant to her:

> *Gloria: … that's a hopeless situation, I've tried working on it, I feel it's something I have to accept, my father just isn't the type of man I'd really like, I'd like somebody more understanding and caring. He cares but not in a way that we can cooperate, or communicate.*

Gloria feels she must accept the disappointing relationship with her father, and yet her sense of hopelessness belies acceptance. Rogers emphatically reflects his understanding of what this means to her:

> *Rogers: Leaves you feeling, nope, that I'm permanently cheated.*

Feelings are the third element of narratives. Feelings can invariably be classified as generally positive or negative to the narrator. Feelings are also attributes of ideas or meanings. How we think about a situation will affect the way we feel about that situation (Spinoza, 1982; Nussbaum, 2001). Consider the case of anger. Imagine that you are sitting on a train, reading a book, and something round and hard stamps hard on your toes and remains there. It is likely that your first response will be one of anger as you look up to attend to the careless person who stepped on you. You do look up, fisting your hand, and before you stands a blind man and you see at once that it was his white cane that struck your toes. Your anger vanishes in a millisecond; you are probably in a state of apology and might even mumble that you are sorry for getting angry, though you might not have said a word. So as not to disturb the blind man you lift his cane from the offended toe and go on your way. It is evident from this illustration that your anger was founded on the premise that the offender was responsible for the offense. Your anger was an attribute of that idea. An understanding of how a person thinks leads more often than not to an understanding of how they feel. The reverse is also true: understanding feelings can illuminate meanings. The reciprocity of the two is apparent in the following exchange between Rogers and Gloria:[12]

> *Rogers: You're trying like hell to be the girl he want you to be.* (On hearing Gloria's narrative of failing to satisfy her father.)
>
> *Gloria: And yet at the same time rebelling. (Rogers: That's right.) Like I almost gloated writing him a letter and telling him, I'm a waitress, which I expect him to disapprove of, I go out at nights, and I almost gloated, hitting him back, like now how do you like me. And I really want acceptance and love from him. I mean I know he loves me.*

---

12. Rogers and Gendlin mistakenly failed to see the two as inherently connected to one another. Both viewed feelings as lumps in the nervous system, accessible only to the introspective therapeutic exercise of focusing. It can be argued that the need for such introspective analysis only underlines the therapist's insensitivity to the meaning of the client's narrative. In this interview Gloria certainly goes from a 'flip' attitude to a mournful one without the benefit of 'focusing' (Gendlin, 1984; Rogers, 1980: 131).

It is here that Rogers empathically reflects on the fourth element of a narrative, and that is the *action* the person takes or considers taking with respect to the situation, the meaning and feelings the client is experiencing:

> *Rogers: So you slap at him and say, this is what I am now, see.*

On hearing this empathic response Gloria delves even deeper into her feelings of hostility.

> *Gloria: Yeah ... you raised me, how do you like it?*

And then, as is so often the case on being understood and on hearing or seeing one's life before one, an alternative perspective is illuminated without any prompting or direction from the therapist. Gloria immediately goes on to say:

> *But you know what I want him to say? I knew this was you all along honey, and I really love you.*

There is a forlorn quality to her utterance. Rogers picks up on it:

> *I guess you really feel badly, that, you think there's very little chance he'll say that.*

That empathic reflection serves as a headline for a more detailed evocation of her relationship to her father:

> *Gloria: No, he won't. I mean he doesn't hear I went, uh back home to him about two years ago really wanting him to know I love him, although I've really been afraid of him. And he doesn't hear me, he just keeps saying things like, Honey you know I love you. You know, I've always loved you. And he doesn't hear.*

The last sentence is pregnant with pathos. Gloria is not speaking *about herself*, but *out of herself. It is an evocative narrative rather than an analytical one, though analysis is embedded in the evocative presentation.* Rogers now empathically reflects on the meaning and the consequent feeling:

> *Rogers: He's never really known you and loved you, and this somehow is what brings the tears.*

The tears are thus inseparable from the meaning and the situation.[13] Imagine how utterly destructive to the narrative it would have been if Rogers attempted to have Gloria 'focus' on her feelings earlier in the interview, when she mentioned her father. Gloria would not have realized that natural harmony of meanings and feelings. A child of three cries when treated badly. A focusing instruction is not necessary. The restoration of this capacity is repeatedly demonstrated in empathic interviews. Gloria recaptures this capacity through the medium of empathic reflections. Here is Gloria's response to Rogers' recognition of her tears.

> *Gloria: I don't know what it is. You know when I talk about it, it feels more flip. If I just sit still a minute it feels like a big hurt down there. Then I, uh, feel cheated.*

---

13. The separation of situation, meaning, feeling and action is entirely arbitrary. A situation would not be a situation for a person unless it had relevance for the person (Dewey, 1896).

Here we see that the 'big hurt' is an attribute of the idea of being 'cheated'. Rogers empathically connects the two:

> Rogers: It's much easier … It's much easier to be a little flip, because then you don't feel that big lump inside of hurt.

While Rogers for the most part empathically reflects the meaning of Gloria's therapeutic narrative, there are moments when he departs from empathy and offers his own version of the therapeutic narrative. At the end of the interview Gloria speaks of the meaning of speaking to Rogers:

> Gloria: Um hum, that's why I like substitutes, like I like talking to you, and I like men that I can respect, doctors and I, I keep sort of maybe, underneath feeling like we're really close you know, and it's sort of like a substitute father.

Instead of offering an empathic reflection such as: 'I may not be the real thing but if you can't have a loving father then someone like me, someone you look up to, maybe, can be a good substitute.' Gloria may have replied:

> Gloria: Yes, maybe but it is just pretending …

But Gloria never gets the opportunity on her own to realize on a more profound level the counterfeit quality of her striving for a respectable man, because Rogers does not empathize but instead offers his own view of their therapeutic encounter.

> Rogers: I don't feel that's pretending.
> Gloria: Well you're not really my father. (Somewhat startled)
> Rogers: No, I meant about the real close business.
> Gloria: Well, see I sorta feel that's pretending too because I can't expect you to feel very close to me. You don't know me that well.
> Rogers: Well all I can do is what I am feeling, that is, I feel close to you in this moment.

It is evident that the emotional meaning for this encounter is quite different for Rogers and Gloria. The empathic dialogue that preceded this moment testifies to the capacity of empathy to bridge these differences.[14]

Rogers departs from non-directive therapy at another point, when he offers an

---

14. It is important to note the difference between sympathy and empathy. Sympathy involves a sense of identification with the narrator in a rather concrete way. One student, a single and divorced mother, on watching the film with other unmarried students was very sympathetic to Gloria. She could not understand why other unmarried, childless students were amused by her plight. The student in question was in the same quandary as Gloria and sympathy was her bridge. Gloria seemed old-fashioned to the other students. However, the student who was a divorced mother also had trouble empathizing with Gloria. Empathy requires a more abstract understanding of a narrative. I could empathize with Hitler and appreciate how betrayed he felt by his generals in particular and the German population, but I have no sympathy for him. Sympathy also conveys an acceptance of the other that is entirely absent in empathy, although it is often the case that empathic understanding seduces people into feeling a sense of kinship with the interviewer (Malcolm, 1990; Shlien, 1997).

analytic interpretation by referring to her unconscious defenses, when Gloria presses him for the third time to express his opinion as to whether to tell her nine-year-old daughter that she engages in sex with men, despite the absence of love.[15] In this case Gloria seems to enthusiastically accept the interpretation, only to slip seconds later into a 'hopeless' abyss. Her sense of hopelessness might be called resistance, since it may be viewed as a disproportionate affective response to the interpretation and thus a flight from coping in a realistic way with the interpretation.

> *Gloria: Do you feel that could hurt her?* (Informing her about her having sex without love.)
>
> *Rogers: ... I guess, uh, I'm sure this will sound evasive to you, but it seems to me, perhaps the person you're not being fully honest with is you?*

In this interlude Rogers has shifted from an empathic attitude, which relies on Gloria's capacity for evolving her narrative and perhaps realizes her unwillingness to face the 'truth' of the matter, to a more directive Socratic stance; to his credit he announces this in a straightforward way when he says: '... but it seems to me ...' Rogers then asserts that Gloria is in a defensive mode when he refers to her unconscious self-deceptive strategy in the sense that a person cannot consciously be dishonest with herself.[16] Consequently Gloria cannot either agree or disagree with Rogers, as she can when he is offering an empathic reflection. Instead, she has to listen to his version of her life, rather than proceed with her own. Rogers in his turn explains, as any good psychoanalyst would, what he means by her lack of self-deception.

> *Rogers: ... because, I was very much struck by the fact that you were saying, 'If I feel alright about what I've done, whether it's going to bed with a man or what, if I really feel alright about it, then I don't have any concern about what I would tell Pam or my relationship with her.*

In effect, he explains that the concern for Pammie is a displacement: a cover over her own guilt about having loveless sex. Evidently he feels Gloria would not have realized this insight on her own, which is curious since the perennial critique of client-centered

---

15. This question, like so many questions clients may ask, has no definitive answer. Nothing in the training of a psychologist or psychiatrist provides them with the wisdom to approach such a question. To evade this problem the directive therapist generally decides that the question is symptomatic of the illness. In contrast, Rogers generally appreciates that the answer to the question must be forged by the client, with the full awareness that regret may always be in the wings. However as we shall see in this particular instance Rogers does view the question as a symptom.

16. A person cannot be said to lie to themselves since that person would know the truth. Self-deception depends on the construction of two minds: conscious and unconscious. Rogers is here saying that conscious Gloria is denying the unconscious Gloria entry into awareness. Rogers never abandoned Freud's model of unconscious defense mechanisms, despite his phenomenological approach to therapy. Unlike Freud, Rogers seemed to feel that a therapeutic relationship that offered consistent unconditional positive regard and empathic reflections would invariably impress the client that defenses were not necessary. In contrast, Freud never abandoned the notion that defenses were always operative even in the fully functioning person.

151

criti qk uf J. C.

\|| therapy has always been the presumed failure of empathy to undo unconscious defenses. In departing from empathic reflections Rogers is, in effect, agreeing with his critics when he suggests more directly to Gloria that she is unconsciously deceiving herself. In any case, Gloria switches gears and instead of further developing her own narrative attends rather closely to the narrative that Rogers is offering:

> *Gloria: Right. Alright. Now I hear what you're saying. Alright then I want to work on, I want to work on accepting me then, I want to work on feeling alright about it. But that makes sense, that that'll come natural and then I won't have to worry about Pammie.*

At this point Gloria is upbeat. She seems relieved that Rogers has finally heard her requests for traditional therapeutic direction. She is redirected. The solution seems easy to her now. Her manner and voice seem optimistic. How simple: if she can accept herself, then her worry about Pammie will cease. She has accepted Roger's interpretation of unconscious displacement and is now ready to work on the real target: herself! But if indeed Pammie is a displacement-concern, as Rogers and other psychoanalysts might suggest, then simple awareness of the displacement will not extinguish the unconscious motive that established it.[17] And this becomes immediately apparent to Gloria as well when she states thoughtfully, without the upbeat quality of her former declaration:

> *Gloria: ... But that makes sense, that that'll come natural and then I won't have to worry about Pammie. (All said in an upbeat way) But when things do seem so wrong for me and I have an impulse to do them, how can I accept that?*

Rogers' direction and analytic interpretation has failed. She is back where she started. Gloria suddenly realizes that self-acceptance is not possible unless there are grounds for self-acceptance. The seeming direction offered by Rogers has done nothing more then return her to ground zero. How can she accept herself when she does so much that is unacceptable? This was a perfectly reasonable question that had been detoured for a few moments. At that point, Rogers does not enter into a further directive dialogue, but instead returns to the empathic mode of responding which quickly leads to Gloria's utter sense of hopelessness, as is so often the case when one has been led to experience a shallow optimism.

The client may be only dimly aware of these elements of his/her narrative, in the same way that a person might sit down to write a letter and be only dimly aware of what he/she is going to write. How often does this dim awareness of the content of the letter result in a many-paged letter in which the writer is surprised, if not shocked, to discover how much he/she had to say? How does this happen? The letter writer, on acknowledging the first sentence or two, is in effect empathizing with his narrative and then inspired to write further, and so this process of writing and acknowledging what has been written results in a lengthy letter. In effect, the letter writer is empathizing with him/herself. In

---

17. Furthermore, it could be argued that Gloria's rejection of herself is a displacement of the historical rejection she felt at the hands of her father. Would Rogers suggest that Gloria was not being honest with herself unless she came to this realization? This is the slippery slope that Rogers commenced when he suggested to Gloria that she was not being honest with herself.

effect, empathic reflection is an effort to communicate these elements of the client's narrative. In effect, the client is writing a letter on the parchment of the non-directive therapist's sensibility.[18] The non-directive therapist conveys an understanding of situation, meaning, feelings and action *only when* the client commences an examination of these elements. In commencing the subject, the client shows a psychological readiness to confront the problematic issue. The empathic therapist will never say: 'Do you know what I mean?' Instead, he/she might say: 'Is this what you mean?' Resistance is not possible, since the effort of the therapist is to capture the feature of the narrative that the client wishes to explore and thus a rejection of the therapist's efforts demonstrates therapeutic misunderstanding rather than client resistance. This is true even if the client subsequently acknowledges that the therapist's previously rejected reflection was indeed accurate. Consider the following hypothetical dialogue:

Client (1): My father was quite short with me.
Therapist (1): You could see that he was upset with you.
Client (2): No, not upset, a little frustrated maybe.
Therapist (2): He wasn't angry and in that sense upset, just frustrated because of what you said.
Client (3): I don't know why I'm splitting hairs here. You were right he was upset. I guess I don't like to think of my father being upset with me.

From Rogers' point of view the client came to realize his father was upset only on hearing the mistaken empathic reflection (Therapist 2). The client may view him/herself as being defensive (splitting hairs), but such a defense was mobilized against a mistaken empathic reflection.

What is the purpose of an empathic dialogue? After all, a person may realize a perfectly clear and coherent narrative as a result of an empathic dialogue, but clarity can turn out to be only a diagnosis of what has passed so far, rather than a guide for a better future. Clarity may be necessary for change, but is not sufficient.[19] It is here that most therapists feel they must take an active and directive stance. But recall that the meaning of the narrative is, for the client, an effort to improve their life in the future. The client

---

18. In effect, the therapist may be seen as illuminating the tacit knowledge of the client. Tacit knowledge refers to knowledge that a person may possess but lacks a medium for expressing that knowledge. Polanyi gives the example of a witness to a crime who cannot provide a description of the offender when asked directly, but when taken to a police artist succeeds bit by bit in providing hairline, eyebrows and jaw line and so the final sketch is a reasonable facsimile of the offender's face. In this context, empathic reflections serve the same function (Polanyi, 1958).

19. Although this is problematical, in that clarity when coupled with self-acceptance may be sufficient to inspire a person with a sense of resolution, there is a moment in Rogers' interview with Gloria when she exclaims that she feels so much better—though she hadn't solved anything at all. It is evident that in experiencing a moment of utter clarity and acceptance by Rogers she had accepted her problem, and in so doing felt a momentary resolution. Of course such moments do not last, for the next moment brings a fresh perspective, and clarity and self-acceptance are thrown once more under the shadow of doubt. Few people, if any, attain such clarity in a permanent way.

is not there for clarity, but change. The narration is an exercise in self-examination and criticism for the client. As we have seen, that is indeed why he/she has entered therapy.[20, 21] But an obstacle remains. This author has given more than a hundred graduate students the following exercise. They are to engage in an empathic dialogue with themselves, first by offering a comment and then an empathic reflection, and pursue the dialogue for thirty minutes. The vast majority stop after ten minutes. Moreover they find that they are suddenly blocked. It is as if they cannot go on. In reviewing these dialogues with students who wish to share them with me, I am able to offer an empathic reflection that often stuns them. Empathy is not sufficient to induce a change in the student's narrative. This is true also for clients. The client's self-respect, as it is for the students engaged in the exercise, is eclipsed by the threat of self-criticism. The therapist, in offering unconditional positive regard in addition to empathic understanding, allows the client to confront conditional positive self-regard. The general could not overcome his conditional self-regard when he faced Socrates, and Socrates did nothing to enable the general to experience being unconditionally accepted. Not surprisingly, self-examination for the general came to a hostile halt.

The client-centered therapist never states: 'You know you have my unconditional positive regard,' but instead shows by the absence of judgment and consistent empathic reflection the meaning of unconditional positive regard.[22] In this vital sense the client's attention is *directed* towards the therapist's attitude towards him/her. To the extent the client perceives and accepts the unconditional positive regard of the therapist, he/she will feel enabled to further question their perceived inadequacies. *Self-respect must always exceed self-contempt if self-examination is to have positive results.* The knowledge of the non-directive therapist does not reside in the whys of the client's feelings and conduct, but instead on how to conduct a conversation with a client that provides a climate of self-acceptance. At first the unconditional positive regard of the therapist allows the self-examination to proceed. Hopefully at the conclusion of the therapeutic encounter, the

---

20. Rogers has never put the matter in terms that describe the client's motive to enter psychotherapy as an opportunity to be self-critical. If he had, then perhaps he would have appreciated the enormous difference in attempting to treat hospitalized schizophrenics (Rogers *et al.*, 1967) who for the most part failed to show that they were interested in a therapy that encouraged self-criticism. Indeed, these subjects were characterized as being uncooperative. The creation of a relationship with an uncooperative patient requires more than providing unwanted empathic understanding. Is it any wonder that empathic reflections failed to encourage uncooperative subjects to reconsider the nature of their realities?

Instead of talking about therapy as an opportunity for the client to be self-critical, Rogers posits an innate motivational force towards the actualization of the individual's genetic blueprint to enter into the cooperative enterprise of society that permits the evolution of the individual, even as it furthers the individual's appreciation of their place in humanity.

21. The involuntary patient in a hospital setting may offer a narrative when one is requested, but may not have initiated a self-critical motive and so may fail to accomplish any more than a passively received clarity through the empathic responses of the therapist.

22. Certainly the parent who feels obliged to tell their child he/she loves him/her implicitly realizes that their actions may have conveyed the absence of love. Similarly when a therapist feels obliged to tell a client that he/she is not being judged, a similar realization exists that certain comments on their part may have led the client to feel quite judged.

unconditional positive regard has been internalized and has become self-respect.[23] What is the source of this unconditional positive regard? Rogers speaks of human nature in the voice of Rousseau (the pro-social 'Noble Savage' is corrupted by society), rather than Hobbes ('In the state of nature life is nasty, brutish and short.'), who expresses the sentiments of Freud. For many psychologists today these generalizations are unconvincing. The more we learn of the nature/nurture controversy, the less inclined we are to proffer generalizations. Nevertheless, it has been argued by Plato that human beings would never choose to be less than optimal. A person could not go to a campus and offer students drugs that would enable them to be lazy, greedy and selfish. No one would buy them. Consequently students—and faculty, for that matter—who possess these qualities did not choose them, but became personifications of them nonetheless. I could have unconditional positive regard for Hitler or Stalin prior to and during their execution or life-long incarceration, on the assumption that neither of them chose to be who they turned out to be any more than a rabid dog chooses to be rabid. And just as I could tenderly euthanize that dog, so I could offer unconditional positive regard to Hitler and Stalin. The premise of unconditional positive regard in this context is that human beings are always doing their best to realize their contribution to humanity, despite their woeful failures to achieve that result.[24]

THE EMPATHIC REFLECTIONS OF TWO NON-DIRECTIVE INTERVIEWS

In what follows are two interviews that I conducted, with a husband one week and his wife the next. In presenting these interviews I would like to make explicit the contrast between directive and non-directive therapy. An effort will be made to provide a textual analysis of my empathic reflections, and in so doing illuminate the narrative elements of situation, meaning, feelings and action, as well as the tacit understanding that is manifested by non-directive empathic reflections.

The first dialogue is with a person who was told a month before that he might have terminal cancer. This was our second interview. He is in his early forties, married and has two young children. After I present a portion of my interview with him, I will provide a second interview I had with his wife one week later. In each narrative the word 'courage' is never mentioned, but certainly courage is one of the vital themes under consideration. In

---

23. Non-directive therapy provides the client with two kinds of learning. First, the client is in a position to discover the enormous power of empathy in their relationships with significant and perhaps not so significant others. Second, the client may learn to appreciate the importance of fully accepting someone else in helping that person to accept him/herself.

24. The failure to appreciate that at any given moment we are doing our best to achieve an optimal expression of our purposes may be due to our learned tendency to judge ourselves in dichotomous categories. Consequently, we may often be able to say how we could have done something productive rather than watching television half the afternoon. However there was a third alternative. We could have done something much worse than watching television. We could have smoked opium all day. If we view ourselves in terms of what we did in light of what we could have done (better *and* worse), we might realize that the actual behavior was the best compromise we were capable of.

these interviews I made a concerted effort to be non-directive, or client-centered. That is, to the best of my ability I offered only my empathic understanding. Even prior to entering my office I assume that the client is engaged in self-critical examination. Consequently, I am not needed to induce a self-critical attitude: merely to facilitate it. At the conclusion of the interview, I would prefer that these clients have difficulty in locating any 'insight' I might have given them, or in being able to point to the role I played in helping them to have an enhanced sense of understanding and control in their lives.[25] This is because my aim is to embed myself in their narrative, rather than have them locate their meaning in my perspective. To the extent that the client feels I am wise or knowledgeable by way of a theory of the human condition, I will feel that I failed, for then I would have accomplished little more than empower my status at some cost to their own.

Client: (*sighs*) 'Well (*pause, sighs*) I got a second opinion … Same as the first.

It is not evident to me what this initial situation means to him. Is he resigned, angry, despondent, challenged? I offer a tentative empathic reflection to underline the possible meaning of this 'second opinion' for him. I am aware, of course, of how most people might react to such news but here, as always, I never assume the individual before me is *'everyman'*. Consequently, theory and research dealing with the reactions of people to negative life events can actually interfere with my understanding of this particular person's reaction to having a terminal illness.[26] I do have a notion of how I might react to such news but here, as always, I never assume that the person before me is like me. I never confuse identification with empathy.[27] However, the register of his tone, his pause and sigh suggested to me the following reflection.

Therapist: Exactly what you dreaded?

It is a real question. As I said above, the meaning and feelings he has about this situation are not evident to me. In offering it as a question, I am assuming the client will understand me that way. In effect, the client must be empathic as well.[28]

Client: Dreaded? No, but it is exactly what I didn't want to think about.

---

25. Once a client tearfully expressed to me: 'Christ, you really know how to walk in my shoes.' That is perhaps the only compliment a non-directive therapist might like to hear.

26. Broyard wrote a day-by-day account of his terminal cancer and entitled his book *Intoxicated by my Illness* (Broyard, 1992). Cancer and impending death offered Broyard an intellectual and emotional challenge. Socrates did not fear death, but instead engaged in the life he had conducted until the final moment—so why not he, Broyard? For all I know this client may be similar to Broyard, and view his illness as no less a challenge than the climbing of Mt Everest.

27. For this reason, in teaching students how to express empathy, it is a mistake to ask them to imagine how they would feel in a similar situation and respond accordingly.

28. The client is required to empathically understand every statement of the therapist. In this case I employed the word 'dread', and the client must assume he knows what this word means to me and how it might apply to him. In this respect all conversation requires mutual empathy.

My empathic response was inaccurate. 'Dread' failed to capture the meaning of his pause and sigh. In spite of my effort to see the individual nature of his response to the diagnosis, I may have been viewing him in too normative a way. Obviously I was not certain of my understanding, since I offered my understanding as a question. The client corrects me. He explains that he simply did not want to dwell on the subject. The emotional landscape of his response to the situation was not relevant so far as he was concerned. On the positive side, the fact that the client corrected me shows that he understands that I am simply trying to understand him.

Therapist: Yes, I see the difference. Dread has nothing to do with it. You tried not to give your medical condition any thought until you had to.

When making an inaccurate empathic reflection it is crucial that the client recognize that you appreciate being corrected. As I stated above, in non-directive therapy the therapist is a model for the client, for the latter's relationship to others. The client may learn that just as he/she appreciates being empathically understood and trusted to evolve his/her own solutions, so his/her friends and family may appreciate his/her acting similarly. In showing him that I can appreciate his distinction I am in effect modeling a non-defensive attitude.

Client: What the hell was the point in worrying about it? *(Raised voice)* You either have it or you don't.[29]

Therapist: You knew you would know the second diagnosis soon enough and now you ***do*** know. And there seems to be an edge of anger in that for you, though I may be mistaken there.

I sensed from his raised voice that he might be angry. On the other hand, perhaps it was just the voice of resolution. I could have asked if he was angry at being stricken with cancer. I could have asked whether he was angry at someone in particular. These questions, like all questions, imply that I, a therapist, like Socrates, am necessary for asking such questions—but as a non-directive therapist I believe just the opposite. The client will explore the nature of his anger—if anger it is—as well as the target of his anger, if and when he is good and ready. It is most important that he know that I have every confidence he can direct appropriate questions to himself. He hopefully discovers my confidence in him by my lack of probing. If I were a directive therapist, I could also be thinking about his comment in normative terms. In saying 'You either have it or you don't,' I might suspect a note of macho bravado and keep this in mind for future reference, when I felt he could appreciate the relevance of such an insight. However, as a non-directive, strictly empathic therapist, the thought does not even occur to me.

---

29 His narrative is evocative in nature rather than analytical. In asking questions the directive therapist may encourage analytical, highly intellectualized narratives which are then ironically considered to be a resistance against the expression of feelings.

Client (shouting and more evidently angry): Is that so crazy? Is that what you call being in denial? I despise that word. Last week I heard my wife … she was on the phone telling her friend I was in denial. She didn't know I was behind her, hearing every f—— word. I went ballistic.[30]

The situation or scene has changed. It is no longer what the doctors told him, but rather his wife's reaction to his way of relating to cancer. A directive therapist might wonder if the change of scene was prompted by his alarm at being told his prognosis. I simply follow the evolution of his narrative in the direction that he, the client, chooses. Because I did not ask questions, he is allowed to speak directly *through* me to his wife. I could almost experience her presence in the room with us. He seems to feel that his wife totally misunderstands his way of dealing with the diagnosis and prognosis of cancer. But, more importantly perhaps, that misunderstanding depicts him in a very insulting way. As a non-directive therapist I am not interested in *why* this is the case, but only *whether* this is the case. I also do not wonder whether his reaction is disproportionate to the nature of her misunderstanding. Such considerations are normative in nature and assume that the way most people react is the correct way to react.[31] This kind of normative diagnostic assessment is utterly inconsistent with empathic listening. Instead, I make an effort to underline the meaning of his wife's statement to him, as well as his feelings about it.

Therapist: It was appalling to you to see how she can so misunderstand you … Believing you were acting out of fear.

I felt certain that it was appalling to him and so I do not pose it as a question. Nevertheless I am confident that if I am wrong he is likely to correct me.

Client: I am not a coward!

Without being directed and asked, the client provides the tacit meaning of his wife's use of the word denial and the rationale for his outrage. It implies for him a running away from threatening truths. His wife had totally misunderstood him. As a directive therapist

---

30. The concept of denial is central to Rogers' theory of defenses, which is identical to Freud's though lacking the detailed analysis of the latter. Rogers' concept of unconscious defenses is inconsistent with his psychotherapeutic approach and will be discussed in greater detail in a subsequent paper.

31. Such normative thinking is endemic to directive therapeutic models. Consider a philosopher, who on hearing she has terminal cancer has a panic attack and seeks a therapist, because she regards the panic attack as shameful. She relates how she has been teaching Plato and the death of Socrates for more than thirty years, and she is ashamed to discover that her fear of death does not bear any resemblance to the reaction of Socrates to death. How many directive therapists would regard such a comparison as over-idealized, if not grandiose, and in effect inform the philosopher-client that her reaction is in fact quite normal, even if her shame over her reactions may not be? This is normative and, finally, prescriptive psychotherapy. In contrast, the non-directive therapist reflects the philosopher's surprise and shame and leaves it to the client to find a suitable point of reference, as well as a basis for compassion for herself in failing to meet the high standards she has set for herself.

I could raise the question that perhaps his wife did not mean it that way. Perhaps she was not suggesting he was a coward, but in fact may regard such avoidance on his or anyone's part as reasonable under the circumstance. I could suggest the possibility that perhaps his wife was having trouble accepting the prognosis and might, in some way, be projecting her own fears onto him. I could have speculated with him on these points in order to inspire some compassion for his wife as well as himself. However, this would be directive and would mean, as in any case of direction, that I believe the client requires me for such direction because he is incapable of providing it for himself. In being non-directive I maintain the basic premise that this self-critical client will make an effort to see the situation from his wife's perspective *if and when* he is prepared to do so. My role remains the same. I wish to respond to his last statement in such a way that he is given the opportunity to reflect on what he is saying, by stating in as succinct a way as I knew at the time his way of dealing with the uncertainty of the original diagnosis.

Therapist: You were just not about to anticipate the worst until you had to. Fear has little or nothing to do with it!

We can see how wrong I was earlier when I employed the word 'dread' to capture his feelings with the doctor. I was unwittingly viewing him in a way that was similar to the way he thought his wife viewed him.

Client: 'Right … That's right … exactly. Now I have it (*loudly*) Alright, the big C … Cancer. See … I can say it. Now what am I supposed to do? Bawl? Ask, why me? Why not you? Is that what Liz calls being in denial?

It seems to me that it is at this point that the client views me as a medium for self-examination. When he states: 'Why not you?' he is not speaking to me but to a collective 'you', as if my presence has become his sounding board. He does not expect me to answer. I suspect that if I were a directive therapist I might hear his final question as a question to me and make some effort to reply. A directive therapist might also wonder whether his attack on the concept of 'denial' was an indirect and hostile attack on psychologists in general and psychotherapists in particular, and thus the client's attention might be drawn to this possibility, since such hostility could undermine the cooperative nature of a psychotherapeutic interview. Since the client is not offering any such analysis, I do not even consider that possibility.

Therapist: You feel somehow that unless you get absolutely hysterical Liz will not believe that you *are* facing the reality of your situation.

I did not say the 'grim' reality of his situation, since he has not characterized the meaning of that reality yet for himself.

Client: (*Long pause, maybe two minutes*) And I won't get hysterical. I am going to go just

one step at a time. Have you ever seen this film, *Merrill's Marauders?*
Therapist: No, I'm afraid I haven't.

If I had seen it I would have told him so and added that I did want to know what special meaning it had for him. Since I hadn't seen the film, I simply assumed that he'd know I wanted to know the point of his reference to the film.

Client: Well ... it's supposedly a true story about this company of Marines who are dead on their feet, having trudged through miles of jungle to accomplish some mission. After completing one horrendous mission their captain or commander, I think the actor was Jeff Chandler, gets word that they will have to continue their march and accomplish yet another and more dangerous mission and trudge another bunch of miles and battle the Japanese forces at some place or other. When he tells the company ... about this new mission ... no one moves. They're wiped out. He implores them to get up and that all it takes is to take one step at a time, just one step at a time. Slowly one by one they get up and move through the jungle to accomplish the mission, going one step at a time.
Therapist: And that's going to be your way. Face each situation, each medical procedure, each decision a step at a time and let the future be whatever it is ...
Client: Yes, that's my way. *(Long pause)* Christ, and I don't even like Frank Sinatra.
Therapist: So you're not in denial but you have to do it your way, despite Frank Sinatra and despite Liz.

He has been able to fully articulate the premise of his actions and feelings. He makes utter sense to himself. Tacit knowledge has become explicit knowledge. He no longer has to justify himself.

Client: *(Minutes pass)* Look, I can appreciate how terrified she must be ... We have children ... I know she loves me, but I have got to fight this battle.

Liberated from the task of self-justification, he is free to reconsider the situation his wife is facing. Had I spoken about considering his wife's situation before he might have 'resisted', and I might have wondered, like so many therapists, why he is so threatened by such a consideration. Fortunately my non-directive responses are not guided by such speculations. When he states that he knows his wife loves him but he still has to deal with his situation, as a directive therapist I could ask why the two objectives have to be mutually exclusive. But here, as always, I allow him to narrate his own story and fully embody the fate of his story. I would no more think of suggesting that the two objectives need not be mutually exclusive than I would suggest to Shakespeare that Romeo and Juliet could end happily if only they would ...

Therapist: You do have this concern for her and you appreciate how worried she might be, but what else can you do given what you are facing?

Instead of suggesting that the two concerns are not mutually exclusive, I empathically reinforce his conviction that they may well be.

Client: Yes … You see we're facing different things. I am trying to keep a cool head in an effort to survive and she is trying to imagine life with me dead.

How many people would have the imagination, originality and courage to articulate in so clear a way the difference in his situation and his wife's? Had I interfered with his narrative as a directive therapist, and suggested that the two objectives may not be mutually exclusive, I might well have robbed him of the opportunity of stating his situation in so decisive a way. He stated the word 'dead' with a finality that phonetically resonated with the cessation of life. The aftermath of heaven was unimaginable for me when he said, 'life with me dead'.

Therapist: You see the two of you in completely different places.

I uttered the words 'in completely different places' by putting a special beat on each word as well as a slight pause between each word, as though to show my understanding that the two of them existed on two separate islands of concern.

Client: *(A few minutes pass)* Yes … I guess I am saying that. But why? I don't understand. *(Voice breaks and he is a little tearful)*

On hearing me say 'two different places' in so definitive a way, I suspect that the client 'reflects' on whether he is actually saying such a thing. The client questions himself and realizes the possible tacit meaning of his own prior assertions and states that he guesses that he is saying what I understand him to be saying.[32] For the first time he wonders *why* such is the case. I try to capture why this is so problematic for him, because I think he is wondering about that. A directive therapist might have offered some guidance: 'Perhaps you're pushing your wife away.' Such a comment, however true, would create a totally novel context in which to view his actions. Indeed, the client might have been grateful. In my non-directive way I did nothing of the kind.

Therapist: How could two people … married … having children, seemingly sharing a life, be in such different and separate places at so critical a time.

It could be argued that I am reinforcing his feelings of isolation from his wife by offering

---

32. It could be argued that my attempted empathic reflection was inaccurate and I led the client to accentuate the distance between him and his wife. If so, it would have only a momentary effect because the tacit meaning of the client's robust narrative could not suffer such a detour, if indeed it was a detour. After all, I did not detour his narrative when I suggested he might have 'dreaded' the diagnosis and prognosis that the doctor gave him. He simply corrected me. Recall also how Gloria corrects Rogers when he is mistaken.

these purported empathic responses. From my perspective, I am reinforcing his *questioning* of this separation. This indeed could have the consequence of widening the gap between him and his wife, but it also could have the consequences of bridging the gap. There is no way for me to know. There is no way for any therapist to know. From my own non-directive perspective the consequences of an empathic response remain the client's affair, not mine. I see no special virtue in helping to sustain his marital relationship. I would regard such a concern as patronizing and consistent with the goals of the religious right.

Client: *(Long pause)* I wish I could talk to her about this, but I'm afraid.

What is he afraid of? I sense that he is afraid that she will not understand his appreciation of her plight, but I am not sure.

Therapist: Somehow you can't imagine that she will understand your appreciation of her situation?
Client: Yes, she may think that I am accusing her of being selfish.
Therapist: Even though you *do* appreciate that it's natural for her to be worried about herself and the children.
Client: Absolutely! Hell, I'm worried about them too.

He has bridged the gap. I have not asked a single question. I have not provided a single insight that went beyond his own frame of reference. I have not underlined how his emotion got in the way of his reasoning. I have not suggested he focus on the elements of his feeling. I have not offered an interpretation that related to unconscious feelings or the connection between his wife and his relation to his mother.

Therapist: You're both in the same place on that!

On hearing me the client looked a bit bewildered for a second, showing by that bewilderment that I had not quite understood him. He wasn't viewing his worry about the children as bridging any gap. I had anticipated him rather than followed him. Nevertheless I was close enough.

Client: I guess so … I guess I am afraid. I don't like to think of her without me. She'll be so alone with the kids. I can't bear to see her that way. *(Crying; minutes pass)* You see, if I allow myself to think of her that way I won't be going one step at a time …
Therapist: You would have to widen your time perspective and contemplate the worst if you were to fully consider her plight.

This reflection states rather precisely the difficulty of fully bridging the gap between the client and his wife, as well as the nature of that gap.

Client: *(Minutes pass)* If I want to be with her *(very softly spoken)*.

Therapist: To embrace her … to be together.

Client: Yes … I … I'm not sure I know how to do it.

Therapist: You do want to be with her but you don't like to think that far ahead, to go more than that one step at a time.

Client: *(Long pause)* I'm not angry anymore … I don't like saying it but I did resent her …

Therapist: You have an expression on your face as though you were looking at her right now.

Client: I am … Maybe for the first time in a long while.

Therapist: You're smiling.

Client: I'm with Liz again *(starts to cry)*.

Therapist: *(After a few minutes)* Perhaps this is a good time to stop.

A few weeks later Liz came to see me and once again I attempted a non-directive, empathic interview.

Client: *(After a minute or so of silence)* Well now that I'm here, I don't know what to say … John found it really helpful to talk to you and urged me to come.

Body language and facial expression frame verbal communications. It is difficult at the time, if not impossible, for the therapist to know the weight of this nonverbal influence on his responses. Somehow I sensed that the relevant part of her opening comment was unrelated to John's urging her to come.

Therapist: And you draw a blank.

Client: It's just that I don't know where to begin.

She empathizes with me by showing her understanding as to why I would reflect on her drawing a blank.

Therapist: Everything seems just so urgent.

Client: Impossible to tweeze apart. *(A minute passes)* I hate saying this but I have this feeling. It just won't leave me. I know John is going to die. I understand that he just began his treatment and perhaps I'm being morbid but I have this sense … In two months, six months, maybe a year I won't have John.

As a non-directive therapist, I am not there to make her feel better. I am not there to give her hope. I am not there to spell out that perhaps she is being morbid. I am not there to ask her about her pessimism and where she thinks it comes from. These are reasonable questions for a directive therapist to ask. As a non-directive therapist I have only to make sure I am following her, in the hope that in following her she is able to follow herself to whatever illumination she could discover for herself.

Therapist: From an objective point of view the future is uncertain. You know that. You know that perhaps John might survive, but yet you have these intuitive feelings … this terrible sense that everything will come to naught. Your husband, this man you can now reach out and touch, is going to die.

Her sentence—'I won't have John'—sensitized me to the intimacy of their relationship, or so I thought. My response was a fleshing out not only of her sense of possible morbidity when I employ the word 'objectively,' but her closeness to her husband. I am doing this because I wish to show my empathic understanding of her narrative.

Client: (Crying for a few minutes) … There are times when I look at him, having dinner, playing with the children and when I wake up, I will find he is gone and that I had been dreaming.

There is not the slightest temptation on my part to comfort her. I am no different from a surgeon in my concentrated effort to simply understand the meaning of what she is saying. I am there for her and not myself, and so the question of my own feelings simply does not arise. On the other hand, I do have the strong conviction that empathic listening is the most comforting thing I could do.

Therapist: As if you have to be on your guard and remind yourself against believing he is alive even as we speak.

I added 'as we speak' to emphasize the ongoing nature of her vigilance.

Client: Exactly. You have it exactly. And I feel just awful about it. I'm so guilty. How can I share that with him? It's not fair. He's being so brave. But we make love and right after, and sometimes even during, I remind myself he's going to die and this is not real.

I do not have a PhD in wisdom or ethics. Consequently, I do not know whether her

---

33. The paper was given as a talk to an academic community. While reviewing my empathic reflections to the wife, one woman, (X), in the audience protested rather vehemently and with barely concealed anger that my reflections augmented the client's morbidity. For example, I might have told her that her feelings of being alone when her husband died were perfectly normal. She was utterly alone in this reaction. Other members in the audience were surprised that the ordinarily sedate X had spoken in so hostile a tone. Later I was told that the woman in question had just lost her husband to cancer. I would suggest that she confused the client's reality with her own, because she was too sympathetic. Sympathy is based on the assumption that you can understand the other person simply through identification as a result of being in a similar circumstance. How many people actually believe that only a man can understand another man, or a woman another woman, or a black person another black person? X viewed the efforts of my client to be morbid in nature and my following the client's narrative as less than helpful. In sharp contrast to sympathy, empathy is an effort to discard one's own frame of reference in order to understand the other as another. In effect, empathy must overcome sympathy if a therapist, or even a friend for that matter, is trying to understand the narrative of another human being.

guilt is appropriate or not. Is it fair or unfair to be preoccupied with her future when her husband is alive and breathing next to her? I feel no more in a position to resolve these issues or direct her in writing her story than I would feel capable of helping Tolstoy write a short story.

Therapist: Even as you feel the strength of his embrace you warn yourself the time left is not only limited but non-existent.[33]

Client: (*Nods; a long silence*) Sometimes I cry when he holds me at night. He doesn't know it or if he does he pretends not to … and I catch myself to be there for him.

Therapist: Somehow you censor yourself to be the woman he is holding.

I believe that the client is spelling out the sensual nature of her present intimacy with her husband. Even her seeming non-participation is rendered sensual by the very nature of her grief. The expression of grief is a sensual act.

Client: He has always been there for me. Always. Whenever I went off the deep end there would be John telling me either what I was afraid of, was crazy, or even if what I was afraid of happened, just what we might do … But I can't talk to him about this.

The client has gone from speaking of the situation (the likely death of her husband), the meaning it has for her (the loss of a loved one) as well as her feelings (grief, guilt and marginal helplessness), and now has come to wonder about what action to take in light of the above.

Therapist: You can't imagine how he could help you here … how he could reassure you on this matter.

I do not spell out the nature of that matter since she has already done it so well. Empathic understanding is not mechanical repetition. Hopefully by now this is only too evident.

Client: What's he going to say? Can you wait and bury me when I'm dead? He'd be right to be bitter.

Therapist: Your fears would understandably disgust him and perhaps rightfully turn him against you.

Here, as in the interview with her husband, it could be argued by a directive therapist that I am reinforcing her fears, rather than encouraging her to confront them. But isn't the client confronting her fears and isn't my empathic response reinforcing that confrontation? *At this moment* in that confrontation the client can see only how her husband would not appreciate her concerns, but rather her concerns would be viewed by him as trivial compared to his own. As for the next moment, that is in the hands of the client, not the therapist, from the non-directive perspective.

Client: I would if I were in his place.

Therapist: And you say that with considerable conviction as it that was very evident to you.

Client: (A couple of minutes pass) I have got to grow up. John will either survive or he will die.

Is this a change of subject? Is she instead realizing that she doesn't have to go to John for help, and that she has the resources to deal with the situation if only she can grow up? I did not have to encourage her to think about her own resources. She did not require my cognitive direction.

Therapist: You have to find a way of getting more mature or gain some perspective in order to face the future in a constructive way for John.

Client: You know, maybe I would understand John if I was in his place and he was in mine. If I ... if I was possibly going to die, he would miss me. I would be able to understand how we might be preparing himself for the worst.

Therapist: You wouldn't think that he was so unfair for having these concerns then.

Client: *(There is a four- to five-minute silence.)*

Therapist: You're thinking about that?

Silence is a therapeutic communication. I thought she might be considering what I just said, but I wasn't sure. In commenting on her thoughts I may have unwittingly conveyed my right to know what she was thinking about. As a non-directive therapist I do not feel I have any such right. I sensed that she would not construe me in this way when I asked my question.

Client: Well ... yes ... kind of ... I'm thinking ... I'm terrified ... truly terrified ... Maybe for the first time ... Not of John's dying ... but me and the children ... alone afterwards ... I don't know what I'll do.

Perhaps, in realizing that her concerns for herself were not selfish in nature, she is able to liberate these fears in a full way for the first time. Freed from guilt for having such concerns, she is able to express them. As a directive therapist I might feel obliged to explain why what is happening is happening so as to put a cork on her terror. As a non-directive therapist I wish only to be extraordinarily sensitive to the meaning and feelings that she has at this point in her narrative.

Therapist: Being a mother with a father ... a wife with a husband ... together with someone you love dearly is one thing, but being utterly alone as a woman and mother is something else altogether. Will you know how to do it?

A directive therapist such as Ellis might suggest she read his article on single mothers. Gendlin might suggest that she try to focus on the experiential element of her uncertainty as a mother. From a feminist perspective it might be suggested that she is afraid of being able to do a competent job, because that might mean she doesn't need to depend on her husband and perhaps she feels guilty about that, and such guilt undermines her confidence. Such considerations and perhaps a dozen more occur to me as I write this paper, but none of these thoughts occurred to me at the time of the interview.

Client: Yes, I get anxious just thinking about it … It will be just me and the kids.
Therapist: How will you manage without your co-captain?
Client: *(A full four minutes pass and her face, so grave the past few minutes, seems to lighten and I can see the possible trace of a smile)* How very odd … I just got this thought. Timmy got a toothache and I have to take him to the dentist.
Therapist: One step at a time?
Client: John told you that.

It struck me that her reference to her son's hypothetical toothache was illustrative of a single step. Moreover, her reference to that step came immediately after I referred to her husband as a co-captain, and the *one step at a time* was, after all, his mantra and so it seemed to me inevitable that he had offered that advice many times before. Indeed, previously she referred to the ways in which his counsel helped her in the past. In any case the interview came to an end a minute or so later.

NON-DIRECTIVE EMPATHY

It is doubtful whether there are more than a handful of therapists, if that many, who consistently employ empathic reflection as their sole therapeutic response. Certainly even those who refer to themselves as person-centered therapists view reflection as but one kind of empathic response.[34] This is, of course, quite true. All human communication rests on the premise that there is an empathic understanding between the communicants. If a person asks me the time and I look at my watch and tell him the time, that person feels I understood him perfectly well. I will not talk to someone unless I believe he/she understands or can understand, my narrative from my point of view. I do not, however, require their empathic reflections to assure me that such is the case.

Since all conversation assumes an empathic base, empathy has come to be equated to any response the therapist makes to a client. This has happened because therapists have lost sight of one vital function of therapeutic non-directive empathy. The function of empathic reflections is to enable the client to reflect exclusively on the nature of their assertions. Only empathic reflections enable the client to consider *exclusively the trajectory of their own narrative*. By way of contrast, in conversation I attend to the narrative of the

---

34. See, for example, Bozarth's discussion on 'emergent' empathic responses (Bozarth, 1997). For a more in-depth discussion of this issue see Frankel and Sommerbeck 'Two Rogers and Congruence', Chapter 4 this volume.

other and to my perspective in light of the other's perspective. The narrative of the other thus provides me with a contrasting view against which to see myself. In a therapeutic context the empathic reflective response of the therapist enables me, as client, to examine my narrative against some standard of my own. My critical imagination is thus the point of contrast to understand and control the narrative that constitutes the meaning of my life.

John's 'single step' prescription for conduct, so cogently illustrated in a film, was his standard for confronting illness, and likely death, rather than mine. It certainly was not a standard of any psychological theoretical model that I may represent. Empathic reflections permitted him to apply this standard to himself and to also realize its shortcomings. This was accomplished by my following and his leading. Empathic reflections serve an important function for the therapist as well. The non-directive counselor who relies only on empathic reflections does not have to worry about whether his/her knowledge, direction, wisdom or insight will discourage, rather than encourage, the richness of the client's narrative by providing too low an intellectual or moral ceiling.

By relying on empathic reflections we have no doubt that we could follow narratives of Proust, Tolstoy and Wittgenstein in no less a way than we could follow the narratives of any other client. However, it is difficult for us to imagine that in offering these individuals the insights of Freud or Ellis, or the behavioral exercises suggested by laboratory experiments with rats and pigeons, that we would accomplish anything more than depressing their interest in speaking to us again—despite the fact that our 'insights' are framed and certified by the PhD that hangs on the wall. One has only to read Wittgenstein's critique of Freud to see how ineffectual the latter would be in proposing his speculations on Wittgenstein's narrative as verities. But can we doubt how extraordinary Freud's empathic reflections would be if he devoted himself to that practice?

Despite the evident virtues of the exclusive use of empathic reflection, and despite the fact that the considerations raised in this paper may be difficult to refute, empathic reflections are often done as a means to an end rather than an end in themselves. Even the self-defined person-centered therapist may empathically reflect one minute, only to offer a question or a comment the next, as Rogers did in his interview with Gloria. However, in doing so the person-centered therapist forfeits the non-directive attitude, and joins the ranks of Socrates, Freud, Perls, Ellis, Gendlin and the rest.

REFERENCES

Botton A de, (2000) *The consolations of philosophy*. New York: Pantheon Books.

Bozarth JD (1997) Empathy from the framework of client-centered theory and the Rogerian hypothesis. In AC Bohart & LS Greenberg (Eds) *Empathy Reconsidered*. Washington, DC: American Psychological Association, pp. 81–102

Broyard A (1992) *Intoxicated by my Illness*. New York: C Potter.

Dewey J (1896) The reflex arc concept in psychology. *Psychological Review*, 3, 357–70.

Duncker K (1939) Ethical relativity? An inquiry into the psychology of ethics. *Mind*, 48, 39–57.

Ellis A & Harper RA (1975) *A New Guide to Rational Living*. New Jersey: Englewood Cliffs.

Gendlin ET (1984) The client's client: The edge of awareness. In RF Levant & JM Shlien (Eds) *Client-Centered Therapy and the Person-Centered Approach*. New York: Praeger, pp. 76–107.

London P (1982) *The Modes and Morals of Psychotherapy*. Washington: Hemisphere Publishers Corp, ch. 12.

Malcolm J (1990) *The Journalist and Murderer*. New York: Vintage Press.

May R (1992) The problem of evil: An open letter to Carl Rogers. In RB Miller (Ed) *In The Restoration of Dialogue*. Washington, DC: American Psychological Association, pp. 306–13.

Nussbaum MC (2001) *Upheavals of Thought: The intelligence of the emotions*. Cambridge: Cambridge University Press.

Polanyi M (1958) *Personal Knowledge*. Chicago: University of Chicago Press.

Rogers CR (1951) *Client-Centered Therapy*. Boston: Houghton Mifflin.

Rogers CR (1965) Transcript of Rogers and Gloria. In EL Shostrom (producer) *Three Approaches to Psychotherapy. Part 1: Client-centered therapy* (Film and Transcript). Corona del Ma, CA: Psychological and Educational Films.

Rogers CR, Gendlin ET, Kiesler DJ & Truax CB (1967) (Eds) *The Therapeutic Relationship and its Impact: A study of psychotherapy with schizophrenics*. Madison, WI: University of Wisconsin Press.

Rogers, CR (1980) *A Way of Being*. New York: Houghton Mifflin.

Shlien JM (1997) Empathy in psychotherapy: A vital mechanism? Yes. Therapist's conceit? All too often. By itself enough? No. In AC Bohart & LS Greenberg (Eds) *Empathy Reconsidered*. Washington, DC: American Psychological Association Press, pp. 63–80. Reprinted in JM Shlien (2003) *To Lead an Honorable Life: Invitations to think about client-centered therapy and the* person-centered approach. [P Sanders (Ed)]. Ross-on-Wye: PCCS Books, pp. 173–90.

Spinoza B (1982) *The Ethics and Selected Letters*. Indianapolis: Hackett Press.

CHAPTER 10

NON-DIRECTIVE THERAPY WITH CLIENTS DIAGNOSED WITH A MENTAL ILLNESS[1,2]

LISBETH SOMMERBECK

Abstract

This chapter deals with the questions that, in my experience, are the most frequent concerns of client-centred therapists in their work with clients diagnosed with a mental illness. I hope it will support therapist confidence in the non-directive attitude when working with clients who are sometimes very difficult to understand empathically, and with whom the therapist's capacity to put his or her own frame of reference out of the client's way is often put to the test.

Furthermore, and still with the intent of supporting therapists in their non-directive attitude, I will give my reasons for regarding client-centred therapy, with its pre-therapeutic extension, as the only suitable psychotherapeutic approach to working with the most disturbed patients in the backyards of psychiatry.

The chapter is written on the basis of many years of experience working in a small psychiatric hospital in Denmark.

Before continuing with the main points of the chapter, I will comment on the terms found in its title.

THE TERMS OF THE TITLE

'Non-directive therapy'

The therapeutic factor in client-centred therapy is assumed to be the client's experience of the therapist's unconditional positive regard for and empathic understanding of him or her.

Therefore, I regard client-centred therapy as synonymous with non-directive therapy. In order to maximally reduce the risk of conveying conditional regard to the client, the client-centred therapist consistently receives and follows the client's expressive process with acceptant empathic understanding. Doing this, the therapist's attitude is non-

---

1. With kind permission from the publishers, this chapter contains several excerpts from Lisbeth Sommerbeck (2003): *The Client-Centred Therapist in Psychiatric Contexts: A therapists' guide to the psychiatric landscape and its inhabitants.* Ross-on-Wye, UK: PCCS Books.
2. The author is deeply grateful to the editor of this book, Brian Levitt, for his patient work turning the language of this chapter into proper English.

directive, since empathic understanding is post-dictive, not pre-dictive.

'Clients'

The clients in the original client population of client-centred therapy actively sought out the help of the therapist and were well motivated in therapy. This cannot always be expected in psychiatric settings where some clients are only minimally motivated in therapy and are lacking any clear notion of what psychotherapy is about. The false expectations of the therapists in the 'Wisconsin Project' (Rogers *et al.*, 1967), were a major reason for the disappointing results of this project (see Sommerbeck, 2002). In addition, if the therapist wants to work with the most disturbed patients of psychiatry, it will be the therapist who initiates the contact, not the patient. These patients do not define themselves as psychotherapy clients in their relationship with the therapist. For these patients the term 'client' is, therefore, somewhat of a misnomer, but for lack of a more appropriate term, I will take the liberty of speaking about 'clients' throughout this chapter, acknowledging, though, that some of these 'clients' do not define themselves as such.

'Diagnosed'

In client-centred therapy the conditions necessary and sufficient for facilitation of the client's most constructive potentials are trusted to be the same for everybody, regardless of diagnosis. The client-centred therapist, therefore, does not change his or her approach according to the psychiatric diagnosis of the client. However, some of the questions that can become concerns for the therapist are often related to the client's psychiatric diagnosis. Thus, it is for descriptive reasons that terms like 'psychotic', 'depressive', 'maniac', etc. are used in the chapter. There is no prescriptive intention implied.

'A mental illness'

The question 'Do mental illnesses exist?' is a very legitimate question for two reasons. First, nobody really knows whether mental illnesses exist as discrete, well-delineated disease entities, although present-day, biologically oriented psychiatry mostly pretends that they do.

My own experience tells me that they do not; the symptoms and problems of psychiatric patients seem to me to blend imperceptibly into each other on a continuum from what is considered normal to what is considered a mental illness. Likewise, there does not seem to exist a well-defined limit between the assumed mental illnesses of, say, schizophrenia and depression. Patients rarely fit nicely into one diagnostic category or the other, and the use of psychiatric diagnoses is very unreliable.

Second, one can doubt that mental illnesses exist, as such, because psychiatric diagnoses are purely symptomatological. In all other branches of medicine, diagnoses tell about the cause of the diagnosed illness. Nobody, however, really knows what the causes are of the conditions seen in psychiatry, so diagnoses are made on the sole basis of a patient's presenting similarity with this or that list of symptoms. This is another reason I am doubtful about the existence of mental illnesses, as such. The term 'assumed' is therefore implied whenever I use terms like 'mental illness', 'psychopathology', etc.

171

FREQUENT QUESTIONS

WHERE IS THE RED THREAD?

It can sometimes be difficult to follow the narrative of psychotic clients because they often jump seemingly incomprehensibly from one issue to another, and sometimes even a single sentence seems disconnected from the one preceding it and the one following it. In the worst cases, psychiatry speaks of 'word salad'. There is no sense of a 'red thread' that one is used to following with more ordinary clients. It is therefore important for the therapist to have a great tolerance for 'missing links'.

The therapist will understand the psychotic client in bits and pieces, but he or she must tolerate the lack of connection between these bits and pieces. What the client says can seem very fragmented, and in following this, the therapist's responses will be fragmented, too: one response feels dissociated from the preceding one and from the next to come. Therapy with these clients is an exercise in 'holding and letting go'. It is important that the therapist not hold on to the understanding of one moment, in order to save his or her own sense of continuity. Rather, the therapist must let go of this understanding in order to follow the client's next move, even if it seems contradictory to the one preceding it. The frequent lack of the experience of a red thread belongs to this type of process. It is not a sign of therapist incompetence.

An example of dialogue with a psychotic client will follow the next section, and it contains examples of seemingly incomprehensible jumps in the client's narrative.

AM I COLLUDING WITH PSYCHOTIC IDEATION?

It can, of course, be difficult to follow a client with empathic understanding in a psychological world that is radically different from the therapist's world or the world of 'consensual reality'. The psychotic client's world is a world that, from the therapist's point of view, is full of hallucinations and delusions. The therapist's capacity to suspend his or her own concept of reality is put to a hard test in therapy with clients whose ideation seems manifestly psychotic. With these clients it is particularly important to remember that empathic understanding is neutral as far as confirmation or disconfirmation of the client's concept of reality is concerned.

The idea of the neutrality of empathic understanding is often not fully grasped in psychiatric circles. In these circles, empathic understanding is often thought of as validating or confirming the other person's concept of reality. In psychiatric circles, a myth exists that empathic understanding of psychotic ideation is a kind of psychosis-reinforcing collusion with the client, and therefore harmful. Most professionals in psychiatry respond to expressions of psychotic ideation with prompt efforts at 'reality correction', as it is commonly called.

Contrary to this myth of collusion, it has been my own experience that it is 'reality correction', not empathic understanding, that is potentially harmful to clients diagnosed with psychosis. 'Reality correction' is, by its very nature, confrontational. Patients with a diagnosis of psychosis, in comparison with other clients, ordinarily feel more threatened by confrontational approaches. Confronted with 'reality correction' they frequently tend to defend their conception of reality, thereby rigidifying and solidifying it and often expanding upon it with more psychotic details and nuances, thus developing their psychotic ideation further. In short, clients can become more psychotic when confronted with 'reality correction'.

In contrast, accurate empathic understanding, non-confrontational as it is, gives the client no reason to defend his or her perception of reality. It is, precisely, the safe and acceptant climate of the empathic context that leaves the client feeling free to explore his or her perception of reality and, eventually, to formulate alternatives to it. This is not surprising from a client-centred point of view, since 'reality correction' is, basically, an expression of negative regard for the client's own perception of reality. In client-centred therapy, unconditional positive regard for the client is, as already mentioned, ordinarily seen as the primary therapeutic agent.

The following excerpt of dialogue is an example of (1) fragmentation, and (2) the typical transition from expression of relatively more to relatively less psychotic ideation in the course of a client-centred therapy session. It illustrates the client's jumps between seemingly unrelated issues, and it illustrates that empathic understanding (and the contact reflections of pre-therapy that characterise the first part of the session) is in no way reinforcing of, or colluding with psychotic ideation. The excerpt is from the sixth session of therapy, and the therapist is the one who has taken, and still takes, the initiative in establishing contact with the client. The therapist sees this patient in the patient's room on the ward.

T: I thought that maybe … if there was anything you might like to tell me today, about how you feel, and about your situation, how you look on it?

C (in a very matter of fact, 'there's no discussing it', way): I feel well.

T: You say you feel well and you look at me very determined.

C: Yes, I feel well, and that's a fact.

(Pause; C looks down on his lap)

T: You say it's a fact you feel well, and now you look down and are quiet.

C: Yes, I feel well when I drink coffee, juice, and things like that, but water is no good— and I've stopped eating.

T: As long as you can drink something that tastes good you feel well, but you've lost your appetite?

C: Yes, and I also feel well because I'm now totally out of the church.

T: It's a relief to be finally out of it.

C: Yes, well, I'm not totally out of it, I still receive their newsletter, and I can't read it, it was a mistake that I joined the church, I'm confused about it—I have to tell them to stop sending the newsletter.

T: The church was really too much, and now you need to get that newsletter off your back, that'll be a relief?

C: Yes, that's it, I need to stop the newsletter and to have my mail delivered here, then I can feel fine—but I do feel fine here.

T: You like to be here, and if you had these things settled you could enjoy it better, be more at ease?

C: Yes, precisely, that would be nice.

(Pause, C moves his head around in abrupt jerks, staring at different spots)

T (slightly mirroring C's movements): You turn your head this way and that way and look around.

C (grinding his teeth): My father is Satan.

T: You grind your teeth and say 'My father is Satan'.

C: He has slaughtered my mother, he is the real Satan, and the Danes are his devils and devils' brood.

T: He is the real Satan, because he has slaughtered your mother, and the Danes are his devils and devils' brood.

C: Not all Danes, people here are nice to me, but he has slaughtered my mother and if he does it again I'll slaughter him.

T: You feel you'll slaughter him if ...

(C interrupts eagerly)

C: Yes, he has terrorised my mother all her life, psychological terror ... her name is Maria, if Satan harmed Maria ... Joseph would slaughter him; I'm Joseph.

T: You say 'I'm Joseph' and you feel like you think Joseph would feel if Satan harmed Maria, is that it?

C (nodding his head and smiling): Yes, and I'm not afraid of Satan, I'm not afraid of anything.

T: You smile at the thought that you are not afraid of Satan or ...

C (interrupting): Yes, I'm not afraid, I'm glad of that, but why does he always have to be so rotten, last time he visited he brought some fruit from his back garden; it smelled awful and then I took a bite and it tasted hellish ... I threw it all away.

T: You think that everything he brings ...

C (interrupting): Yes, why does he have to be so provocative?

T: Like 'Why the hell can't you buy me some good fruit that I like, instead of bringing me the rotten leftovers from your back garden?'

C: Yes, I think he never spreads anything but shit around him—I can't bear being near him.

The client spends the rest of the session exploring his relationship with his father in a way that seems much more coherent and less infiltrated with psychotic ideation than in the first part of the session. This does not mean that the psychotic ideation does not recur. It did with this client, and with most psychotic clients it does, so processes like the one depicted will be repeated many times with more or less variation. Slowly and gradually, though, the client's psychological world normally becomes more continuously compatible with 'consensual reality'.

Note the sudden jumps from insisting on his well-being, to his eating habits, to his relationship with the church, and to his father. One can wonder about the connection between these issues, but one will probably never know. Further, the therapist's responses are as fragmented as the client's expressions.

Note also how the generalisation about Danes becomes modified, and how his conception of his father is modified. At first the client's father is, literally, Satan; later he takes on more humane proportions and is 'merely' unbearably provocative. Also, 'slaughter' becomes 'psychological terror'. I feel convinced that if someone had pointed out to him that his identification of his father with Satan was unrealistic, in the name of 'reality correction' and out of fear of colluding with his psychotic ideation, he would have persevered more rigidly in this idea in order to convince the other that he was right. Openness to corrective experiences is a sign of maturity that is not characteristic of psychotic people. It was acceptant empathic following of his journey in his own psychological landscape that created the safety and space for him to consider alternatives in his conception of that landscape.

The excerpt contains some examples of the so-called 'contact reflections' of pre-therapy (Prouty, 1994). Such contact reflections occur frequently in work with psychotic clients, and the next session will deal with this issue in more detail.

I HAVE NO IDEA WHAT IS GOING ON IN THE CLIENT—WHAT DO I DO?

Some psychiatric patients, typically with a diagnosis of schizophrenia, are experienced as being 'out of contact' ('autistic'), either for long periods of time or for shorter, more fleeting instants. One has no idea what is going on in them. I used to feel that I had nothing to offer these patients, because there seemed to be nothing for me to empathise with in my contact with them. This has changed since I learned about Garry Prouty's Pre-Therapy (Prouty, 1994). Now my answer to this predicament is to add the contact reflections of pre-therapy to the ordinary empathic understanding responses of client-centred therapy.

Pre-therapy can be seen as an extension of client-centred therapy that allows the therapist to relate therapeutically with the most seriously disturbed psychiatric patients. In pre-therapy the ordinary empathic understanding responses of client-centred therapy are replaced by so-called contact reflections, which offer the therapist an appropriately concrete way of following the client's overt 'being in the world' with unconditional acceptance. The contact reflections empathise with the client's expressive process as such, not with something the client might wish the therapist to understand about his or her inner goings-on. These clients do not seem to entertain a wish for this kind of understanding—or they take it for granted. The concrete level of empathising with these individuals is reminiscent of empathising with small children. When little Peter claps his hands in jubilation at seeing the train pass by, I think the accepting and empathising parent will, more likely than not, clap his/her hands, too, with an expression of jubilation on his/her face. Grownups spontaneously and lovingly reflect babies and small children literally. They say: 'My, aren't you crawling fast', or 'Oh, what a big smile', or 'Now you paint it red all over', etc., and they look forward, lovingly, to the infant's 'next move'.

Thus contact reflections are totally literal reflections of conspicuous elements in the client's immediate surroundings, of the client's posture, movements or facial expressions, or of the client's words. They are just what I need when I have no idea what is going on in the client. They have also made it possible for me to approach, on my own initiative, the patients in the remotest backyards of psychiatry with unconditional acceptance.

As I have become more experienced with the application of contact reflections and as I have experienced the positive effects of contact reflections in establishing contact with the patient, I have come to experience the concreteness of these reflections as a gentle expression of my wish to get in contact with the client. They express my acceptance of the client, my wish to be with the client, and my empathy with the conspicuous features of the client's behaviour in relation to his or her immediate environment. Most of my contact reflections hover softly somewhere between a declaration, which would have been a mockery of the client's expression, and a question, which would not only have been a mockery of the client's expression, but also an intrusion into the client's expressive process.

In my practice, today, I fluctuate rather effortlessly, and without really noticing it, between the empathic understanding responses of client-centred therapy, when I feel I have a sense of what is going on in the client, and the contact reflections of pre-therapy, when I do not. The following example illustrates this fluctuation between the empathic understanding responses of client-centred therapy and the contact reflections of pre-therapy. In the example, ER refers to ordinary empathic understanding responses (empathic reflection). SR, BR, FR, WWR and RR refer to the contact reflections of pre-therapy (situational reflection, body reflection, face reflection, word-for-word reflection and reiterative reflection, respectively).

In our first three therapy sessions, Lillian, diagnosed with paranoid schizophrenia, talked rather freely of her conviction that her new neighbours were out to kill her. The consequence of this conviction was that she started living in her apartment as if she were not there. She stopped going out, opening windows, turning on the light, using radio and television, flushing the toilet, etc. Finally she mustered all her courage and phoned the police, and told them in a whisper of her predicament. The police offered to come and take her to the hospital. She accepted this offer with relief and took part in the various activities of her ward with great pleasure, feeling safe and comfortable in the hospital.

In the fourth session Lillian's condition has changed. All energy seems drained out of her, she sits with her head bent down so I cannot see her face, and she does not start talking eagerly as she did in the former sessions. She sits like this for some minutes, and I have no idea what is going on in her.

T: We sit in silence and you have bent your head down. (SR, BR)
(L stays in the same position for a while. Then she raises her head a little and takes both her hands to her head, pulling her hair and using her hair as 'handles' to shake her head.)

T (Mirroring her gesture): You shake your head with your hair. (BR)

(L lets her hands sink into her lap and turns to look at me with what to me seems like an expression of hopelessness in her face and eyes.)

T: You look hopeless? (FR)

L (Looking down again): Yes ... I don't know.

T: You said: 'Yes', and 'I don't know'. (WWR)

L: I don't know what to say—I'm so tired.

T: Too tired even to talk; is that how you feel? (ER)

L: Yes ... Yes.

(There is a long pause, when T stays silent and L remains motionless, with her head bent down, as at the start of the session. Then the loud 'cock-a-doodle-doo!' of a nearby cock is heard and L raises her head and looks towards the window.)

T: You look up at the sound of the cock. (BR, SR)

(L Turns towards me and smiles at me, and I smile at her.)

T: You looked up at the sound of the cock and now we smile at each other and you look glad. (RR, SR, FR)

L: We used to have lots of animals at home when I was a kid; cocks, too; sometimes they kept everybody awake (giggles).

T (smiling): Feels good and funny, recalling that, right? (ER)

L: Yes, (looking sad), I wish I could be there again.

T: You look sad when you think of how you miss being at home as a kid. (FR, ER)

L: Yes, I wish I had my family, I feel so lonely, and I don't know what to do, I'm scared of returning home.

T: If I had a family to return home to, I wouldn't feel so lonely and scared, is that it? (ER)

L: Yes, my contact nurse proposed the other day that I try to go home to my apartment with her, one of these days, to see how it feels; I think they want to dismiss me from hospital soon.

T: You think they see you as being ready to be dismissed soon, but you don't feel ready at all. You feel they hurry you a bit? (ER)

L: Yes, but I think I should try to go home with her.

T: You feel you ought to give it a try? (ER)

L: Yes, I really don't know what to do, how I shall manage at home. I'm not so scared of the neighbours anymore, but still, maybe I'll do something that disturbs them, so they'll complain about me to the janitor and have me thrown out of the apartment, that's what I'm thinking about all the time.

T: You just worry so much that you won't do things right at home, that you'll somehow displease your neighbours? (ER)

L: Maybe—they have two children so they are four and I'm alone, and their apartment is the same size as mine ...

T: Feels as if you haven't got the right to occupy that much space when they have so little? (ER)

L: I know I've got the right, of course, but still ... I guess I feel somehow guilty about it

... but that's only ... it's weighing me down, the thoughts; they keep turning and turning around in my head. (Bends her head down and away again, saying this.)

T (again feeling somewhat out of contact with L): You said 'It's weighing me down' and you bend your head. (WWR of the part of the client's statement that seemed most meaningful to her, combined with BR)

L (after a long pause, almost inaudible): I don't think I can go home with K (contact nurse); do you think she will be annoyed with me?

T: I don't know, I wish I could tell you for sure that she wouldn't be, 'cause I guess you are really afraid to displease her? (Answer to L's question and ER)

L: Yes, she has done a lot for me and she offers to escort me home, and then I can't even think of trying.

T: Like there'd be nothing you'd wish more than to feel able to accept her offer and feel helped by it, but instead you feel burdened by it, is it something like that? (Normal ER.)

L: Yes, very, and I don't know how to tell her.

T: Mhm, hm, How shall I tell her?

L: Mhm. (Stays silent for quite a while, looking rather thoughtful.)

T: You look thoughtful (FR)

L: Maybe if we postponed it a week or two, maybe that would be OK with K, after all I haven't been in hospital very long, not nearly as long as many of the other patients.

From this point on, Lillian seemingly stays in contact for the rest of the session. In this session and in the succeeding ones, which follow much the same pattern as above, Lillian expresses much deeper feelings of worthlessness, loneliness and anxiety about managing on her own. The problems with the neighbours are just the last event in a long and hard struggle to live a life as close as possible to what she considers normal.

The fluctuation between empathic reflections and contact reflections that is illustrated in this example is characteristic of much of my work with psychiatric clients and I experience no sharp distinction between the ordinary empathic understanding responses (empathic reflection) of client-centred therapy and the contact reflections of pre-therapy. Instead they seem to me to change imperceptibly into each other.

DO I DISTURB THE CLIENT'S PROCESS WITH MY WISH TO UNDERSTAND?

Particularly with clients diagnosed with manic and megalomanic psychoses, I sometimes feel that I might as well not be there, that the client might as well be talking to the wall, that the client talks for the sake of talking, without any wish that I understand anything. John Shlien wrote (1961: 296) that communication means taking into account the other, and that 'acknowledging the other is essential to the existence of mind, from beginning to end'. The clients I am talking about certainly do not seem to take me, as the other, into account. In their apparently unreflective stream of talking they do seem quite mindless, as if they were talking machines. Furthermore, this has nothing to do with whether the content of their talking is considered psychotic or not. I used to find it hard to pay attention to what these clients were saying. The reason for this was that the client, seemingly, did not reach out for my attention and understanding. I used to feel lost, not knowing what to say and do, because attending to the client's communication, with the intention of understanding it empathically, was what I assumed my work to be about. Eventually I decided to find a way to do my job, rather than just let the client's stream of talk pass in one ear and out the other so that I felt left behind at the station with the train long gone. I decided to do what was necessary to check my tentative empathic understanding with the client, which meant, sometimes quite forcefully, interrupting the client's monologue with a cry of: 'Wait a minute! Is this what you are saying?' (followed by my idea of what the client was talking about). It has turned out that this normally engages the client in a dialogue for a short while, until monologuing takes over again, and the process is repeated. Slowly, however, the client normally starts to demonstrate an interest in my interest in him or her. The periods of dialogue become longer, and the energy invested in upholding them is more equally distributed between the client and myself.

Barbara Brodley (1998: 25) discusses five criteria for making tentative empathic understanding responses, characterizing one of these as follows: 'when the therapist feels an impulse or desire to express and communicate him- or herself while immersed in the attempt to empathically understand'. Brodley further expands on this:

> This impulse or desire to express oneself, which is resolved through expression of understandings, probably originates in the interpersonal and interactional nature of the psychotherapeutic relation. Inherent in an interpersonal relation is an expectation of an exchange—a back and forth characteristic of the interaction. The deeply empathically engaged therapist, however, seldom will experience any specific content from his or her own frame of reference that could serve as a vehicle for self expression. Thus, when the interaction involves almost exclusive focus and attention on the client member of the dyad, the therapist may feel the desire to be responsive and expressive through the vehicle of tentative empathic understandings. (p. 25)

It is this desire of the therapist that makes the difference between monologue and dialogue with many manic and megalomaniac clients.

Sometimes it is difficult to strike the right balance between the therapist's wish to understand the client and the therapist's wish not to disturb the client's process. Welcome interest and disturbing interference seem close neighbours with these clients. There is a quality of 'getting on' and 'getting off' about the process, as the therapist takes heed of the client's signals about the appropriateness, to the client, of the therapist's interest in understanding the client. I do not always strike the right balance, and the result can be an impatient exclamation from the client: 'Stop interrupting me!' A little vignette can, perhaps, render some of the flavour of this kind of interaction.

> *I am seeing David in the ward, where he paces the floor of his room incessantly. He sometimes passes out into the hallway while talking out loud and very fast in a monotonous voice, and without looking at me once during the half hour I am there:*

179

'The colour is wrong, the colour is wrong, it should have been yellow, yellow is good, blue is bad, I'm poisoned by the paint, the name is David with yellow, the colour must be corrected, it's blue, wrong, the sun is yellow ...'

The only way I can stay attentive and interested is by pacing the floor alongside him and interrupting at times to check if I have got this or that phrase or word right. That interruption is loud enough to capture his attention, which means that it is very loud. For a fleeting instant, David, without looking directly at me, acknowledges my presence nonetheless by saying, 'Yes, that's it,' or something to that effect. He may also do this by saying, with irritation, 'No, you don't understand anything, do you?', before he is off on his monologue again. Any understanding of more coherent meanings is far beyond me, just getting the literal wording right is an effort, but enough of a meaningful effort for me to capture my interest and attention.

WILL THE CLIENT COMMIT SUICIDE?

The possibility of suicide is always painfully present, particularly with clients diagnosed with psychotic depression. Rogers (1951) addressed the difficult issue of suicide when he wrote:

> Does the counsellor have the right, professionally or morally, to permit a client seriously to consider ... suicide as a way out, without making a positive effort to prevent this choice? Is it a part of our general social responsibility that we may not tolerate such thinking or such action on the part of another? These are deep issues, which strike to the very core of therapy. They are not issues which one person can decide for another. Different therapeutic orientations have acted upon different hypotheses. All that one person can do is to describe his own experience and the evidence which grows out of that experience. (p. 48)

Over the years, as my confidence in my competence as a therapist has grown, I have become increasingly less inclined to do anything to interfere with clients' suicidal ideation and intentions. I have learned that a client's disclosure of plans to commit suicide is still one or more crucial steps away from actually committing suicide. I have also learned to become more trusting of that flicker of hope implicit in the client actually being there with me, and in the client's feeling of reduced isolation and abandonment as a result of my willingness to listen to, and try to understand, his or her suicidal ideation, although the client may be unable to express this for quite a while. Finally, and perhaps most importantly, I have become more convinced that the best precautionary measure I can take, as a client-centred therapist, with respect to suicidal risks, is to remain the client's client-centred therapist, and nothing else. It can still happen, though, that the courage to act according to this conviction fails me, especially when the relationship with the client is of a very short duration. Such was the case with Betty:

In our third session, Betty tells me that she is considering suicide. Her life is a hell of meaningless despair; she is a burden to others, there is no light at the end of the tunnel, and committing suicide would be such a relief. She has also made a concrete plan of walking to the nearby railway and throwing herself in front of the train. At the end of the session she says that during sessions with me she has started to feel a little better, a little relieved, and this also happens in talks with her two contact nurses. However, when these talks end she feels just as despairing as before, or even worse. Still, her talks with the nurses and me are like little oases of light to her in a desert of darkness.

After the session, I had some thinking to do. I knew Betty had not talked about suicide before, and my evaluation was that her suicidal thinking was grounded in temporary, reversible psychotic ideation. She was a typical client whom the psychiatric system was expected to prevent from committing suicide. In addition, because until that moment she had been delusional in a quiet, non-destructive way (she was convinced that she was to blame for the massacres that took place during the civil war in former Yugoslavia), she was in an open ward from which clients often went out for a stroll in the surrounding park and forest without anybody noticing. She had ample opportunity to get to the railway tracks.

Should I pass information about her suicidal plans on to the staff members of her ward? What would be the consequences of passing it on? Would there be more or less forceful interventions? Forced transfer to a closed ward? I wondered about risks to the therapy process. Might she lose confidence in me? Particularly, might she lose confidence in my confidence in her? Might she feel betrayed by me? Might she feel that I had left her isolated in her hell? On the other hand, suicide would be the end of any therapy, which I would find quite tragic in light of the likely reversibility of her condition.

How much importance could I attach to her statement that she had started to feel a little relief in her relationships with me and her primary nurses? Would these very new, albeit positive, relationships be enough to 'hold' her? What about the consequences for myself? How would I feel, if she committed suicide and I hadn't told anyone I knew about her plans? I felt convinced that it would be a very painful experience. In addition, it would be a great relief for me to pass on this information, to share the burdensome feelings of worry, doubt and responsibility with my colleagues in the ward. I also felt that not telling would be a breach of my contract with the hospital. As well, I wondered if I would jeopardise my trustworthiness to my colleagues if I did not tell.

In the end, in this case, I decided that the consequences of telling would be less negative than the consequences of not telling. I made this decision, however, with an uneasy feeling of betraying the client-centred philosophy and the client, by making myself the expert on the client, because I had decided to take steps to interfere with what the client might find to be the best decision for herself.

The question of suicide is, in my experience, the hardest of all the questions that arise in client-centred therapy in psychiatric settings.

ARE WE GETTING ANYWHERE?

When the therapist engages in a relationship with a severely psychotic patient, he or she must be prepared for the possibility that this may develop into a lifelong relationship, or at least a relationship that will last until the therapist retires. Some clients, but far from all, will continue to want help from the therapist with their struggle towards full 'normalcy' when the more intense and regular therapy relationship has terminated. Although they find themselves satisfied with their own gains from therapy, they will want the therapist as a sort of 'security net' for help in crisis situations, in order for them to get through these situations in constructive rather than destructive ways, i.e. by opening up to their experiences rather than denying and/or distorting them. This may entail prearranged sessions with very long intervals (which clients sometimes cancel because they have better things to do—and the therapist should welcome this), or the client may just want to phone the therapist to arrange for a few sessions when he or she feels in crisis. It is important to accommodate these wishes from (formerly) psychotic clients. They signify a healthy dependence on the therapist, because these clients do seem to continue to be more prone to develop psychotic distortions of experiences, when under stress, than most people. It seems that although psychotherapy with a very long time-perspective can help psychotic clients in a profound way, it cannot 'remove' a biological/hereditary disposition to be more easily overwhelmed and overburdened in crisis situations, with a concomitant risk of psychotic breakdown. In my experience a continuous, open-ended therapy relationship, on a very elastic schedule, reduces the risk of psychotic breakdown and augments the chances that the client will learn from a crisis situation to a very considerable extent. Furthermore, it is my experience that such a relationship is no burden to the therapist at all: rather, it is a joy; the therapist will be amazed at how little effort it takes for these clients to feel that they have received what they wanted, when they need 'emergency help'. In addition, it feels like a privilege to me to be allowed to follow another person's development so closely, for such an extended period of time.

Most psychotic clients, though, do not continue this far and this long in psychotherapy. Some clients terminate therapy when they have become able to live in a sheltered facility and continue their development there. Some terminate when they have become able to live outside an institution, in a satisfying manner, and with the protection of disability benefits and sheltered day-care centres. Some terminate for reasons extraneous to the therapy and some terminate only to return later, which they may do several times. In short, the arrangements that need to be made for therapy with these clients are much more unpredictable than with the clients seen by the client-centred therapist outside the psychiatric setting.

As may be surmised from the discussion above, patience, patience, and still more patience is a must in psychotherapy with psychotic clients. A tolerance for the absence of narcissistic gratification or the gratification of one's need to feel helpful as a therapist is also a must. With many clients, it can happen that for several sessions in a row there will be no sign of progress. Both client and therapist may have to look back over a span of many months to realise that progress has taken place. The experience of the client deepening his level of self-exploration will be rarer with these clients than with non-psychotic clients. Furthermore when the client does deepen his level of self-exploration, it is often only to revert to his former and more superficial level in the next moment. In addition, clients may not indicate in any way that the sessions with the therapist are helpful to them, at least not until the later phases of therapy or the 'steady state' crisis intervention phase. On the contrary, they may indicate that therapy is of no benefit to them, that other patients might need the help of the therapist more, etc.—but with the continued wish to renew their appointment with the therapist. In combination with the fact that progress is slow to come about, and that relapses with psychotic episodes may well occur in the first long phases of therapy, the absence of more evident indications of being helpful can be a strain on the therapist's self-confidence.

Sometimes, though, there are exceptions to this ordinary state of affairs. To the surprise of the therapist there are the rare clients who terminate after one or two sessions with expressions of gratitude for the help they have received; they feel much better and in no further need of therapy.

Schedules and duration of therapy with a psychiatric client population will thus be far more variable and elastic than is ordinarily the case outside of psychiatric settings. The following are a few examples.

Three clients who started with me in the 1980s have asked when I will retire and whether I will consider continuing with a few private clients after retirement.

One client, who started therapy three months ago, felt relieved by the first session and has continued to want weekly appointments that he either uses for 10 minutes to say that he feels fine and then decides to leave; or he cancels the appointment by phone with a request for a new appointment the following week. The last time he came in he did not want a new appointment, but he did want reassurance that he could phone me to arrange an appointment if he found himself in need of it.

There is another client I have not seen for 5 years. Before that time, we had a rather regular one-session-a-week therapy for a couple of years. However, she telephones each year in the month of December to cancel our once-a-year appointment, to tell me a little about her life, and to make an appointment for December the following year.

REASONS FOR THE UNIVERSALITY OF CLIENT-CENTRED THERAPY WITH PSYCHIATRIC CLIENTS

THE THERAPIST'S NON-DIRECTIVE ATTITUDE POSES NO DEMANDS ON THE CLIENT

It is common practice in other schools of psychotherapy to regard people with the most severe psychological disturbances as being 'beyond psychotherapeutic reach'. The basic reason for this is that other therapeutic approaches normally demand some degree of cooperation from the potential client, apart from this person allowing the therapist to make a 'perceived or subceived difference' (Rogers, 1959: 207) in his/her experiential field. At the very least, therapists of other approaches depend on experiencing a minimal degree of client interest in and ability to (1) keep a sustained focus of attention, (2) make him- or herself understood by the therapist, (3) change something about him- or herself and (4) receive input/interventions from the therapist's frame. For various reasons, though, therapists will not have these experiences with many of the patients in the backyards of psychiatry. Floridly psychotic patients rarely keep a sustained focus for any substantial length of time. Withdrawn, so-called autistic patients seem without any wish that others understand anything about them. People diagnosed with delusions of persecution apparently do not feel the need for help to change anything about themselves; rather, they feel a need for relevant authorities to put a halt to their persecution. People diagnosed with delusions of grandiosity seem to think that it is everyone else who is in need of their help, not the other way around. People diagnosed with a psychotic depression seem so depleted of energy and hope that they cannot contribute anything in a therapeutic relationship. Finally, people diagnosed with a manic psychosis feel happy, elated, without any worries about which they might wish a therapist's help. These groups of patients are all either incapable of, or uninterested in, receiving input/interventions from the therapist's frame of reference. Since they are people whose behaviour is often within the area of applicability of laws governing the use of force in psychiatry, they are frequently involuntarily admitted to hospital, and involuntarily treated with medicine. Offers of help from psychiatry that they are actually free to refuse, such as psychotherapy, they normally do refuse.

Of course, this list is a crude generalisation; it is stereotypical and leaves out nuances, degrees and important variations. Still, within these stereotypes lie the reasons these patients are normally considered 'beyond psychotherapeutic reach'. They are, however, not beyond the reach of the non-directive approaches of client-centred therapy and pre-therapy, which are often seamlessly combined. The reason for this is that the client-centred therapist's interest in following the client's own process, fully on the client's own terms (the therapist's non-directive attitude), is totally independent of any collaborative contribution from the patient. Many patients who refuse an offer of help, do appreciate an offer of interest. That offer is the essence of client-centred therapy.

THE THERAPIST'S NON-DIRECTIVE ATTITUDE IS NOT CONFRONTATIONAL

It is common practice in most psychotherapeutic approaches that the therapist, in some way or other, confronts the client with what the therapist, from his or her own frame of reference, regards as inconsistencies in the client's expressive process. This, of course, does not happen in client-centred therapy, where the other person's 'inconsistencies' are assumed to exist solely in the eyes of the beholder. In other words, perceived inconsistencies in the client are, in effect, therapist misunderstandings of the client. The client-centred therapist recognises and acknowledges them as such. These 'inconsistencies' disappear as the therapist's understanding of the client increases. Furthermore, not understanding does not justify judgementally attributing deficiencies to others.[3] This is one reason why client-centred therapy is eminently suitable for clients diagnosed with a mental illness,

---

3. The client-centred therapist's benign view of human nature (the conviction that the inherent pro-social nature of the organismic valuing process exists) implies a belief that people always have perfectly good reasons for behaving as they do. It may be difficult for the person in question, and for others, to understand the reasons for this behaviour. Nevertheless, human beings are consistent, as are all other animal species, whether or not their behaviours are understood as such.

since these clients tend to feel either threatened by this kind of confrontation with their 'inconsistencies' (and not without good reason), or to find it meaningless.

There is, however, one aspect of client-centred therapy, as it is often described in the literature, that entails a risk of being experienced as confrontational by the client: the stress on the I–Thou relationship, on the two participants in the therapeutic dyad being separate individuals with different experiences of reality. The very use of the pronouns 'I' and 'Thou' can sometimes feel threatening to the most disturbed psychiatric clients. Let me expand a little on this issue. In the therapy excerpt with Lillian (p. 176), there is an instance where my empathic understanding response is in the first-person singular mode ('If I had a family to return home to, I wouldn't feel so lonely and scared', is that it?). I respond as if literally identifying with the client, and I often find myself doing this with psychotic and near-psychotic clients, who typically do not feel much trust in others; rather, they tend to feel quite distrustful, isolated and scared in their relationships with others. In my experience, responding in the first-person singular mode can help these clients feel more safe and less isolated, because it allows for a clearer 'we-relationship' as opposed to the 'I–thou relationship' that is implied in the 'You feel (or think, etc.)' type of response, which psychotic and near-psychotic clients can sometimes experience as confrontational, threatening and alienating. Responding in the first-person singular mode seems sometimes to promote these clients' trust that I am fully with them. It also seems to help them better perceive my empathic understanding of and my unconditional positive regard for them.

In the same vein, I sometimes find myself using the client's first name in my responses to those who are typically less self-expressive than Lillian (examples of this can be found in Prouty, 1994). This is my reaction to an impression I sometimes have that these clients can feel threatened by the sheer experience of themselves as the seat of their own experiences. Addressing them by their first name; i.e., 'John looks sad' or 'John hears a menacing voice,' sometimes feels natural as a way of expressing acceptance of the client's difficulty with experiencing himself as an 'I'. It also seems to be a way of being respectful of the degree of closeness with his or her experiences that is currently tolerable to the client. Likewise I sometimes talk with clients, about them and their experiences, in the third person, as if we were literally talking about somebody else, referring to the client as 'he' or 'she'. Fundamentally, I think, this is no different from the situation with more self-expressive clients, where therapist and client sometimes talk about different, less well-integrated aspects of the client's self-concept in a somewhat distancing way ('Part of me/you feels angry' or 'The helpless me/you', for example). Addressing a client by his or her first name, though, and talking with the client about the client in the third person, is certainly more comprehensive than speaking about parts of the client, encompassing, as it does, that central aspect of a person that is experienced as 'I'. With these clients the atmosphere of the relationship is sometimes reminiscent of an old couple sitting side by side on a bench without looking at each other: just commenting, on and off, on what they see and hear, or talking about the old days or about something else of common interest. It is more or less the opposite of what is normally meant by an 'I–Thou' relationship (and those pronouns are rarely used). However, in its emotional, low-key intensity, it can feel close in a very comfortable and safe 'we' way that makes it possible for these clients to appreciate the relationship with the therapist.

The two chairs in my office, where I and clients sit, do not face each other. They are not side by side either. They are somewhere in between, so the client and I can easily fluctuate between a side-by-side 'We'-relationship' and a face-to-face 'I–Thou' relationship.

Again, it is, of course, basically the non-directive attitude of the client-centred therapist, when he or she attentively, sensitively and empathically follows the client's own process, that assures the safety of this non-confrontational contact.

THE THERAPIST'S NON-DIRECTIVE ATTITUDE STRUCTURES THE RELATIONSHIP

It is common in psychiatric circles to believe that patients diagnosed with psychosis need 'structure'. What is meant by 'structure', though, is rarely defined. The practical implications of the conviction that psychotic patients need structure are normally that staff members in psychiatric hospitals try to make the patient follow a rather tightly scheduled daily routine; that 'limit setting' is an important concept; and that an appropriate psychotherapeutic approach is assumed to be one that is goal directed and where the therapist structures the process by trying to keep the patient's focus on a certain issue, or on several issues in an ordered sequence. As a consequence of the belief that psychotic patients need 'structure' of the kind mentioned above, the non-directive attitude of the client-centred therapist is often thought of as being potentially harmful, because it is wrongly seen as a passive, 'laissez-faire' attitude that leaves the psychotic client helpless in his/her world of hallucinations and delusions. What is ignored is that the most important aspect of the notion of 'structure' is the reliability of the social environment of a person. Patients diagnosed with psychosis are, in my experience, more vulnerable than people at large to 'surprises' in the way their significant others relate with them. In this sense, I think it is true that patients diagnosed with psychosis 'need structure'. They seem to thrive better (and exhibit fewer psychotic symptoms) when they know rather precisely what they can expect of others and when expectations of theirs, once established, are not nullified or invalidated at a later time. One could also say that they, more than most other people, seem to need others to relate consistently (or congruently) with them. In this sense, client-centred therapy is probably the most structured of all psychotherapeutic approaches. Any client, including a client diagnosed with psychosis, quickly learns what they can expect from their client-centred therapist: the therapist's very best effort at acceptant empathic understanding, neither more nor less. This is the consistent non-directive attitude of the therapist throughout the course of therapy. The client-centred therapist does not change his or her attitude to make occasional directive interventions in sudden and surprising ways, which the psychotic client would potentially find to be provocative or over-stimulating.

The client-centred therapist's non-directive attitude is, of course, precisely a consequence of the therapist's very active effort at following the client's process with acceptant empathic understanding. There is nothing 'passive' about it, no 'laissez-faire', no unstructured letting the client down, or leaving the client to his or her own devices, isolated and unaccompanied. It is truly unfortunate and sad that the therapist's non-directive attitude in client-centred therapy has been misunderstood in this way; and to the degree that 'non-directive' is confused with 'unstructured' it is particularly unfortunate and sad for patients diagnosed with psychosis, because this confusion is one of the reasons why client-centred therapy has been dismissed as unsuitable for these people—when the truth is, in my experience, that it is eminently suitable for them.

There is another aspect of client-centred therapy with psychiatric clients that structures the relationship for the client:

In the example with Lillian, (p. 176) many of my tentative empathic understanding responses take the form of relatively explicit questions: i.e., I ask explicitly, in one way or another 'Am I understanding you correctly?' In therapy processes, where the therapist cannot rely on a stable, solid and continuous experience of the inner frame of reference of the client (the client seems 'out of contact'), it is my experience that it is sometimes helpful to be explicit with one's intention to try to understand empathically. One can do this by formulating one's tentative understanding as a question, verbally, not only with one's tone of expression. The main reason for doing this is, of course, that the therapist will normally feel more insecure about his/her empathic understanding with these clients, than with more self-expressive clients. As a result, asking comes naturally. However, a welcome 'by-product' of asking explicitly is that it helps structure the therapy process for the client. In effect, by asking explicitly, the therapist says repeatedly and clearly to the client: I am here to try to understand you; this is what our talking together is about—I can't read your mind, and I'm not an expert on you.

THE THERAPIST'S NON-DIRECTIVE ATTITUDE ENTAILS NO RISK OF HARMING THE CLIENT

It is also common in psychiatric circles to misunderstand client-centred therapy as an in-depth exploratory approach on a par with psychodynamic therapy. Again, this is unfortunate and sad for patients diagnosed with psychosis. These patients are, in psychiatric circles, assumed not to benefit from an in-depth exploratory approach. On the contrary, these patients are assumed to be easily harmed by such an approach. The consequence of this misunderstanding is, therefore, that client-centred therapy is deemed unsuitable for these people.

In my experience it is true that people diagnosed with psychosis are easily harmed by an in-depth exploratory approach that, more or less subtly, directs the client to still deeper levels of experiencing, and to still closer contact with emotionally stimulating material. The therapist who is biased towards 'deep is better than shallow' and 'close is better than distant', and therefore more or less systematically aims in the direction of 'deeper' and 'closer', does pose a risk to psychotic clients who can easily be overwhelmed and over-stimulated by what is normally regarded as 'deep' and 'close'.

If this bias, that 'deep' is better than 'shallow', is held by client-centred therapists, they should not work with clients diagnosed with severe psychopathology. Unfortunately the bias does exist among client-centred therapists, probably because most of them

187

work with less disturbed clients in private practices, university clinics, outpatient clinics, etc. They work, in short, mostly with clients who have never set foot in a psychiatric hospital and never will. With these clients, the bias that 'deep and close is better than shallow and distant' is probably inconsequential and may even be helpful. However, it is also questionable that one can remain non-directive and still hold such a bias, and I shall return to this point below.

The existence of this bias among client-centred therapists is illustrated with the notion that 'additive empathy' (Mearns and Thorne, 1999: 45) or empathic understanding of 'edge-of-awareness experiences' (*ibid.*: 52) is preferable to accurate empathy with what the client, in this moment, wants the therapist to understand about his or her psychological landscape. If I have understood Mearns and Thorne correctly, the client-centred therapist should, according to these authors, aim at additive empathy and empathy with edge-of-awareness experiences, as opposed to 'ordinary', accurate, empathic understanding of the client's inner frame of reference or psychological landscape. This preference is, apparently, supported by research: Sachse (1990: 300–2) has shown that clients typically react with a deepening of their level of experience when the therapist systematically strives for 'deep' empathic understanding responses and succeeds in this. However, the clients in this research were ambulatory clients, not in-patients in a psychiatric hospital. In-patients in a psychiatric hospital are, of course, more seriously psychologically disturbed, probably psychotic or in a so-called 'borderline' condition. They will typically react with withdrawal and/or intensification of psychotic symptoms to any effort to direct them to deeper levels of experiencing, whether by aiming systematically at 'additive empathy' or empathy with 'edge-of-awareness experiences' or by any other means. The tacit assumption that a deepening of the level of experiencing during the session is synonymous with therapeutic progress is not true for clients diagnosed with psychoses.

Therapist efforts at directing the client towards deeper levels of experiencing is, of course, an in-depth exploratory approach. But is it truly client-centred therapy? I think not, because the therapist who more or less subtly directs the client towards deeper levels of experiencing is, surely, process directive and this has, in my mind, nothing to do with client-centred therapy, where the therapist is non-directive not only with respect to content but also with respect to process. Raskin (1988: 33) puts it beautifully when he differentiates between systematic and unsystematic therapist responses and says that therapists making systematic responses have 'a preconceived notion of how they wish to change the client and work at it in systematic fashion, in contrast to the person-centred therapist who starts out being open and remains open to an emerging process orchestrated by the client'. Rogers has the following to say (1959: 229–30) about in-depth exploratory approaches:

> In the freedom of therapy, as the individual expresses more and more of himself, he finds himself on the verge of voicing a feeling which is obviously and undeniably true, but which is flatly contradictory to the conception of himself which he has held ... Anxiety results, and if the situation is appropriate [a later section discloses that this means that the core conditions are dominant

(this author's comment)], this anxiety is moderate, and the result is constructive. But if, through overzealous and effective interpretation by the therapist, or through some other means, the individual is brought face to face with more of his denied experiences than he can handle, disorganization ensues and a psychotic break occurs.

Aiming systematically at 'additive empathy' or empathy of 'edge-of-awareness experiences' is, in my experience, precisely such an 'overzealous' approach which can easily bring clients diagnosed with psychotic or near-psychotic conditions face-to-face with more of their denied experiences than they can handle. The usefulness of client-centred therapy to clients diagnosed with psychosis or other forms of severe psychopathology hinges on the non-directive attitude of the therapist with respect to the process, as well as to the content. Psychotic clients, and clients with a 'borderline' diagnosis, will often flatten their level of experiencing, as a sort of healthy recuperation, before they deepen it again. These clients can therefore talk about the latest fashion in shoes in one moment, only to talk about exceedingly painful experiences the next. The therapist should follow the client in both of these directions with equal interest and respect. The importance of a non-directive approach is not surprising, when one considers how easily these clients are overwhelmed and over-stimulated and disposed to process their experiences, particularly their emotionally disturbing experiences, in psychotic ways.

Dave Mearns (1994: 80–3) writes that a characteristic feature of clients with a 'borderline' diagnosis is the externalised locus of evaluation of these clients, and I quite agree. As a matter of fact they seem, in order to have 'dependency wishes' satisfied, to be masters at sniffing out conditional regard, which they also oppose in order to have 'independency wishes' satisfied. The consistent, non-directive, empathic following, which maximally reduces the risk of conveying conditional regard, is, therefore, necessary for them if they are to struggle constructively with their conflict as an internal conflict. Deviations from this non-directive practice are typically experienced as conditional regard of one or the other side of the conflict, or as conditional regard of the struggle itself. This will often result in an externalisation of the conflict, which they will then experience, and not without reason, as taking place between themselves and the therapist.

The following is an example of the harmful effects of an 'in-depth' exploratory intervention that I engaged in as a consequence of being overly impressed by the theory that traumatic experiences must be 'worked through' in therapy.

Hannah is 33 years old. She has a long history of impulsive, self-destructive behaviour in stressful situations. She cuts her wrists, swallows sharp objects, overdoses on tranquillisers, etc. She is hospitalised as a consequence of one of these self-destructive episodes and seems to profit from the various hospital activities she is engaged in, including psychotherapy. The following excerpt is from the sixth session with Hannah.

Hannah has spent most of this session talking about the events of the week, listing them without much reference to her thoughts and feelings about them. Towards the end of the session, after a rather long pause, she starts talking about the death of her mother when she, Hannah, was in her teens:

H: It was awful. I've tried to forget about it, but I can't. It feels so bad, I don't know what to do about it, somehow it's always with me, but I've never really talked about it before.

T: Maybe you'd like to try to talk a little about it now? To say a little more about that bad feeling?

H: She died of cancer. It took a very long time. Towards the end her face was … not right … it … it … (obviously uncomfortable and distressed, fighting with tears) … it just looked awful, I couldn't bear to look at her.

T: You wanted so much to be close to her, look at her, but it was horrible to do so.

H (between sobs of crying): Yes, I've felt so guilty about it, I just turned away, didn't look at her, she looked too hideous, her eyes were all swollen … I never kissed her goodbye … she smelled …

T: She was just too abhorrent to be close to, to touch and kiss and you've blamed yourself for feeling like that … and, telling about it, it hurts so awfully much.

H: Yes … (crying desolately for a while, then rather abruptly, and surprisingly to the therapist, she takes a grip on herself) … It's too silly to cry about now, it's such a long time ago, and it can't be changed.

T: Annoyed with yourself that you cannot just let bygones be bygones.

H: Yes, that's right, there's no point in dwelling on the past—I do feel a little relieved though.

T: Relieved and annoyed—well, I think time is about up for today.

After a few small-talk remarks, Hannah leaves.

The next day the therapist is informed that shortly after the end of the session, Hannah swallowed three sewing needles and was brought to the intensive care unit of the nearest general hospital.

The emotions stimulated by the successful attempt of the therapist to have the client explore her feelings concerning the death of her mother were evidently more than the client could tolerate. In a later session it became clear that anger at the therapist, for having forced her to talk about her mother's death, had been the most troubling feeling.

An inaccurate or, rather, incomplete tentative empathic understanding response, which only demonstrated the therapist's understanding of the client's pain, and not of the client's wish to forget about the pain, might have easily been followed by the same sequence of events as the directive, probing question. So might have efforts at 'additive empathy' or empathy with 'edge-of-awareness experiences' that moved the client closer to her experience of her mother's death. 'Deeper' or 'closer' is *not* better with a psychiatric client population.

BEYOND PSYCHOTHERAPEUTIC REACH?

In the preceding sections, I hope I have demonstrated that the non-directive approach inherent in a combination of client-centred therapy and pre-therapy can reach those who are traditionally considered unreachable. By this, I do not claim that they are, necessarily, 'cured'. They do, however, become able to share a greater part of life with the rest of us, to the satisfaction of themselves as well as their social environment.

Psychiatric nurses where I work, who participate in a training group that I facilitate in pre-therapy, do not ask: Is this patient too disturbed to benefit from the approach? On the contrary, they ask: Is this patient too little disturbed to benefit from the approach? I feel touched by this because it is evidence, to me, that non-directive therapy, in the form of client-centred therapy augmented with pre-therapy, is an approach that can reach the unreachable; an approach for those who are the worst off; an approach that gives to those who have nothing, by regarding them as just as potentially understandable as the rest of us. It is not only a myth that the client-centred therapist's non-directive attitude is useless, or even harmful, with clients diagnosed with severe psychopathology; it is the opposite of the truth.

REFERENCES

Brodley BT (1998) Criteria for making empathic responses in client-centred therapy. *The Person-Centred Journal*, 5(1), 20–28

Mearns D (1994) *Developing Person-Centred Counselling*. London: Sage Publications.

Mearns D & Thorne B (1999) *Person-Centred Counselling in Action*. London: Sage Publications.

Prouty GF (1994) *Theoretical Evolutions in Person-Centered/Experiential Therapy: Applications to schizophrenic and retarded psychoses*. Westport: Praeger.

Raskin NJ (1988) What do we mean by person-centered therapy? Paper presented at the meeting of the Second Association for the Development of the Person-Centred Approach, New York.

Rogers CR (1951) *Client-Centered Therapy*. Boston: Houghton Mifflin Company.

Rogers CR (1959) A theory of therapy, personality, and interpersonal relationships as developed in the client-centered framework. In S Koch (Ed) *Psychology: A study of a science, Vol. 3*. New York: McGraw-Hill, pp. 184–256.

Rogers CR, Gendlin ET, Kiesler DJ & Truax C (1967) *The Therapeutic Relationship with Schizophrenics*. Wisconsin: The University of Wisconsin Press.

Sachse R (1990) Concrete interventions are crucial: the influence of the therapists processing proposals on the client's intrapersonal exploration in client-centered therapy. In G Lietaer, J Rombauts & R Van Balen (Eds) *Client-Centered and Experiential Psychotherapy in the Nineties*. Leuven: Leuven University Press, pp. 295–308.

Shlien JM (1961) A client-centered approach to schizophrenia: first approximation. In A Burton (Ed) *Psychotherapy of the Psychoses*. New York: Basic Books, pp. 285–317. Reprinted in JM Shlien (2003) *To Live an Honorable Life: Invitations to think about client-centered therapy and the person-centered approach*, [P Sanders (Ed)]. Ross-on-Wye: PCCS Books, pp. 30–50.

Sommerbeck L (2002) The Wisconsin watershed—Or the universality of CCT. *The Person-Centered Journal*, 9(2), 140–57.

CHAPTER 11

AN EXPLORATION OF NON-DIRECTIVE WORK WITH DRUG AND ALCOHOL USERS

SUE WILDERS

INTRODUCTION

Most people will have had a drink or been drunk at some point in their lives. Many will also have some experience of recreational drugs. Human beings have used substances in every known society in order to change, or maintain, their mental, physical, or emotional state. For some, this use becomes a defining feature of their lives, because of the extent of the use, its effects, or the meaning the use has for that person. This chapter is an exploration of the types of issues that may arise when working as a non-directive person-centred therapist with people whose substance use has become a defining feature. Although this can be very satisfying and rewarding work for the therapist and the client, I think it is important to acknowledge that at times, for the practitioner, it can also be highly challenging.

UNPREDICTABILITY AND SUBSTANCE USE

Drugs and alcohol affect people in many different ways. Many people who use drugs or alcohol report common or similar experiences relating to their use. This is no different from people reporting similar experiences to other life events, such as bereavement or falling in love. Despite some common reactions, each person who uses a substance will experience their own unique effects from it, and this will even vary within the same person at different times. This is because one effect of drugs and alcohol is to enhance or suppress mood. Therefore, experiences will vary as a consequence of a particular mood interacting with a particular mood-altering effect of a drug. As therapists, we may experience our clients as appearing sharp, articulate, lucid, and highly emotional. In contrast, they may appear emotionally distant, or introverted and with little intellectual awareness. The extremely varied effects can make it difficult to predict how clients who use substances might present during a therapy session. Although we aim as person-centred therapists to stay with our clients 'in their world as if it were our own', moment by moment, this lack of predictability can be disconcerting.

Within the context of therapy, we may still expect to encounter some predictable social norms, perhaps taking for granted and anticipating certain forms of behaviour as a result. Within a relatively wide experiential band, we can reasonably expect a certain degree of distance or intimacy. In the context of a therapy session, different clients with varying emotional stresses, or having varying cultural norms, may step a little closer or a little further away from us psychologically or emotionally, and yet remain within the bounds of commonly understood cultural behaviour. Some norms are common to almost all clients; eg., a greeting, or a clear beginning and end in our therapeutic encounters. These norms may be present among clients who are experiencing the effects of drugs or alcohol, but sometimes they are not. There may be times when substance users step outside the norms of society, especially when having a strong reaction to the substances they have used. It is at those times—when our clients are most strongly affected by substances—that our commitment to non-directivity, our respect for the sovereign human being and her right and imperative to choose her own path, may receive one of its greatest tests. This is the case, not only because of the effects that substances may have on the individual, but also because of the immediacy of that experience for the therapist.

Clients may talk about issues like self-starvation, cutting themselves, social isolation, and other behaviours that may, at least on the surface, be considered as self-harm, or harmful to the organism. These behaviours are usually brought into therapy sessions through the client's description of them. However, clients who use drugs or alcohol may demonstrate their use, not in an abstracted way through a descriptive narrative of the act, but concretely and immediately through their actual presence and presentation within a session. They may meet us while intoxicated, hallucinating, or in other ways strongly affected by the substance they have used. Any strong reaction to a substance or subsequent behaviour is demonstrated before our very eyes.

THE CHALLENGE OF EMPATHY

When a client's ability to reason cognitively is inhibited by the use of substances, we may not be able to rely on any degree of common intellectual understanding. Our client might not be making much sense to us intellectually. Our empathy must be attuned to the whole person, rather than solely to his thoughts. This is the challenge of having our clients attend a session with us while drunk or high. Although writing about clients with even less access to relationships than those who are strongly intoxicated, or hallucinating because of substance use, Garry Prouty (2002) nonetheless expressed this way of being with the whole person with beautiful simplicity: 'A therapist needs to look as much as listen' (p. 12). This elegantly stated insight is of course applicable to all clients.

Our clients usually assist our empathic understanding by sharing their thoughts and thought processes. Even when our clients' words contrast with their emotions, their words do help us to develop our empathic understanding of them, and of their frame of reference. When this cognitive aspect is missing and our clients are unable to, or are disinterested in, articulating their own thoughts or process, our commitment to their self-determination is brought sharply to the fore. Is this stumbling, barely coherent person really capable of governing his own life? In this situation, not only are we obliged to either maintain or reject our non-directive attitude, but we are forced to make this choice immediately, in the moment.

While this immediacy is present in all therapeutic interactions, we might consider whether there is any fundamental difference between listening non-judgementally to our clients as they recount behaviours, and listening non-judgementally, being non-directive, while our clients *demonstrate* those very behaviours. There is certainly no distinction within person-centred theory in our way of relating in these two scenarios. In either scenario, our aim to non-judgementally understand our client remains the same. Empathy is the process by which we immerse ourselves in our client's world without losing ourselves. As fully as we are able, we allow ourselves to really understand how it is for our client. Therapist congruence is also an integral part of the picture. Jerold Bozarth (1998: 52) put it like this:

> Empathy in client-centred theory is a concept that is integrated with the conditions of congruency and unconditional positive regard. It exists within a context of non-directivity and is predicated on the foundation block of the actualising tendency.

By meeting our clients while they are under the influence of drugs and alcohol, the opportunity exists for a deep connection in which the client is wholly accepted. I doubt if it is possible to overstate the importance of accepting our clients during their immersion in this experience. Drug and alcohol users will at times think about, feel and experience the world under the influence of substances. For some this state is their most common or regular condition—they may be more often under the influence of substances than not. That may be their preferred way of being in the world; but it is also a less acceptable way of being insofar as much of society is concerned. The everyday experience for many substance users is one of receiving external judgements, hostility, and discrimination. By meeting with our clients while they are in this state of intoxication we are at least potentially able to offer them unconditional positive regard, whatever their state of consciousness or ability to articulate. When we offer the core conditions (Rogers, 1957) at these times, we demonstrate that our acceptance is genuinely toward the whole person. Our acceptance is not offered as a reward for sobriety. Or put another way, our positive regard is truly unconditional.

WORKING WITH CLIENTS WHO ARE UNDER THE INFLUENCE OF SUBSTANCES

Many therapists are wary of offering therapy while clients are under the influence of substances. Some of this wariness has simply been absorbed without question from the theories of directive, non-person-centred approaches. Most directive models of therapy include a belief that it is not possible to work therapeutically with people who are under the influence of substances. Proponents of these approaches have been so successful in promoting this viewpoint that many therapists have simply accepted their assertions as though they were facts; however, they are not facts.

There are fundamental differences between the theory and practice of person-centred therapy and the theory and practice of other, directive approaches. Directive therapists seek to dissuade their clients from following their own internal choices, thoughts and feelings, in favour of external ideas and suggestions that emanate from the therapist, based on the therapist's theory. This is at least the case when the client is not coincidentally moving in the direction preferred by the directive therapist. A major aim of directive approaches is to 'put the client in touch' with some particular aspect of himself, such as 'underlying feelings', or to alter his thinking. Substance use may indeed be a barrier to these aims, since drug and alcohol use affect thought processes and emotions and can therefore be an obstacle to therapists who would seek to interfere with their clients' thinking. Substance use frustrates directive therapists in their aim of changing their clients.

Person-centred therapists have very different criteria and intentions from those of directive therapists. Since our sole intention as person-centred therapists is to offer the core conditions of congruence, empathy, and unconditional positive regard to our clients in order for them to find their own path, our client's way of being cannot possibly present an obstacle to our therapeutic approach. Their state of intoxication and its effects are merely another variable for us to encounter and understand.

THE CORE CONDITIONS IN THE CONTEXT OF WORK WITH SUBSTANCE-USING CLIENTS

Some therapists may question whether a strongly intoxicated client is capable of *receiving* the core conditions. We could ask the same question about any client. And yet, by whichever means we assess the impact of the core conditions on our non-substance-using clients, those same criteria could be applied to substance-using clients. There is no significant, observable difference in the responses of our drug and alcohol-using clients to unconditional positive regard and empathy in comparison with any other client's responses. This has been my observation in the thirteen years I have worked with this client group. As with other clients, substance users who undertake therapy do affirm feeling understood and accepted in person-centred therapy. They may demonstrate this in their body language; for example, nodding their heads in confirmation, smiling, and giving appropriate and sustained eye contact. They may also demonstrate it verbally by such comments as, 'Yes, that's exactly it', 'No one has ever really listened to me before', or 'You don't seem to judge me'. Our substance-using clients also refer to changes in their lives, movement in a positive direction following the onset of therapy. They may, for example, describe improved self-esteem, or leaving a violent relationship. Clients may also report changes in relation to their substance use, but that is not always the case.

In non-directive therapy the client cannot obstruct the therapy, whereas in directive therapy the client may unwittingly obstruct it, e.g., by coming to the session under the effects of a substance. Any obstacles we may encounter in non-directive therapy are within the therapist, not the client. There may be obstacles in terms of the therapist's ability to offer the core conditions. Drug and alcohol-using clients may at times behave in idiosyncratic ways. Their speech patterns may be accelerated or disjointed. Their levels of alertness, or even consciousness, may be quite varied. Such unusual behaviours can be experienced as dissatisfying or disconcerting by therapists. These reactions in the therapist, emanating from the therapist's internal frame of reference, are understandable. However, they are bound to run counter to the therapy.

The content and detail of our substance-using client's movement will inevitably be unpredictable, just as with any client. This truth can be challenging for a therapist if she has an expectation that the therapy will result in clients abstaining from drug or alcohol use. If the therapist is harbouring a desire to see her client give up the use of substances, then this directive attitude, even if unspoken, is likely to interfere with the therapist's ability to offer unconditional positive regard. A therapist's expression of great pleasure or positive regard over her client's reduction of, or abstention from, drug or alcohol use may be accurately perceived by the client as conditionally acceptant in relation to her substance use.

Offering unconditional positive regard is not always a simple or straightforward matter for the non-directive therapist. In reality, at times any individual client or particular issue may trigger feelings in us as therapists, and we may then experience some difficulty in maintaining the core conditions of congruent acceptance and understanding. If our clients respond in 'normal', socially accepted ways within a therapeutic relationship, then there is little choice but for us to look inside ourselves. This may be done in supervision or in our own therapy, to attempt to lessen our discomfort and enable us to continue with the therapeutic relationship.

QUESTIONING WHETHER TO ENGAGE IN WORK WITH SUBSTANCE-USING CLIENTS

The question, 'Can I work therapeutically with this particular client?', if it arises at all, generally arises at some point *after* the onset of therapy. This is quite different from the process that many therapists engage in when faced with the possibility of working with someone who is a frequent, heavy, or chaotic drug or alcohol user. If this use of substances exists prior to the onset of therapy, the therapist may ask herself the question of whether she is at all able to proceed to a therapeutic relationship.

For the non-directive therapist faced with the prospect of working with such a client, the first ethical and theoretical issue is one of non-directivity. Should the decision over whether or not to start a therapeutic relationship belong to the therapist, belong to the client, or be a joint process? As therapists, whether directive or non-directive, we hold an understanding of the basic process of therapy. We have a theoretical framework and an expectation of what we intend to offer within the relationship. So if, for example, it appeared to us that a potential client had a very different idea about the nature of the relationship from the one we ourselves held, I believe it would fall to the therapist to make this explicit. If a potential client were to say something like, 'I'm coming to see you so that you can tell me where I should invest my money', more explanation would be required from the therapist in order to prevent the client from being dissatisfied with the relationship and from feeling misled about its purpose. However, it is unlikely that the non-directive therapist would make a judgement over starting a therapeutic relationship with this client without involving the client in the decision. Any ensuing discussions would be along the lines of a joint process in which the therapist would make clear the nature of the therapeutic exchange. Ultimately for the non-directive therapist, the decision over whether or not to start a therapeutic relationship would be made by the client.

What if our potential client understands the purpose and process of therapy, but the therapist is anxious, fearful, or feels for some reason unable to enter into a therapeutic relationship? Does our non-judgemental, non-directive imperative begin only after therapy has begun, or does it start earlier than this, at the point of referral? Because we often identify clients ahead of time, a therapist with fears or prejudices towards people of different backgrounds or status to her own may be able to avoid engaging in therapy with such people. In so doing the therapist would be making an external judgement about the client, presupposing who he is and how he may relate in the relationship. This may be the case for therapists with clients whose use of substances is known prior to the onset of therapy.

There may be arguments, based on person-centred theory, in support of such avoidance. The theory underpinning the person-centred approach describes six conditions as necessary and sufficient for therapy to proceed. Conditions two and three state:

2. That the first person, whom we shall term the client, is in a state of *incongruence*, being *vulnerable*, or *anxious*.

3. That the second person, whom we shall term the therapist, is *congruent in the relationship*. (Rogers, 1957: 96, original emphasis)

It would be very difficult to proceed with person-centred therapy in a situation where the therapist was more anxious or more incongruent than the client. Furthermore, a therapist who felt unable to genuinely offer the core conditions of empathic understanding and unconditional positive regard might create or compound internalised judgements within the client. As such the conditions would not exist to enable the client to free himself from conditions of worth. Therapeutic, life-enhancing movement would be inhibited.

Declining a client is a far from simple issue. There can be many reasons for a therapist to feel reluctant to take on a client. Fear or hostility toward the client is one reason, but there may be others, such as uncertainty or fear of being out of one's depth. By making a decision not to take a client, the therapist assumes an expert role, even if this decision is based on the therapists' acknowledgement of her own inexperience or incompetence. That is to say, the therapist assumes knowledge of what is in the best interests of the client. In theoretical terms, the client's internal locus of evaluation is rejected in deference to the therapist's assessment. This runs counter to the basic aims and principles of client-centred therapy, in which the client is trusted as the expert in his own life. There may also be circumstances in which a therapist rejects a client because she feels it is in *her own* best interests to do so. Sometimes (extremely rarely) this may feel unavoidable although it would inevitably be directive and therefore counter-therapeutic.

In declining a client the therapist imparts an external judgement or a condition of worth to the client. The counter-therapeutic aspect of rejecting a client would be common to all clients; however, clients belonging to sections of society suffering from oppression or discrimination would also receive a societal condition of worth. Along with the impact of negative judgements on his personality, and rejection of his ability to make sound judgments as a sovereign human being, the client may also hear that the therapist 'agrees' with the negative views about the 'group' to which the client belongs. In this case, societal attitudes and discrimination towards those it designates as 'junkies' and 'drunks' will coincide with the judgements the client receives from the therapist: he is not appropriate or acceptable to the therapist. Furthermore, he is not able to judge for himself the potential usefulness of the therapy.

It is not possible to avoid these issues if we decline a client. Consequently a double bind exists for a therapist who feels unable to offer the core conditions. Either the therapist assumes the 'expert' role by declining the client, and thereby giving the client a condition of worth; or else the therapist accepts the client but is unable to offer the core conditions of congruent and empathic unconditional acceptance.

THERAPIST RESPONSIBILITIES

Supervision and personal therapy are helpful for gaining awareness and resolution of our blocks to empathy, and in rekindling feelings of unconditional acceptance towards our clients. Probably one of our most important responsibilities as therapists is to remain aware of any inability to offer unconditional positive regard and to work on removing these blocks. No matter how much we work on ourselves, it would be impossible for anyone to know if they were completely self-aware. Lack of self-awareness is denied to our awareness. It is for this type of reason that it is probably a good idea for non-directive therapists to be extremely cautious about commenting from their own frames of reference.

There are times when we have sufficient self-awareness to know that we are holding value judgements, either toward an individual client or toward clients with similar characteristics. It would be unrealistic to imagine that there would never be a situation in which an individual therapist might find herself unable to shift judgemental feelings and therefore feel unable to work with a particular client. It is worth repeating that the starting point for these decisions is the recognition of difficulties in the therapist, rather than any notion of 'problematic' clients.

It is more usual for judgemental feelings to emerge once therapy has begun. Often such feelings are transient and are altered by the impact of the relationship. The non-directive stance requires each person to take personal responsibility for his or her own actions and process. Although it is only the client who shares details and information about his life as a regular and integral part of the therapy, the relationship is far from one-sided. Every action creates a reaction. There is a dynamic that exists between client and therapist, a growing relationship in which congruence within both is always a developing process.

PSYCHOLOGICAL CONTACT AND THE THERAPEUTIC RELATIONSHIP

The core conditions exist within, and as part of, the relationship between therapist and client. Although as person-centred therapists we consciously seek to experience the core conditions in relation to our clients, it is often the case that clients will also develop empathy and, to a certain extent, even unconditional positive regard for their therapist. The relationship between therapist and client is personal and intimate. In fact the relationship is so important in person-centred therapy that Rogers (1957: 96) included this as the very first of the six therapeutic conditions of person-centred therapy: 'that two persons are in psychological contact'. Although the word 'psychological' was omitted in Rogers' important 1959 paper, the meaning of this first condition remains the same if we consider it within the context of the overall theory. The therapist endeavours to offer genuine acceptance and empathy to the client within their relationship. This acceptance has no conditions placed on it over how the client chooses to use the session. The client is free to work on issues, sit in silence, be rational or be incoherent, emotional or distant. There is no requirement that she engage actively with the therapist—she can if she chooses be inward looking throughout the session.

Some might question whether it is possible to be in psychological contact with someone who is heavily under the influence of substances. This question might be raised especially if the client is incoherent for some, or all, of a session. I believe it is a question that emerges when we confuse cognitive ability with psychological contact.

It might be helpful for a therapist to ask herself, 'Is the client able to receive the core conditions'? The following example might provide some clarity over this issue. Clients may attend a session highly agitated and under the influence of substances. However, when we are able to experience unconditional positive regard and empathy toward a client who is in this state, our clients will almost certainly become less agitated. The opposite is also true. When agitated clients feel judged or confronted, their level of agitation is likely to increase. In this scenario the outcome of the psychological contact is clear and visible. There is no reason to assume that psychological contact is not present when our clients are withdrawn or subdued, rather than agitated. To a certain extent, when agitated, our clients exhibit psychological contact in the relationship between therapist and client externally. Or they do so sufficiently for us to realise the genuineness of the psychological contact between therapist and client. Yet it makes no sense to assume that the lack of demonstrable behaviour equates to a lack of psychological contact. Contact of this kind is about an internal experience, and is not about how the client communicates.

Sometimes the only signifier of psychological contact is that the client attends the session. Attendance demonstrates both the awareness of the relationship and its importance to the client. In fact for non-directive person-centred therapy to proceed, I would suggest that client attendance is the only requirement necessary. The client, by self-directing himself to the session, has chosen to engage with the therapy. Since person-centred therapy is based on the relationship, it is equally accurate to say that the client has chosen to engage with the therapist. The contact, the 'psychological' contact, is expressed through the client's decision to be present in the session.

THE IMPORTANCE OF THE CLIENT'S FRAME OF REFERENCE

Accepting and supporting the self-direction of our clients is fundamental to person-centred therapy. This is true not only of the broader questions, such as whether or not to engage in therapy at all, but is also true of the way in which the therapy progresses. Non-directivity requires us to stay with our clients in both detail and essence. Only by remaining entirely focused on our client's frame of reference can we avoid influencing the direction of the therapy with our own evaluations and preferences. In our work with substance users this means carefully following the client's preference, even regarding whether or not to look at their use of substances. Some clients are not interested in discussing any aspect of their substance use, whereas others may spend hours discussing the smallest detail of their use.

Clients may be sensitive to any indication from the therapist that she has a preference over whether or not her client looks at his substance use in any detail. Clients attending drug or alcohol services are often required by those services to discuss their substance use. Even when they are not required to do so, clients may well believe that it is expected of them. In contrast, clients who find a private therapist may avoid looking at the specifics of their use, believing that they should concentrate on their feelings or choices instead. There is a palpable sense of relief when a client discovers that he can address *any* issue in *any* detail without judgement from the non-directive therapist. This is especially the case with any issues in which the client might anticipate receiving value judgements from his therapist. Drug and alcohol users in particular receive external judgements and sanctions from many different people and institutions: friends and family may be critical; access to children may be denied; jobs and relationships may be lost; medical care may be denied; and people may be imprisoned either for the use itself or because of related issues.

Not all substance users will experience these problems, or be affected by them emotionally. However, awareness of the wider issues in society might enable therapists to have a better understanding of the ways in which any conditional feelings within us could coincide with wider, societally held conditions of worth. Therefore, as therapists, we might want to spend a little while considering our own feelings and assumptions about drug and alcohol use. Is there a level of alcohol use that we consider 'too much'? Are there some drugs that we think of as 'hard' and others that we think of as 'soft'? Most of us hold some kind of assumptions or feelings about these types of issue. In thinking about these issues, we can gain an understanding not only of our own assumptions, but also of where these ideas came from. It is likely that each person reading this chapter will have some views that she or he has taken for granted, and that would be very different from other people reading these same words. I am not suggesting that as person-centred therapists we should be aiming to relinquish any of our own thoughts or ideas; rather, as with any issue, our aim is to put those thoughts and ideas to one side in order to enter our client's frame of reference.

INFORMATION IS NOT ADVICE

By entering our client's frame of reference we submit, without critique, to our client's direction. However, very rarely, there may be times when we would deliberately, consciously, speak from our own frame of reference. There are times when we may have information available to us that our client is not aware of. Usually a non-directive therapist would not offer information from her own frame of reference purely because she knows something that the client does not know. However, on very rare occasions, a non-directive therapist might want to offer information to a client.

The type of information that I would offer to substance-using clients is related either to harm minimisation, or to information about where or how to access specific assistance. In the case of harm minimisation, I would offer this information if my client had some risk attached to their practice that they might not be aware of. For example, if someone has a physical dependency on alcohol, stopping suddenly without medication can be fatal, and is a common cause of death amongst people with an alcohol dependency. I would probably offer this information to a client who had an alcohol dependency. Additionally, if a client expresses a wish to enter some specific form of treatment, I would give my client information on where or how to access it.

As with all our input as therapists, the ethics that guide our work will influence the meaning of our interactions. Deciding whether or not to offer information to a client is an individual and ethical question for each therapist to consider. I believe that the significant issue is not whether we offer information, but whether we maintain a non-directive stance. There is, in my mind, a world of difference between giving information and giving advice. This difference lives not only in the words we use, but also in our intent, manner, and attitude. Is it our intention to push our client in a certain direction, or are we offering information to the client without concern for what he does with it? In informing my client of overdose risks, will I be as accepting of her rejection of this information as I would be of her decision to refer to it?

CONCLUDING COMMENTS

This chapter was written with therapists in mind, but I hope it is also relevant to anyone in contact with substance users. Indeed, the non-directive person-centred approach is relevant in any relationship or interaction with substance users, especially within drug or alcohol agencies. It is my opinion that if we approach our clients from the standpoint of the non-directive core conditions, it is of no great importance whether we sit in a small office room and call our relationship therapy, or we sit in a smoky bedroom while someone injects heroin into a vein and calls our relationship 'outreach'. If both parties choose to be present, if the core conditions are present in the therapist, and if the client is able to be the way he is at that moment and is accepted, I believe that the venue and external description of the meeting is unimportant. Drug and alcohol use are merely things that people do; substances that people use. The reasons for drug and alcohol use and their meanings are as numerous as the people who use these substances. What it means to be a person who uses a lot of drugs or alcohol becomes apparent only when we listen to the unique journey of each individual as they share it with us, in our utter acceptance of the sovereign right of each human being to self-direct her or his own life.

REFERENCES

Bozarth JD (1998) *Person-Centered Therapy: A revolutionary paradigm*. Ross-on-Wye: PCCS Books.

Prouty GF (2002) Pre Therapy and Existential Phenomenology. In GF Prouty, D Van Werde and M Pörtner, *Pre-Therapy: Reaching contact-impaired clients*. Ross-on-Wye: PCCS Books, pp. 11–13.

Rogers CR (1957) The necessary and sufficient conditions of personality change. *Journal of Consulting Psychology, 21*(2), 95–103.

Rogers CR (1959) A theory of therapy, personality and interpersonal relationships, as developed in the client-centered framework. In S Koch (Ed) *Psychology: A study of a science, Vol. 3, Formulations of the person and the social context*. New York: McGraw-Hill, pp. 184–256.

CHAPTER 12

THE ART OF NON-DIRECTIVE 'BEING' IN PSYCHOTHERAPY[1]

JEROLD D. BOZARTH

Abstract

This chapter discusses the art of 'being' in psychotherapy from the perspective of the author's experience and study as a non-directive, client-centered/person-centered therapist. Several conclusions about psychotherapy are presented within a quasi-autobiographical context in order to permit readers to know the source of such conclusions. Among these conclusions are that: (1) effective psychotherapy is as much about what the therapist does not do as what the therapist does in therapy; (2) the client is her own best expert about her life; and (3) it is a virtual myth that there are specific treatments for particular psychiatric dysfunctions. The art of psychotherapy in Rogers' theory is the presence of the therapist's unconditional positive self-regard, creating an atmosphere of unconditional positive regard towards the client within an empathic context. It is the unconditional empathic reception of the client with trust in the client's own direction, way and pace that is the art of psychotherapy. It is this presence that is the crux of success for all psychotherapy.

INTRODUCTION

If I keep from commanding people, they behave themselves
If I keep from preaching at people, they improve themselves
If I keep from meddling with people, they take care of themselves
If I keep from imposing on people, they become themselves
Lao Tzu

Therapist 1: Have a nice day.
Client: Oh no, more pressure!

Therapist 2: You must accept yourself.
Client: Please, I have some standards.

---

1. Published under the title, 'The Art of "Being" in Psychotherapy'. *The Humanistic Psychologist*, Special Triple Issue: The Art of Psychotherapy. 29, 1–3, Spring, Summer, Fall, 2001. Reproduced with permission of the American Psychological Association, Division of Humanistic Psychology (Division 32).

Psychotherapy means different things to different people. The 1985 Phoenix Conference on the 'Evolution of Psychotherapy' dramatically illustrates this point (Zeig, 1987). It was reported in *Time* magazine that the notable experts did not agree with each other. In a report on the promotion of scientific psychotherapy, Joseph Wolpe described the conference: 'as a babble of conflicting voices' (Wolpe, 1987). There is little evidence that there has been much change twenty years later. The advent of 'empirically supported treatments' (EST) and subsequent reactions may have accelerated the babble.

The therapeutic orientations represented at the Phoenix Conference exemplified two general assumptions about psychotherapy. One of these assumptions is that humans are reactive beings. That is, there is the assumption that humans are primarily reactive either to external stimuli (e.g., Skinner) that reinforces their behavior, or reactive to internal stimuli identified as inner motivations (e.g., Freud). The second assumption is that humans are in the process of becoming. Individuals have free will and freedom of choice (e.g., Rogers). Rogers referred to this process of becoming as the 'self-actualization process', a developmental process of the self that becomes congruent with the organismic 'actualizing tendency' when individuals are free to experience themselves with unconditional positive self regard (Rogers, 1959). It is this latter view that is more often considered to be akin to the practice of psychotherapy as an art.

Art, in this instance, is viewed as embedded in the relationship of the therapist and client, and in the development of the client's potentials within an empathic relationship of unconditional acceptance.

The two views of psychotherapy have been discussed in terms of differences and commonalities. They have also been discussed as 'relationship therapy' and 'behavior therapy' (Patterson, 1966, 1968). The difference between the views has also been emphasized as general treatment factors versus specific treatments (Patterson, 1984, 2000; Duncan and Moynihan, 1994; Stubbs and Bozarth, 1994,;Bozarth, 1998a; Hubble, Duncan and Miller, 1999). The fundamental difference in values between these views creates problems in the discussion of the art of psychotherapy. The differences raise such questions as: 'Is psychotherapy a science or an art?' 'Is psychotherapy both an art and a science?' 'Are some psychotherapies art and others science?' Perhaps others will explore answers to such questions. I will, however, discuss the art of psychotherapy from the bias of my own experiences and from my involvement with the theory and practice of non-directive client-centered therapy. Rogers succinctly identified the conditions of the therapeutic process (Rogers, 1957, 1959). He identified the therapist conditions as congruence, unconditional positive regard, and empathic understanding of the client's frame of reference. The postulates of Rogers' theory are inherently non-directive for the therapist. The therapist with a non-directive stance trusts that the client is the person who directs her/his own life. It is the client who provides the way, the pace and the direction.

I have chosen to examine the art of psychotherapy in relation to the primary axiom of client-centered theory; i.e., the necessary and sufficient conditions of therapeutic personality change (Rogers, 1959: 213). As well, I concur with Rogers that the axiom of certain necessary and sufficient conditions is the foundation for all successful therapy (Rogers, 1957). This foundation is inherently a non-directive way of being for the therapist. The direction of the client's life is a natural 'organismic' direction that emerges from the therapist's non-directive attitude of experiencing the conditions of unconditional positive regard towards the client and empathic understanding of the client's frame of reference. However, it can be noted from my title that I have become more specific about the art of psychotherapy. I suggest that it is the art of the therapist's 'being' in psychotherapy. This, too, is consistent with Rogers (1980), as he titled one of his books, *A Way of Being* and also with the advent of his book *Client-Centered Therapy* (Rogers, 1951), focused on the therapeutic conditions as therapist attitudes.

My inquiry is presented from a perspective reflecting my personal/professional journey as clinician, educator, theoretician and researcher of psychotherapy. Hopefully, such an approach will allow the reader to be aware of some sources of my bias as well as to know the basis for my conclusions. I will begin with a statement of my current conclusions about psychotherapy.

MY CURRENT CONCLUSIONS ABOUT PSYCHOTHERAPY

The following statements provide a succinct summary of several of my conclusions about psychotherapy that have a bearing on the art of psychotherapy:

- Effective psychotherapy is as much about what the therapist does not do as what the therapist does in therapy.
- The client is her own best expert about her life.
- Success in psychotherapy is determined and developed by clients when they are free enough to experience their own unconditional, positive self-regard.
- The process formulation of psychotherapy is a questionable concept for measuring psychotherapeutic progress; and is a concept that leads therapists to impose on the client's individual process.
- It is a virtual myth that there are specific treatments for particular psychiatric dysfunctions.
- The evidence from psychotherapy outcome research identifies the critical variables as the client/therapist relationship and extratherapeutic variables (e.g., client resources).

These conclusions may perhaps strike some readers as extreme. I hope that sharing experiences that stimulated me to such conclusions will clarify my view of the art of being in psychotherapy.

NON-DIRECTIVE CLIENT-CENTERED THERAPY: THE CLIENT AS AN ARTIST'S ARTIST

The client is her own best expert on her life! This is the parsimonious and resounding exclamation of non-directive client-centered/person-centered therapy (I use these terms interchangeably). Ironically, client-centered theory 'instructs' the therapist to be a certain

205

way even although it is a non-directive theory (Brodley, 1997; Bozarth, 2000a). It is an approach that rests in the 'creative ability and skill' and the potential resources of the client.

I doubt that Rogers would have agreed that the axiom of the 'conditions of the therapeutic process' is an instruction for the therapist to be a certain way (Rogers, 1959: 213). However, I contend that his statement can be viewed as 'instructions' for the client-centered therapist (Bozarth, 1998a, 2001c). Rogers' theory requires that the therapist experience unconditional positive regard (UPR) towards the client and experience empathic understanding (EU) of the client's frame of reference. The therapist must be congruent (C) while experiencing these two attitudes. There are no particular behavioral referents to the therapist's 'way of being'. Unfortunately, response repertoire often replaced the importance of therapist attitudes, resulting in mistaken notions about client-centered therapy (Bozarth, 1984, 1998a, 2001a, 2001b, 2002a; Bozarth and Brodley, 1986). In this way, the art of 'doing' replaced the art of 'being' in the understanding of even client-centered/person-centered therapy (Bozarth, 1998a: 97–101). However, Rogers' 'instructions' are that the therapist consistently *experience* the two attitudes of UPR and EU while being congruent.

THE ART OF PSYCHOTHERAPY FROM A PERSON-CENTERED PERSPECTIVE

In a request for information from individuals involved in client/person-centered practice, one individual's comment summarized many of the responses to my question: 'Any ideas about psychotherapy as an art?' She said, 'Therapy may be just the art and science of being the person who is with the client, providing necessary and sufficient conditions no matter what the approach' (Teresa Clarke, personal communication, December 12, 2001). Another respondent explained person-centered therapy in relation to art in the following way: 'Clients talk about the magical world they discover when they find, understand, feel an answer. Harmony is therapeutic, so is the inner order achieved by therapy. The same when you listen to music or look at an agreeable synthesis. Art is harmony and order' (Ioulios Iossifidis, Rogerian Forum Network, December 14, 2001). Another individual identifies her struggle as a 'client-centered therapist'.

> Sometimes I'm quite concerned that I'm a 'cold' person—well, maybe I am, and so be it, then—because I'm really not very interested in being helpful. I'm interested in understanding, and that's the reason I enjoy doing CCT [client-centered therapy]. So I count myself extremely fortunate that CCT *is* helpful, so I can earn my living doing what I like—much like a musician, I guess, just to mention one example of professionals who do what they enjoy doing, and then, luckily, people find it useful. Actually, I'd feel more precisely identified by the term 'client-centred understander', than by the term 'client-centred therapist'; that would give people a better idea of what they can expect from me. Had it not been for the existence of CCT, I think, I'd never have become a therapist, because I've always felt somewhat at a loss, and I still do, when

people relate to me as some kind of doctor, who knows what it will take for them to solve their problem(s), or relieve their symptom(s). At the same time, I think the term 'therapist', with its connotations of 'treatment' or 'healing', do give people some kind of right to expect some kind of helpful activity from me. So, again, I feel very lucky that CCT *is* helpful. (Lisbeth Sommerbeck, Rogerian Forum Network, January 4, 2002)

In the final analysis, reference to the art of psychotherapy is simply a way to generally refer to activities that can be more specifically defined. The truth of the matter is that art is defined in a way that could also describe science. For example, one definition of art states: 'Human effort to imitate, supplement, alter, or counteract the work of nature' (www.dictionary.com). Art is the 'conscious production or arrangement of sounds, colors, forms, movements, or other elements in a manner that affects the sense of beauty ...' (www.dictionary.com). It is, perhaps, that different therapies accomplish such arrangements in different ways. It is within different frames of logic that the therapist is attentive to the other person. The logic of science in therapy calls for prediction and control of the human experience. The core of art in therapy calls for the individual expression of meaning and feelings. It is not the logic of behavioral change that results in behavioral change. It is the complex, organismic feelings that guide the ebb and flow of the artistic interaction in therapy. The attention of the therapist to the client's momentary frame of the world opens the way for the client's development of unconditional self-regard. Coulson touches on the crux of the artistic interaction of client and therapist in his comments about the expressions of feelings in client-centered community groups. He states:

Feelings come from an unspeakable zone of experience represented by a center of consciousness in the right brain hemisphere, the same center in which poetry and other artistic expressions develop.

As we are capable of recognizing the truth in poetry, we are capable of seeing it in one another's feelings. Feelings are thus both an expression of the deeper self—and a way of making contact with the world. But they can't be justified. They aren't an argument. They are a source of contact with life, which, though available to us, is beyond us, never fully manageable. With feelings, as with life, there are no experts. (Coulson, 1977: 58)

Coulson's comments capture a primary difference between most humanistic therapies and the more reactive-oriented therapies. They reflect the fundamental differences of the two views of psychotherapy characterized in the conference on the evolution of therapy. As profound as these differences might be, all effective therapies involve the art of being. I reach this conclusion even though strongly biased in the fundamental principles of the person-centered approach and guided from the basic axiom of client-centered therapy. I consider Rogers' client-centered/person-centered therapy to be a revolutionary paradigm (Bozarth, 1998a). It is revolutionary because of the therapist's extreme trust in the client's self-determination and self-authority. As such, the emphasis of the therapist

207

is upon the relationship rather than upon the intent to change something about the client or even to focus on problems. Nevertheless, the art of being in psychotherapy is as pertinent for those who operate from the reactive perspective. This way of being may simply be part and parcel of the attitudes of the therapist and present in any therapeutic model of operation. As Tom Malone stated in the 1980 reprint of *The Roots of Psychotherapy*, 'the experiential psychotherapist is one who finds techniques and theoretical systems that are most congruent with his/her person, and so allow him/her the fullest and most feeling expression of their personality and character in relating to patients' (Whitaker and Malone, 1980, xxviii). It is such expression that brings the therapist into the client's world. Remembering that it is the client who is the true artist in therapy allows a great deal of latitude in the therapist's behaviors. The therapist must be comfortable with her model of therapy to be congruent with herself in the therapy session. The therapist's responsiveness and trust of the client is impossible without her own congruence in the session.

AN EVOLUTION OF LEARNINGS

My leanings toward certain conclusions about psychotherapy were developed during the first five years of my professional career in counseling and psychotherapy. Retrospective review of this experience cast my beliefs into more explicit statements, and only now do I find that I more readily cast my lot with therapy as an art—the art of being in psychotherapy. I haven't really thought much about psychotherapy as an art or as a science. Neither do I think of any particular theory of therapy when I think about, or am involved in, a session with another person. It is more accurate for me to say that I seek the 'theory' of the client. I haven't changed much in that respect from the assumptions that I developed in my first professional position.

I was hired in 1958 as a Psychiatric Rehabilitation Counselor in a State Mental Hospital to develop a department of vocational rehabilitation. The program was a pilot project in the state hospitals of Illinois. I was 26 years old, recently discharged from the army and was an unemployed construction worker when I applied for the job. I had a bachelor's degree with concentration in sociology, social studies, speech, political science and psychology. I had no particular interest in clinical work, nor any experience or knowledge about 'pathology'. I had neither experience nor training to work with such clientele. I had no idea of what the job would actually be, and neither did anyone else. The charge was to develop a 'rehabilitation program' that would help individuals to leave the hospital and live independently and, it was hoped, become employed. There was a wide range of freedom to accomplish these goals. It turned out that most of the people referred to me were 'chronic psychotics' who had been in the hospital for decades. Most of them were referred by ward attendants or by other 'patients'. I mention all of this to point out a context that was particularly important. I had no preconceived ideas about 'mentally ill' individuals. My great discovery was that, not knowing what to do to help, I learned to depend upon clients to provide their own direction. They discovered what they wanted to do and could do. I discovered that to just be with them, to listen to them and to give them attention and respect were powerful ways of helping them. The resources of training funds and job placement were helpful, but a distant second to just being with any particular individual. To my surprise, many of these individuals quickly started to demonstrate progress by becoming 'more normal', by working on assignments in the hospital, by being more interpersonal. Their improvements were buttressed by objective evidence of reduced recidivism rates, functional employment, independent living, self-evaluations and increased quality of life. It was a relief and a great discovery that such 'dysfunctional' individuals could find their own ways without guidance.

GUIDELINES FROM 'CHRONIC PSYCHOTICS'

I discovered two of Carl Rogers' writings during this time (Rogers, 1951, 1957). He provided a structure for helping people in a way that I had stumbled into by random behavior and inadequate training. He had written his 'integration statement' about the time that I started working on my first job at the state hospital (Bozarth, 1998a: 103–9; Rogers, 1957). Moreover, Rogers had formalized a couple of my personal conclusions about psychotherapy/counseling (he also agreed with my conclusion that there was no difference between psychotherapy and counseling). These conclusions were: (1) the self-direction of the client could be trusted, and (2) the relationship and the resources of the client were the primary treatment factors. Below are brief vignettes of my experience with several clients who influenced me.

Client vignettes

> **Howard** *had been in the hospital for over twenty years, diagnosed as Schizophrenic, Paranoid Type. He spent several years in a special institution for the criminally insane because of brutal knife attacks on several people. When we first met, he said that he had heard about me from other residents and had asked his physician to refer him. We met for two or three formal appointments, during which time he talked mostly about his jobs in the hospital. He had a paper route, delivering the local paper to hospital staff who lived on the grounds. As well, he did yard work for some of the staff. We also discussed some of the resources available through the rehabilitation program, including support for vocational training. He said that he was interested in some kind of training but that staff had tried to help him get out of the hospital numerous times. It just never worked out. He then concluded that he was really too afraid to get out of the hospital and decided not to see me for any more appointments. He felt that he would not be able to function outside of the hospital. Over the next year, we casually chatted in the coffee shop or under a shade tree about his girlfriends, his work activities, and sometimes about world events. Nearly a year after our initial contact, Howard asked for an appointment and immediately picked up on our conversation of the first formal meetings as though there had been only a few days' lapse. He thought that he might be interested in going to 'barbers' school'. We talked weekly for several months, having what might be considered normal conversations about*

209

normal things. Somewhere in that discussion, Howard decided to pursue training to become a barber. He was accepted for the program, but had to wait six months to begin the next class. He decided during the interim to try to find work outside of the hospital. Hospital staff members were quite skeptical of his search for work, since the industrial community was in a severe recession. I agreed with Howard's wish to meet before and after his job interviews. However, Howard missed most of those meetings and came by at the end of the week to report that he had three job offers. He decided to take the job where he would 'prep' hospital patients for surgery. Howard finally went to barbers' school and was a barber until retirement twenty years later. I was able to follow his life to some extent because my mother was the Chief Medical Records Administrator for the state hospital and was also acquainted with Howard's daughter. It still strikes me as ironic that this 'knife-wielding paranoid' and 'incarcerated psychotic' became a solid contributor to society through employment that involved the use of razors and scissors.

There were many variables that converged to help Howard return to society. If I were one of those helpful variables, what did I do that helped? One of my activities helped me to examine this question. I kept copious notes of the sequential verbal responses of individuals, recording them immediately after sessions. I would then try to determine the thematic 'I' statements of the individuals. Interestingly, I seldom included my responses except in a very general way. Howard's overall theme sequence was something like:

> *I'm curious about this rehabilitation program.*
> *I'm pretty successful in the hospital at making a little money.*
> *I have it made here. I have security and don't have to worry about a lot of things. I have girlfriends. I have spending money. I have a certain kind of respect.*
> *I don't think I could make it outside.*
> *I wonder if I could make it?*
> *I could give it a try. I could go to school while I am still in the hospital.*
> *I am pretty sure I can do it but I have to get out right away or I might change my mind. I can't wait for the starting date of the school.*
> *I am a successful man. I'm employed. I have contact with some of my family who disowned me years ago.*

My sequential themes were along the following lines:

> *I am willing to meet with Howard to just listen to him.*
> *I accept his fear of getting out of the hospital and will support him in his decision not to leave the hospital.*
> *I will go with Howard in his decision to seek employment, even though others think that he 'is crazy' to search.*

In short, my way of being with Howard was to be involved, responsive, and willing to help him find ways to implement his decisions. I had no goals for him to get out of the hospital. I trusted his decisions at every level. I was willing to be with him on his terms.

If I doubted his decisions, I would have shared this with him in depth as I did with many clients.

I learned from Howard, as well as from others, that clear improvements did not depend upon exploration of their internal experiences; that they did not delve into self-exploration; and that they did not focus on their feelings in the ways that are usually considered important in therapy.

Gerald, *a 21-year-old, was diagnosed as Schizophrenic, Paranoid Type. He had been on a locked ward for about six months owing to violent behavior at admission two years earlier, as well as due to recent 'aggressive episodes'. He worked on the hospital garbage disposal truck when not locked up. Gerald asked his doctor for permission to start talking with me about a job. We met in an abandoned kitchen that was to be renovated for office space. Gerald seldom had much to say and most of the first half-dozen sessions were spent in silence. He seemed to exude anger. Now and then, I would find myself visualizing him as pulling a meat cleaver from one of the kitchen drawers and striking me. I would sometimes tell him that I felt afraid of him. I even told him about my imagining that he was chasing me with a meat cleaver. This brought a slight smile to his face that somehow relieved me. He kept asking me to help him obtain an off-grounds pass in order for him to look for a job. He wanted me to take care of things for him. As I have written elsewhere in more detail (Bozarth, Zimring and Tausch, 2002), our interaction suggested that we both acknowledged that he wanted me to do things for him and that I struggled with my willingness to accommodate him. I did accompany him to the employment office and to other job interviews a couple of times. At his request and to my relief, I waited for him in the car. We discussed one of the trips, but then Gerald stated that they were going to pay him for working on the garbage truck in the hospital, and that he would be unable to meet with me for a while. During one session, Gerald talked about his family and reported that he might be discharged to live with them. This was surprising, because much of his anger was thought by his psychiatrist to be towards his family. But then he was suddenly discharged. He had a job and was going home to live with his family. He did stop by to see me prior to discharge, but I was not in the office. I did not hear any more from him until three years later, when he wrote me a letter thanking me for my help and for 'believing' in him. However, nearly fifteen years later, I learned more about what happened with Gerald. I was discarding graduate student files in a university over a thousand miles from the locale where I met Gerald. One of the folders was that of Gerald. He had been in military service, received an honorable discharge, worked as a successful insurance agent, and had received a graduate degree in a 'helping' profession. My summary of thoughts about this therapeutic experience is expressed in the following quote:*
There were no great empathic understanding responses in the dialogue, no noticeable 'moments of movement', but Gerald had a relationship with someone who supported him and went with Gerald's feelings, expressions and internal frame of reference on a moment-to-moment basis, sometimes when logic might dictate otherwise. Gerald's resources, both internal and external, were predominant factors. His motivation to get out of the hospital

and his eventual perception of his family as supportive of him were variables that supported his own theory of change. Many potent factors must have come into his life over the years. Nevertheless, Gerald viewed the relationship as helpful to him over three years later. His motivation to get out of the hospital and his desire to work, along with a new type of family support that was not available to him earlier in his hospital stay, were later variables that supported his own 'theory of change' (Hubble *et al.* 1999). (Bozarth, Zimring and Tausch, 2002: 176–7)

What was my relationship with Gerald? We seemed to have a nonverbal understanding of each other. He knew that I was aware of his anger but that I wasn't really afraid of him. We communicated with our smiles to each other. He smiled at my discomfort of doing things for him.

While reconstructing my memory and pieces of notes of my experience with Gerald, I am struck with his initial view of his family as part of his problem. He was angry with his family; they were even part of his illness. Later, his view of his family became one of his strongest resources. His family became one of the extratherapeutic variables for his change. Extratherapeutic variables include a range of client and environmental factors such as intelligence, support groups, family, education, values, luck, and money. Gerald's situation with his family suggests to me that the therapeutic relationship actually fosters the client's initiative to develop his own resources, as Gerald did with his family.

> **Eleanor** *was in her late forties. A ward attendant referred her. She had been diagnosed in her twenties as Schizophrenic, Undifferentiated Type. I have also reported my experience with her in previous articles (Bozarth, 1998b, 2001a). I was initially shocked in my first meeting with Eleanor. I met a woman with a semi-toothless grin who was sitting on the floor playing with her feces. After muttering some things about my role as a psychiatric rehabilitation counselor and asking some general questions for the record, I settled myself enough to be in the relationship. I explain this as follows:*
> I was acutely aware of my words being attempts to dissipate some of my anxiety, aware of my tendency to want to 'get out of there' and aware of my discomfort with the odors of the ward. She did stop playing with her feces shortly after I introduced myself. I was also aware of my increasing desperation. I felt that she was aware of me, but I could not be sure. I asked myself, 'Why am I asking these questions?' My only goal was to experience some sense of her frame of reference, but I did not feel that I was accomplishing this with Eleanor. Near the end of the session, I made the 'spontaneous' statement: 'Do you think that you might want to go to beauty school?' Immediately, I thought: 'Oh no, why did I say that?' She did not respond. Shortly after, I asked her if she would like for me to return in a few days. She nodded affirmatively. When I returned the next week, Eleanor was washed and neatly dressed. She was patiently waiting in a chair. We started to meet once a week. (Bozarth, 2001a: 193–4)

Eleanor started working on an in-hospital job assignment within a month of our contact. I do not think that she ever got out of the hospital, but her quality of life changed considerably. My thoughts are that my acceptance of my own anxiety increased my trust in Eleanor, and that increased my own unconditional positive self-regard in the moment. I could be with Eleanor in murkiness and uncertainty. My great learning from Eleanor was that very ill individuals may be depended upon to find their own ways of growing.

Howard, Gerald and Eleanor (not their real names) were characteristic of those individuals who taught me psychotherapy. At least three of my conclusions about psychotherapy were strongly imbedded in me when my focus shifted from clinical work to research and education. These conclusions were the following:

• **Effective psychotherapy is as much about what the therapist does not do as what the therapist does in therapy.**
My conclusion is consistent with the statement by Lao Tzu at the beginning of this chapter. It is when one does not presume, evaluate and impose that the individual feels free to change. Gertrude Stein's characterization of Paris is a reasonable metaphor of the art of being in psychotherapy. She said something to the effect that it isn't what Paris gives; it is what she doesn't take away. I did give these three clients my attention, trust, interest and involvement. I did not try to change them, diagnose them, try to decrease their 'problems' or try to convince them to leave the hospital. Rogers wrote about this point early in his career. He commented:

> Therapy is not a matter of doing something to the individual or of inducing him to do something about himself. It is instead a matter of freeing him for normal growth and development. (Rogers, 1942: 29)

It was, and is still, the freedom of the individual's growth and development that resolves the client's problems in person-centered therapy. Later, Rogers further delineated the therapist's way of being that facilitates such freedom.

• **Success in psychotherapy is determined and developed by clients when they are free enough to experience their own unconditional positive self-regard.**
I wasn't familiar with the term unconditional positive regard when I first reached this conclusion; however, it fits the way these clients determined their direction and achieved progress in their own ways. Howard pondered getting out of the hospital and returned to sessions after a year behaving as though he had been in therapy weekly, making an important decision to be trained as a barber. Gerald's view of the therapist as 'believing in' him seemed to form a large part of his progress towards a normal life in society. Eleanor's bizarre behavior changed to more constructive behavior in a short time after a very confusing interaction with the therapist. One common denominator seemed to be that these three individuals were treated as people rather than as 'patients'. I viewed them as people exploring training and work in the same way that 'normal' people might go about such exploration. Mostly, I think that I trusted them to find their own ways and own directions.

213

• **The client is her own best expert on her life.**

This conclusion is similar to the previous two, although a more radical exclamation. Trust of the client's self-determination and self-authority are the crux of the therapist's art of psychotherapy. It was probably with Eleanor that I felt most shaken about my capacity to work with her. It was a great lesson for me to trust this woman playing with her feces to take some control of her life. It was a greater lesson to observe her discovery of the capacity to work.

CONUNDRUMS OF CLINICAL PRACTICE

By the time I moved to a research-and-education state hospital, my views of therapy were pretty well integrated. I pursued formal education as well as workshops concerning many therapeutic approaches. I developed a psychiatric rehabilitation program in which I saw many clients, but also supervised doctoral interns from universities including the universities of Illinois, Iowa, Southern Illinois and Chicago. More formal education involved Adlerian, psychodynamic, gestalt, behavior modification, cognitive behaviorism, and vocational counseling and guidance. I was both student and student supervisor with students from many theoretical orientations. It is interesting that I had no formal training or education in client-centered therapy, with the exception of one course at the University of Chicago taught by Fred Zimring. Fred had become a psychologist studying perception. He became involved with client-centered therapy after an experiment studying perception. The subjects reported psychological changes to Fred because of the non-directive listening of those conducting the experiment. He became intrigued with the power of a non-directive stance.

I periodically undertook research inquiries to satisfy my own curiosity. One of those projects opened additional thoughts for me about therapists' perceptions of their clients. I had some questions about the usefulness of diagnosis and evaluation of clients when I moved to the psychiatric teaching hospital. It was clear that in the conventional state hospital diagnoses were related to particular physicians, rather than to any successful treatment procedures. Identify the diagnosis and one would have identified the physician who led the charge for any particular diagnosis. I wondered if the influence of staff would be just as true with diagnoses and behavioral assessments in a psychiatric training setting. The clerical staff helped me in this project by eliminating all identifying information, including client information and staff information on reports of referrals to me. The upshot was that I could seldom identify the appropriate client with descriptive information from the reports. I could, however, nearly always identify the author of the report. Observations of this nature would later coincide with inquiries into research studies on psychotherapy effectiveness.

THE SOURCE OF CLINICAL SUCCESS

My opportunity to function concomitantly as a student, clinician and clinical supervisor afforded fertile soil to ponder. The source of clinical success left me with ambiguous conclusions. What was the relevance of diagnosis and evaluation when such assessments appeared to be far from the reality of the client? How was it that most clients seemed to change regardless of the type of treatment? How was it that clients changed without any clearly defined treatment? Either the therapies have something in common and/or clients just use and adjust to what is available to them. Client change seemed less related to diagnosis, evaluation or type of therapy than to particular therapists. Moreover, client change was often not even related to particular therapists. I learned that a behaviorist had documented that two-thirds of therapy clients change, and two-thirds of comparable clients change without therapy (Eysenck, 1952). It was ten years later before I realized that this documentation stimulated an influx of research on psychotherapy effectiveness. It was over forty years later when I realized that investigation of the postulate of the therapist conditions (Rogers, 1957) was an important response to Eysenck's conclusions (Stubbs and Bozarth, 1994). The consistent findings were that therapists who measured higher on the conditions postulated by Rogers had clients who significantly improved. Therapists who came out low on the conditions had clients who actually deteriorated. A temporal theme that emerged was that the therapy relationship was 'for better or for worse'.

Later, I realized that Rogers' postulate of the necessary and sufficient conditions in 1957 was not about client-centered therapy, but concerned all therapies and helping relationships. It was really an 'integration' or 'conditions theory' statement (Bozarth, 1998a: 103–9; Stubbs and Bozarth, 1994; Barrett-Lennard, 1998). It was this statement that I had earlier adapted as a model, because it allowed me to do many things as a therapist within the focus of the client's frame of reference. For example, as a Psychiatric Rehabilitation Counselor I could help individuals to obtain training, find employment, acquire appropriate living accommodation or be involved in other actions, while being a certain way in relationships with clients. In short, Rogers' postulates of the necessary conditions captured the essence of my clinical experiences and provided a frame for therapy that requires a certain way of being with clients. This way of being is, from my perspective, the art of psychotherapy.

OTHER EXPERIENTIAL INFLUENCES

My conclusions about psychotherapy have also been strongly influenced by my group experiences. Again, it was my group experience with the people in the state hospital that convinced me that the art of being was more important than leadership or intervention. My first formal group therapy experience consisted mostly of individuals who had moved to community homes after decades as patients of a state mental hospital. The members had been diagnosed with such labels as 'schizophrenic, paranoid type'; 'schizophrenic, hebephrenic'; 'chronic brain syndrome'; 'alcoholism'; 'mentally retarded'; a 16-year-old diagnosed with 'acute schizophrenia'; 'manic depressive'; and 'sociopath'. We usually met under a shade tree and the 'patients' directed the meetings. The weekly meeting was the only formal treatment available to them. They were all considered likely to be readmitted to the hospital. As it turned out, not one of them returned to the hospital. Most of them were eventually discharged and half of them were employed. I later learned in graduate school that nearly everything about the group was antithetical to proper group treatment. My way of being in that particular group was that I depended upon the clients for the substance and direction of our activities. It seemed natural for me to later become involved in 'basic encounter groups' and large community groups (Bozarth, 1998a: 149–59, Bozarth, 2005: Chapter 16 this volume). I could probably be identified as a group junkie, as I explored groups ranging from National Training Lab groups, gestalt groups, TIGER training, Transactional Analysis and Jungian group training. From 1974 up to the present day, I have continued involvement with person-centered groups. My involvement has included the La Jolla program, community groups and international groups facilitated by Carl Rogers and different colleagues. In 1987, five individuals (Barbara Brodley, Nat Raskin, David Spahn, Fred Zimring and myself) founded the Warm Springs Person-Centered Workshop. The program turned out to be an experiment with the principles of the person-centered approach, sometimes challenging our trust and perseverance. We started with designated facilitators, which was discarded along with other structures that are usually imposed on groups. The eighteenth program occurred in February, 2004. Part of what I have learned from group experiences is the following:

> I learned from these groups to trust individuals and the individuals as a group, to trust myself more, to absorb the happenings, and to say little most of the time. I came to believe that an atmosphere of freedom, a safe place for individuals to struggle, a place for individuals to be accepted as they are, were the main ingredients for growth. Empathic understanding and facilitator expertise seem less and less important for personal growth in groups. If this were true, I pondered the implications for individual therapy and for the theory. (Bozarth, 2000b: 35)

My pondering still continues. The most consistent implications for me are that successful therapy is highly related to two major variables. The first variable is the way of being of the therapist. That way is closely related to Rogers' postulates of the three therapist conditions. The second variable is that of the remarkable resiliency and capacities of human beings. Rogers, of course, referred to this as the actualizing tendency.

INDWELLING OF THEORY AND RESEARCH

This quasi-autobiographical approach to unravel my view of the art of psychotherapy is a bit burdensome for me to write, but I hope helpful rather than distracting to readers. To clarify a bit further, my experience was heavily focused on clinical work from 1958 through 1963. I worked on my doctorate at the University of Iowa from 1963 to 1966. Counseling and psychology at the university was largely behaviorally oriented and dedicated to scientific-method empirical research. I entered academia in 1966 and was involved with teaching, writing and various administrative positions such as chairperson and director of departments and programs. I was heavily involved in supervising clinical work, but carried only small client loads.

INDWELLING RESEARCH

My indwelling from 1968 to 1980 was heavily focused on empirical research. I was particularly interested in examining the therapist conditions through empirical research. My interest in the therapist conditions took me to the University of Arkansas to work with Charles Truax and Kevin Mitchell in 1968, because of their major studies on the therapist conditions. It was there that we examined the conditions as related to outcome for a nationwide sample of psychotherapists and, in a separate study, of rehabilitation counselors. I will note a couple of the influences that bear on my thoughts about art in psychotherapy. The 'Arkansas Study' on psychotherapy (Mitchell, Bozarth and Krauft, 1977: 484–8) was disappointing in that the therapist therapeutic conditions were not related to outcome. There was modest improvement for most clients but not differential improvement. The study on rehabilitation counselors (Bozarth and Rubin, 1975) did identify relationships of the counselor conditions to outcome. There were several problems with the psychotherapy studies pointed out by Mitchell *et al.* (1977) and, in a later review, by Patterson (1984). I was intrigued with the fact that nearly all of the therapists and counselors were low on the rating scales of the conditions. Perhaps this meant that the scales were not really valid. However, reviews of other studies by Mitchell *et al.* and others suggested the same phenomenon. That is, therapists with higher ratings were compared with lower-rated therapists, but the higher ratings were *not* high. If the operational definitions and the scales are valid, this means that the truly high levels of the conditions have not been examined.

It turns out that minimally facilitative therapists are compared to non-facilitative therapists. Few of these comparisons involve client-centered therapists. Even so, studies on the conditions from the 1960s through the 1980s suggest that the higher conditions are associated with client improvements (Bozarth, Zimring and Tausch, 2002). This can be interpreted as good news in that just moderately high therapist conditions are associated with client improvement. In general, the operational definitions of the lower scale levels characterize the therapist as being disinterested, off of the mark, and directive in behavior. It is to the client's credit that she might overcome such therapist behavior by not deteriorating. This finding fitted my assertion that it as much what the therapist does not do in therapy as what she does in therapy that helps. I also concluded from my involvement with quantitative research that the conclusions and directions of psychotherapy outcome research were misleading. They seemed to me more politically determined than due to a search for effectiveness of therapy. The art of psychotherapy is sucked out of being by the reliance on the quasi-assessment of psychotherapy. My uneasy feeling about psychotherapy research led me to concentrate more on examining the research findings.

In 1998 I examined the conclusions of the major research reviews on psychotherapy outcome and re-examined my own inquiry. The most prominent conclusions in my opinion were the following:

> 1. Effective psychotherapy is primarily predicated upon (a) the relationship between the therapist and the client, and (b) the inner and external resources of the client.
>
> 2. The type of therapy and technique are largely irrelevant in terms of successful outcome.
>
> 3. Training, credentials and experience of therapists are irrelevant to successful therapy.
>
> 4. Clients who receive psychotherapy improve more than clients who do not receive psychotherapy.
>
> 5. There is little evidence to support the position that there are specific treatments for particular disabilities.
>
> 6. The most consistent of the relationship variables related to effectiveness are the conditions of empathy, genuineness and unconditional positive regard. (Bozarth, 1998a: 165)

I noted that, three decades later, the research reviews reflected the major notions observed by Berenson and Carkhuff (1967) and the Strupp, Fox and Lessler (1969) survey. Specifically, the core of these notions was: 'the importance of the client's involvement in their own treatment and the minuscule influence of "interventive" techniques' (Bozarth, 1998a: 167).

INFLUENCE OF RECENT STUDIES

There were two studies that particularly solidified my thoughts about psychotherapy. Duncan and Moynihan (1994) summarized reviews of quantitative research studies and proposed a model of psychotherapy predicated upon the conclusions of the research. They suggested the utility of intentionally utilizing the client's frame of reference. Their view of empathy, apparently without realizing it, resonated the Rogerian view as 'a function of the client's unique perceptions and experience and requires that therapists respond flexibly to clients' needs, rather than from a particular theoretical frame of reference or behavioral set' (Duncan and Moynihan, 1994: 295).

The second study was a qualitative study of psychotherapy outcome research (Stubbs and Bozarth, 1994). At the Third International Forum of the Person-Centered Approach in 1987, I had reported that the prominent conclusion of the time concerning Rogers' hypothesis of the necessary and sufficient conditions for therapeutic personality change was that the conditions were necessary, but not sufficient. My review published six years later (Bozarth, 1996) and included in my book (Bozarth, 1998a: 35–42) did not find a single study supporting this position. Dr Stubbs independently examined the literature several years later, in an unpublished paper, and also found no empirical support for the assertion. This led us to the qualitative study, which turned out to reveal much more than expected. The conclusion of 'not sufficient' was, at best, an extrapolation of flawed logic without one direct study to support the assertion. We found evolving temporal categories of research investigations and reported the research conclusions in each category. The major implications of the study in relation to effective psychotherapy were reported in the following way:

> The major implications ... are that: (1) the major thread running through the four-plus decades of efficacy research is the relationship of the therapist and client, and that a strong part of those data refer to Rogers' attitudinal conditions of the therapist; and (2) the research foundation for the 'specificity question' has abysmal research support and the precursor of the 'specificity' assumption is the unsupported theme of Rogers' conditions being necessary but not sufficient. (Stubbs and Bozarth, 1994: 168)

It became clear that the increased investigation of specificity was not based on the results of previous research.

Several articles and books started to identify the client as her own best generator of self-change. One review asked, 'What makes psychotherapy work?' and answered with, 'the active client' (Bohart and Tallman, 1996). They conclude that it is not only the client's frame of reference and more reliance on the client, but also that 'we must truly understand that it is the whole person of the client who generates the processes and solutions that create change' (p. 26).

One book summarizing research findings and clinical discoveries (Duncan, Hubble and Miller, 1997), resulted in the conclusion of the 'clients' frame of reference, their world view, as the determining "theory" for our work' (p. 206). Another is an edited book of reviews of psychotherapy research (Hubble, Duncan and Miller, 1999). Although extensive and comprehensive, the crux of this book is its emphasis on the common factors culled from reviews of research studies. The research (Lambert, 1992; Lambert, Shapiro and Bergin, 1986) suggests that 30 percent of the outcome variance is accounted for by the common factor of the client/therapist relationship. Techniques account for 15 percent as does placebo effect. Forty percent of the variance is accounted for by extratherapeutic change variables (factors unique to the client and her environment).

It is from the above evidence that I find additional support for the following conclusion about psychotherapy: The evidence from psychotherapy outcome research identifies the critical variables as the client/therapist relationship and extratherapeutic variables (e.g., client resources).

This conclusion was further buttressed by my involvement in a review of research on client-centered therapy (Bozarth, Zimring and Tausch, 2002). Within a host of conclusions, several stand out as especially significant.

First, research on client-centered therapy decreased to practically nothing in the United States after Rogers' (1957) integration statement. The studies shifted to studies of the necessary and sufficient conditions, regardless of theoretical orientations. I discovered this in an earlier review of the research in the United States (Bozarth, 1983) and found the re-emergence later (Bozarth *et al.*, 2002). The research on the conditions dominated psychotherapy outcome studies during much of the 1950s through to the

1980s. During this time there was substantial research supporting Rogers' postulates of the attitudinal conditions. Confirmation of the research support for over two decades of findings was dismissed by many researchers, with the rationale that the conditions had been found to be 'necessary but not sufficient' and that more specificity was needed. The assumption that the research did not support the conditions was predicated upon fewer than a half-dozen reviews. In addition, these reviews were not analyses of the research findings but calls for increased vigor of research designs. These discoveries led me to have increased skepticism about specific treatment models for psychiatric dysfunction, and to an even stronger belief in the importance of the art of being in psychotherapy. By now, I assume that the reader has gathered that this way of being is non-directive, centralized on the relationship and on the client's self-authority, self-determination and self-developing resources. All of this buttressed my conviction in the following conclusion.

• **It is a virtual myth that there are specific treatments for particular psychiatric dysfunctions.**
This conclusion has been further buttressed by my thoughts about the 'empirically supported treatment' proposals of the Task Force of Division 12, Clinical Psychology, of the American Psychological Association. Their efforts are founded upon the assumption that there are specific treatments for particular dysfunctions (Task Force on Promotion and Dissemination of Psychological Procedures, 1995: Bozarth, 2002b). I argue that this proposal is the epitome of the 'specificity myth', a term referring to treatments based upon specific treatments for specific dysfunctions, and that the premise is fallacious for the treatment of psychiatric conditions. My article reviews the credibility of diagnosis, as well as the deceiving pattern of psychotherapy outcome research. In addition, intrinsic flaws of EST are identified and discussed. All in all, research in psychotherapy outcome brings us closer to the art of being in psychotherapy.

INDWELLING THEORY

Over the last couple of years, I have pondered more about client-centered/person-centered theory. I will briefly share several of my conclusions concerning this indwelling, since these thoughts have moved me closer to my constellation of the 'art of being'.

First, Rogers' (1957) integration statement brought us closer to realizing the common art in all therapies. It is important to reassert that his statement is not about client-centered therapy, but about all therapies and helping relationships. He provides the context for what the therapist should be in psychotherapy, regardless of theoretical orientation. It is after this statement that research in the United States on psychotherapy outcome became focused on the integration statement, also labeled 'conditions therapy theory' (Barrett-Lennard, 1998). It was somehow possible for therapists to communicate these attitudes through various sources and techniques. In fact, techniques and activities were, to Rogers, only as good as the extent to which they communicated the attitudes (Rogers, 1957; Stubbs and Bozarth, 1996; Bozarth, 1998a, 103–9).

Second, the therapist attitudes postulated by Rogers are highly integrated and, functionally, one phenomenon. From Rogers' (1959) *magnum opus* writing, I suggest (a) a reconceptualization of the conditions in terms of their relationship to each other (Bozarth, 1998a: 43–9); (b) that Rogerian empathy always includes unconditional positive regard (Bozarth, 1997, 2001b, 2001c); and (c) that congruence is a special 'way of being' incorporating the therapist's experience of UPR and EU, and is the very presence of the therapist in client-centered therapy (Bozarth, 2001a). In fact, my succinct conclusions about congruence in CCT are as follows.

> Congruence cannot exist without the integral relationship with unconditional positive regard and empathic understanding, otherwise client-centered therapy is threatened as a viable theory. (p. 197)

And a more specific definition:

> Congruence is the manifestation of unconditional positive self-regard (UPSR) and can be identified as the therapist's presence in client-centered therapy. Unconditional positive regard towards, and empathic understanding of, the client's frame of reference characterize this presence. (*ibid.*: p. 197)

I interpret Rogers' *magnum opus* presentation of his theory as ultimately suggesting that it is the therapist's UPSR that begets UPR and EU. He is quite explicit about this in his applications of the theory to family life (Rogers, 1959: 241).

TRUST OF CLIENT'S DIRECTION

One important question that is often taken for granted is the trust of the therapist in the client's self-direction. Although the bedrock of Rogers' theory is the natural constructive growth force (actualizing tendency), most of his focus, along with others, has been on the therapist's role in psychotherapy. One of the things that I noticed about students and practitioners alike, shortly after I started studying various psychotherapeutic approaches, was that most students and therapists seldom learn the potency of simply going with the client's direction. Indicative of this is the belief that the therapist is a process expert, helping the client towards her own experiencing. My opinion is that it misses the point to focus on process, or feelings, or any other specific thing. Such ideas plummet me back to my early experiences with hospitalized psychiatric clients. Most of them didn't go through any noticeable process, no 'moments of movement', nor necessarily any great increase in their 'I' statements. However, they did change on multiple outcome criteria. Apparently, my view is different from most other therapists, including Carl Rogers. He once sent me a paper that he wrote, entitled 'Moments of Movement'. He said that he very much liked the paper and hoped that I would too. I did like the paper, but my thought is that many individuals do not have such moments. Rogers referred to a point in his work with Jim Brown (also Mr Vac) that was one of these moments (Bozarth, 1996). My view was that the moment was more meaningful for Rogers than it was for Mr Brown. I suggested that Rogers giving him cigarettes, loaning

221

him money and being willing to sit in silence with him were more meaningful in terms of Mr Brown's frame of reference than the moments Rogers focuses on. Jim Brown's most important and consistent statement seemed to me to center on his comment in a letter to Rogers after discharge from the hospital. He said that it felt good to be able to say, 'To hell with it'. Here are a couple of more brief examples of client experiences outside of the hospital that further influenced my thinking.

> **Mary**, *a woman in her early thirties, came to the counseling clinic because of the extreme behavioral problems of her three-year-old boy. I probably remember this instance because I was studying behavioral analysis. Mary discussed the disturbing, uncontrollable behavior of the boy, stating that it created tension between her husband and herself and that she was always worn out from dealing with him. She wanted some ideas of how to handle him. The boy's behavior fitted the behavioral analysis guidelines, making it tempting to work out a behavioral program with Mary. If I ever really had any intention to do so, I stalled too long and our time elapsed. She somewhat reluctantly said that she would schedule another appointment. To my surprise, Mary did not mention her son in the next session, or ever again over our sessions. This second session, she revealed that she was having an affair with one of her neighbors. But this too was dropped after the second session, as she expressed her feelings of not being appreciated by her husband; and that too changed to expression of her feelings of inadequacy and incompetence. Eventually she renewed a comfortable relationship with her husband and reported being much less anxious, as well as more capable of dealing with her life. Her boy had become a normally adjusted three-year-old after the first session.*

My relationship with Mary was primarily to listen and be present.

The following vignette is slightly different in that I was supervising a therapist.

> **Harry** *was a 12-year-old boy who had been referred to the counseling center because of behavioral problems at home and school, as well as for receiving failing grades in school. Harry was friendly to the therapist and would answer questions from the therapist, but would then fall into silence. At my suggestion, the therapist allowed Harry to talk about anything; Harry spent several sessions talking about horror movies. For example, he depicted vivid pictures of the gory scenes in the movie* Alien. *The therapist was concerned that they weren't accomplishing anything, and also could not stand listening to the gory descriptions. The supervision involved my listening to the therapist's difficulty with the gore and violence of the movies. But Harry simply continued his depiction over, perhaps, a half-dozen sessions. I suggested to the therapist that he rent a videotape of one of the movies. He did so and found that he increased his capacity to listen to Harry. The therapist felt that discussion of the movies was easier, but still felt that they weren't getting anywhere. I simply told him to keep listening, not to worry about accomplishing change. It was after about eight sessions that Harry's parents came in for a session and brought records from his school over the past couple of months. Harry had changed in all aspects of his violent behavior and was now receiving 'As' in school. Needless to say, the parents were thrilled by*

the success. In a later interview, Harry said to his therapist, 'You know, I am something like that alien ... well, I used to be ...'

The therapist and I learned something about the potency of the attentive presence of listening and being with another person.

I wrote about my perception of my role as a therapist with several clients when exploring Rogers' concept of congruence (Bozarth, 2001a). This summary is apropos here as well:

> My role as a therapist in the above therapeutic interactions might be summarized as 'naive' and 'non-interfering'. My conscious intentions were to have no preconceptions about what the person might do, be or become. My only intent for action is to experience the person's frame of reference. This means that I am open to the person's immediate view of the world, including her feelings and ideas. This includes acceptance of murkiness, as in Eleanor's world, or acceptance of not knowing the world, as in Lawrence's sessions. [*Lawrence was a client not reported here.*] It includes the extreme trust of the client's constructive inner motivation. I also do not want to impose my empathic understanding on the client. I think that these intentions are shown in the above interactions. It seems to me that my unwavering trust in the other individual results in greater trust in myself. It is as though the more I trust the other individual, the more I trust my own experiences in the relationship. The more I trust myself, the more I trust and experience the client. I do not have any intention to share my experiences with the client, but I am willing to share them when they are 'persistent', a term which Rogers used periodically when discussing congruence. I am also open to sharing them if they are spontaneous, with high intensity in myself. I never think about my UPSR or about my congruence. My focus is upon the client's world with the intention of setting my self aside or, perhaps, blending my self with (or in deference to) the client's self. My only intention is to be with the client in her world. Ideally, all of my specific behaviors and responses will emanate from this facet of our interaction. I am free to be a certain way in the relationship. Being this way, I feel free to 'do' many specific things out of the client's frame of reference. (Bozarth, 2001: 196–7)

At the risk of overdoing it, one more story of a client in a counseling center taught me a valuable lesson. Prior to going to work at the University of Arkansas, I was a therapist subject in the psychotherapist study being undertaken by Truax and Mitchell. This meant that my randomly selected client was tested several times by a psychometrist. The tests included a battery of outcome tests including the Psychiatric Status Schedule, Minnesota Multiphasic Personality Inventory and self-concept measures. All recorded sessions were rated for therapist's levels of the conditions of congruence, unconditional positive regard and empathy. I was consciously focusing on being as empathic as possible with the client. She tended to blame everything on external problems. I did not feel connected with her and when I confessed my difficulty to her, she simply dismissed it. She kept returning for weekly appointments, and I kept trying to stay with her. We had our last appointment before I left for the job with the directors of the research project. I was feeling that I simply was not very helpful to her. But then she started telling me how much she had changed since beginning therapy. She understood things better; her marriage had been salvaged; she felt more confident; and so forth. A couple of years later, I could not resist checking her improvement scores while working on the research project. She had significant changes on many of the measures, corresponding to her self-exclamations at the last session. The tape ratings for my levels of the conditions were moderate, but hardly outstanding. I relate this story because of her last statement at the last session. By the time she finished relating her satisfaction of feeling so improved, I had started to feel something like, 'I am a pretty good therapist after all; I didn't know I did so well.' My recall is that I was feeling a bit cocky. Then she hit me with her last statement—something like: 'Yes, I am doing so much better and it is all because *I took up golf.*' This story has always been important to me for several reasons. It reminds me that it is important to be humble as a therapist. It is important that client perceptions of reasons for change may be significantly different from our psychological explanations. It is important to realize that our perceptions of ourselves as therapists are perhaps significantly different from the clients' perceptions.

SUMMARY

The art of psychotherapy that has evolved for me from clinical experiences, research findings and indwelling of Rogers' theory is that a certain presence of the therapist frees the client to help herself. This presence is characterized in the relationship and fosters the client's utilization of extratherapeutic variables. The presence is not characterized by particular response styles often associated with empathy (Bozarth, 1984). Also, the relationship is not the 'therapeutic alliance' that is predicated on the intent to seduce the client into complying with therapeutic goals. The relationship is what happens between two individuals. As such, it is highly idiosyncratic and may involve a wide array of specific behaviors. The art of psychotherapy in Rogers' theory is the presence of the therapist's unconditional positive self-regard, creating an atmosphere of unconditional positive regard towards the client within an empathic context. It is the unconditional empathic reception of the client with trust in the client's own direction, way and pace that is, in my view, the art of psychotherapy and the crux of success in all models of psychotherapy.

Author's note: Correspondence may be directed to Jerold D. Bozarth, 1160 Hunting Creek Lane, Watkinsville, GA 30677, or <jbozarth1@charter.net>.

REFERENCES

Barrett-Lennard GT (1998) *Carl Rogers' Helping System: Journey and substance.* London: Sage.

Berenson BG & Carkhuff RR (1967) (Eds) *Sources of Gain in Counseling and Psychotherapy.* New York: Holt, Rinehart & Winston.

Bohart, AC & Tallman AC (1996) The active client: Therapy as self help. *Journal of Humanistic Psychology, 36,* 7–30.

Bozarth JD (1983) Current research on client-centered therapy in the USA. In M Wolf-Rudiger and H Wolfgang (Eds) *Research on Psychotherapeutic Approaches: Proceedings of the 1st European Conference on Psychotherapy Research.* Trier, Frankfurt: Peter Lang, pp. 105–15.

Bozarth JD (1984) Beyond reflection: Emergent modes of empathy. In R Levant & J Shlien (Eds) *Client-Centered Therapy and the Person-Centered Approach: New directions in theory, research, and practice.* New York: Praeger, pp. 59–75.

Bozarth JD (1996), A silent young man: The case of Jim Brown. In BA Farber, DC Brink & PM Raskin (Eds) *The Psychotherapy of Carl Rogers: Cases and commentary.* New York: Guilford Press, pp. 240–50.

Bozarth JD (1997) Empathy from the framework of Client-Centered Theory and the Rogerian hypothesis. In AC Bohart & LS Greenberg (Eds) *Empathy Reconsidered: New directions in psychotherapy.* Washington DC: APA, pp. 81–102.

Bozarth JD (1998a) *Person-Centered Therapy: A revolutionary paradigm.* Ross-on-Wye: PCCS Books.

Bozarth JD (1998b) Remembering Eleanor: A way of contact. *Person-Centered Journal, 5*(1), 36–8.

Bozarth JD (2000a) Non-directiveness in client-centered therapy: A vexed concept. Paper presented at the Eastern Psychological Association (March 20), Baltimore, MD.

Bozarth JD (2000b) Forty years of dialogue with the Rogerian hypothesis. In D Bower (Ed) *The Person-Centered Approach: Applications for Living.* New York: Writers Club Press, pp. 27–54.

Bozarth JD (2001a) Congruence: A special way of being. In G Wyatt (Ed) *Rogers' Therapeutic Conditions: Evolution, theory and practice. Vol. 1: Congruence.* Ross-On-Wye: PCCS Books, pp. 184–99.

Bozarth JD (2001b) An addendum to Beyond Reflection: Emergent modes of empathy. In S Haugh and T Merry (Eds) *Rogers' Therapeutic Conditions: Evolution, theory and practice. Vol 2: Empathy.* Ross-on-Wye: PCCS Books, pp. 144–54.

Bozarth JD (2001c) Client-centered unconditional positive regard: A historical perspective. In JD Bozarth & P Wilkins (Eds) *Rogers' Therapeutic Conditions: Evolution, theory and practice. Vol. 3: Unconditional positive regard.* Ross-on-Wye: PCCS Books, pp. 5–18.

Bozarth JD (2002b) Empirically supported treatment: Epitome of the Specificity Myth. In JC Watson, RN Goldman & MS Warner (Eds) *Client-Centered and Experiential Psychotherapy in the 21st Century: Advances in theory, research and practice.* Ross-on-Wye: PCCS Books, pp. 168–81.

Bozarth JD (2005) Non-directive Person-Centered Groups: Facilitation of freedom and personal power. In BE Levitt (Ed) *Embracing Non-Directivity: Reassessing person-centered theory and practice for the 21st century.* Ross-on-Wye: PCCS Books, pp. 281–302.

Bozarth JD & Brodley BT (1986) Client-centered psychotherapy: A statement. *Person-Centered Review, 1*(3), 262–71.

Bozarth JD & Rubin SE (1975) Empirical observations of rehabilitation counselor performance and outcome: Some implications. *Rehabilitation Counseling Bulletin, 19*(1), 294–8.

Bozarth JD, Zimring F & Tausch R (2002) Client-Centered Therapy: Evolution of a revolution. In D Cain and J Seeman (Eds), *Handbook of Humanistic Psychotherapy: Research and practice.* Washington DC: American Psychological Association, pp. 147–88.

Brodley BT (1997) The non-directive attitude in client-centered therapy. *Person-Centered Journal, 4*(1), 18–30.

Coulson WR (1977) The foreignness of feelings. In WR Coulson, DL Meador & B Meador (Eds) *The La Jolla Experiment: Eight personal views.* La Jolla, CA: The La Jolla Program, pp. 45–58.

Duncan BL, Hubble MA & Miller SD (1997) *Psychotherapy with 'Impossible' Cases: The efficient treatment of therapy veterans.* New York: WW Norton.

Duncan BL & Moynihan D (1994) Applying outcome research: Intentional utilization of the client's frame of reference. *Psychotherapy, 31,* 294–301.

Eysenck HJ (1952) The effects of psychotherapy: An evaluation. *Journal of Consulting Psychology, 16,* 319–24.

Hubble MA, Duncan BL & Miller SD (1999) *The Heart and Soul of Change: What works in therapy.* Washington, DC: American Psychological Association.

Lambert MJ (1992) Implications of outcome research for psychotherapy integration. In JC Norcross & MR Goldfried (Eds) *Handbook of Psychotherapy Integration.* New York: Basic, pp. 94–129.

Lambert MJ, Shapiro DA & Bergin AE (1986) The effectiveness of psychotherapy. In SL Garfield & AE Bergin (Eds) *Handbook of Psychotherapy and Behavior Change.* 3rd edn. New York: Wiley, pp. 157–212.

Mitchell KM, Bozarth JD & Krauft CC (1977) A reappraisal of the therapeutic effectiveness of accurate empathy, non-possessive warmth, and genuineness. In AS Gurman & AM Razin (Eds) *Effective Psychotherapy: A handbook of research.* New York: Pergamon, pp. 482–502.

Patterson CH (1966) *Theories of Counseling and Psychotherapy.* New York: Harper and Row.

Patterson CH (1968) Relationship therapy and/or behavior therapy. *Psychotherapy: Theory, Research and Practice, 5,* 226–33. Reprinted in CH Patterson (2000) *Understanding Psychotherapy: Fifty years of client-centred theory and practice.* Ross-on-Wye: PCCS Books, pp. 35–45.

Patterson CH (1984) Empathy, warmth, and genuineness in psychotherapy: A review of reviews. *Psychotherapy, 21*(4), 431–8. Reprinted in CH Patterson (2000) *Understanding Psychotherapy: Fifty years of client-centred theory and practice.* Ross-on-Wye: PCCS Books, pp. 161–73.

Patterson CH (2000) *Understanding Psychotherapy: Fifty years of client-centred theory and practice.* Ross-on-Wye: PCCS Books.

Rogers CR (1942) *Counseling and Psychotherapy.* Boston: Houghton Mifflin.

Rogers CR (1951) *Client-Centered Therapy: Its current practice, implications, and theory.* Boston: Houghton Mifflin.

Rogers CR (1957) The necessary and sufficient conditions of therapeutic personality change. *Journal of Consulting Psychology, 21*(2), 95–103.

Rogers CR (1959) A theory of therapy, personality, and interpersonal relationships as developed in the client-centered framework. In S Koch (Ed) *Psychology: Study of a science: Vol. 3. Formulation of the person and the social context.* New York: McGraw-Hill, pp. 184–256.

Rogers CR (1980) *A Way of Being.* Boston: Houghton Mifflin.

Strupp HH, Fox RE & Lessler K (1969) *Patients View their Psychotherapy.* Baltimore: Johns

Hopkins Press.

Stubbs JP & Bozarth JD (1994) The dodo bird revisited: A qualitative study of psychotherapy efficacy research. *Journal of Applied and Preventive Psychology, 3*(2), 109–20.

Stubbs JP & Bozarth JD (1996) The Integrative Statement of Carl Rogers. In R Hutterer, G Pawlowsky, PF Schmid and R Stipsits *Client-Centered and Experiential Psychotherapy: A paradigm in motion.* Frankfurt am Main: Peter Lang, pp. 25–33.

Whitaker CA & Malone TP (1980) *The Roots of Psychotherapy.* New York: Brunner/Mazel.

Wolpe J (1987) The promotion of scientific psychotherapy. In JK Zeig (Ed) *The Evolution of Psychotherapy.* New York: Brunner/Mazel, pp. 133–42.

Zeig JK (1987) *The Evolution of Psychotherapy.* New York: Brunner Mazel.

Chapter 13

NON-DIRECTIVENESS AND THE PROBLEM OF INFLUENCE

Marjorie Witty

Psychotherapy is the name we give to a particular kind of personal influence ... but who is to say whether or when such interactions are helpful or harmful, and to whom?

Thomas Szasz

INTRODUCTION

All psychotherapies may be analyzed as occasions of social influence. In order to justify the continued significance of non-directiveness as a defining criterion of identity in client-centered/person-centered therapy, and to illustrate its usefulness as a helpful compass for the therapist, this chapter explores conformity to social norms, compliance with the authority of the therapist, person-perception, and attributional errors as sources and mediators of influence in the therapy situation. The point of the analysis is to illustrate the helpfulness of non-directiveness in order to limit iatrogenic influence while preserving therapeutic influence. While it is impossible to avoid harm to the client in therapy, this impossibility should not lead us to abandon the attempt to minimize this harm. By committing to being guided by non-directiveness, the client-centered therapist may experience more personal freedom while doing less harm.

Meaningful differences exist between client-centered/person-centered therapies and experience-centered/process-directive therapies, and may become more distinct through the lens of social influence. Process theorists (Gendlin, 1974; Greenberg, Rice and Elliott, 1993; Lietaer, 1998) picture non-directiveness as an outmoded rule which inhibits the therapist as a person and constrains the therapy process. Further, Lietaer argues that the social status of highly-trained therapists is warranted and desirable as a source of influence and, as such, should be claimed and deployed on behalf of the client (Lietaer, 1998).

While client-centered therapists agree that offering oneself as a source of help to another person as a psychotherapist must imply expertise, the expertise is that of being a person *practiced in acceptant understanding* who is open to being affected and influenced in the encounter with a person seeking help (Grant, 1990; Brodley, 2002; Schmid, 2004). Process-directive theorists define expertise as a use of therapist influence with the goal of returning the client's attention to the experiencing process, or to other therapist-defined tasks (Lietaer, 1998; Greenberg, Rice and Elliott, 1993), and with this process goal argue that non-directiveness is a non-issue since the client is being invited to return to the 'original source' of meaning (Hendricks, 2002). This chapter suggests that all therapeutic approaches purvey iatrogenic effects which issue from directiveness, as well as other types of social influence. Client-centered therapy, with its characteristic therapist attitude of non-directiveness, is defended as one way of working with clients that minimizes iatrogenic effects.

I. SOCIAL INFLUENCE IN THERAPY

THERAPY AS A SOCIAL SITUATION

The therapeutic situation is a *social situation* and is, therefore, a human relationship subject to interpersonal, contextual, social and situational influences which arise when two persons are communicating with each other—in this particular case, the situation being defined as one in which the therapist contracts to provide the service of helping to the voluntary client. Client-centered therapy is a situation in which social influence flows bidirectionally from therapist to client, and from client to therapist, in a fluid, dynamic way. It is useful to analyze forms of influence in the therapy situation in order to correct misunderstandings about client-centered therapy. In this section I review three instances of influence (power in action): therapist influence, client influence and situational factors. *Therapist influence*, which arises from the person of the therapist in relation to the client and from the therapy itself, will be examined with reference to the authority of the therapist in stimulating compliance and conformity with social norms. *Client influence,* which stems from the person of the client in relation to the therapist, will be examined in terms of the automaticity of person-perceptual processes which affect the client's reactions to the therapist. *Situational factors* will be instanced with reference to the socially inculcated dispositional bias, in which persons tend to attribute responsibility for problems in living to dispositions within persons, instead of situational factors which can be shown to account for a greater share of causal influence (Nisbett and Ross, 1997).

POWER

Before examining these three forms of influence, the construct of power is explored in more detail. Broadly defined, *power is the ability to exert social influence* (Fiske, 2004: 521). 'Power is potential influence, and influence is power in action' (Ng cited in Fiske, 2004: 521). Power can be further broken down conceptually into types. French and Raven (1959), in their classic treatment of types of power in the interpersonal domain, describe five kinds of power which involve both a 'target' of influence and perception by the target. *Reward power* is the target's perception that the other person controls benefits, whereas *coercive power* is the perception that the other person controls punishments. *Referent power* is described by the target's identification with the other; *expert power,* by the target's perception that the other is knowledgable; and *legitimate power*, by the target's perception of the other's right to influence (Fiske, 2004: 520). All of these forms of power can be found relevant within the context of psychotherapy.

Client-centered therapists, as well as most other therapists, possess all five of French and Raven's forms of power. Therapists 'control' benefits such as care, acceptance, concern, etc., and punishments such as refusing to take phone calls at times the client may want to call, refusing to reduce or forgive fees when the client loses her employment, and the most fundamental refusal—to be an equal in personal disclosure and vulnerability; to move the relationship into the world as a mutual friend. Therapists function under the aegis of 'expert knowledge' which is ratified by academic degrees and licenses from the state. They are likely viewed as sources of legitimate influence by clients, and they may be viewed as persons who are worthy of emulation and identification. Clients, by virtue of their situation in therapy, can be said only to have reward power in that they can leave the therapist and deprive him or her of income and the client's presence. Clients may have different kinds of expert power that can tend to equalize the power in the therapeutic situation. Overall, though, by virtue of the structure of the relationship, the therapist has more and different kinds of power, and thus the ability to influence.

In her analysis of the dynamics of power within the therapy context, Proctor (2002: 37) points out that this complex construct has variously been defined as coercive force (power-over), as a motivational source within the self to affect one's interpersonal environment (power-from-within), and as collaboration of two autonomous persons (power-with). Proctor argues that older models of therapy have emphasized the power of the therapist to effect change in the client, a kind of unidirectional flow of influence. Her own analysis elucidates that power is shared collaboratively in all therapeutic relationships, and in particular in person-centered therapy which consciously advocates client self-authority and the movement away from external influence as the goal of therapy. However, the acknowledgment of the client's internal sources of power does not finally erase the imbalance of power in the therapeutic relationship.

Research in social psychology has focused on interpersonal processes that involve the flow of social influence, the factors that contribute to possession of social influence, and the ways in which day-to-day, ordinary, human cognitive and emotional functions lead to cognitive biases. Some of these processes involve deliberate efforts to influence others, e.g., the effort to market a workshop to therapists which will help them develop a 'market niche'. Social influence also comes into play as an aspect of person-perception and attributions of competence, such as the client's perception of the therapist as a professional who possesses legitimacy by virtue of having attained credentials and licensure.

Within the therapy relationship, both parties to the relationship possess power and thus both parties' influence affects therapy outcomes (DeVaris, 1994). As Rogers (1951) asserted, the influencing process (which includes the core conditions) depends upon personal perceptions. The client perceives the socially ascribed role of the therapist as one of legitimate expertise even before encountering the therapist in person. Patterson states:

> *Therapy is an influencing process.* The intent of the therapist is to influence the client. If this were not so, the therapist would not be practicing. The issue is

not directiveness–non-directiveness. Rogers recognized the irrelevance of this as an issue when, as Cain (1989) notes, he abandoned consideration of the issue. The relevant issue is the nature and extent of this influence that is consistent with the philosophy and assumptions of client-centered therapy. (Patterson, 2000: 182, original emphasis)

Opposing Patterson's charge of irrelevancy, I think that debates within the person-centered/ experiential approaches over directiveness and non-directiveness are, in fact, a focal site of difference which necessitates continuing attempts to define inclusionary criteria for identity across the many 'tribes' of the 'person-centered nation' (Warner, 2000; Lietaer, 2002). Patterson points out, correctly I think, that the fundamental issue has to do with what kinds of influence are consonant with the theory and values of the client-centered approach.

IMPLICATIONS OF THERAPY AS AN INFLUENCING PROCESS

The question arises as to whether an essentialist approach that makes categorical statements about human nature—including approaches followed by adherents of the 'actualizing tendency', 'focused experiencing' and 'processing of meaning'—is necessarily going to result in methods which systematically diminish the client's own possibilities for self-creation. Approaches which define process-diagnostic categories such as 'levels of experiencing' or 'fragile process', may stimulate the therapist to provide either interpersonal solutions or guidance, with the aim of remedying precisely that which the approach defines as a problem.[1] This is where non-directive client-centered therapists part company with focusing-oriented or other process-directive therapies—they do so in the belief that influence effects must necessarily enter in with the application of *deliberate methods* which are not products of the natural, spontaneous, and personal encounter between client and therapist. The criticism is that the client is necessarily 'given a lesson in his or her inferiority' (Gergen and Kaye, 1992: 171) when he is directed, invited to focus, advised; in fact, even when he is attended to in some other-than-ordinary way. For the therapist to attend to the client with some intensity, attributing specialness to the utterances of the client, can communicate implicitly that what is happening between client and therapist is not a conversation, but a specialized process which only the therapist fully understands.

---

1. According to Held's generic model (1995), which aims to encompass current systems of therapy, modernist systems typically posit three terms in the therapy equation: (A) the '*problem*' to which the therapy is the (B) '*solution*'. The linkage between the constructions of 'problem' and 'solution' most often leads to the (C) *categorization* of clients and/or types of problems (diagnoses). For instance, in a cognitive-behavioral model, the problem (A) is often described as 'irrational, negative, and self-defeating attributions', while the solution (B) involves directing the client's attention to these irrational thought patterns in order to replace them with rational ones. The third term (C) of client/problem categories may range from the *general* ('psychotic' versus 'non-psychotic') to the *particularized* (represented by diagnostic distinctions such as 'phobic', 'rejection sensitive', 'borderline') to the *non-defined*, (therapy systems which eliminate categories altogether). Systems which make no commitment to defining clients' problems in advance of the encounter are considered *postmodern* and *antisystematic* (Held, 1995: 58).

Essays by Moon (2005) and Grant (2005) in this volume variously acknowledge an influencing process and advocate an ethical posture of respect for the client, culminating in a disciplined constraint of influence through defining the target of empathic understanding as the clients' intended communications (Grant), and the realization of congruence as inclusive of spontaneous responses from the frame of reference of the therapist (Moon). Consideration of spontaneous versus non-spontaneous therapist-frame responses (Moon, 2005; Brodley, 1999) represents a deep concern with the impact of the power of the therapist. As Tomlinson and Whitney (1970) point out in their article 'Values and Strategy in Client-Centered Therapy', means and ends should be consistent in the moral domain of therapy practice. If one's end is to empower the client, one cannot employ disempowering means to do so on the assumption that means have no effects in and of themselves.

If we endorse aims such as 'empowerment' or 'freeing the client's potentials for self-realization', are we necessarily—at the level of practice—setting goals for the client? Brodley (1999) has addressed this problem by discriminating the objective scientific language of the theory from the actual practice of being with a client. She argues that there is no necessary conflict between articulating goals in the theory and being non-directive in practice, although no matter how non-directively the therapist realizes the core conditions, it does not negate the possibility of communicating the therapist's values regarding personal authority and power. That is, to the extent that the client accurately perceives the non-directive attitude, he or she can extrapolate values which inform this therapeutic stance.

DELVING FURTHER INTO FACTORS OF INFLUENCE: THERAPIST INFLUENCE

The question I turn to now is the issue of whether the influence that arises as a by-product of empathic understanding, as well as other therapist intentional behavior, evokes submission to the authority of the therapist. Obedience may be defined as a change in belief or behavior in response to pressure from a figure perceived to hold authority (Gergen and Gergen, 1981: 497). Most of the time, voluntary therapy relationships are not appropriately described as involving obedience to the therapist's authority since, most of the time, clients have of their own volition sought out the therapist for help and, if they are not helped, have the power to fire their therapists.[2] Compliance is perhaps the more relevant concept, along with conformity and belonging. Compliance may be defined as involving acceding to requests in order to gain rewards or to avoid punishment for nonconformity. Additional possibilities for compliance are numerous in a situation in which the client is confronted with an ambiguous situation

---

2. However, as one thinks about the actual number of non-voluntary clients—children, mothers who have lost custody of children through Child Protective Services, persons remanded to therapy for substance abuse, involuntary psychiatric prisoners, persons incarcerated for crimes who are ordered to receive 'treatment', teenagers sent to boot camps by their parents for being queer—the scope of the problem with authoritarian power, as Szasz (1978) puts it, the problem of 'salvific coercion' in therapy—becomes evident. This discussion, however, is limited to the situation of voluntary therapy.

in which socially accepted norms for behavior are not explicitly identified, and in which he or she is anxious to be accepted. Client-centered therapists do not ask leading questions and rarely pose questions of any type except questions for clarification (Brodley, 1999). It seems unlikely that clients in client-centered therapeutic relationships are actively complying, but the possibility exists nonetheless because clients do not necessarily recognize or believe that they are participating in a relationship which strives to protect their autonomy. Given the past experiences of many of us with authorities, it is quite possible that clients may experience the threat of the therapist's power in spite of many, many hours of experiences which would contradict the idea that the therapist wishes to wield power or control over the client.

Client behaviors or beliefs which lead to conforming to social norms in order to gain acceptance and belonging are a significant aspect of compliant behavior in therapy. As several authors in the person-centered approach have shown through the examination of Rogers' therapy behavior (Brodley and Brody, 1990; Merry, 1996), empathic understanding responses represent the majority of responses to clients. As such, empathic understanding responses should be explored as sources of 'perceived meta-communications' of therapist influence that pertain to aims which the client seeks. These various aims are idiosyncratic to clients because clients are unique. However, common therapist responses that may influence by implication, because of these aims, may be seen in the following statements: 'I understand what you just said. It is important to me and I want to understand more.' 'You are comprehensible to me.' 'I accept you and care about what you are saying to me.' To a significant extent, the implicit meanings which accompany explicit empathic understanding responses express the attitude hypothesized to centrally effect personality change: unconditional positive regard (Bozarth, 1998; Patterson, 1984). This is the pure 'elixir' of therapeutic influence, which is wholly beneficent. However, the possibility exists that some clients may be interpreting the therapist's empathic responses (and the generally warm and acceptant presence) as *rewards for conformity to norms which clients believe to be governing the therapy situation.*[3] This erroneous conclusion could result in the client's belief that his or her in-session behavior has elicited the acceptant and caring responses from the therapist, leading to another erroneous assumption (see Cooper, 2005). It is not the behavior of the client that elicits unconditional positive regard; it is the *person* of the client. In this case, we may surmise that the client's appraisal of the therapist's regard is conditional, but that she enjoys some degree of efficacy in eliciting that conditional regard. The basic impact of unconditional positive regard is diluted, but may still be regarded as therapeutic as opposed to iatrogenic.

In addition to querying the array of possible effects of empathic responses, it is necessary to ask whether the empathic understanding response process (Brodley, 1996, 1997) elicits conformity through selective reinforcement. Lietaer (1998) has argued that we cannot avoid selectively reinforcing aspects of clients' narratives, and that the therapeutic avenue is the selective reinforcement of client utterances which are deemed

---

3. I recall a client who told me, in a state of anguish, that he had the eyes of a rapist. As he was leaving my office, I looked into his eyes and commented that he didn't look much like a rapist to me. He dismissed my remark with 'You *have* to like me; you're my therapist.'

to arise from authentic experiencing, because contact with immediate bodily experiencing leads toward a self-propelled process of personality change (Gendlin, 1970). From a client-centered vantage point, if you are giving yourself the instruction to listen for the *point of the client's communication*, you are trying as best you can not to deflect the client away from his or her intended, self-generated thread in conversing. The therapist is consciously devoting her/himself to the client's intended narrative. Empathic responses, from within this context, if they can be said to reinforce selectively, reinforce the point the client is attempting to bring out in the moment and, conceivably, may reinforce the *general* behavior of the client's relating a personal narrative. However, it is entirely conceivable that errors in understanding—which may occur without the therapist's awareness when the client does not correct the therapist's error—may reinforce a *particular* aspect of the client's communication; but the presumed randomness in errors of understanding would tend to counteract selectivity effects. Selective reinforcement *does* seem an accurate description of focusing prompts or invitations, because the client is selectively directed toward 'depth', or 'inner flow of experience', or 'deeper levels of experiencing' and away from 'dead end discussions' (Gendlin, 1996: 7).

Nonetheless, it is easy to imagine that clients experience pressure to conform to certain expectations in the situation of therapy. Unquestionably, therapists carry both overt and covert expectations; for their clients to arrive roughly on time, for clients to remain clothed, for clients to respect the personal space of the therapist, to at least minimally acknowledge the presence of the therapist, etc. Although we cannot with certainty assume that clients *want* our empathic acceptance, they seek from us ... something; something that will help. And they bring with them internalized social norms which guide behavior in the therapy situation; our expectations for them may be deliberately undefined and wide open, but the clients' own prior social learning provides scripts (Schank and Abelson, 1977) for behavior in interpersonal interactions such as therapy. Insofar as the client is not yet able to discriminate the uniquely nonjudgmental, unconstrained character of the therapy situation, he or she may erroneously perceive it as a situation in which he or she is expected to 'behave' by being deferential to the expert or legitimate power of the therapist.

PERSON-PERCEPTION AS AN INSTANCE OF CLIENTS' INFLUENCE

An aspect of the client's internalization of social norms may be described by the notion of 'person-perception'. Fiske notes that automatic perception processes are activated in the first moments of meeting another person. 'Subtle prejudice builds on this kind of automatic perception process. People are extremely good at categorizing, within a fraction of a second, people's race, sex and age, based on visual cues that are highly practiced. These categories activate stereotypic associations which may then be applied to the individual' (Fiske, 2004: 411). Our awareness of these practically automatic processes in ourselves alerts us to our being classified and categorized by our clients. In this respect, clients have a kind of power in that their favorable or unfavorable reactions to us make some degree of difference, even though our vulnerability to these judgments diminishes with experience and the self-perception of competence.

Factors which may work against the perception that we can be successful in helping our clients are often a concern for developing client-centered therapists. If the therapist is young and inexperienced, he or she may worry about not being 'believable' as a therapist. Additionally, therapists have concerns about the possibility of clients' biases or prejudices, particularly if they belong to a stigmatized group based on race, age, gender, social class or sexual orientation. Therapists who suffer from health problems or grievous losses which alter their appearance have expressed concern about clients' reactions (Gershon and Mitchell, 1996). Part of the concern is the legitimate issue of whether the therapist's youth, race, health, etc., will distract the client, leading the client to feel the need to explore concerns which were not present initially or to worrying about the therapist's comfort, availability and reliability. The other part of the concern regards— or so it has seemed to me—the desire to be perceived as a 'legitimate' helper. The point here is that clients' perceptions of us as therapists affect our comfort and security in the therapy situation. With years of experience, client-centered therapists are much less concerned with their clients' perceptions and are able to be themselves spontaneously and easily, no matter who the client is. This probably is due to the greater degree of experience of the therapist in knowing how to meet the issue of how he or she is being perceived. Therapists as human beings are sensitive to the positive regard of others, including clients, and to its lack.

A client-centered colleague who is still new to doing therapy describes her anxiety about being perceived as competent by new clients.

> I think my initial response is that I feel differently depending upon the situation ... When I first began my practicum, and I was meeting five clients for the very first time, I was absolutely terrified. I was so anxiety ridden, I really had to work to soothe myself. What was I afraid of? I think a host of things. I had doubts that I knew what to 'do', I had doubts I could be of any use to clients. I really questioned the weight of the responsibility. (K. Strickland, personal communication, March 20, 2005)

In this case, the 'reward' power of the client to affirm or reject the therapist is made clear, and often, if the client elects not to return for a second or third session, the therapist will not really know why, thus threatening the therapist's sense of 'legitimate power' in her role as a professional capable of providing a highly skilled practical art. It is an instance in which non-directiveness prohibits challenging the decision of the client, although the therapist has the freedom to inquire about whether or not she has been of help or whether she has done or said something which has hurt the client. The point is that the client-centered therapist absorbs the rejection without turning on the client.

SITUATIONAL INFLUENCE: ATTRIBUTIONAL BIAS

When a person labels him/herself as deserving of a partner's violent behavior, he or she exhibits a common pattern of thinking which has been called the 'fundamental attribution error' identified by Lee Ross in 1977 (cited in Nisbett and Ross, 1980: 31). The fundamental attribution error describes a person's assertion that he or she is responsible for negative outcomes when, in fact, observers would attribute more weight to situational (as opposed to dispositional) factors. The person blames herself for provoking the violence by 'talking back' to her partner. While recognizing this provocation as a proximal factor in the series of violent events, the observer would see many more causal factors in the situation, such as frustration from unemployment, alcohol or drug levels in the partner's body, the partner's history of corporal punishment as a child, etc.

In my experience, many therapists who hear clients asserting their own blameworthiness in situations which are largely beyond their control are, if not moved to counter this self-incriminating, self-defeating behavior, at least caught in the experience of being between a rock and a hard place. The 'rock' is allowing the client to persist in self-blame which strikes the therapist as unbearably unfair and inaccurate; the 'hard place' is that by asserting one's opinion from one's own frame of reference, one places one's perception of truth above that of the client—one makes the client wrong.

The contradiction of some feminist therapists lies in taking the didactic road at the expense of the sovereignty of the client they are aiming to empower. Kitzinger and Perkins (1993) observe this selective validation amongst feminist therapists.

> [T]herapists are selective about which experiences they will or won't validate in therapy ... Few lesbian/feminist therapists, for example, will uncritically validate a survivor of child sexual abuse who talks of being to blame for her childhood rape because of her seductive behavior; instead, she is likely to be offered an analysis of the way in which victim blaming operates under heteropatriarchy. (Kitzinger and Perkins, 1993: 190–1)

From a client-centered framework, it is unlikely that a political analysis would be offered to counter the fundamental attribution error, but some of us *have* fallen into a covert way of correcting the client under the guise of empathic understanding. 'I'm just trying to understand why you take responsibility upon yourself for the beating. Could you explain it more?' (This question, were it not motivated by the desire to have effects on the client's way of perceiving and symbolizing her own reality, would be acceptable as a question for clarification.)

Dwelling in the non-directive attitude guides the therapist to continue in a process of empathic understanding. In this instance, the client-centered therapist's compass of non-directiveness constrains this didactic impulse, allowing the client to blame herself unsparingly. The therapist remains interested in understanding this assertion—noting her internal disagreement with the client's fundamental attribution error, yet not becoming incongruent by *accepting her own internal reaction*—and expresses her understanding of the client's expression of self-blame. By functioning in this way, the iatrogenic influence of the therapist is inhibited in favor of legitimate therapeutic influence: acceptance, respect for the client's views, and empathic attunement to the client's immediate wish to assert herself as the author of her own fate. In this instance a person who has been objectified and is without power experiences the power of her own truth, 'power-from-within' to express, to explain, even to defend the abusive partner.

It is important to note that this practice is not the same as 'validating' the client's experience, perceptions or personal theories. The person may experience validation from the process of empathic understanding in the context of non-directiveness, but this experience is distinct from being validated by the therapist who speaks from the standpoint of 'knowing', saying in essence, 'I think you're really onto something there; I think that's the better way to think about your abuser.' 'I'm relieved that you're not blaming yourself! You've stopped being a victim.' In these albeit well-meaning statements, the therapist has usurped the authority of the client, has placed the client in the role of the 'good student', and has reinscribed the authority of the therapist as the one who can sniff out 'bad thinking'.

THE HEGEMONY OF PSYCHOTHERAPEUTIC SYSTEMS: LOOKING AT THE BIGGER PICTURE

Gergen and Kaye (1992) assert that all psychotherapy systems are hegemonic; that is, their creators wish to establish their primacy in the practice arena of the therapy industry, as well as in the contest for legitimacy in the realm of research, even when their critique calls positivist science into question.

> By implication (and practice), the ultimate aim of most schools of therapy is hegemonic. All other schools of thought and their associated narratives should succumb. Psychoanalysts wish to eradicate behavior modification; cognitive-behavioral therapists see systems therapy as misguided, and so on. Yet, the most immediate and potentially injurious consequences are reserved for the client. For in the end, the structure of the procedure furnishes the client a lesson in inferiority. (Gergen and Kaye, 1992: 171)

Gergen and Kaye, while describing the schisms and internecine conflicts that characterize the field of psychotherapy, are also pointing to the problem of iatrogeny that inheres in all therapy approaches. Iatrogenic influence may be defined as psychological, social, or economic harm that occurs as a result of the therapeutic relationship, including the role of the therapist, the communications of the therapist and the social/political meanings which arise from the therapy situation.

In taking account of iatrogenic effects in the person-centered context, Brodley (2002) has asserted that all unequal relationships are injurious—however common they may be, and however important they are for human development. Even though the disparity in power may vary greatly within therapeutic dyads (see Brink, 1987; Burstow, 1987; Proctor, 2002), it is particularly salient and problematic in a relationship which exists by definition as one in which a person calls out for help to another, within the context of a socially legitimated profession.

Disagreements within the person-centered approach between non-directive client-centered therapy and process-directive therapies reflect this concern about what is ethically supportable practice. These tensions also reflect our commonly shared value in preserving and promoting practices that speak to the *human person*, in a period of history where human beings are caught up in global struggles for hegemonic influence and are daily sacrificed as so much 'collateral damage'. Within the person-centered and experiential approaches, elucidating differences and commonalities serves our need for debate based upon accurate understandings. However, this effort of clarification is rendered particularly difficult by virtue of the nonsystematic nature of idiosyncratic relationships which are expected to change within the therapy session and over time, and by the personal embodiment of attitudes which necessarily lead to unique expressions within therapy. In this respect, systematic approaches such as emotion-focused therapy tasks may be easier to conceptualize and communicate about. It is true that in client-centered sessions, almost anything can happen. Because of this and because of the difficulty in describing in general terms what is of necessity particular, client-centered therapists are sometimes accused of using non-directiveness as a litmus test of faith. The importance we accord to this attitude/value, however, does not originate in our desire for hegemony amongst humanistic therapies. Instead, we emphasize non-directiveness because experiential and process-directive theorists fail to address the potential harm which may issue from practice guided by the therapist-as-expert.

II. ANSWERING CRITIQUES OF NON-DIRECTIVENESS

In the early formulations of client-centered therapy, the therapist's realization of the gestalt of the core conditions implied a non-directive attitude (Rogers, 1942; Raskin, 1948). This attitude expressed trust in the client's inner resources to grow in autonomy and self-direction, although Rogers regarded this trust as an operational hypothesis with each new client (Rogers, 1951). The meaning of this attitude over the years has been elaborated and more clearly defined, and is now described both as a non-directive *sensibility* or attitude, which is an aspect of the therapist's phenomenology (Brodley, 1997), and as *a principled ethical position* representing respect for the right of persons to self-determination (Rogers, 1951; Brodley, 1997; Grant, 1990, 2004).

Just as the construct of non-directiveness has grown and developed over the last 60 years, so have myriad misconceptions regarding its meaning, definition and significance, both within and without the person-centered approach. The most common misconception of client-centered therapy holds that non-directiveness requires rigid adherence to empathic understanding responses, to the exclusion of other forms of response such as spontaneous therapist-frame responses or the willingness to answer questions. It is also argued that non-directiveness is impossible because all therapies influence clients (Lietaer, 1998; Kahn, 1999). Another view challenges non-directiveness as a concept evoked in order to support what is essentially a false notion of the equality of the two persons in the therapy relationship (Barton, 1974; Burstow, 1987). Additionally, client-centered therapy as a whole is seen as less effective owing to the constraints of the non-directive attitude (Burstow, 1987; Kahn, 1999). The approach is said to deny influence effects while actually indoctrinating the therapist's narrative and beliefs (Pentony, 1981). Lietaer, theorist from the experiential, process-directive wing of the person-centered approach, argues that directing the client's process is a legitimate function of therapist expertise and that the debate over non-directiveness should be put aside (Lietaer, 1998).

This chapter tries to correct some of these misconceptions. It posits that non-directiveness results in a therapy that carries a unique form of social influence, insofar as the relationship that evolves between a client and a non-directive therapist is figuratively the furthest number of standard deviations from a systematized, professional, contractual relationship, while still remaining one. A client-centered relationship, resting on the foundation of the non-directive ethical position, approaches mutuality most fully while retaining the necessary inequality (Burstow, 1987), which structurally defines helping relationships.

NON-DIRECTIVENESS IS AN ILLUSION

In his book *Models of Influence in Psychotherapy*, Pentony (1981) presents the position that client-centered therapy fails to recognize the therapy as a vehicle for the inculcation of a new value system. He quotes Barton:

> the client-centered theorist–therapist is totally enraptured within the natural attitude by the purity, depth, and intensity of the feelings emerging from within the client-over-there. He is *in principle*, by virtue of his theory, its biases, and the very enrapture of client-centeredness, unable to notice the fundamental structure of what he is doing. He can only understand himself as understanding, empathizing, or expressing the feelings that belong to the client. He cannot understand himself *in principle* as transformer, selector, emphasizer, indoctrinator of ideology, teacher of theory, convinced articulator of a view of reality, life, and values or understand the actual centering of the process in that space-between shaped by client and therapist together. In short, he is not able to make focal, thematic, and theoretical what is actually going on in the 'lived-world-space' between his client and himself ... (Barton, 1974: 245–6, as quoted in Pentony, 1981: 95–6)

Let me try to spin out what Barton might be onto in his critique. From the perspective of theory, Rogers expressed the idea that human development moved away from compliance to authority and the control of others (heteronomy) in the direction of trusting one's inner experience as a trustworthy guide for living (autonomy). The direction toward full functionality involved expanding one's awareness of inner experiencing so that the full range of visceral organismic data could be tapped and absorbed into the more differentiated self. Rogers' theory of 'pathology' was simply the resolution of incongruence between experience and self-concept—the growing capacity to allow contradictory, sometimes threatening aspects of experience into awareness. This process was hypothesized to accelerate within a relationship in which the client was unconditionally accepted, respected and understood. The question raised by Pentony (via his reference to Barton's critique) is whether the therapeutic goals of autonomy, inner congruence and greater reliance on the experiencing organism are, in fact, inculcated through non-directive client-centered therapy. This would be of particular concern to cross-cultural theorists who critique the emphasis on individuality and autonomy in western psychology.

I reject Barton's criticism as an inaccurate description of client-centered practice. All of the client-centered therapists I know considered the question of whether or not the empathic understanding response process (Temaner, 1977)—also described as the 'empathy cycle' (Barrett-Lennard, 1999)— necessarily conveys systematic meta-level meanings early in their development as client-centered therapists. As the client-centered therapist commits to the ethical stance and sensibility of non-directiveness, he or she necessarily asks what the limits of non-directiveness are. As noted above, the meta-message of empathic responding may incorrectly be heard as agreement with the client's assertions. But in any case, client-centered therapists are aware of their in-therapy behavior as a source of various types of influence.

As early as 1951, Rogers remarks:

> Many issues in personality theory and the therapeutic process center around the problem of values. One of the cardinal principles in client-centered therapy is that the individual must be helped to work out his own value system, with a minimal imposition of the value system of the therapist. *This very commitment is, of course, itself an expression of a value which is inevitably communicated to the client in the intimate course of working together.* This value, which affirms the individual's right to choose his own values, is believed to be therapeutically helpful. The suggestion of an array of other values by the therapist is believed to be therapeutically harmful, possibly because, if they are presented by the therapist, they will inevitably carry the authority of the therapist and constitute a denial of the self of the client at the moment. The therapist cannot simply express a value for what it is worth; *his expression has a clear direction, an inescapable relevance to the client. The client must actively cope with it.* (Rogers, 1951: 292, italics added)

Clearly, Rogers was acutely conscious of the issue of his influence in particular and of the issue of power in the therapeutic relationship in general. In fact, the 'new' postmodern therapies—discursive, narrative, feminist, and collaborative—espouse ideas which were central to Rogers' work 50 years ago. 'Modern' therapies, amongst which client-centered therapy is grouped,[4] along with psychoanalysis, as representatives of a 'resocialization model' (Pentony, 1981), are roughly and inaccurately characterized as non-collaborative,

---

4. In the case of client-centered therapy, this theoretical classification may be misleading—by virtue of Rogers' emphasis on the unique person and the process which being a person means, the *practice* of non-directive client-centered therapy must of necessity be a completely individualized practice, both in terms of the uniqueness of the client as well as in Rogers' belief that one had to find one's own way to be a therapist (Rogers and Sanford, 1985). At the level of person-to-person meeting, client-centered therapy is always idiosyncratic, given the unique 'private mixture' of two sovereign beings who relate to each other; as personalities, with unique learning histories, and with an unknown and dynamic path ahead (Keys, 2003).

monological as opposed to dialogical; hierarchical and diagnostic as opposed to egalitarian; and non-diagnostic. By contrast, postmodern therapies are not diagnostic but collaborative and conversational (Kitwood, 1990; Jordan, *et al.*, 1991; McNamee and Gergen, 1992), with the client regarded as the expert (Anderson and Goolishian, 1992; Strong, 2002), and where meaning is fluid and not inevitably anchored in objective reality (see Rogers' corollary on perception, 1961: 341). Plus ça change, plus c'est la même chose …

My concluding point about non-directiveness as an illusion and as inculcation is that meta-level meanings *may* be conveyed through the practice of empathic understanding as a way of being. Those meanings are not 'systematic' (are not experienced in the same way as focusing invitations or process-directive procedures) in the lived experience of the client; the meanings are unique, authentic expressions from a congruent therapist, and are in no way prescriptive as they bear on the content of what the client brings up or as they bear upon the manner in which the client presents self or relates in the situation. To acknowledge this nonsystematic, nonprescriptive influence is not to agree that non-directiveness is illusory or impossible. In fact the therapist's being guided by reference to the principle of non-directiveness results in a kind of influence 'decanted', if you will, from any 'will-to-power.' This 'depotentiated distillate' of non-directive empathic understanding itself is probably (different with each client) apprehended as a meta-value of the therapist's. It says 'I respect your freedom as a person; your views, your ways of figuring out what to do; I don't want to harm you through my possibly (though not inevitably) powerful influence.' Non-directiveness would be negated if the therapist conveys that the client always be ready to 'kill the Buddha!' It implies that no authority can be trusted; that resistance and defiance are desirable.

The first and only time I met Carl Rogers, I told him that when I saw him on film, I experienced the impulse to bow in respect. He responded with 'I hope you get over that!' I felt hurt because he seemed to assume that my respect was an instance of hero-worship or of uncritical awe. This was clarified and worked out, which relieved me. One really ought to be able to show respect and even adoration without it being assumed that that feeling is reflexive or unconsidered.

Thus a correct understanding of non-directiveness should not lead to our promoting autonomy over dependency—we accept both wholeheartedly, since we do not know what is best for the client at any given time. Theoretically, a client may depend on a therapist over many years as an authentic expression of his or her own considered needs and desires.

Granting this meta-influence and its reception by the client *as* influence, I differentiate this form of influence from the process-directive approach, which does involve 'selective reinforcement'. Lietaer illustrates his position:

> Being experience-oriented implies selective reinforcement. Rogers and other client-centered therapists, too, freely admit it. Not every statement of the client receives equal attention. We always try to move from the narrative to the feelings, from the theoretical-abstract level to what is actually experienced. (Lietaer, 1998: 68)

241

I agree that empathic responses given by an experienced client-centered therapist may at times be unwittingly selective, even when the only instruction to self is to grasp the 'point' of the client's intended communication (Zimring, 2001; Grant, 2005). But I surmise that the lack of intention to lead the client in a particular direction of 'depth of experiencing' or 'focused experiencing' creates a freer interpersonal environment. To encourage centering on inner experiencing implies that we know that that is best for the client.

Many years ago I had a client who used his sessions to discuss ideas from theology and politically oriented publications such as *The Nation*. I listened to his ideas and occasionally responded with my own ideas—feeling guilty and worried that this couldn't be therapy. Years later he came back to therapy and commented in passing one day, (referring to the work he had done with me years before), 'That was during the time I was working out my moral and political philosophy.' Today I would have clarified with him what he was doing in engaging me in theological and political discussion, to make sure that was how he wanted to use the time, which included allowing me to freely converse with him. I am sure that although this was one person's idiosyncratic behavior in therapy, it was indeed his choice and his legitimate use of therapy. It was an example of a client inviting my personal influence. A question arises as to whether process-directive approaches would have endorsed this client's process in therapy.

NON-DIRECTIVENSS INSTILLS A FALSE SENSE OF EQUALITY

Critics charge that non-directiveness implies a *false equality* between client and therapist, leading thusly to a *passivity* and failure of the therapist to lead (Burstow, 1987). In her personal account of her own therapy with a client-centered therapist, Burstow (1987) criticizes client-centered therapy in terms of an unthinking and naïve embrace of the notion of the equality of the therapist and client. She presents in detail the issue as it emerged in the dialogue between Martin Buber and Carl Rogers (in Buber, Rogers and Friedman, 1965).

The essence of the disagreement between them was that Buber contended that the structure of the therapeutic situation—its cultural, social and political meanings—trumped the personal differences in power which might characterize the two persons in the therapy dyad. Rogers maintained that the interpersonal encounter in the therapeutic situation was experienced by both therapist and client as authentic and mutual. By way of example, a particular client I had many years ago was a personal-injury attorney who brought millions of dollars to his law firm every year. I was a graduate student and a woman. In terms of social status, real economic power and gender identity, my client outranked me. Nonetheless, Buber would argue that the client who comes for help cannot 'mutualize' the situation by inviting me to discuss my personal problems, or even ask me about which movie I went to over the weekend, without undercutting the structure that permits a therapeutic relationship to occur. I agree that there is a structure which must hold up in order for the therapeutic relationship to work in the service of the client. However, Rogers' passionate rebuttal to Buber was that in the lived experience of the relationship, he experienced and believed that his client experienced a genuine meeting—a human encounter in mutuality as persons.

Burstow depicts this situation as one of 'necessary inequality' which should be acknowledged openly by the therapist. To fail to do so is to fall into a false belief in the mutuality and to miss the vulnerability of the client and the relative invulnerability of the therapist. I agree with Burstow in her assertion. However, in her article she proceeds to attack client-centered therapists for being deluded about the autonomy and self-direction of clients. She asserted that in her own case, when in desperate need of direction, she could not get the leadership from the client-centered therapist.

This is a misunderstanding of the practice of client-centered therapy. If the therapist is open to the client in all modes of being, then she will be open to a client's attempts to solicit help and direction. She may even say, 'You appear to be circling around whether or not to ask me something. I would be glad to try to answer if you want that.' The client may say, 'I need you to tell me what to do. I am so upset I am afraid and can't think.' Of course, the therapist will be at pains to stay within the client's frame of reference, but ultimately will find a way to help. There is disagreement on this point between client-centered practitioners (e.g., Sommerbeck, 2003), but I would argue that attunement and response are, in fact, consistent with the principle of non-directiveness.

Burstow's experience of client-centered therapy, in my view, was not representative of good client-centered therapy, but was rather uncharacteristically nonresponsive, passive, and rigid. Client-centered therapists who have theoretical clarity and enough experience to have worked through many situations in a non-directive way are highly attuned to their clients, responsive to both verbal and nonverbal behavior, and psychologically free to act in ways which meet even extreme needs of their clients.

There is indeed a danger to clients who ask for and receive help from the therapist, in taking on the belief that the therapist's ideas and guidance are going to be consistently better than their own. But respecting the choice of the client in his or her appeal for response is consistent with non-directiveness *and* is possibly iatrogenic in the long run. In my personal experience, it often seems that more vulnerable clients do not solicit responses from my frame of reference, as if they are protecting themselves from my potential influence. Clients who are psychologically independent occasionally ask questions and solicit my views. One client has told me explicitly not to worry about her taking my views too seriously; that if she asks me a question, I can be free to answer spontaneously because she is ultimately going to consider what I say as my own fallible opinion.

CONCLUSION

Analyzing therapy through the lens of social influence can clarify our theoretical thinking about therapy. Non-directiveness, which becomes integral to the therapist's own sensibility, and which may be expressed as a principle for functioning in accordance with the value of respect for another's right to self-determination, is still relevant in discriminating different kinds of person-centered therapy practices from process-directive practices. Both desired therapeutic social influence and undesired iatrogenic influence are inevitably conveyed within the therapy relationship. The concept of non-directiveness leads the way to a disciplined freedom on the therapist's part and to containment of possible iatrogenic impact on the client.

Author's note: I wish to thank my colleagues at the Illinois School of Professional Psychology, Drs Sue Bae and Scott Pytluk, for their helpful insights about social psychology. Barbara Brodley, Nat Raskin, Susan Pildes, Kathy Moon and Jerold Bozarth have also supported me in writing, and have my gratitude. Barry Grant helped me clarify a number of points and aided in the process of revision. To Brian Levitt go many thanks for his generosity and encouragement and very helpful revision in reducing the number of papers to one.

REFERENCES

Anderson H & Goolishian H (1992) The client is the expert: A not-knowing approach to therapy. In S McNamee & KJ Gergen (Eds) *Therapy as Social Construction* Thousand Oaks, CA: Sage Publications, pp. 25–39.

Barrett-Lennard GT (1999) *Carl Rogers' Helping System: Journey and substance.* London: Sage.

Barton A (1974) *Three Worlds of Therapy: An existential-phenomonological analysis of the therapies of Freud, Jung and Rogers.* Palo Alto, CA: National Press.

Bozarth JD (1998) Unconditional positive regard. In *Person-Centered Therapy: A revolutionary paradigm.* Ross-on-Wye: PCCS Books, pp. 83–8.

Brink DC (1987) The issues of equality and control in the client- or person-centered approach. *Journal of Humanistic Psychology, 27*(1), 27–37.

Brodley BT (1996) Empathic understandings and feelings in client-centered therapy. *The Person-Centered Journal, 3*(1), 22–30.

Brodley BT (1997) The non-directive attitude in client-centered therapy. *The Person-Centered Journal, 4*(1), 18–30.

Brodley BT (1999) Reasons for responses expressing the therapist's frame of reference in client-centered therapy. *The Person-Centered Journal, 6*(1), 4–27.

Brodley BT (2002) Client-Centered: An expressive therapy. *The Person-Centered Journal, 9*(1), 59–70.

Brodley BT (2002, July) With and without the non-directive attitude. Colloquium on psychotherapy and counseling presented at the Carl Rogers centennial conference, San Diego, CA.

Brodley BT & Brody AF (1990, Summer) Understanding client-centered therapy through interviews conducted by Carl Rogers. Paper presented in panel, 'Fifty Years of Client-centered Therapy: Recent research' presented at the Annual Meeting of the American Psychological Association, Boston.

Buber M, Rogers CR & Friedman M (1965) Dialogue between Martin Buber and Carl Rogers. In M Friedman (Ed) *The Knowledge of Man.* New York: Harper & Row.

Burstow B (1987) Humanistic psychotherapy and the issue of equality. *Journal of Humanistic Psychology, 27*(1), 9–25.

Cain DJ (1989) The paradox of nondirectiveness in the person-centered approach. *Person-Centered Review, 4,* 123–30. Reprinted in DJ Cain (Ed)(2002) *Classics in the Person-Centered Approach.* Ross-on-Wye: PCCS Books, pp. 365–70.

Cooper M (2005) The inter-experiential field: Perceptions and metaperceptions in person-centered and experiential psychotherapy. *Person-Centered & Experiential Psychotherapies, 4*(1), 54–68.

DeVaris J (1994) The dynamics of power in psychotherapy. *Psychotherapy, 31*(4), 588–93.

Fiske ST (2004) *Social Beings: A core motives approach to social psychology.* Hoboken, NJ: Wiley.

French JRP Jr & Raven BH (1959) The bases of power. In D Cartwright (Ed) *Studies in Social Power.* Ann Arbor, MI: Institute for Social Research, pp. 150–67.

Friedman M (1985) Healing through meeting and the problematic of mutuality. *Journal of Humanistic Psychology, 25*(1), 7–40.

Gendlin ET (1970) A theory of personality change. In JT Hart & TM Tomlinson (Eds) *New Directions in Client-Centered Therapy.* Boston: Houghton Mifflin, pp. 129–73.

Gendlin ET (1974) Client-centered and experiential therapy. In D Wexler & LN Rice (Eds) *Innovations in Client-Centered Therapy.* New York: Wiley, pp. 211–46.

Gendlin ET (1996) *Focusing-Oriented Psychotherapy.* New York: Guilford Press.

Gergen KJ & Gergen MM (1981) *Social Psychology.* New York: Harcourt Brace Jovanovich.

Gergen KJ & Kaye J (1992) Beyond narrative in the negotiation of therapeutic meaning. In S McNamee & KJ Gergen (Eds) *Therapy as Social Construction* Thousand Oaks, CA: Sage, pp. 166–85.

Gershon B & Mitchell S (Eds) (1996) *The Therapist as a Person: Life crises, life choices, life experiences and their effects on treatment* (Vol. 6). New York: Analytic Press.

Grant B (1990) Principled and instrumental non-directiveness in person-centered and client-centered therapy. *Person-Centered Review, 5*(1), 77–88. Reprinted in DJ Cain (Ed)(2002) *Classics in the Person-Centered Approach.* Ross-on-Wye: PCCS Books, pp. 371–7.

Grant B (2004) The imperative of ethical justification in psychotherapy: The special case of client-centered therapy. *Person-Centered and Experiential Psychotherapies, 3*(3), 152–65.

Grant B (2005) Taking only what is given: Empathy and self-determination in non-directive client-centered therapy. In BE Levitt (Ed) *Embracing Non-directivity: Reassessing person-centered theory and practice in the 21st century.* Ross-on-Wye, UK: PCCS Books, pp. 248–60.

Greenberg LS, Rice LN & Elliott R (1993) *Facilitating Emotional Change: The moment-by-moment process.* New York: Guilford Press.

Hart JT & Tomlinson TM (Eds) (1970) *New Directions in Client-Centered Therapy.* Boston: Houghton Mifflin.

Haugh S & Merry T (Eds) (2001) *Rogers' Therapeutic Conditions: Evolution, Theory and Practice. Vol. 2: Empathy.* Ross-on-Wye: PCCS Books.

Held BS (1995) *Back to Reality: A critique of postmodern theory in psychotherapy.* New York: WW Norton.

Hendricks MN (2002) Focusing-oriented/experiential psychotherapy. In DJ Cain & J Seeman (Eds) *Humanistic Psychotherapies: Handbook of research and practice.* Washington, DC: American Psychological Association.

Jordan J, Kaplan A, Baker-Miller J, Stiver I & Surrey J (1991) *Women's Growth in Connection.* New York: Guilford Press, pp. 221–51.

Kahn E (1999) A critique of non-directivity in the person-centered approach. *The Journal of Humanistic Psychology, 39*(4), 94–110.

Keys S (Ed) (2003) *Idiosyncratic Person-Centered Therapy: From the personal to the universal.* Ross-on-Wye: PCCS Books.

Kitwood T (1990) Psychotherapy, postmodernism and morality. *Journal of Moral Education, 19*(1), 3–13.

Kitzinger C & Perkins R (1993) *Changing our Minds: Lesbian feminism and psychology.* New York: New York University Press.

Lietaer G (1998) From non-directive to experiential: A paradigm unfolding. In B Thorne & E Lambers (Ed) *Person-Centred Therapy. A European perspective.* London: Sage, pp. 62–73.

Lietaer G (2002) The united colors of person-centered and experiential psychotherapies. *Person-Centered & Experiential Psychotherapies, 1*(1&2), 4–13.

McNamee S & Gergen KJ (Eds) (1992) *Therapy as Social Construction.* Thousand Oaks, CA: Sage.

Merry T (1996) An analysis of ten demonstration interviews by Carl Rogers: Implications for the training of client-centered counselors. In R Hutterer, G Pawlowsky, PF Schmid & R Stipsits (Eds) *Client-Centered and Experiential Psychotherapy: A paradigm in motion* Vienna: Peter Lang, pp. 273–83.

Moon K (2005) Non-directive therapist congruence in theory and practice. In BE Levitt (Ed) *Embracing Non-directivity: Reassessing person-centered theory and practice in the 21st century.* Ross-on-Wye, UK: PCCS Books, pp. 261–80.

Natiello P (1994) The collaborative relationship in psychotherapy. *The Person-Centered Journal, 1*(2), 11–18.

Nisbett R & Ross L (1980) *Human Inference: Strategies and shortcomings of social judgment.* Englewood Cliffs, NJ: Prentice-Hall.

Patterson CH (1984) Empathy, warmth, and genuineness in psychotherapy: A review of reviews. *Psychotherapy, 21*(4), 431–8.

Patterson CH (2000) On being non-directive. In CH Patterson (Ed) *Understanding Psychotherapy: Fifty years of client-centered theory and practice.* Ross-on-Wye: PCCS Books.

Pentony P (1981) *Models of Influence in Psychotherapy.* New York: The Free Press.

Proctor G (2002) *The Dynamics of Power in Counselling and Psychotherapy.* Ross-on-Wye: PCCS Books.

Raskin NJ (1948/2004) The development of non-directive therapy. *Journal of Consulting Psychology, 12,* 92–110. Reprinted in NJ Raskin (2004) *Contributions to Client-Centered Therapy and the Person-Centered Approach.* Ross on Wye: PCCS Books.

Rogers CR (1942) *Counseling and Psychotherapy.* Boston: Houghton Mifflin.

Rogers CR (1951) *Client-Centered Therapy.* Boston: Houghton Mifflin.

Rogers CR (1961) *On Becoming a Person: A therapist's view of psychotherapy.* Boston: Houghton Mifflin.

Rogers CR (1977) *On Personal Power.* New York: Dell Publishing.

Rogers CR & Sanford R (Presenters) (1985) *PeterAnn, Evolution of Psychotherapy Conference Phoenix, Arizona* [Motion picture]. Milton Erickson Institute.

Schank RC & Abelson RP (1977) *Scripts, Plans, Goals and Understanding: An inquiry into human knowledge structures.* Hillsdale, NJ: Erlbaum.

Schmid PF (2004) Back to the client: A phenomenological approach to the process of understanding and diagnosis. *Person-Centered and Experiential Psychotherapies, 3*(1), 36–51.

Sommerbeck L (2003) *The Client-Centred Therapist in Psychiatric Contexts: A therapists' guide to the psychiatric landscape and its inhabitants*. Ross-on-Wye: PCCS Books.

Spinelli E (1997) *Tales of Un-knowing: Eight stories of existential therapy*. New York: New York University Press.

Strong T (2002) Collaborative 'expertise' after the discursive turn. *Journal of Psychotherapy Integration, 12*(2), 218–32.

Szasz T (1978) *The Myth of Psychotherapy*. Syracuse, NY: Syracuse University Press.

Temaner BS (1977) The empathic understanding response process. Unpublished manuscript, Chicago Counseling and Psychotherapy Center Discussion Papers, Chicago.

Tomlinson TM & Whitney RE (1970) Values and strategy in client-centered therapy. In JT Hart & TM Tomlinson (Eds) *New Directions in Client-Centered Therapy*. Boston: Houghton Mifflin, pp. 453–67.

Warner MS (2000) Person-centered psychotherapy: One nation, many tribes. *The Person-Centered Journal, 7*(1), 28–39.

Zimring F (2001) Empathic understanding grows the person. In S Haugh & T Merry (Eds) *Rogers' Therapeutic Conditions: Evolution, Theory and Practice. Vol. 2: Empathy*. Ross-on-Wye: PCCS Books, pp. 86–98.

CHAPTER 14

TAKING ONLY WHAT IS GIVEN: SELF-DETERMINATION AND EMPATHY IN NON-DIRECTIVE CLIENT-CENTERED THERAPY

BARRY GRANT

Don't take things that are not given.
Dae Gak (1997) and others

The practice of non-directive client-centered therapy can be justified solely in terms of the principle of respect for clients' right to self-determination (Grant, 2004). In this ethics-only understanding of non-directive client-centered therapy, person-centered theory has little role in guiding, explaining, or justifying practice. Empirical research has no role at all. Ethics-only non-directive client-centered therapy takes the *practice* described by Rogers (1951/1965), Bozarth and Brodley (1986), Brodley (n.d., 1997b, 1999), Bozarth (2001), and others, abstracts it from its 'home' in theory and research, and places it on the ethical foundation of the right to self-determination. The essence of this practice is experiencing and expressing the attitudes of acceptance, understanding, and genuineness. The person-centered literature describes many ways of living these attitudes. Not all of them respect clients' right to self-determination. This chapter examines one of the attitudes—empathy—and argues that the object or target (Zimring, 2001) of empathy consistent with respect for self-determination is what clients give: that is, clients' intended meanings.

An ethics-only conception of client-centered therapy is based on an argument that all psychotherapies require ethical justification and on a personal desire to give a coherent account of a form of psychotherapy that is independent of formal psychological theory and research (Grant, 2004). Most non-directive client-centered therapists would justify their work in ways that refer to theory and research. Though they may not share my rejection of Rogers' theorizing, they may find value in the clarity an ethics-only approach can bring to understanding empathy.

I share Zimring's (2001) and Brodley's (2001) concern with explicitly defining a target or object of empathy. Zimring (2001) defines a target as 'what, in the speaker's message, we should try to understand and respond to' (p. 86). Brodley (n.d., 1996, 1997a, 1997b, 1999, 2000) offers an explicit and very useful account of how to do non-directive client-centered therapy—a manual, almost, for beginning therapists. This chapter is not a manual of any sort. It does not consider empathic understanding in relation to the other therapeutic attitudes, nor does it locate empathic understanding fully in the context of a relationship between particular individuals with particular negotiations of a therapeutic relationship. The understanding of empathy I propose is based on the ethical principle of the right to self-determination, a conceptualization of motivated action, and assumptions about human communication. This chapter sketches the main implications of the right to self-determination only for empathic understanding, not for the entire practice of non-directive therapy.

A FRAMEWORK FOR ANALYZING CONCEPTIONS OF EMPATHY

Definitions and descriptions of empathy fill the person-centered literature (see especially Bohart and Greenberg, 1997a; Haugh and Merry, 2001). Rogers (1975/1980) describes empathy as a process, a way of being, a state, an experience, a perception, a sensing, and an action. Empathy has cognitive and affective (Cooper, 2001), aligned and traditional (Mahrer, 1997), and modern, and postmodern (O'Hara, 1997) varieties. Bohart and Greenberg (1997b) posit five dimensions to empathy—cognition, experience, action, relationship, and validation.

My framework for analyzing conceptions of empathy is based on the assumption that empathy is a goal-directed activity. People *do* empathy. Persons engaged in empathy or any other goal-directed activity are motivated to carry out actions that have an intended goal and focus and result in consequences. The structure of empathy is similar to that of many other activities, particularly those involving interactions with others—loving, criticizing, encouraging, being genuine, being accepting, even riding a bike and eating a meal. The framework is neutral as to the content, nature, and meaning of empathy and, in principle, allows every version of empathy to be mapped and compared. It serves as an analytic lens that can expose logical inconsistencies in theory, ethics, motivation, intention, and the enactment of intentions. It also serves the more modest goal of providing a structure for my analysis of empathy as taking what clients give.

Motivation—*the therapist's reasons for attempting to understand, why the therapist does empathy, the internal 'source' of the therapist's empathic activity.* Common motivations for doing empathy in therapy include desires to act in ways consistent with a philosophy of life and beliefs about the rights and capabilities of others. On the analysis proposed here, empathy is *defined* first as an activity, not an attitude. An attitude, by definition, includes the sense of a disposition to act. A disposition is a motivation. Logically, the action has to be defined prior to the disposition. One cannot have the disposition to perform an undefined activity.

Persons can be rightly said to have the *attitude* of empathy when they are *disposed* to act empathically toward others and when they have beliefs and values that support the disposition. Rogers (1951/1965) refers to the 'attitude and orientation' of the counselor and an 'attitudinal orientation'. If empathy is understood only as therapeutic activity, not as action rooted in one's philosophy, ethics, and inclinations, then it is a technique. As Rogers (1951/1965) describes the implementation of the therapeutic attitudes, the attitude of empathy and the actions of empathy reciprocally shape each other. Conceptual understanding, skill and disposition influence each other as one reads, reflects, practices therapy, and receives consultation.

Intention—*the therapist's conscious goals for empathizing, what the therapist tries to accomplish by empathizing.* The activity of empathizing has a purpose, a goal. In the person-centered literature, the goal is typically to provide a condition for growth (Rogers, 1986/89) or a stimulus to growth, for example, to help clients further their experiencing (Rice, 1974; Rogers 1975/1980). Therapists' goals in doing empathy should be consistent with their motivations, conceptions of the target of empathy, and their actions.

Object or target—*what the therapist tries to empathically understand or empathize with.* The grammar or logic of empathy requires that empathy has an object. We use the word incorrectly if we say, without further elaboration, 'I felt empathy' or 'I understood empathically.' Empathy must be with, for, toward, or about something. Greenberg and Elliott (1997, cited in Zimring 2001: 93) list 'feelings ... emotional experiences ... self-concept[s] ... self-evaluations ... motivations and defenses, wishes and fears' as the objects of empathy. In Zimring's (2001) view, the targets are self-sense and self-reactions, intentions, and representations of the world. Rogers described the object of empathy in a number of ways, including: 'the feelings and personal meanings that the client is experiencing ... [including] even those just below the level of awareness' (Rogers, 1975/1980: 142); and '... perceiv[ing] the internal frame of reference of another with accuracy and with the emotional components and meanings which pertain thereto ... sens[ing] the hurt or the pleasure of another as he senses it and ... perceiv[ing] the causes thereof as he perceives them' (Rogers, 1975/1980: 140).

No object of empathy can be grasped directly. Witch doctors and yogis may have unmediated experiences of feelings, intended communications, self-evaluations, or other objects of empathy. For the rest of us to 'get' any of these, we must perceive sense data, understand language, 'read' gestures, and maybe even tune in to certain vibrations. Shlien (1997) claims that empathy 'operates at what we might think of as primitive levels, cellular, glandular, olfactory, chemical, electromagnetic, autonomic, postural, gestural, and musical–rhythmical, more than lexical' (p. 77). Every conception of empathy has or should have 'directions', operationalizations of what to do covertly and overtly to receive or grasp or get the object of empathy.

Covert actions and processes—*what the therapist does internally in empathizing.* Most of the work of empathy is internal. Therapists think, imagine, feel, direct attention, generate images, suspend judgment, bracket points of view, monitor thoughts, and so forth. Rogers (1975/1980), for example, says empathy:

> involves being sensitive, moment to moment, to the changing felt meanings which flow in this other person, to the fear or rage or tenderness or confusion or whatever, that he/she is experiencing. It means temporarily living in his/ her life, moving about in it delicately without making judgments, sensing meanings of which he/she is scarcely aware. (pp. 142–3)

Observable actions—*what the therapist says and does overtly in empathizing.* Rogers, for example, refers to 'communicating your sensings' and 'frequently checking with [the client] as to the accuracy of your sensings, and being guided by the responses you receive' (Rogers, 1975/1980: 142–3). Cooper (2001), in an account of embodied empathy, refers to therapists spontaneously mimicking clients' behavior. Bozarth (2001) argues that therapist communication of personal experiences can be expressions of 'emergent modes' of empathy.

Reception or consequence—*the effect of the therapist's actions; how clients experience, or what they make of or do with, the therapist's actions.* The reception and consequences of empathy can be quite varied, ranging from annoyance and frustration to joy or nothing at all. Rogers (1959), Zimring (2001), Bohart (2004), and others propose theories of how empathy affects clients.

THE RIGHT TO SELF-DETERMINATION

The concept of the right to self-determination has its history in the tradition of political liberalism (Gauss and Courtland, 2003). The right to self-determination is the core element of 'the liberal idea of freedom ... [which] claims for man, by reason of his humanity, the right, within limits ..., to order his life as seems good to him' (Plemenatz, 1973: 36). J.S. Mill says of this idea of freedom:

> The only freedom which deserves the name, is that of pursuing our own good in our own way, so long as we do not attempt to deprive others of theirs, or impede their efforts to obtain it. Each is the proper guardian of his own health, whether bodily, or mental and spiritual. Mankind are greater gainers by suffering each other to live as seems good to themselves, than by compelling each to live as seems good to the rest. (Lerner, 1961: 266)

The self-determination of one's life is the 'liberty to do anything which does not coerce, restrain, or injure another person' (Benn, 1967: 198). In this view, one is free to act as one wills, provided one does not infringe on the right to self-determination of others. One is an agent, surveying the inner and outer world; identifying with a tradition, humanity, a group, or nothing; deciding, choosing, and acting, impulsively or deliberately. One is sovereign within the realm marked out by the right—the boundary of the sovereignty of others. *Everything* one does that does not infringe on the sovereignty of others and which is not a consequence of one's own sovereignty being infringed upon is an exercise of this right. One has this right by virtue of being a person, not by virtue of meeting skill or rationality requirements.

The right to direct one's life is an ethical, not a psychological or empirical concept. All persons who are free from coercion, restraint, and threat of injury—those depressed, miserable, suicidal, without hope or initiative, as well as those who are confident and have a sense of self-efficacy—are exercising their right to self-determination (Grant, 2004). The question of whether young children or impaired adults have this right is not answered by a rationality or ability assessment. It is answered through imagination, empathy, and a willingness to negotiate terms and create a space for these persons to act by their lights. In some situations (e.g., children in the path of a car) other ethical principles trump respect for the right to self-determination. But the right may be

251

overridden only with great care. Persons who are not regarded as free to determine their way in the world are treated as less than human, as less than oneself: 'For if one denied a man this right, it would be open to others to use him, like their beasts and their tools, for their own purposes and as they chose' (Benn, 1967: 198).

Non-directive client-centered therapists, in my view, have no desire to impose on clients any goals, schemas, agendas, conceptualizations, diagnoses, or visions of mental health or fully functioning lives. They do not believe that clients should talk about some things rather than others. They believe that everything clients do—talking, sitting, staring out of windows in silence, holding legs and rocking—expresses their right to determine their lives.

Of course, non-directive therapists negotiate fees, schedules, and other matters as they exercise *their* right to self-determination to create the conditions under which they are willing to offer a relationship. Otherwise, they aim only to act responsively, empathically, genuinely, and nonjudgmentally. They wish to respect clients' right to self-determination not because they are morally prissy, but because respect for clients' rights is part of their respect for persons in general and clients in particular. They care about being responsive, real, accepting, and empathic because they believe that this is how they can, at their best, respect clients as persons from whom they want nothing. Because they have no goals for clients and want nothing from them, clients necessarily 'fill' most of the therapy relationship space. They fill the space mostly with speech.

Speaking is sense-making/expressing. We speak with voice and movement to make, or try to make, sense to an audience. With few exceptions (e.g., talking aloud to oneself or 'artistic' uses of speech such as concrete poetry), speakers seek to convey meanings to an audience. Speakers desire and intend to be understood (Witty, 2004). We may have other more important intentions, such as clearing a room ('Fire!'), deflecting a conversation, or making a promise, but their realization depends on conveying meaning.

We can bring to a communication any interpretive scheme, preconception, or procedure we choose. We can make any sense we wish of any communication. Among all the meanings that can be construed of a communication, however, are some that the speaker would acknowledge as the intended meanings. These are the meaning speakers *give*, the ones they seek to get across to listeners. Even vague and muddled meanings and meanings discovered in the act of speaking can be meanings a speaker would recognize as the intended ones.

Only one object of empathy is consistent with respect for clients' right to determine their lives: what clients give, their intended meanings. Brodley (2001) and Raskin (2001) make this point. Brodley describes the target as 'the client's intended immediate communication and expression' (p. 18). Raskin's (2001) definition of 'empathic' refers to 'what the client is aware of and trying to convey to the therapist' (p. 13). Non-directive client-centered therapists seek only to understand what clients *give*. They do not attempt to *take* what can be found or construed in client communication but is not offered. Intentionally taking what is not offered is an impertinence, an insult, an abrogation of a client's right to self-determination. It necessarily requires having goals for or theories or ideas about clients that specify what in client communication deserves special attention. In this case, therapist ideas, not client communications, guide what the therapist seeks to understand. In taking—that is, in intentionally (and perhaps carelessly) construing or adding meanings not offered—therapists do something *to* clients. They do not receive and follow, but push, lead and direct.

Consider these examples from Rogers (1986/1989):

> 1. *Jan: I have two problems. The first one is the fear of marriage and children. And the other one is the age process, aging. It's very difficult to look into the future, and I find it very frightening.*
>
> *Carl: Those are the two main problems for you. I don't know which you'd rather pick first.* (p. 139)

> 2. *Jan: The older I get, though, the stronger I feel about the marriage situation. Now whether the two are related, I don't know. But the fear of getting married, and being committed, and children—I find it very, very frightening. And it's getting stronger as I get older—*
>
> *Carl: It's a fear of commitment, and a fear of having children? And all that seems to be a growing fear, all those fears seem to be increasing.* (pp. 141–2)

What does Jan give in the first example? She says she has two problems, two fears: marriage and children, and getting older. Her last sentence is ambiguous. Her fear of the future could have to do with aging alone, or aging and family, or something else. Does Carl show that he only gets what she gives? No. He names Jan's problems as her main problems, which Jan did not do. He also suggests that she address the problems in order. Of course, we do not know Rogers' intentions. Perhaps he wanted only to take what Jan gave him and was wrong. But when, as it were, Rogers opens his hand to show what he has taken from Jan, more is there than she gave him. In the second example, Rogers has in his hand only what Jan gave him: a description of her experience of the relationship between getting older and her 'marriage situation' and a question about the relationship between her fear of marriage and her fear of having children.

THE STRUCTURE OF NON-DIRECTIVE EMPATHY

MOTIVATION

Non-directive client-centered therapists' motivations for doing empathy are the belief that clients have a right to determine their lives, an attitude of acceptance, and a desire to express acceptance through empathy that respects self-determination. This motivation fits perfectly with Rogers' description of the 'philosophical orientation of the counselor' (Rogers, 1951/1965: 20–1).

253

Intention

In seeking to understand, non-directive therapists seek only understanding. They do not seek understanding in order to make clients feel understood, promote 'safety and trust in the self', model how clients should relate to themselves, establish a therapeutic relationship, 'facilitate' the accessing of 'deep experiencing potential' (Bohart and Greenberg, 1997a: 8–9), or make anything else happen in, for, or to clients.

Object

The meanings the client intends to communicate are the object of empathy in non-directive client-centered therapy. The notion of an 'intended meaning' is best explicated in terms of the processes one engages in to understand another's intended meaning: that is, in terms of the operationalization of, rather than a definition of, the concept. I do this in the next section.

Here it is important to note that one implication of empathy as taking what is given is that the client's frame of reference cannot be an object of empathy. According to Rogers, one of the necessary and sufficient conditions of personality change is that 'the therapist experiences an empathic understanding of the client's internal frame of reference and endeavors to communicate this experience to the client' (Rogers, 1957/1989: 221). The ability to 'perceive the internal frame of reference of another with accuracy and with the emotional components and meanings which pertain thereto as an ability if one were the person, but without ever losing the "as if" condition' (1959: 210) is perhaps one of Rogers' strongest and best-known descriptions of empathy. By internal frame of reference Rogers' (1959) means:

> all of the realm of experience which is available to the awareness of the individual at a given moment. It includes the full range of sensations, perceptions, meanings, and memories, which are available to consciousness. The internal frame of reference is the subjective world of the individual. Only he knows it fully. It can never be known to another except through empathic inference and then can never be perfectly known. (p. 210)

A frame of reference is made of experiences, not communications. We have one even if we communicate nothing, and we cannot *give* a frame of reference even if we wanted to. By definition, part of a frame of reference is available to consciousness, but not *in* consciousness, and so cannot be articulated or implied. We cannot know that what we become aware of later is something that was available to consciousness earlier. The picture of 'sensations, perceptions, meanings, and memories' as sitting in our consciousness, like items on a grocery shelf waiting for us to direct our attention to them, is false. We as much create our experience as become aware of preexisting items of consciousness (Gendlin, 1997).

A 'frame of reference' is an abstraction—an item, actually—in therapists' theories, not in clients' communications or consciousnesses. Therapists who aim at understanding clients' frames of reference will direct clients' attention to matters they may not even be thinking of, let alone communicating. Brodley and Brody's (1990; Brodley's 1994, 2001) analysis of Rogers' work shows, though, that Rogers rarely took the liberty that this conception of empathy offers.

COVERT ACTIONS AND PROCESSES

Non-directive client centered therapists try to understand what clients communicate. This activity is very similar to understanding a text or other verbal material. It is 'reading' an improvised and ongoing text, qualified, nuanced, and amplified with gestures and expressions. Actually, 'empathic' understanding is redundant. Understanding personal communication *is* empathic understanding—understanding what someone is saying, someone's intended meanings, not just any meanings that can be given to the person's words.

Meanings, of course, do not exist as isolated entities that can be apprehended directly, and speakers do not deliver intended meanings with identifying tags. Listeners construct, read, and interpret intended meanings in a speaker's communications. In order to understand what someone is saying, one must at least understand or be familiar with:

- the language the person uses
- jargon and slang the person uses
- the world the person refers to, including the world of cultural understandings of human motivations, dilemmas, and tasks
- the person's previous communications
- the person's intentional, non-verbal communications
- cultural norms for organizing speech
- the person's idiosyncratic ways of organizing speech.

In empathic understanding, knowledge of the organization or structure of communication is especially important. Brodley's (n.d.) first instruction to beginning therapists includes asking, 'What is the client succeeding in "getting at", or what is the client trying to get at?' (p. 2). Zimring (2000) refers to the 'client's intention in communicating' (p. 49) and the client's 'present reaction to and interest in his or her problem or concern' (p. 54). Speech is not simply one utterance after another. Speech has an organization and a hierarchy. We usually speak to 'get at' something, to make a point. We express some meanings to lead up to or establish a basis for other meanings. At least most Westerners seem to do this; persons from other cultures may structure communication in other ways.

Listening for (a), a client's frame of reference; (b), what a client gives, without appreciating how speech is structured; and (c), what clients give, while being sensitive to the structure of speech, can be illustrated in reference to these words from a hypothetical mother in Zimring (2000):

Things are pretty frantic right now. My kids are just starting school and I am

255

starting a new job so I can't be home with them and it doesn't feel right. So they have to be over at my mother's and she is very inconsistent in the mother's treatment of them. (Zimring, 2000: 108)

Listening for (a), the mother's full range of sensations, perceptions, meanings, and memories, which are available to consciousness, we might refer to her frantic feelings, her uneasiness about leaving her kids with her mom, her judgment of her mother's treatment, or even feelings of loss of control, guilt and fear that might be 'under the surface'. Listening for (b), what she gives, without appreciating how her speech is structured, we might give a summary of what she said. We would have no sense of anything she says being more important to her than anything else, no sense that she is trying to get at something, and so no reason to do other than repeat or summarize what we have heard. Listening for (c), what she gives, while being sensitive to the structure of her speech, we probably would not say anything, as we would not perceive a point. We would feel that we do not know yet what in all of this matters to her at the moment, what she is doing with it, what she is getting at in communicating these words. As Zimring says, once she adds, 'It's not as bad as it was before. I can sort of see the shape of some of the roots of the turmoil' (*ibid.*: 94), we would feel we have an idea of what she is getting at and might say, 'You are understanding better the source of the turmoil about your mom and your kids, and you feel better about the situation.'

The target and proximal targets of non-directive empathy are texts or text-like. They are not experiences or inner worlds or felt meanings or frames of reference. They are communications, explicit or implied. The person's 'inner world', or what it is like to be in the person's shoes, or the person's 'frame of reference', and related concepts serve well as heuristics in understanding clients' communications. They capture the idea that empathic understanding requires imagination, interpretation, and attention to the whole of what a person says and does, but they cannot be objects of understanding.

Rogers' (1975/1980) account of empathy as a sort of swimming in the experience and inner world of another person may be also useful, but taken literally it is inconsistent with non-directive empathy. Zimring's (2001) three targets of empathic work also serve as aids to understanding, but not as operationalizations of the target of empathy. Clients often 'give' points that have to do with self-states and self-reactions (e.g., liking something) and intentions and transactions (e.g., figuring out the cause of an event or the meaning of someone's reaction). Noticing whether a client is depicting the objective world of public events or the subjective world of meanings and reactions helps to follow meanings.

We do not know enough about understanding to give beginning therapists a set of instructions on how to understand, on what to do 'in their heads'. as they listen to clients. Brodley's (n.d.) first instruction to beginners does not say *how* to get what clients are getting at. Maybe the best instruction at this point in our understanding of how to do empathic understanding is: Bring everything you have to the task—use your imagination, track the client's logic, listen for themes, attend to spontaneous images, put yourself in the client's shoes. Experiment. See what works.

The literature on reading comprehension probably has great relevance to teaching non-directive empathy. I suspect that key elements of the task are: developing schemas for organizing communication; following 'markers' (e.g., 'and', 'so', 'however') that speakers use to organize speech; and generating hypotheses about intended meanings and testing the hypotheses against other parts of the text or speech or checking with the speaker. Brodley (1996) and Zimring (2001) describe the latter sort of a process.

Non-directive therapists not only intend to understand, they are committed to the task of understanding accurately. This is because the motivation to do empathy is rooted in respect for persons: A commitment to accuracy is an expression of respect. One does not express respect through casual, indifferent attempts to understand. Ideally, one brings everything one has to trying to get exactly what the client gives, and one strives to acquire the skills, knowledge, and dispositions that allow one to understand.

As Brodley (1997b) shows, feelings of understanding and not understanding guide the process of empathic understanding. Therapists create meaning out of clients' words and gestures. They feel they have understood when they have made a sense that makes sense as being the client's intended sense. When they do not feel they have understood, they check their understanding, or they wait, hoping more material will resolve confusion or dissolve uncertainty.

OBSERVABLE ACTIONS

Covert and overt actions are two aspects of the task of empathy. Most of the work of understanding happens covertly (Brodley, 1996). Empathic responses are adjunctive, not essential. The key overt actions of non-directive therapists are empathic understanding responses—attempts to confirm tentative understandings or resolve ambiguities or other responses that in some other way serve understanding (Brodley, n.d., 1997b). If a therapist intends only to get what clients give, the reasons for speaking must serve getting what clients give.

In order for empathic responses to actually help therapists understand clients, clients must understand the responses. The responses are roughly of the form: 'I'm saying what I think you are saying in a way I think you will understand and which expresses my intention only to understand.' The client is the judge of whether or not the therapist has gotten what was given (Brodley, 1997a; Rogers, 1986/2002).

RECEPTION

How clients receive or experience therapists' words and actions is largely irrelevant to the practice of non-directive empathy. Therapists do not intend that clients feel understood, but because they try to state their understandings so that clients can understand them, clients often do feel understood.

SUMMARY

I have attempted to draw out the main implications of the right to self-determination for an ethics-only view of non-directive empathy. The result is, I hope, an ethically consistent account of a form of non-directive empathy. Client-centered therapists who share this ethics-only view are motivated to do empathy primarily by the belief that clients have a right to determine their lives. They draw on their knowledge of the world, language use, jargon, how clients structure communication, and any other means that work to make sense of client communication. Guided by their experiences of understanding and not understanding, they check understandings with clients to ascertain their accuracy. They intend that clients understand their checking responses, but otherwise they do not concern themselves with how clients receive their responses. They seek only to understand what clients give.

REFERENCES

Benn S (1967) Rights. In *The Encyclopedia of Philosophy*, Vol. 7. New York: Collier Macmillan, pp. 195–9.

Bohart AC (2004) How do clients make empathy work? *Person-Centered and Experiential Psychotherapies*, 3(2), 102–16.

Bohart AC & Greenberg LS (1997a) Empathy and psychotherapy: An introductory overview. In A Bohart & LS Greenberg (Eds) *Empathy Reconsidered: New directions in psychotherapy.* Washington, DC: APA, pp. 3–32.

Bohart AC & Greenberg LS (1997b) Empathy: Where are we and where do we go from here? In A Bohart & LS Greenberg (Eds) *Empathy Reconsidered: New directions in psychotherapy.* Washington, DC: APA, pp. 419–47.

Bozarth JD (2001) An addendum to beyond reflection: Emergent modes of empathy (August 2001). In S Haugh & T Merry (Eds) *Rogers' Therapeutic Conditions: Evolution, theory and practice. Vol. 2: Empathy.* Ross-on-Wye: PCCS Books, pp. 144–54.

Bozarth JD & Brodley BT (1986) Client-centered psychotherapy: A statement. *Person-Centered Review*, 1(3), 262–71.

Brodley BT (n.d.) Instructions for beginning to practice client-centered therapy. Unpublished paper.

Brodley BT (1994) Some observations of Carl Rogers' behavior in therapy interviews. *Person-Centered Journal*, 1(2), 37–47. Reprinted (amended) in BE Levitt (Ed)(2005) *Embracing Non-directivity: Reassessing person-centered theory and practice in the 21st century.* Ross-on-Wye: PCCS Books, pp. 96–111.

Brodley BT (1996) Empathic understanding and feelings in client-centered therapy. *Person-Centered Journal*, 3(1), 22–30.

Brodley BT (1997a) The non-directive attitude in client-centered therapy. *Person-Centered Journal*, 4(1), 18–30.

Brodley BT (1997b) Criteria for making responses in client-centered therapy. *Person-Centered Journal*, 5(1), 20–8.

Brodley BT (1999) Reasons for responses expressing the therapist's frame of reference in client-centered therapy. *Person-Centered Journal*, 6(1), 4–27.

Brodley BT (2000) The therapeutic clinical interview: Guidelines for beginning practice. In T Merry (Ed) *Person-Centred Practice: The BAPCA Reader*. Ross-on Wye: PCCS Books, pp. 110–15.

Brodley BT (2001) Observations of empathic understanding in a client-centered practice. In S Haugh & T Merry (Eds) *Rogers' Therapeutic Conditions: Evolution, theory and practice. Vol. 2: Empathy*. Ross-on-Wye: PCCS Books, pp. 16–37.

Brodley B & Brody A (1990) Understanding client-centered therapy through interviews conducted by Carl Rogers. Paper presented in the panel 'Fifty Years of Client-Centered Therapy: Recent Research', at the American Psychological Association annual meeting in Boston, MA, August.

Cooper M (2001) Embodied empathy. In S Haugh & T Merry (Eds) *Rogers' Therapeutic Conditions: Evolution, theory and practice: Empathy*. Ross-on-Wye: PCCS Books, pp. 218–29.

Gak Dae (1997) *Going beyond Buddha: The awakening practice of listening*. Boston: Charles Tuttle.

Gauss G & Courtland SD (2003) 'Liberalism'. In EN Zalta (Ed) *The Stanford Encyclopedia of Philosophy* (Winter 2003 Edition). <http://plato.stanford.edu/archives/win2003/entries/liberalism/>.

Gendlin ET (1997) *Experiencing and the Creation of Meaning: A philosophical and psychological approach to the subjective*. Evanston: Northwestern University Press.

Grant B (2004) The imperative of ethical justification in psychotherapy: The special case of client-centered therapy. *Person-Centered and Experiential Psychotherapies, 3*(3), 152–65.

Haugh S & Merry T (2001) (Eds) *Rogers' Therapeutic Conditions: Evolution, theory and practice. Vol. 2: Empathy*. Ross-on-Wye: PCCS Books.

Lerner M (1961) (Ed) *Essential Works of John Stuart Mill*. New York: Bantam Books.

Mahrer A (1997) Empathy as therapist–client alignment. In A Bohart & LS Greenberg (Eds) *Empathy Reconsidered: New directions in psychotherapy*. Washington, DC: APA, pp. 187–213.

O'Hara M (1997) Relational empathy: Beyond modernist egocentrism to postmodern holistic contextualism. In A Bohart & LS Greenberg (Eds) *Empathy Reconsidered: New directions in psychotherapy*. Washington, DC: APA, pp. 295–319.

Plemenatz J (1973) Liberalism. In *Dictionary of the History of Ideas, Vol. III*. New York: Charles Scribner's Sons, pp. 36–61.

Raskin NJ (2001) The history of empathy in the client-centered movement. In S Haugh & T Merry, T (Eds) *Rogers' Therapeutic Conditions: Evolution, theory and practice. Vol. 2: Empathy*. Ross-on-Wye: PCCS Books, pp. 1–15.

Rice LN (1974) The evocative function of the therapist. In D Wexler and L Rice (Ed) *Innovations in Client-Centered Therapy*. New York: Wiley, pp. 289–311. Reprinted in S Haugh & T Merry (Eds)(2001) *Rogers' Therapeutic Conditions: Evolution, theory and practice. Vol. 2: Empathy*. Ross-on-Wye: PCCS Books, pp. 112–30.

Rogers CR (1951/1965) *Client-Centered Therapy*. Boston: Houghton Mifflin.

Rogers CR (1957/1989) The necessary and sufficient conditions of therapeutic personality change. In H Kirschenbaum & V Henderson (Eds) *A Carl Rogers Reader*. Boston: Houghton Mifflin, pp. 219–35.

Rogers CR (1959) A theory of therapy, personality, and interpersonal relationship as developed in the client-centered framework. In S Koch (Ed) *Psychology: A study of a science, Vol. 3*. New York: McGraw-Hill, pp. 184–256.

Rogers CR (1975/1980) Empathic: An unappreciated way of being. In C Rogers, *A Way of Being*. Boston: Houghton Mifflin.

Rogers CR (1986/1989) A client-centered/person-centered approach to therapy. In H Kirschenbaum & V Henderson (Eds) *A Carl Rogers Reader*. Boston: Houghton Mifflin, pp. 135–52.

Rogers CR (1986/2002) Reflection of feelings. In D Cain (Ed) *Classics in the Person-Centered Approach*. Ross-on-Wye: PCCS Books, pp. 13–14.

Shlien JM (1997) Empathy in psychotherapy: Vital mechanism? Yes. Therapist's conceit? All too often. By itself enough? No. In A Bohart & LS Greenberg (Eds) *Empathy Reconsidered: New directions in psychotherapy*. Washington DC: APA, pp. 63–80. Reprinted in. JM Shlien (2003) *To Lead an Honorable Life: Invitations to think about client-centered therapy and the person-centered approach*. [P Sanders (Ed)] Ross-on-Wye: PCCS Books, pp. 173–90.

Witty M (2004) The difference directiveness makes: The ethics and consequences of guidance in psychotherapy. *Person-Centered Journal, 11*(1–2), 22–32.

Zimring, F (2000) Empathic understanding grows the person. *Person-Centered Journal, 7*(2), 101–13. Reprinted in S Haugh & T Merry (Eds)(2001) *Rogers' Therapeutic Conditions: Evolution, theory and practice. Vol. 2: Empathy*. Ross-on-Wye: PCCS Books, pp. 86–98.

CHAPTER 15

NON-DIRECTIVE THERAPIST CONGRUENCE IN THEORY AND PRACTICE

KATHRYN A. MOON

This chapter is a foray into the meeting place of client-centered theory, ethics and practice. It began as an attempt to elucidate the meaning of Carl Rogers' (1957, 1959, 1961, 1980) term *congruence* in light of the non-directive values of his theory. My reading of Rogers' writings leaves me with a strong impression that he was consistent in his therapeutic intentions throughout his career from 1946 to 1987. If not examined closely, it can seem as if Rogers never explicated the meaning of congruence, particularly therapist congruence, into an unambiguous whole. However, I believe that congruence was present as a finished concept in 1951, even before it had been named, and that same concept was integral to Rogers' theory and practice from then forward. It was present in his descriptions of the individual who has completed therapy (1951: 522–4, 1961, 1969; Rogers and Russell, 2002) and in his discussions of theory and practice late in his life (Baldwin, 1987; Rogers, 1986; Rogers and Russell, 2002). The point of this essay has been to clarify for myself the Rogerian concept of congruence in a manner that answers some tension and confusion I have experienced as a non-directive practitioner.

The primacy of the non-directive attitude in the mind and heart of the therapist is intrinsic to this discussion. This attitude informs my work with a political stance that shelters, asserts and respects the human right to self-determination. I feel ethically compelled to practice therapy under the auspices of a belief in free will. Working in relationship with a person who has sought help, I am contracted to give a high quality of service. Given my values, I do so by dedicating myself to the client's direction. Whether or not free will exists, the non-directive attitude serves clients by fostering psychological freedom and protecting them from harm by me.

I define therapist congruence for the client-centered therapist as the experiencing of psychological freedom to be a non-directive, phenomenologically oriented therapist who is choosing to be engaged responsibly in a client-centered relationship. My conclusion is that the practice of client-centered therapy is definitionally shaped by guiding ethical principles, in which a congruent—that is experientially open and psychologically free— therapist experiences acceptance and understanding toward another. The following discussion begins with an exploration of Rogerian theory, particularly in relation to congruence, and ends with my present thoughts concerning its implementation in practice.

I. CLIENT-CENTERED THEORY

Carl Rogers founded client-centered theory upon the hypothesis that all living organisms are inherently motivated to maintain and fulfil themselves as best they can, each 'according to its nature' (Goldstein, 1934 [in German]/1995: 163). This constructive life force is called the actualizing tendency. Actualization is believed to be the primary motivation, a universal need or drive to self-maintain, flourish, self-enhance and self-protect (Bozarth, 1998; Bozarth and Brodley, 1991; Brodley, 1999b; Merry, 2003; Rogers, 1946, 1951, 1959, 1961, 1963, 1980; Patterson, 1964/2000; Raskin, 1996/2004; Van Belle, 1980).

Rogers posited six necessary and sufficient conditions for effective psychotherapy (1957, 1959), three of which (the 'core' conditions) give therapists a facilitative way 'to be' with clients. These three conditions, sometimes referred to as the 'therapist conditions' (Bozarth, 1998: 105)—unconditional positive regard, empathic understanding and congruence—when embodied in the therapist, meld together into a manner of therapeutic presence (Brodley, 2000) that is trusting and respectful of the client. I consider this therapeutic presence to be protective and sheltering of the client's ways of being, doing and perceiving. Rogers' theory was put forward as inductively derived: given the universality of the actualizing tendency, *if* certain necessary and sufficient therapeutic conditions are present in a relationship, *then* the individual will self-maintain and flourish.

In simple terms, client-centered therapy gives therapists a way to have a relationship with clients that is therapeutic, because it clears a fertile space in which the client is trusted to thrive according to his nature, values and choices. The six necessary and sufficient conditions of this 'If … then …' assertion are:

1. That two persons are in *contact*.
2. That the first person, whom we shall term the client, is in a state of *incongruence*, being vulnerable, or *anxious*.
3. That the second person, whom we shall term the therapist, is *congruent* in the *relationship*.
4. That the therapist is *experiencing unconditional positive regard* toward the client.
5. That the therapist is *experiencing* an *empathic* understanding of the client's *internal frame of reference*.
6. That the client *perceives*, at least to a minimal degree, conditions 4 and 5, the *unconditional positive regard* of the therapist for him, and the *empathic* understanding of the therapist. (Rogers, 1959: 213, original emphasis)

Rogers' major theoretical statements (1957, 1959) are inductively reasoned and rest upon the biological construct of the actualizing tendency. Nevertheless, the trajectory of Rogers' theory is phenomenological in nature and forces client-centered therapy and the person-centered approach out of an objectivist, positivist medical model, and into a philosophical paradigm (Rogers, 1951: 532, 1959: 251, see also 1946).

CLIENT-CENTERED THERAPY AND THE NON-DIRECTIVE ATTITUDE

Most client-centered therapists share a large degree of consensus in defining two of Rogers' three therapist conditions, namely unconditional positive regard and empathic understanding. *Unconditional positive regard* might be defined as the therapist's acceptance of the client's experiences and self-representations without judgment and without discrimination of some communications from the client as more valid or compelling than others (Standal, 1954; Moon, Rice and Schneider, 2001). The major vehicle for communicating unconditional positive regard is the therapist's dedication to *empathic understanding* (Brodley and Schneider, 2001), a dedication to following and receiving the client. Empathic understanding is never certain, never complete. It often manifests itself as an interactive process wherein the therapist, imbued with the nonjudgmental mind-set of unconditional positive regard, follows the client and sometimes checks with the client to see if the therapist is indeed accurately grasping the client's experiences, intentions, meanings and communications (Brodley, 1996; Brodley and Schneider, 2001; Raskin, 1947/2005, cited in Rogers 1951: 29). How this process appears in practice can vary, depending upon the unique expressive qualities of the client and the style and temperament of the therapist who is being freshly attuned not only to each individual client, but also to each new moment with the same client.[1]

Devotion to experiencing unconditional positive regard and empathic understanding can result in therapist behaviors that are likely non-directive in effect. I qualify this as merely 'likely' only because therapists are fallible human beings, and we can never know how a client will perceive or experience the therapist's behaviors. We can say that the client-centered therapist, when busily engrossed in the task of empathically and nonjudgmentally receiving the client, has no agenda other than the agenda of the client, and, as a consequence, is working non-directively.

Some client-centered writers (Grant, 1990, 2004; Moon, 2001; Brodley, 2005; Levitt, 2005, Chapter 1 this volume; see also Brodley, 1997; Prouty, 2000; Schmid, 2001b, 2002; Witty, 2004) embrace the non-directive attitude as an ethical stance that is foundational to practice. From that standpoint we can say that an ethically viewed choice not to manipulate, divert or estrange the client from his own path determines the therapist's choice to immerse herself in the exclusive client-centered task of acceptant empathic reception. Rogers' instructions for being client-centered, that is, to experience the inherently non-directive therapist conditions, give a non-directive therapist such as myself a constructive way to be in relationship with a client. A sincerely client-centered therapist tends to work in a non-directive manner. A non-directive therapist finds client-centered therapy to be a natural fit.

By 1951 Rogers had stopped calling his approach 'nondirective therapy'. In his

---

1. The third condition, therapist congruence, and the sixth condition, that the client perceive the therapist's empathic understanding and unconditional positive regard, are not addressed by me at this juncture. Perhaps it would be accurate to say that I regard them as concepts that are primarily theoretical rather than practical in nature. The theoretical aspects of therapist congruence will be addressed in the following section.

oral history in 1986–1987 (Rogers and Russell, 2002: 253), he said that the term was rebellious of mainstream psychology and was dropped in favor of a more positive, confident name for the approach: 'client-centered therapy' emphasized the therapist's intention to accept and understand the client's frame of reference (Raskin, 1948/2004). The idea of the 'non-directive attitude' so eloquently described by Nathaniel Raskin (Raskin 1947/2005, 2001/2004; Rogers, 1951: 29) was salvaged by Barbara Brodley (1997, 2002), Jerold Bozarth (1998, 2000, 2001a) and Barry Grant (1990). These writers emphasize how the non-directive attitude imports a positive, revolutionary thrust into the therapy. It imbues the therapist with a level of trust in the client, a 'non-directive acceptance' (Raskin, 1948/2004) that defines client-centered practice. Bozarth emphasizes unconditional positive regard as the theoretical and therapeutic core of Rogers' therapy; unconditional acceptance leaves no room for directivity (1998: 56, 2001a). Brodley's and Grant's emphases are ethically based. Brodley suggests that 'client-centered therapists are unique in the extent of their commitment to be of help without disempowering their clients' (1997: 18). Grant describes the non-directive attitude as 'being humbled before the mystery of others and wishing only to acknowledge and respect them ... an almost aesthetic appreciation for the uniqueness and otherness of the client' (1990: 83).

The hypothesis of the actualizing tendency and the proven sturdiness of Rogers' theoretical conditions bolster and shape my work but are secondary to my ethically based choice to be a non-directive, client-centered companion and not an expert. The term 'person-centered', as the general name of the Rogerian approach to such vocations as teaching and parenting, accurately heralds my psychotherapeutic premises: (1) every being's perceptual experiences, meanings and intentions are unique and to be respected; and (2) the experience of meaningful acceptance (i.e., unconditional positive regard in a context of feeling understood) facilitates resilience and growth.

I have been distracted at times by possible tensions between the theory and practice of client-centered therapy. Rogers' guideline that the therapist be *congruent in the relationship*' (Rogers, 1959: 213), can raise the spectre of a potential conflict between therapist congruence and therapist devotion to the discipline of empathically accepting the client. Nevertheless, I have come to think that in client-centered theory there is no need to choose between therapist discipline and therapist congruence, or between the concept of congruence and the non-directive attitude. The remainder of this discussion will be a study of Rogers' theoretical construct of *congruence* and its implications for a therapist in non-directive practice.

CONGRUENCE IN ROGERS' THEORIES OF PERSONALITY AND THERAPY

Whether discussing congruence or incongruence, Rogers is addressing a universal human, fluid condition. In terms of Rogers' personality theory, congruence refers to personal wholeness and adjustment (as opposed to maladjustment), a relative absence of self-conscious constrictions and anxieties, and a consequent *intra-personal* openness between awareness and experience allowing for *inter-personal* openness between awareness, experience and self-expression. According to Rogers, incongruence begins in human development at an early age. The newborn is a natural experiencer and born congruent. Infants seek, enjoy, cry and gurgle, organismically responding to the mixed experiences of being alive. However, highly dependent upon the care of others, the small child develops increasing sensitivity to the concrete, practical, even protective, emotional and psychological demands of caregivers, and surrenders experiential freedom in the interest of self-maintenance. The child learns to muffle himself, intrapsychically as well as interpersonally.

Rogers' 1959 personality theory statement relies heavily upon the language of Stanley Standal (1954; Moon, Rice and Schneider, 2001). Standal hypothesized a universal need for positive self-regard which thrives with consistent experiencing of positive regard from significant others (*ibid.*). In the course of perceiving nonacceptance from caregivers, the child develops (or incorporates) conditions of worth: inner limits which block the flow of the newborn human's genuine, perhaps purposeful, responses to perceived reality (Rogers, 1951: 494), which Rogers called the 'organismic valuing process' (1951: 522–3). It is the nature of the human species that we are born into need for others. It is the law of the jungle that we must appease those whose willingness to aid and abet us may be contingent upon our cooperation. The point is that in order to maintain life-sustaining relationships we become psychologically alienated from ourselves, from our natural way of being. Through the waywardness of life and the self-suppressions that can arise even from receiving love and protection in the course of a relatively happy childhood, everyone is burdened with intrapsychic snarls and interpersonal constrictions.

According to Rogers' theory of therapy, it is through experiencing optimal relationship that we can regain psychological freedom. It is through acceptant reception by another that we shed our anxieties and become more freely alive. The task of therapy is to free the intrapsychic experiencing of the individual, yielding him more inner and interpersonal freedom, option and choice.

For a helping relationship to be optimal, the therapist needs to experience a necessary degree of congruence. The therapist must be 'congruent in the relationship' (1959: 213). Rogers offered the following basic definition of therapist congruence:

> the therapist should be, within the confines of this relationship, a congruent, genuine, integrated person. It means that within the relationship he is freely and deeply himself, with his actual experience accurately represented by his awareness of himself. It is the opposite of presenting a façade, either knowingly or unknowingly. (1957: 97)

Jerold Bozarth (1998, 2001b: 189), Barbara Brodley (1998/2001) and John Shlien (2003), extrapolate from this and other similar descriptions by Rogers that congruence is an integrated state that allows the therapist to be fully present, acceptant and empathic with a client. 'It is *the ability to listen* … without being impeded by the reverberations in oneself' (Shlien, 2003: 15). Peter Schmid suggests that congruent therapists are 'patient, curious and full of the ability of being astonished and surprised' (2001a: 222).

Bozarth (1998, 2001b) equates therapist self-acceptance to congruence and relates it to Rogers' 1959 statement of the application of client-centered theory to family life: it is through congruence, which flows from the therapist's in-the-moment self-acceptant

265

openness to her own experience, that the therapist can most fully and openly attend to the client. This means that in therapy, through 'experiencing genuine and true interest … [and empathic] acceptance from the therapist, the client, in a growing state of congruence, experiences increasing self-acceptance, openness to self and other' (Moon, 2002: 136). This idea of openness to self and other was present in proposition XVIII of Rogers' 1951 theory of personality:

> When the individual perceives and accepts into one consistent and integrated system all his sensory and visceral experiences, then he is necessarily more understanding of others and is more accepting of others as separate individuals. (1951: 520, original italics)

This idea, along with Rogers' awareness of the immanent philosophical thrust of his theory, is also present, along with the word 'congruence,' on the last page of his 1951 personality theory chapter:

> This theory is basically phenomenological in character … It pictures the end-point of personality development as being a basic congruence between the phenomenal field of experience and the conceptual structure of the self—a situation which, if achieved, would represent freedom from internal strain and anxiety, and freedom from potential strain; which would represent the maximum in realistically oriented adaptation; which would mean the establishment of an individualized value system having considerable identity with the value system of any other equally well-adjusted member of the human race. (Rogers, 1951: 532)

The construct of 'congruence,' in client-centered theory, present in 1951, makes a complete circle containing the incongruence and the congruence of both client and therapist (Bozarth 1998, 2001b; Merry, 2001; Moon, 2002). 'The development of congruence is … a development of the human potential for experiencing' (Haugh, 2001: 127). A therapist who is congruent in the relationship is present to facilitate the development of congruence in the client. A beginning therapist, partly through client-centered consultation, changes and grows just as does the client of the consultee (Merry, 2001; Worrall, 2001). A therapist's working self-acceptance is further enhanced through practice as the therapist experiences making a positive difference in the self-experiences of clients (Standal, 1954; Moon, Rice and Schneider, 2001). Over time a therapist at work likely tends to experience congruence more and more consistently.

If therapy were ever completely, perfectly finished, a 'fully functioning person' would emerge from that process. Such a person is merely an abstraction, an ideal (Rogers, 1969: 295). This is because, theoretically, every person is always in process, always developing and changing, such that a consistent experience of congruence, a truly complete openness to self and other is never fully achieved. This ideal person is accurately aware of his experiencing. His self structure is fluid—not a fixed or assessable object, but instead an active living experiencing subject, 'a fluid gestalt changing flexibly in the process of assimilation of new experience' (Rogers, 1959: 234). To Rogers, the person is not only always in process, always maturing; he *is* a process, an alive, self-actualizing process (Van Belle, 1980: 70–1).

> The good life, from the point of view of my experience, is the process of movement in a direction which the human organism selects when it is inwardly free to move in any direction ... (Rogers, 1961: 187)

Congruence can be defined as integration, self-awareness, realness, genuineness, authenticity, transparency, openness, and psychological freedom. It is freedom to be oneself, to experience and to become not only that which I am in the moment, but also that which in an unencumbered state I value and choose. For the therapist it is freedom from self-conscious constraint, preoccupation and anxiety, such that she can be therapeutically available, empathically attending and able to experience unconditional positive regard for the client.

Client-centered theory is a holistic, growth theory viewed by Rogers as applicable to all helping relationships. The 'existing subjective person' (Rogers, 1959: 251), is every person, each one always maintaining, self-furthering, becoming and changing. The alive and becoming person is central to Rogers' theories of personality and therapy. Also central in the theories of personality and therapy is a relationship wherein two existing subjective persons reside. In theoretical terms the therapist has engaged herself to serve as helper to the other and has engaged herself to be 'congruent in the relationship' (1959: 213). In nontheoretical terms, in the working terms of a contract, one person is the favored member of the relationship, the recipient of service. The client-centered therapist concedes dictation of direction to the client. All the while, both individuals are fallible human beings, ever in the process of becoming and experiencing varying degrees of congruence and incongruence. However, for therapeutic potency, the therapist needs to be sufficiently congruent to be truly present and attending in relationship with the client.

THE PERCEPTUAL STANCE OF THE FULLY FUNCTIONING THERAPIST

Rogers' (1961) description of the idealized person who has completed therapy, the fully functioning person, gives a picture of near-perfect congruence. He tells us how congruence might influence the internal attitude and self-expression of the fully functioning person, and, by extension, the internal attitude and self-expression of the congruent client-centered therapist. His congruence 'corollary' (Rogers, 1961: 341) describes the congruent individual who holds a phenomenological worldview, an 'attitude of personal perceptions' (Brodley, 1998: 94). With the corollary he articulates the perceptual nature of the non-directive attitude and perhaps offers a clue as to the language a congruent therapist might speak.

> If an individual is at this moment entirely congruent, his actual physiological experience being accurately represented in his awareness, and his communication being accurately congruent with his awareness, then his communication could never contain an expression of an external fact. If he was congruent he could not say, 'That rock is hard'; 'He is stupid'; 'You are

bad'; or 'She is intelligent.' The reason for this is that we never experience such 'facts'. Accurate awareness of experience would always be expressed as feelings, perceptions, meanings from an internal frame of reference. I never know that he is stupid or you are bad. I can only perceive that you seem this way to me. Likewise, strictly speaking I do not know that the rock is hard, even though I may be very sure that I experience it as hard if I fall down on it ... If the person is thoroughly congruent then it is clear that all of his communication would necessarily be put in a context of personal perception. This has very important implications. (Rogers, 1961: 341)

A congruent non-directive therapist follows and accepts the client's experience with an empathic, acceptant *perceptual* attitude. This means accepting the experiential reality relative and essential to this individual in this moment. This means that the therapist enters into the client's experience without over-identifying, over-investing, judging or objectifying. Practicing client-centered therapy, embodying the non-directive attitude, means accepting reality as perceptual and being humble before the universe of the unknown, including the yet-to-be-discovered experience of the client who lives in his own separate perceptual world.

A client-centered therapist, working within a phenomenological mindset, like the fully functioning person, functions rationally (because she is contracted to be responsible and so chooses to function accordingly) with an attitude of perception. In the corollary statement, Rogers suggests that a congruent therapist would not communicate her perceptions as objective facts.[2] We can infer from this that, according to Rogers, when making an 'I statement', the congruent client-centered therapist would wish to be transparently, politically clear that the therapist does not intend to be making a factual statement about the client. The therapist would likely make this clear through her manner of self-expression: 'This is only my thought ...' or, 'I was wondering ...' or, 'I think I understand what you mean, but I was distracted for a moment by the thought ...'

To work effectively, a client-centered therapist needs to maintain a sufficient level of congruence to be fairly consistently present in interested attendance to the phenomenology of the client. However, engaged in an ethical commitment to be present and available for the client, the therapist's work is complicated because she is human and fallible. This is perhaps part of Rogers' emphasis upon congruence as the foremost necessary condition: the therapeutic task of empathic acceptance is complicated. The therapist is aided in this task, able to experience the therapeutic conditions, by stepping into the job of accepting a perceptual view of reality. The therapist is congruent in the role of experiencing the therapist conditions and perhaps functionally enhanced during the therapeutic hour by her working therapist level of congruence. She is open to the experiencing of both self and other,

---

2. Bert Rice (2004, personal communication) has suggested that Rogers' congruence corollary statement (1961: 341) is inconsistent with the notion that free will exists. When Rogers says that the congruent individual 'would never ...', he is limiting the options of the congruent individual. Rogers' statement appears inconsistent with an assertion of the *existence*, as opposed to the *perception*, of free will. Is the congruent individual determined to speak in a particular manner?

congruent enough to be personally available for relationship with the other, and not invulnerably ensconced in a role of expert scientist. It is her choice and her commitment to engage herself as a responsible companion (see also Schmid, 1998: 86).

II. THERAPIST CONGRUENCE IN CLIENT-CENTERED PRACTICE

The therapeutic relationship exists as a service to the client. In the client-centered relationship a congruent therapist is dedicated to following the client's lead by experiencing unconditional positive regard and empathic understanding. My working therapist congruence is in part based upon a theoretically driven vocational stance of 'sensitive and sincere "client-centeredness"' (Rogers, 1946, cited in 1951: 30). My best therapeutic attitude incorporates trust in the client, trust in the ethical foundation upon which I work, trust in client-centered theory and trust in myself as an engaged person able to embody my therapeutic values. My professional stance is to trust myself and the other person. The client-centered therapeutic task might be defined as the discipline of client-centered therapy, the discipline of experiencing empathic understanding and acceptance. Therapist congruence is the ability of the therapist to practice the discipline.

The idealized, fully functioning, congruent client-centered therapist would never be distracted from the task of empathic acceptance. But, in the real working world, the fully human world, therapists are sometimes incongruent. 'Moment to moment, the therapist experiences "mines of complex responses to the client"' (Susan Pildes, email communication, 2004). Therapist congruence, the ability to be present, attending and open to experiencing, can fluctuate. Sometimes a therapist attitudinally shifts out of the client's perceptual field and into her own. She might feel an intense urge to self-express.

I have moments of incongruence amidst the fluttering of my awareness. These moments include experiences of internal pressure to inform or correct the client. I can be distracted from experiencing empathic acceptance. These instances, which are not so very rare for me, represent my dilemma concerning therapist congruence. Is this a lapse in my working congruence, meaning a lapse in my ability to attend to the client? Or is it sometimes a lapse in what I have come to think of as my *vocational congruence*, a lapse in the *authenticity of my purpose* as I fleetingly wonder if the necessary conditions are really sufficient? Is offering the unique service of non-directive, attentive companionship really the best service I can offer right now? I can temporarily forget how catalytic to life enhancement I have found client-centered therapy to be for myself and for my clients.

Interestingly, these impulses of mine tend to carry a positive emotional feeling in that they seem generated by my compassion, enthusiasm and caring for the client. It is my more positive, sometimes protective, feelings towards the client that can leave me perplexed by what I experience as my congruence dilemma.[3] On the one hand, the

---

3. In this discussion I have ignored Rogers' multiple statements (see footnote 7, p. 275) regarding persistent negative feelings within the therapist. It is my positive, supportive feelings towards clients and not my more rare negative ones that motivated this study of congruence.

theory delineates my helping role as experiencer of unconditional positive regard and empathic understanding. On the other, therapist congruence, that is, therapist psychological freedom, is necessary to doing good therapy. I believe that a unique relationship endowed with the facilitative therapist conditions is the most potent service I can provide to the client. But, I may feel supportive, caring or concerned and might want to share my thoughts.

Amidst the to and fro of everyday practice, there tend to be two kinds of instance when I might wonder if I am deviating from client-centered theory. Both might lead to making a 'therapist-frame' response (Brodley, 1999a), communicating the therapist's rather than the client's frame of reference. For the present discussion, these can be conceived as spontaneous and nonspontaneous therapist-frame responses (see also Brodley, 1987, 1993, 1999a, 1999b; Raskin, 1988).

SPONTANEOUS THERAPIST-FRAME RESPONSES

I have come to think of spontaneous therapist-frame responses within a non-directive client-centered context as expressive of the alive and human presence of the therapist. I consider such expression to be a sign of transparent wholeness, a consequence of the therapist being congruent in the relationship, a consequence of being sufficiently psychologically free to be totally engrossed and immersed in the client's world. In the course of being so engrossed, a therapist can naturally, empathically, make a therapist-frame statement, gesture, or other expression that is symptomatic of being thoroughly with the client, a true companion to the client.

Relatively benign examples of spontaneous responses can include exclamations of agreement, surprise and pleasure (see Brodley, 1999a, for categories of therapist-frame responses). Raskin suggests that:

> The therapist may go further and, in a spontaneous and non-systematic way, offer reactions, suggestions, ask questions, try to help the client experience feelings, share aspects of his or her own life, etc., while maintaining a basic and continuing respect for the client as architect of the process. (1988: 2)

In my opinion, we witness quickening therapist spontaneity in a famous exchange between Rogers (T below) and Gloria (C below) (Shostrom, 1965):

> C57: Yes, and you know what else I was just thinking? I—a dumb thing—that all of a sudden while I was talking to you I thought, 'Gee, how nice I can talk to you and I want you to approve of me and I respect you, but I miss that my father couldn't talk to me like you are.' I mean, I'd like to say, 'Gee, I'd like you for my father.' I don't even know why that came to me.
>
> T57: You look to me like a pretty nice daughter. But you really do miss the fact that you couldn't be open with your own dad.

I understand Rogers' first sentence, a therapist-frame response, to be an utterance that evidences his high degree of involvement in Gloria's experience. Rogers spontaneously meets Gloria in the vicinity of her emotional valence and in his therapist-frame sentence he simultaneously accepts her statement, which she has characterized, as 'dumb'. Rogers' statement is not thought out; it is warmly receiving of Gloria and her disclosures. In his full response to her, Rogers overflows and then rights himself as he returns to empathically following the client's frame of reference: 'But you really do miss the fact that you couldn't be open with your own dad.' We'll never know to what extent Rogers' emotional statement might have deterred or distracted Gloria from pursuing an alternative series of associations. However, through its return in the second sentence to Gloria's frame of reference, Rogers' full response to her expresses his dedication to acceptant empathic following.[4]

I observe this in my own work. I will be so immersed in the client's narration that when the client asks me a question, without any sort of checking as to whether or not I understood the question or whether it was rhetorical or explicit on the client's part, I spill out my honest response to the question. Then I might catch myself and say something to return to the client's frame of reference or to check if my response was to what the client had been asking. I consider this sort of thorough engagement with the client as intrinsic to the client-centered therapeutic relationship. It is a sign that I am functioning with openness to myself and consequently to the client.

Should my view of therapist spontaneity as being within the purview of the theory be contingent upon its degree of frequency? Perhaps. Certainly if I form a habit of spontaneously responding to clients in a supportive or dubious manner, then I am departing from Raskin's *non-systematic spontaneity* (1988: 2) into the non-client-centered terrain of systematic therapist disclosure. In a study of ten of Rogers' transcripts, Merry (1996: 281) noted that while Rogers 'was not averse to communicating something of his own emotional state, or his own experience ... actual examples of him doing this are quite rare ...'

In certain contexts, my spontaneous therapist-frame responses can occur frequently. Therapist animation can evidence itself in the unpredictability of client-centered child therapy; this is especially likely when a child's wish is that the therapist actively engage in the play. It also occurs in sessions with mature, adult clients whose clear preference is that the therapist just talk, share her thoughts or brainstorm with them. Also, therapist spontaneity surfaces frequently in facilitated person-centered group therapy, as well as in couple and family therapy where the therapist enters into the family or couple as part of a working team (Pildes and Moon, 2004).

Sometimes therapist self-representations are responsive to clients' wishes, questions or intentions (Brodley, 1999a) and might occur frequently. Faced with a client's immediate question or long-standing directions to me, I shift back and forth between the client's

---

4. Bert Rice suggests that Rogers' first sentence in this response can actually be classified as an 'empathic understanding response' (Brodley, 1994, 1996), because Rogers is effectively understanding and accepting Gloria's somewhat embarrassed and tentative statement. He suggests that Rogers' meaning would have been no different had he said: 'You'd like to say, that I could be your father. But you really do miss ...' Such a response would be a more literal empathic following statement, but not as emphatically acceptant in response to Gloria's embarrassment as was Rogers' actual statement.

frame of reference and my own. In order to do so, I must make many therapist-frame self-representations. I tend to self-represent in the manner described in Rogers' congruence corollary, that is, in language that communicates my attitude of perception. My participation in the relationship as a whole is client-centered in that I am responsive to the client's lead. I am willing to weave back and forth between perceptual world views at the beck and call of the client. I am following the client's directions to me and maintaining an acceptant perceptual attitude. I consider these sorts of situational responses of mine to fall generally into the category of 'spontaneous' therapist-frame responses. As Bozarth says:

> The therapist goes with the client, goes at the client's pace, goes with the client in his/her own ways of thinking, of experiencing, of processing. The therapist can not be up to other things, have other intentions without violating the essence of Person-Centered Therapy. To be up to other things—whatever they might be—is a 'yes, but' reaction to the essence of the approach. (1998: 11)

My point concerning therapist spontaneity is that therapist aliveness is necessary to a therapist being sensitively available and open to the client. A therapist's psychological freedom is fundamental to therapist congruence and thus central to the therapy. My inner freedom, that is my very ability to be fully present, can lead me to self-express in a manner that can appear to be technically incorrect. In fact, these self-representations can potentially be harmful both personally and existentially to the client, as well as to the potency of the therapy. Nevertheless, client-centered theory requires the therapist to be spontaneously present.[5]

NONSPONTANEOUS THERAPIST-FRAME RESPONSES

I sometimes make a different kind of deviation from the practice of experiencing unconditional positive regard and empathic understanding. These deviations are not spontaneous and are indeed 'yes, but' (Bozarth, 1998: 11, 2001a: 146) reactions to the client's phenomenology. Like my spontaneous responses, these tend to be triggered by positive, warm feelings I have for the client. But I wonder if they are more signs of incongruence than congruence, actually a lapse in unconditional positive regard. I am referring to times when, aware of being stirred by the content of the client's self-expression, I speak consciously and directively from my own frame of reference. I am aware of feeling stimulated; my awareness is a sign of congruence. But my choice to self-represent is perhaps the opposite, a sign of vocational incongruence, a values crisis of sorts. Having lost the capacity to maintain a *perceptual attitude* and to seamlessly experience unconditional positive regard, I have momentarily become less than fully functioning as a client-centered therapist. I might wonder whether or not to self-represent. Because I have contracted to nourish the personal emergence of the client, this may be an ethical fork.

---

5. How the client and therapist assimilate the therapist's overflow requires a separate discussion already broached somewhat by Brodley (1999a).

Some of the risks of informing, countering, or advising the client have been enumerated by Barbara Brodley:

> Time is taken from clients' use of the limited therapy time. Clients may become distracted from their own focus and introspective process. Clients may feel they are being evaluated or judged. They may lose their sense of self-determination and empowerment in the therapy process. In theoretical terms, a client's *locus of evaluation* (Rogers, 1959) may be influenced away from within himself towards the therapist. Clients may become confused or defensive about the therapist's intentions, perceiving the therapist as having his own agenda for them. In addition, comments from the therapist's frame are inherently more difficult for clients to understand than empathic understanding responses. (1999a: 12)

In spite of the risks, I do sometimes speak from my therapist frame of reference to alert, inform, dissuade, self-disclose or, more rarely, question a client.[6] These directive responses tend to be stirred in me in connection with warm caring and concern for the client. Yet, however warmly caring I may feel, therapist support and therapist advice fall outside Rogers' non-directive theory of therapy, outside the nondiscriminating nature of unconditional positive regard.

On the one hand, Rogers was clear that client-centered therapy cannot be a tool; it must be sincere, simple and not manipulative. His theory insistently values the client as subject and not object and values the therapist as human and free. To force the formal theory as a mold upon the therapist's behavior violates these values. On the other hand, at what point does therapy cease to be therapy and become, according to the non-directive view, harmful at worst, negligent and therapeutically diluted at best? At what point does a paradigm shift in practice occur? Is the tipping point quantitative or qualitative?

How existentially violent to the client are these self-assertions that arise from my caring (though essentially judgmental) involvement in the relationship? In terms of the values of client-centered therapy, there is no way to dodge the clear answer. Although the theory trusts the client to be resilient and self-able (even in the face of therapist misfires), there is significant existential risk to the client.

Self-representation might at times be necessary to the therapist's peace of mind, a clearing out of concern or excitement, enabling the therapist to return to offering unconditional positive regard and empathic understanding. Susan Pildes calls these self-representations 'clearing responses' (personal communication, 2004). Marginal glimmers of my frame of reference might carry an element of generosity of feeling toward or cherishing of the client; they can be expressive of an aliveness in my egalitarian, philosophical political stance of being human with the other. They can take some of the scientific Rogerian 'if ... then' (Rogers, 1957, 1959) axiom-driven starch out of my

---

6. I am not referring to what Brodley (1999a: 25) calls 'questions for clarification', which are a version of empathic understanding response, a checking for better understanding the client's experience.

presence: not because they are so intended, but because I am a person who feels and cares. A person who feels and cares is unlikely to cling righteously to a single modality of responsive therapeutic presence.

But, when a therapist departs from the traditional, more medical model or manualized role of expert over the client as object, she assumes a different responsibility: she commits to sheltering and not obstructing the becoming of the client who is regarded as a trustworthy, existentially entitled and self-determining subject. In client-centered therapy, a therapist who feels and cares tends to dwell responsibly and consistently within the client's frame of reference.

Brodley (1997, 1998/2001, 1999a) and (1998, 2001a) have offered discussion relating to my congruence dilemma. Brodley states that while remaining committed to the 'philosophical orientation ... and therapeutic attitudes and the non-directive attitude, the client-centered therapist remains free to behave in whatever way his or her best judgment or therapeutic instincts leads or demands of him or her' (1997: 25). Bozarth emphasizes that Rogerian theory instructs the therapist to *experience,* empathic understanding and unconditional positive regard, but does not prescribe any particular verbal or nonverbal mode or style of response. '[V]alid person-centered responses are located in the centering of the therapist in the world of the client with trust in the client's self-determination' (Bozarth, 1998: 101).

To some extent, the attitude of perception and the language suggested in Rogers' congruence corollary (1961: 341), a language of political transparency and of knowing one does not know, can soften the blow of a therapist's explicit, self-expressive directing of the client. That is, if the therapist explains what she is responding to, or why, or with what in mind, the therapist makes transparent the agenda of her therapist-frame viewpoint; she clarifies that she is speaking subjectively. Of course, if the language of the congruence corollary is used as a tool to offset and excuse therapist-frame intrusions, then the relationship offered by the therapist ceases to meet the Rogerian definition of therapeutic (Rogers, 1961).

We can hope that the therapist's disciplined non-directive habit of acceptantly not knowing what is best for the client will lessen the loss to the client when the therapist chooses to self-represent as an agent within the client's world of experience. That is to say, the therapist's usual intention to receive the client as a self-directing leader in the relationship, the therapist's manner of speaking with a perceptual attitude of accepting the relativity of truth, and the therapist's checking back with the client (Raskin, 1947/2005, cited in Rogers, 1951: 29; Schmid, 2004) may mitigate against harm to the client.

My present thinking is that perhaps on those occasions when the therapist is wondering, 'Should I or shouldn't I insert myself into the client's world?' the most responsible answer is 'No, I shouldn't depart from the client's frame.' I suggest this, not as a rule, but as a thought. The theory rejects the rigidity of rules; it is at heart a phenomenological theory that carries an attitude of humility toward the other, an attitude of relativity, and an attitude of never knowing. In a sense, the client-centered therapist who is feeling an internal pressure to self-express to the client might be described as momentarily suffering from a delusion of knowing.

Do I really want to make a statement as simplistic as 'Spontaneous therapist-frame responses, even though they are apt to have a directive impact and might impose psychological risk to the client, are theoretically acceptable to me; whereas, thought-out, careful interventions are not'? Such a conclusion might seem ludicrous. Nevertheless, theoretically and ethically, this is what I think.

Since I care whether or not the therapy I practice is 'good' for the client, I want to maintain a reflective working awareness. I choose to beware of deviating from the practice I believe to be therapeutic. I am aware that my self-representations might obstruct the emergence of the client or risk the client feeling diminished. My self-expression can shift the political relationship and the intrinsic nature of the therapy. It can detract from the consistent quality of the therapy being offered. It can steal the client's thunder and cast doubt upon the client's sense of trustworthiness.

Simultaneously, I can view moments of choosing to self-express as instances when I am trusting myself as a person and trusting the client as sturdy and capable of handling my incursions into his world. I believe that at times my self-representations, supportive statements, informative tidbits and pieces of advice can be perceived as helpful by the client or by me. Still, even if tangible benefit results for the client, it can be argued that this benefit is worth less than the philosophical and psychological costs of countering the momentum of the client's phenomenological agency or devaluing the client's awareness as less compelling than my own.

Congruence has been defined as psychological freedom, the fluctuating capacity to be open to experiencing both self and other. For the therapist, congruence is part of her immediate psychological state of being within herself and in relationship. As such, given this definition, there is little a therapist can do mid-session to improve her own congruence. It seems to me that the only in-session assistance available to a floundering client-centered therapist is her awareness of her values, her ethical stance and her non-directive attitude. [7]

Aware of being aroused into losing track of her working values, the non-directive therapist can choose to respond to the client in a conservative manner, that is, with empathic acceptance. She knows that this decision likely promises that the client will feel received in being just as he is and will not feel thwarted from construing whatever meanings he attributes to his experience.

---

7. The idea that there is nothing a therapist can do to restore congruence within-session warrants further attention not given here. Such a discussion would entail acknowledging suggestions by Rogers (Baldwin, 1987; Rogers, 1961; Rogers and Truax, 1967) that can appear to be advocating negative or critical-sounding therapist-frame statements made with a transparent attitude of perception. I personally consider judgmental therapist frame statements advisable only when they flow naturally (spontaneously) within a session. When faced with having a negative feeling toward the client, I do subscribe to making an increased effort to experience empathic understanding (Brodley, personal communication, 2003), or an effort 'to employ … [therapist] responses constructively as a basis for further [open-ended] inquiry …' (Patterson, 1985: 63) before making possibly critical sounding therapist-frame statements to the client. This opinion of mine is consistent with my reasoning in this essay that nonspontaneous interventions are theoretically unacceptable.

CONCLUSION

My conclusion is tied to my understanding of therapist congruence in Rogers' theory of personality and to the philosophical non-directive values inherent in Rogers' theory of therapy. To be present and available to attend to and receive the client, the therapist needs to be open to the experiences of self and other: that is, psychologically free within the therapy relationship. A therapist needs to be engrossed in the activity of being with the client and not preoccupied by theory or fear of making mistakes. I believe that a client-centered therapist's deep investment in non-directive values leads to a tendency to shelter from therapist incursions the client's budding meanings, feelings and agency. Accepting the client's perceptual experience is the genuine and freely chosen, customary, ethical and therapeutic behavior of the client-centered therapist.

As client-centered therapists, to the extent we are congruent, we are able to do the work. Because we are alive, always in process and human, we are sometimes incongruent. However, it is when we are congruent that we are most truly in therapeutic relationship with the client. Because we are contracted in service to the client, we owe him respect, responsibility, protection and quality of therapy. Quality of therapy requires a congruent therapist. A congruent therapist is psychologically free. A psychologically free therapist has the capacity to choose to respond to the client in the ethical, client-centered modality of not imposing, but instead honoring, accompanying and being present. Client-centered therapeutic presence entails experiencing unconditional positive regard and empathic understanding characterized by an attitude of perception.

The view of congruence offered here is not dualistic. In Rogers' theory there is no dichotomy or battle between discipline and freedom. The therapist does not self-express as an expression of freedom. Having psychological freedom does not mean that the therapist tends to self-express. The therapist just *is* a free person and thus able to do the job. Unconditional positive regard and empathic understanding are not in competition with congruence and freedom. The client-centered task is one of experiencing the attitudes of unconditional positive regard and empathic understanding. It requires that the therapist is free enough, congruent enough, to do so. In the last year of his life, Rogers said the following:

> Being real does not involve us doing anything we want to do; it means a disciplined approach. That's one thing that I realize I have not stressed enough, and consequently it has been overlooked. I'm quite a disciplined person myself, and it comes naturally to me to think that everyone else is too, but that's not so. (Rogers and Russell, 2002: 284)

The psychologically free, or congruent, therapist tends to be acceptant of herself and of the client and chooses to practice the art of implementing Rogers' non-directive theory of therapy. When self-expressing, she tends to do so with a transparently phenomenological attitude. The non-directive attitude, an ethical, political and phenomenological stance of choosing to shelter the client's self-direction, permeates the being of the client-centered therapist.

Author's note: It is impossible to adequately acknowledge the extent to which my thoughts and words have been influenced by my kind and generous teachers, all patient readers, Jerold Bozarth, Barbara Brodley, Susan Pildes, Bert Rice and Harry Van Belle.

REFERENCES

Baldwin M (1987) Interview with Carl Rogers on the use of self in therapy. In M Baldwin and V Satir (Eds) *The Use of Self in Therapy*. New York: Haworth Press, pp. 45–52.

Bozarth JD (1998) *Person-Centered Therapy: A revolutionary paradigm*. Ross-on-Wye: PCCS Books.

Bozarth JD (March, 2000) Non-directiveness in client-centered therapy: A vexed concept. Presentation at the Eastern Psychological Association, Baltimore, MD.

Bozarth JD (2001a) An addendum to beyond reflection: Emergent modes of empathy (August 2001). In S Haugh & T Merry (Eds) (2001) *Rogers' Therapeutic Conditions: Evolution, theory and practice. Vol. 2: Empathy*. Ross-on-Wye: PCCS Books, pp. 144–54.

Bozarth JD (2001b) Congruence: A special way of being. In G Wyatt (Ed) *Rogers' Therapeutic Conditions: Evolution, theory and practice. Vol. 1: Congruence*. Ross-on-Wye: PCCS Books, pp. 184–99.

Bozarth JD & Brodley BT (1991) Actualization: A functional concept in client-centered therapy. In A Jones & R Crandall (Eds), *Handbook of Self-Actualization*. [Special issue] *Journal of Social Behavior and Personality, 6*(5), 45–59.

Brodley BT (August, 1987) A client-centered psychotherapy practice. Discussion paper at the Third International Forum on the Person-Centered Approach, La Jolla, CA. www/adpca.org

Brodley BT (1993) Appendix. In CJ Topping (Ed) An Equal Prizing: Couple therapy from a client-centered perspective. Unpublished doctoral dissertation. University of Georgia, pp. A1–A7.

Brodley BT (1994) Some observations of Carl Rogers' therapy behavior. *The Person-Centered Journal, 1*(2), 37–48.

Brodley BT (1996) Empathic understanding and feelings in Client-Centered Therapy. *The Person-Centered Journal, 3*(1), 22–30.

Brodley BT (1997) The non-directive attitude in Client-Centered Therapy. *The Person-Centered Journal, 4*(1),18–30.

Brodley BT (1998/2001) Congruence and its relation to communication in Client-Centered Therapy. *The Person-Centered Journal, 5*(2), 83–116. Reprinted in G Wyatt (Ed) (2001) *Rogers' Therapeutic Conditions: Evolution, theory and practice. Vol. 1: Congruence*. Ross-on-Wye: PCCS Books, pp. 55–78.

Brodley BT (1999a) Reasons for responses expressing the therapist's frame of reference in Client-Centered Therapy. *The Person-Centered Journal, 6*(1), 4–27.

Brodley BT (1999b) The actualizing tendency concept in client-centered theory. *The Person-Centered Journal, 6*(2), 108–20.

Brodley BT (2000) Personal presence in Client-Centered Therapy. *The Person-Centered Journal, 7*(2), 139–49.

Brodley BT (2001) Observations of empathic understanding in a client-centered practice. In S Haugh and T Merry (Eds), *Rogers' Therapeutic Conditions: Evolution, theory and practice. Vol. 2, Empathy*. Ross-on-Wye: PCCS Books, pp. 16–37.

Brodley BT (2002) Client-centered: An expressive therapy. *The Person-Centered Journal,* 9(1), 59–70.

Brodley BT (2005) Client-Centered Values Limit The Application of Research Findings: An issue for discussion. In S Joseph & R Worsley (Eds) *Person-Centred Psychopathology: A positive psychology of mental health.* Ross-on-Wye: PCCS Books, pp. 310–16.

Brodley BT & Schneider C (2001) Unconditional positive regard as communicated through verbal behavior in Client-Centered Therapy. In P Wilkins & JD Bozarth (Eds) *Rogers' Therapeutic Conditions: Evolution, theory and practice. Vol 3: Unconditional Positive Regard.* Ross-on-Wye: PCCS Books, pp. 155–72.

Goldstein K (1995) *The Organism: A holistic approach to biology derived from pathological data in man.* New York: Zone Books, 1995 [original German, 1934, *Aufbau des organismus*].

Grant B (1990/2002) Principled and instrumental non-directiveness in Person-Centered and Client-Centered Therapy. *Person-Centered Review,* 5(1), 77–88. Reprinted in DJ Cain (Ed), *Classics in the Person-Centered Approach.* Ross-on-Wye: PCCS Books, pp. 371–7.

Grant B (2004) The imperative of ethical justification in psychotherapy: The special case of Client-Centered Therapy. *Person-Centered & Experiential Psychotherapies,* 3(3), 152–65.

Haugh S (2001) The difficulties in the conceptualisation of congruence: A way forward with complexity theory? In G Wyatt (Ed) *Rogers' Therapeutic Conditions: Evolution, theory and practice. Vol. 1: Congruence.* Ross-on-Wye: PCCS Books, pp. 116–30.

Merry T (1996) An analysis of ten demonstration interviews by Carl Rogers: Implications for the training of client-centered counsellors. In R Hutterer, G Pawlowsky, PF Schmid & R Stipsits (Eds) *Client-Centered and Experiential Psychotherapy: A paradigm in motion.* Frankfurt am Main: Peter Lang, pp. 273–83.

Merry T (2001) Congruence and the supervision of client-centred therapists. In G Wyatt (Ed), *Rogers' Therapeutic Conditions: Evolution, theory and practice. Vol. 1: Congruence.* Ross-on-Wye: PCCS Books, pp. 174–83.

Merry T (2003) The actualisation conundrum. *Person-Centered Practice,* 11(2), 83–91.

Moon KA (2001) Non-directive Client-Centered Therapy with Children. *The Person-Centered Journal,* 8(1), 43–52. A slightly revised version is in JC Watson, RN Goldman & MS Warner (Eds) *Client-Centered and Experiential Psychotherapy in the 21st Century: Advances in theory, research and practice.* Ross-on-Wye: PCCS Books, pp. 485–92.

Moon KA (2002) A dearth of suds for Davey: A therapist's thoughts during a child therapy session. *Person-Centered Journal,* 9(2), 113–39.

Moon KA, Rice BA & Schneider C (2001) Stanley W Standal and the need for positive regard. In P Wilkins & J Bozarth (Eds) *Rogers' Therapeutic Conditions: Evolution, theory and practice. Vol 3: Unconditional Positive Regard.* Ross-on-Wye: PCCS Books, pp. 19–34.

Patterson CH (1964/2000) A universal theory of motivation and its counseling implications. *Journal of Individual Psychology,* 10, 17–31. Reprinted in CH Patterson, *Understanding Psychotherapy: Fifty years of client-centred theory and practice.* Ross-on-Wye: PCCS Books, pp. 10–21.

Patterson CH (1985) *The Therapeutic Relationship.* Pacific Grove, CA: Brooks/Cole.

Pildes S & Moon KA (2004) 'Automatic for the people': Client-centered couple and family therapy. Presentation at the annual conference of the Association for the Development of the Person-Centered Approach, Anchorage, Alaska.

Prouty GF (2000) Carl Rogers and experiential therapies: A dissonance? In T Merry (Ed) *Person-Centred Practice: The BAPCA reader.* Ross-on-Wye: PCCS Books, pp. 30–7.

Raskin NJ (1947/2005) The nondirective attitude. In BE Levitt (Ed) *Embracing Non-directivity: Reassessing person-centered theory and practice in the 21st century.* Ross-on-Wye: PCCS Books, pp. 329–47.

Raskin NJ (1948/2004) The development of non-directive therapy. *Journal of Consulting Psychology, 12*, 92–110. Reprinted in NJ Raskin (2004), *Contributions to Client-Centered Therapy and the Person-Centered Approach.* Ross-on-Wye: PCCS Books.

Raskin NJ (1996/2004) Person-centred psychotherapy: Twenty historical steps. In W Dryden (Ed) *Developments in Psychotherapy: Historical perspectives.* London: Sage, pp. 1–28. Reprinted in NJ Raskin (2004) *Contributions to Client-Centered Therapy and the Person-Centered Approach.* Ross-on-Wye: PCCS Books, pp. 215–44.

Raskin NJ (1988) Responses to Person-Centered vs Client-Centered. *Renaissance, 5*(3/4), 1–2.

Raskin NJ (2001/2004) The history of empathy in the client-centered movement. In S Haugh and T Merry (Eds) *Rogers' Therapeutic Conditions: Evolution, theory and practice. Vol 2: Empathy.* Ross-on-Wye: PCCS Books, (pp. 1–15). Reprinted in NJ Raskin (2004), *Contributions to Client-Centered Therapy and the Person-Centered Approach.* Ross-on-Wye: PCCS Books.

Rogers CR (1946) Significant aspects of Client-Centered Therapy. *American Psychologist, 1*, 415–22.

Rogers CR (1951) *Client-Centered Therapy: Its current practice, implications, and theory.* Boston: Houghton Mifflin.

Rogers CR (1957) The necessary and sufficient conditions of therapeutic personality change. *Journal of Consulting Psychology, 21*(2), 95–103.

Rogers CR (1959) A theory of therapy, personality, and interpersonal relationships as developed in the client-centered framework. In S Koch (Ed) *Psychology: Study of a science: vol. 3: Formulation of the person and the social context.* New York: McGraw-Hill, pp. 184–256.

Rogers CR (1961) *On Becoming a Person.* Boston: Houghton Mifflin.

Rogers CR (1963) The actualizing tendency in relation to 'motives' and consciousness. In MR Jones (Ed) *Nebraska Symposium on Motivation, vol. 11.* Lincoln, NE: University of Nebraska Press, pp. 1–24.

Rogers CR (1969) *Freedom to Learn.* Columbus, OH: Merrill.

Rogers CR (1980) *A Way of Being.* Boston: Houghton Mifflin.

Rogers CR (1986) Client-Centered Therapy. In IL Kutash and A Wolf (Eds) *Psychotherapist's Casebook.* San Francisco: Jossey-Bass, pp. 197–208.

Rogers CR & Russell DE (2002) *Carl Rogers, the Quiet Revolutionary: An oral history.* Roseville, CA: Penmarin.

Rogers CR & Truax CB (1967) The therapeutic conditions antecedent to change: A theoretical view. In CR Rogers *et al.* (Eds) *The Therapeutic Relationship and its Impact: A study of psychotherapy with schizophrenics.* Madison, WI: University of Wisconsin Press.

Shlien JM (2003) *To Lead an Honorable Life: Invitations to think about client-centered therapy and the person-centered approach.* [P Sanders (Ed)] Ross-on-Wye: PCCS Books.

Schmid PF (1998) 'Face to face'—The art of encounter. In B Thorne and E Lambers (Eds) *Person-Centred Therapy: A European perspective.* Thousand Oaks, CA: Sage, pp. 74–90.

Schmid PF (2001a) Authenticity: The person as his or her own author. Dialogical and ethic perspectives on therapy as an encounter relationship. And beyond. In G Wyatt (Ed) *Rogers' Therapeutic Conditions: Evolution, theory and practice. Vol. 1: Congruence.* Ross-on-Wye: PCCS Books, pp. 213–28.

Schmid PF (2001b) Acknowledgement: The art of responding. Dialogical and ethical perspectives on the challenge of unconditional relationships in therapy and beyond. In P Wilkins & J Bozarth (Eds) *Rogers' Therapeutic Conditions: Evolution, theory and practice. Vol. 3: Unconditional Positive Regard.* Ross-on-Wye: PCCS Books, pp. 49–64.

Schmid PF (2002) Knowledge or acknowledgement? Psychotherapy as the 'art of not-knowing'— Prospects on further developments of a radical paradigm. *Person-Centered & Experiential Psychotherapies, 1*(1/2), 56–70.

Schmid PF (2004) Back to the client: A phenomenological approach to the process of understanding and diagnosis. *Person-Centered & Experiential Psychotherapies, 3*(1), 36–51.

Shostrom EL (1965) (Producer) *Three Approaches to Psychotherapy.* [Film] Orange, CA: Psychological Films.

Standal SW (1954) The need for positive regard: A contribution to client-centered theory. Unpublished doctoral dissertation, University of Chicago.

Van Belle HA (1980) *Basic Intent and Therapeutic Approach of Carl R Rogers: A study of his view of man in relation to his view of therapy, personality and interpersonal relations.* Toronto: Wedge Publishing Foundation.

Witty M (2004) The difference directiveness makes: The ethics and consequences of guidance in psychotherapy. *Person-Centered Journal, 11*(1–2), 22–32.

Worrall M (2001) Supervision and Empathic Understanding. In S Haugh & T Merry (Eds) *Rogers' Therapeutic Conditions: Evolution, theory and practice. Vol. 2: Empathy.* Ross-on-Wye: PCCS Books, pp. 206–17.

Chapter 16

NON-DIRECTIVE PERSON-CENTERED GROUPS: FACILITATION OF FREEDOM AND PERSONAL POWER

Jerold D. Bozarth

The goal (and art) of person-centered therapy is to facilitate the creation of a climate in each person and the group of persons. An event in which this takes place is the definition of person-centered group therapy.

John K. Wood, 1983: 239

DEDICATION

This chapter is dedicated to John K. Wood, who died in August, 2004. John was a leader in the development of person-centered groups. He joined Carl Rogers, Natalie Rogers, Maureen O'Hara, Maria Bowen and various other individuals in a unique experiment with large community groups from the early 1970s to the early 1980s.

After working for over a decade with the experiment of large groups, John married the Brazilian artist, Lucila Machado Assumpção. John and Lucila worked a citrus farm in Brazil that evolved into an ecological experiment and was eventually established as an Ecological Reserve. They took a major step toward the application of person-centered group principles to the understanding of social cooperation and the development of Ecological Systems.

INTRODUCTION

This chapter examines the development of, and assumptions that underlie, person-centered groups, leading to the formulation of several postulates about person-centered groups. Person-centered groups are identified as those groups operating on the basic propositions of Carl R. Rogers' theory of therapy and his extended theories of interpersonal relations and the fully functioning person (Rogers, 1959). The range of the person-centered group includes the 'basic encounter group', 'large community group', 'international cultural diversity group', group therapy, person-centered training groups, conflict resolution groups, and person-centered organizational groups (including education, administration and management). The extension of person-centered group principles to the politics of social cooperation and natural processes of interpersonal interaction is considered.

Rogers' (1959) self-proclaimed *magnum opus* theory statement and subsequent minor clarifications (Rogers, 1963, 1975, 1978, 1980) are examined in relation to his expositions on groups (Rogers, 1970, 1977, 1980, 1983). This examination is supplemented by reviews of other publications (Bozarth, 1986, 1988, 1992, 1995, 1998; A. Coulson, 1999; W. Coulson, 1970; Devonshire, 1991; Lago and MacMillan, 1999; MacMillan and Lago, 1993, 1996, 1999; McIlduff and Coghlan, 1991; Raskin, 2004; Stubbs, 1992; Thorne, 1988; Wood, 1982, 1983, 1984, 1994, 1997, 1999).

Rogers' theory is inherently non-directive in relation to the therapist/facilitator. *The premise is that it is the client who directs her own life.*

EXPERIENCES OF THE AUTHOR

A brief delineation of my experience in client-centered/person-centered groups provides a context to help clarify certain aspects of this chapter, and examples that influenced my analysis of person-centered groups are presented here. My experience is elaborated upon in other writings (e.g., Bozarth, 1998: 153–9). Chapter 12 in the present book titled 'The Art of Non-Directive "Being" in Psychotherapy' also offers a more elaborate picture of my experiences and professional journey.

LEARNING 'CLIENT-CENTERED THERAPY'

I learned 'client-centered therapy' from hospitalized psychotic clients in the late 1950s. It was after discovering that I could trust and depend upon clients for the development of their own treatment and growth process that I learned about Rogers' theory of client-centered therapy. Rogers, (1957) 'integration' article provided me with a macro-theory for my personal discovery that disturbed individuals can find their own ways to health and growth. This experience was followed by years of involvement with group activities. I attended groups of every persuasion, including gestalt, Adlerian, psychoanalytic, Transactional Analysis, TIGER training, National Training Lab groups, psychodrama, sociodrama, and therapeutic community groups. I facilitated 'person-centered' groups of hospitalized psychiatric clients; rehabilitation agency clients; and student groups prior to, and after, my first official client-centered training in groups at the La Jolla Program in 1974. Since 1974, I attended a minimum of one community group per year with Carl Rogers and his various colleagues up to the year of his death in 1987.

MY FIRST PROFESSIONAL GROUP

My first professional work experience was with hospitalized 'psychotic' clients. I had to periodically meet with individuals who had moved out of the hospital and the group format became the only practical way to meet with them. I have described my first experience as a 'group leader' as follows:

> My first experience as a group 'leader' in the psychiatric hospital was with a group of about fifteen individuals who had entered a group home outside of

the hospital after twenty or more years as hospital patients. The group was established in order to permit me to meet with all of the individuals during my community trips each week. In short, nearly every aspect of the group violated the traditional knowledge about groups (since I didn't know much about the group literature at the time). The group usually met in the shade of a tree, the structure consisted of my request for us to meet ' ... to see how things are going'. It was a heterogeneous group that was diagnosed with a variety of labels. For example, members included a sixty-year-old male with 'chronic alcoholism; undifferentiated type'; a sixteen-year-old male 'schizophrenic, hebephrenic'; a 'mentally retarded' (IQ: 50s), thirty-year-old woman; a forty-year-old male 'manic depressive'; a thirty-five-year-old female 'schizophrenic, hebephrenic'; a forty-five-year-old male 'schizophrenic, paranoid', and a variety of individuals with still other diagnostic labels. They simply had the opportunity to talk (or not talk) about anything. No rules, directions, orientation were ever given. It was years later that I discovered that nearly everything about the group went against guidelines for groups. Nevertheless, standard criteria suggested that every member made clinically significant progress. (Bozarth, 1998: 150)

I gained a healthy respect for the non-directive group. *I could trust members of the group to direct their own lives.*

A BASIC ENCOUNTER GROUP

I facilitated a small group for three days during my second year in the La Jolla program. My goal as a small-group facilitator had already become that of attempting to maximize my unconditional reception of every person in the group. A sub-goal was to give up the position/role of facilitator for equal participation with others. I thought the latter goal was reached in this group, since at the end of the group few were clear about who was facilitator and one person refused to believe that I was the designated facilitator. I do not remember much of the content of that group except that it was a highly emotional experience for everyone in it. After the last group session, we sat for hours, mostly in silence, with each other. *The experience of our relationship trumped everything else.*

A random observation

I was in a beer garden in Georgia in the late 1970s when I overheard a group discussion. My previous five years had been laden with encounter and community groups—not really prevalent activities in Georgia. The conversation that I could not help hearing included precise descriptions that reflected my experiences and observations in the encounter-group community. It turned out that this group had just returned from a 'barefoot cruise', when they had lived and worked together for a couple of weeks as the crew of a sailboat. *They were free from their usual societal constrictions. They simply had the time together in an intimate situation that was different from most of their experiences.*

A large community group

In the late 1970s, I attended the second of my large community groups, with Carl Rogers and colleagues as facilitators. Nearly 200 participants met in a rustic mountain community for two weeks. It was by far my most difficult group experience; but, perhaps, my most growth-producing one.

Among my experiences: I was sick with a chronic lung infection; I had to be inoculated for exposure to hepatitis; I found myself alone without a small group after the community meeting finally 'decided' to break into small groups; and finally, I was kicked out of the small group facilitated by Carl Rogers.

My reaction to the overall experience can be characterized by my decision to get out of the group environment to associate with something 'real'. I trekked two miles to a local bar in the pitch dark—in pouring rain through mud puddles in the middle of the road, because that was the only way in the pitch darkness to stay on the path.

This scenario may not immediately suggest a very meaningful group experience; however, I confronted some of my fears of rejection, feelings of inadequacy and inability to assert myself. I did this mostly by associating with the hired kitchen workers, one of whom provided me with significant unconditional positive regard.

The struggle itself became part of my growth process. A few people who unconditionally accepted me countered my negative experiences.

The Warm Springs person-centered experiment

The first person-centered workshop in Warm Springs, Georgia began in 1987, two weeks after Carl Rogers' death. The program was formulated and planned in 1986 by a few individuals during the first meeting of the Association for the Development of the Person-Centered Approach Conference in 1986. Founding members of the 'Warm Springs' experience were Barbara Temaner Brodley, Nat Raskin, David Spahn, Fred Zimring, and myself. Chuck Devonshire was added to the staff prior to the first meeting. After a couple of years, designated facilitators were discontinued and I coordinated the program with the help of students. The 'Warm Springs Workshop' reflected the name of the town—the site of the Roosevelt Rehabilitation Institute. The workshop inadvertently developed into an experiment that stretched the commonly perceived boundaries of the person-centered approach. There were 100 or more participants for the first ten years, and 40 to 60 participants in the past several years. The 19th annual workshop took place in March, 2005.

Several observations regarding this 19-year-old 'experiment' are:

1. The event was in large part emergent ...

2. Although there were no designated facilitators, some individuals assumed that there were and identified other participants as facilitators.

3. There were often statements at the end of the workshops that the experience had 'changed my life ...' had 'been an exceptional experience ...', 'will have a major impact on my life ...' After one workshop, I heard a range of explanations to others by participants that included, 'It was a big party ...'; 'It was group

therapy ...', 'great intellectual experience ...', 'it was so terribly intense'.

4. Several times, only a couple of individuals of the community came for the scheduled community meetings, yet, the community group at the end of the workshop was one that reflected cohesion and individual satisfaction.

5. (Owing to leaderless facilitation), [o]ne person was ready to leave and another wanted a refund of her registration fee. The concerned group met for the entire night and the next day had changed their view to that of having had a very positive workshop experience. (Bozarth, 1998: 155)

My views about person-centered groups have been shaped through my experiences with person-centered encounter groups, community groups, and learning groups. In addition, I have implemented the principles of the theory in administration, teaching, and research during my career of forty years as a university professor and administrator. My experiences with the 19-year Warm Springs experiment with non-directive community groups have merged with my observations of other groups across my career and with person-centered (client-centered framework) theoretical principles, leading me to formulate some postulates about person-centered groups. These are presented later in this chapter.

HISTORICAL DEVELOPMENT

Nat Raskin (1986a, 2004) points out that group therapy was one of the extensions of individual client-centered therapy. Group and play therapy, student-centered teaching, and workshops were several domains that were given attention prior to the end of the 1940s. Rogers (1942) cited a paper written by Durkin (1939), a 'relationship therapist', as a significant reference that described a pre-school play therapy group. The therapeutic movement was related to the interpretation of the relationship between the patient and the therapist.

Raskin further indicates that the principles of client-centered therapy were applied more specifically to therapy groups by Hobbs (1951) and related to a variety of groups by Gordon (1951) that eventually included 'Teacher Effectiveness Training' and 'Parent Effectiveness Training' groups. These two authors, along with Dorfman, who wrote about play therapy, had chapters in Rogers' (1951) first complete theory presentation. According to Raskin (2004), group leaders contributed primarily by having '*an attitude of respect for the participants, implemented by disciplined empathic listening and communication*' (p. 135, original emphasis).

In 1956 Rogers, on his election as the first president of the American Academy of Psychotherapists (AAP), was involved in pre-convention workshops of 50 to 150 participants in a 'community' that consisted of small groups, recreation opportunities, and several large-group meetings. There appeared to be a subtle extension of Rogers' emphasis on respect for participants through 'disciplined empathic listening and communication' to the sharing of personal experiences of failures and difficulties. Raskin (*ibid.*) cites Kirschenbaum (1979) quoting Rogers' description of a small-group experience with 12 students in a postgraduate seminar in 1950 in which Rogers comments:

> As we got into it, sharing more and more deeply of our personal experiences, our failures, and our difficulties, it became a moving personal experience. (Cited in Kirschenbaum, 1979: 330)

Rogers was not dismissing the implementation of respect through 'disciplined empathic listening and communication'. He was implicitly expressing the increasing involvement of the facilitator as a group member. The emphasis of the facilitator's role was to embody certain personal attitudes (Rogers, 1951, 1959) which are explicitly defined in the theory as the therapist's experiencing of unconditional positive regard toward others, and of empathic understanding of the frames of reference of others (Rogers, 1959).

The role of the person-centered group facilitator as an involved person took more concrete form and function in the early 1960s during Rogers' tenure at the Western Behavioral Science Institute (WBSI) in La Jolla, California, where the staff increased their involvement with intensive groups of from 8 to 18 individuals. This interest meshed with the encounter-group era and Rogers' 'basic encounter group' was often considered to be the same as other encounter groups. This confusion led critics irrationally and incorrectly to condemn person-centered groups as promoting sexual promiscuity, drug abuse, and counter-cultural activities (Milton, 2002).

Client-centered advocates later complained that Rogers lost the direction of his theory. Boy (1985), for example, proposed that the basic encounter group had been mainstreamed, i.e., it was no different from other encounter groups because the facilitator's behavior did not differ from group facilitators of other theoretical approaches. Frankel (1988) asserted that there was a 'Rogers 1' and 'Rogers 2' after Rogers' inclusion of congruence in his theory. Bill Coulson (1987) posed the 'Californication of Carl Rogers' to explain the view that Rogers lost his direction after Wisconsin. Shlien (2003) considered the Wisconsin research project with hospitalized psychotics in conjunction with the move to California to be Rogers' 'watershed', characterizing the whole experience as a misdirection of theory and practice.

Such vigorous *ad hominem* complaints missed the point that the foundation of Rogers' venture into groups was in his earlier book, *Client-Centered Therapy* (Rogers, 1951). There we find chapters on 'Play Therapy', 'Group-Centered Psychotherapy', 'Group-Centered Leadership' and 'Administration', and 'Student-Centered Teaching'. His theoretical stance then evolved into an explicit theory statement (Rogers, 1959). The foundation for person-centered groups is Rogers (1959) theory of therapy, personality, interpersonal relationship and application. In other words, the conditions of the therapeutic process—as expanded to the theory of interpersonal relationship and the hypothesis of the fully functioning person—provide the theoretical base for person-centered groups.

The basic encounter group and other person-centered groups are as different from mainstream encounter groups as client-centered therapy is different from other therapies. Rogers' basic premise is consistent—that is, that the locus of control resides totally in the individual. The assumption is that the individual determines the way, direction and pace of her life. The 'necessary and sufficient conditions' of the therapeutic process are the assumptions for both individual client-centered therapy and for the person-centered group. As Rogers later stated, he was doing the same whether he was a therapist with an individual in client-centered therapy or as a facilitator in a person-centered group (Rogers, 1987a: 13).

Rogers' association with the La Jolla program in 1966 started a slow shift towards an expanded venture. Bill Coulson, Doug Land and Bruce Meador were the primary innovators of the La Jolla program, which initially involved twenty days of 100 or more participants. They met in small groups—many participated as co-leaders of small groups for two weekends—and all met in a daily community meeting where it was discovered that people could share feelings, talk openly and gain from the large-group experiences of 100 individuals or more. Groups were 'about what people are like everywhere, when they have the time and acceptance to let themselves be met' (Coulson, Land and Meador, 1977: preface). This experience, I believe, opened the way for personal growth opportunities to develop in groups through creation of communities centering on the large-group experience. The other aspects of such communities generally involve small encounter groups, topical groups, presentations, leisure activities and so forth. The decision to further explore this direction took place in 1973 with Natalie and Carl Rogers, John K. Wood, Alan Nelson and Betty Meador as the facilitators. This type of community learning program then continued with a group of facilitators that included Natalie and Carl Rogers, John K. Wood, Maureen O'Hara, Maria Bowen and others, taking place in Europe and Latin America as well as in the United States. The large community group became an observable phenomenon.

Simultaneously—and even prior to the experiences with the community group workshops—client-centered training programs were offered in Europe that had the community group as a central part of the experience, facilitated by Chuck Devonshire and colleagues (Devonshire and Kremer, 1980), including Rogers. These eventually resulted in the spread of formal training programs in European countries including the United Kingdom, France, Germany, Portugal, Italy, Hungary, Czech Republic, Slovakia and Switzerland. Large and small groups became central aspects of these training programs.

Facilitator Development Institute (FDI) workshops were developed and convened in Holland, Germany and France. The first one was held in Glasgow, Scotland. The purpose of the workshops was to provide experience and theory in the facilitation of groups (MacMillan and Lago, 1999). MacMillan and Lago (1999: 29–45) identify several innovative workshops, including one in Zinal, Switzerland, in 1981 and Istanbul 1998 in Turkey.

In 1982, the first International Forum on the Person-Centered Approach was convened by Alberto Segrera in Mexico, and the International Conference on Client-Centered and Experiential Psychotherapy was founded in 1988 through initial efforts by Germain Lietaer—the latter organization becoming the World Association for Person-Centered and Experiential Psychotherapy and Counseling (WAPCEPC) in 2000. The International Forum continued the community group and small groups as part of the meetings. WAPCEPC, however, focused more on academic presentations and developed more formal group protocols for membership interactions.

In 1986, the Association for the Development of the Person-Centered Approach (ADPCA), instigated by David Cain, met for the first time. The organization consisted of mostly US participants but recently took on a more international character, meeting outside of the United States in England in 2001 and France in 2003.

By the late 1960s the impact of client-centered theory on groups had expanded in a subtle and near-unnoticed manner. Student groups became prevalent in some schools. Experiments and research in education were notably present, but mostly ignored by the whole of society. Rogers wrote several books concerned with student-centered education (Rogers, 1969, 1983; Rogers and Freiberg, 1994) and unprecedented research in education was undertaken with positive results in the United States and Europe (Aspy and Roebuck, 1975; Tausch, 1978).

The evolution of person-centered group therapy to include societal change and conflict mediation was reflected in Rogers' activities in the late 1960s, and expanded during the last decade of his life. For example, a two-year encounter group identified as the 'Education Innovation Project' took place with the Los Angeles Immaculate Heart of Mary Catholic school system (Coulson, 1972). The project started with 560 teaching sisters and 60 facilitators. Massive defections and conflicts between the sisters and the hierarchy resulted in the closure of most schools. For better or for worse, only a few dozen sisters were teaching in that system in 2002, leaving some to question the value of the project (Coulson, 1972).

Rogers increasingly concentrated on social impact, mostly through group experiences, and explicitly considered the political impact of client-centered philosophy and practice. (Rogers, 1977, 1982, 1986a, b, 1987a, b, c; Rogers and Ryback, 1984). Rogers and Ryback (1984) analyzed the Camp David meeting of Carter, Sadat and Begin along the line of person-centered principles. One of the especially exciting programs for Rogers was the Rust workshop (Rogers, 1986a), an event which entailed the meeting of leading world diplomats and representatives. In addition, Rogers and Sanford (Rogers, 1986b, 1987b) visited South Africa, Soviet Russia and other countries in the quest to influence world politics with person-centered principles.

RESEARCH

Raskin (1986b, 2004) reviewed research beginning in the 1940s and identified the evolution and type of this research. He states:

> Rogers' formulation of individual Client-Centered Therapy was extended to group therapy as early as 1945. Research on the group process followed, which paralleled that on individual therapy. Verbatim typescripts replaced impressionistic notes, therapist and client behavior were measured, client-centered group therapists were found to respond differently from directive ones, and there was confirmation of the therapeutic effectiveness of conditions

such as empathy, congruence, and warmth even with very disturbed populations. The emergence of interest in intensive groups was accompanied by some research, but it is noted that with this development, there was a decline in research activity and in the general impact of the client-centered school on psychotherapy research. This is related to Rogers' departure from a major university setting, to a heightened interest in the concept of experiencing and in the therapist's own experiencing, and to the difficulties of implementing, up to now, the alternative model of science and of psychological research that Rogers espouses. (Raskin, 2004: 145)

Two recent reviews of research on client-centered/person-centered therapies and humanistic groups include Bozarth, Zimring and Tausch (2002) and Page, Weiss and Lietaer (2002). Page and associates incorporate most of the research on groups reported by Bozarth, Zimring and Tausch and conclude that studies 'have focused on outcomes and processes related to the core conditions originally articulated by Rogers' (Page *et al.*, 2002: 348). They indicate that the findings 'seem to support a strong relationship between therapist-offered and member-offered conditions of empathy, warmth, and genuineness, and positive therapeutic outcomes' (p. 348). The trend of research in their assessment is that European studies are likely to increase and that there will probably be greater involvement of process-oriented, qualitative and case-study research.

The move of client-centered group activities towards larger community groups and societal change groups may require a shift in the type of research. Observational and experiential inquiry appear to be the primary methodologies for current study of the person-centered, large-group phenomenon. One such study of cross-cultural, person-centered community workshops has special relevance to the theoretical base of person-centered groups (Stubbs, 1992).

A HEURISTIC, CROSS-CULTURAL RESEARCH PROJECT

Stubbs (1992) studied individual experiencing in person-centered large-group workshops. She interviewed fifteen individuals from nine countries at four sites. The workshops were embedded in different contexts, i.e. association with (1) the Association for the Development of the Person-Centered Approach (ADPCA); (2) Cross-Cultural Communication Workshop; (3) International Forum on the Person-Centered Approach; and (4) a Person-Centered Training Institute. Stubbs' project is of special interest because she was examining the meaning of the participants' perceptions, rather than pre-conceptions about person-centered theory. The participants also ranged across age, gender and knowledge about the theory and practice of the person-centered approach. The results of the study support:

    1. the construct of the actualizing tendency as the foundation of the person-centered approach in community groups;

    2. the importance of individuals' experiencing of genuineness and uncon-ditional positive regard from other group members;

3. the importance of 'non-directivity' as an important theoretical construct;

4. the importance of facilitators (however, the importance was non-specific);

5. the importance of personal contact was present, as well as the belief that the group was a microcosm of society. (Stubbs, 1992: 2)

The non-specific importance of the facilitators is of interest, since no particular characteristics or behaviors were noted as more important. The characteristics of genuineness and unconditional regard were considered important, but were ascribed to other group members as often as to facilitators. Notably missing was reference to the importance of empathic understanding.

Further research on some of these issues is critical at this juncture.

FUNDAMENTAL VALUES AND PRINCIPLES

This paper asserts that the person-centered group is an event in which there is non-directive facilitation that fosters freedom and personal enhancement of the individual. The theoretical assumption in person-centered theory is that the individual will perceive that unconditional positive regard is being experienced toward her and that there is an empathic understanding of her frame of reference. The individual will then direct her life. In short, the core elements of the therapist's task are non-directive and these core elements for growth are theoretically the same whether or not the event is client-centered individual therapy, client-centered group therapy, student-centered education, the basic encounter group, large community group, or societal change groups.

The assumption of non-directive therapist/facilitator participation is clear in Rogers' (1959) theory. In this writing, Rogers' theory of therapy is the central concept, with peripheral theories revolving around the theory of therapy—all predicated on the same assumptions of the therapeutic conditions. These peripheral theories are presented as the theories of (1) personality, (2) interpersonal relationship, (3) the fully functioning person and (4) application (Rogers, 1959). Applications of these theories include family life, education and learning, group leadership, and group tension and conflict.

The basic principle and value in this set of theories is that the person/participant/client is capable of knowing best about her life and can best realize the direction, way and pace of growth. *The non-directive element of the therapist/facilitator/person is that of allowing and facilitating other individuals to direct their own lives.*

The advent of the basic encounter group and large community group did not change or shift the basic values or the fundamental premise of the therapeutic process (e.g., the conditions of unconditional positive regard and empathic understanding). The *source* of the conditions for growth, however, is expanded with the advent of such groups. *The facilitator is no longer the person who is necessarily perceived as providing the conditions (i.e., experiencing UPR and empathy). The group members are just as likely to perceive the conditions in other participants or perceive the conditions as a pervading psychological climate.*

MANIFESTATIONS OF PRINCIPLES

The issue of how these principles and values are *manifested* is difficult to deal with in individual therapy, even more difficult when considering person-centered groups, and still more so in the extrapolation to societal influence. There are several complicating factors to consider in person-centered groups.

Individual therapy might be viewed as a purer opportunity for the therapist to experience the conditions toward the client, whereas group manifestations of therapeutic conditions are more varied. Alan Coulson (1999) suggests that 'group facilitation is problematic insofar as no one can predict who is going to do or say something which is facilitative for another' (p. 172).

My view is that person-centered groups often lose the basic non-directive premise when facilitators accept assumptions from other theoretical premises. There is often an intention to promote particular behaviors or attitudes. Essentially, this intention is founded upon the encounter group rubric, 'Tune in and talk up.' Minor examples of such contamination are repeated statements from notable client-centered group facilitators like: 'I wish that you would talk more so I can know you better.' 'Thank you for saying that about yourself. Now, I know you better.' These are well-meaning statements, but reflective of the idea that a person should behave in a certain way. The facilitator would like for them to speak! Or others would like for them to express their feelings!

There are more obvious actions of contamination, such as proposing that a person sit in a chair to 'talk' with an aspect of herself (a common Gestalt technique), or pounding a pillow to rid oneself of anger. Notably, however, many client-centered therapists will try to encourage expression of feelings and/or self-exploration by participants. These activities are not always alien to the non-directive premise—they might emerge naturally from the relationships and interactions. However, such comments and actions promoted by facilitators all too often represent an intrusion on the self-direction of individuals. Fortunately, the person's view of a general facilitative atmosphere and perception of even a few participants offering unconditional reception is usually enough to overcome such intrusions.

John K. Wood (1984) and Rogers (1986a) have referred to the setting as an important factor. Certain settings distract individuals from their involvement with the group while other settings are more conducive to participants being open to their experiences. For example, simple things such as institutionally scheduled lunch and dinner hours might conflict with important developments during group meetings. Acoustics might not be good in a large room. Although conveners try to minimize barriers like these, dealing with such challenges can add to group cohesion and strengthen relationships.

The members of the group themselves are, of course, a central factor: there are often several group members who demand excessive group attention; who take up much of the talking space; there might be individuals who display psychological problems or even display psychotic behavior. It is possible that one individual can wreak considerable havoc in a group (Wood, 1997).

Wood (1999) also points out that objectives of group organizers may affect the psychological climate of any particular group. As well, the general purpose of the group may generate a different focus. The basic encounter group has personal growth as its major intent, whereas organizational planning may at times dominate the large community group. Furthermore, the goals of the organization may be antithetical to the psychological environment. Any of these factors might inhibit the freedom of individuals.

My personal observation is that all of the above factors are largely irrelevant as far as effectiveness is concerned. For example, I have been in 'successful' groups that have taken place under shade trees, in classrooms, in an old warehouse, on a nude beach, in an unused commercial kitchen, in the wilderness, and in auditoriums. I have been involved with groups where several people at the same time have become 'psychotic'. I have also been in large groups where extreme conflict resulted in part of the group withdrawing from the main community group. *The crucial factor is the psychological environment that exists.* One conclusion I reached about the previously described Warm Springs Workshop experience was that:

> designated facilitators, workshop format, or the presence or absence of particular individuals are of little relevance. When people feel fundamentally free to be who they are at the moment, they move in constructive directions and it is often in the struggle that they find freedom and growth. (Bozarth, 1998: 156–7)

EFFECTIVENESS OF PERSON-CENTERED GROUPS

A person-centered group can be defined as effective when a significant number of participants become more congruent than they were prior to the group. Congruence, by definition of the theory, is that the individual's self-concept becomes more aligned with her organismic experiences (Rogers, 1959).

One of the necessary and sufficient conditions for therapeutic personality change is that the therapist is *congruent* in the relationship. That is, the therapist is whole and integrated. Another condition is that the client is *incongruent* in the relationship. The client is anxious and vulnerable. Rogers (1959: 215) states that the congruence of the therapist must include their capacity to experience unconditional positive regard and empathic understanding. It is clear in his delineation of the process and outcome variables that congruence is characterized by these two conditions, along with other variables. Congruent individuals are identified as being more empathic to others, less judgmental, having greater internal locus of control and so forth. Those who are 'incongruent' (i.e., individuals who have self-concepts that are distant from their organismic experiences) become more congruent as they perceive these attitudes (specifically unconditional positive regard and empathic understanding) in others with whom they have relationships. *Client congruence is therapeutic personality change! Therapeutic personality change is related to better functioning, more social awareness and greater self-awareness, greater effort in conflict resolution, and increased problem-solving abilities!*

The number of people who change and the extent of change are related to the individuals' perceptions of freedom and to their perceptions of congruence toward others in the group.

The implications of the theory, research, axioms and practice of the large community group have been presented as follows:

> The implications are, simply put, that individuals who can experience the freedom 'to be who they are' (unconditional positive regard) can find themselves becoming freer to experience growth (actualizing tendency). Facilitators/conveners create this freeing atmosphere by trusting the process (hence, acting in ways that promote that freedom), not interfering with struggles, accepting each individual in his or her right as a human being and by being open to whatever outcome might occur. This is the essence of the atmosphere and the role of the convener to promote such an atmosphere in person-centered groups. (Bozarth, 1998: 158–9)

Hopefully, the convener/facilitator is involved in the creation of such an atmosphere, but this may not necessarily be the case. If not, a relevant question is, 'How is the atmosphere created?'

The first and most comfortable answer is that there would be enough participants in the group who do trust the process, do accept unconditionally other individuals' ways of life, and do not have presuppositions about what might occur. In essence, the facilitators/conveners must always be willing to give up their control and to unconditionally receive individuals in their developing relationship. Rogers offers some sense of this when he comments: 'The whole aim is to relinquish any attempt to control the outcome, to control the direction, to control the mood' (Rogers, 1975: 63), and again when he states that his hope as a group facilitator is to 'become as much a participant in the group as a facilitator … Each facet is a real part of me, not a role' (Rogers, 1970: 48–9). It seems as though at least a few of the participants would be engaged in Wood's (1982) 'ground rules' for facilitators; that is, openness to surprise and to their own surrender to unity. Some of the participants are willing to listen to any given individual with respect and without judgment.

A second answer is that a natural process will occur given both appropriate time and a situation that is not hindered by structured activities. William Coulson's (1970) early speculations introduce the idea *that the necessary and sufficient condition for the encounter is that there be the occasion for it.* As he puts it:

> This occasion, this sole necessary and sufficient condition of the encounter, is one of stopping the action long enough for people really to come to see one another, for them gradually to have with one another the things which are so simple—to weep, to be held, to be loved—that people ordinarily are too embarrassed to mention them. (Coulson, 1972: 10)

Coulson cites the importance of facilitators as that of being able to '… help individuals to not … while away the time chit-chatting, vying for leadership, or in other ways avoiding honest expression' (p. 10). Coulson further deliberates on the role of the facilitator:

> But put a facilitator in the room, imply that s/he knows what she's doing and then suggest to him that s/he not do anything, except perhaps to gently express his/her own feeling from time to time, and this assignment of leadership will both prevent people from wasting time with such social maneuvers as contending over leadership themselves, and also give them sufficient permission to speak honestly. People need an excuse at first to speak honestly, and the mere presence of an 'expert' can be sufficient excuse—he (she) doesn't have to do anything special. (1972: 110)

These observations resonate with the importance of the non-directive attitude, lack of interference, and trust in the actualizing tendency. However, there is no particular reason that these conditions need to be created by designated facilitators. The facilitation of the natural growth process of individuals (the actualizing tendency) is dependent upon a given person's perception of the experiencing of unconditional positive regard and empathic understanding toward her, and this may come from anyone in the group. Those who are congruent during particular interactions in the group create the therapeutic atmosphere. Hence, they entrust themselves to:

> (1) trust 'group wisdom' as well as individual wisdom; (2) become participants in the group ... [and facilitators on occasion]; (3) trust the inherent therapeutic potential of all members, realizing that any particular person may be more therapeutic with any particular group member than any of the facilitators; (4) combine the spontaneous, genuine responsiveness with their desire and efforts to understand; and (5) relinquish control of outcome, direction, or mood. (Bozarth, 1988/1998: 153)

The observation that the *occasion itself* is the sole necessary and sufficient condition for the encounter group, to be consistent with client-centered theory, must assume the natural development of the psychological conditions in the group. That is, *individuals in a non-directive and unstructured group will move naturally toward the therapeutic psychological environment. Individuals will become increasingly self-directive and congruent.*

CONCLUSIONS AND POSTULATES

The core motivational principle of client-centered theory and, subsequently, of person-centered groups is the *actualizing tendency*. This is the function of the whole organism that 'is perhaps best conceptualized as a tendency toward fulfillment, toward actualization, and enhancement of the organism' (Rogers, 1963: 6). Rogers' credo is that the basic nature of human beings is constructive and trustworthy. This basic nature of the individual is accentuated when the individual is functioning freely. The individual is increasingly free from conditions of worth garnered from introjected values of significant others in society.

Five postulates related to person-centered groups are:

1. The person-centered group is an event where the therapeutic psychological environment promotes freedom for individuals to become increasingly more congruent.

There is a particular *psychological climate* that creates freedom. *A succinct statement of the criterion of success of person-centered groups is that each individual becomes more congruent.* An individual's self-concept increasingly corresponds with her organismic experiences. Hence, the individual moves toward the ideal of the *fully functioning person* (Rogers, 1959: 234–40). The specifics of being *congruent* include Rogers' process and outcome variables (e.g., experiences herself as the locus of evaluation, experiences greater unconditional positive self-regard, is less anxious and vulnerable, more realistic, more objective, able to problem solve better). Specific improvements cited in different types of person-centered groups, such as reduction of interpersonal tensions in conflict resolution, or increased grasp of knowledge in student-centered teaching, are predicated on the overall development of the individual.

The person-centered group is an *event* in which a *psychological environment* is created that facilitates freedom for the individual to be in touch with her organismic valuing process.

Individuals are increasingly able to deal with their problems, increase their efficiency and, as well, are more likely to form meaningful relationships with others. This is true whether reference is to group therapy, a therapeutic community group, basic encounter group, large community group, education, conflict resolution, or societal change groups.

2. The therapeutic psychological environment is fostered by individuals who are congruent in their relationship with any given person at a particular time.

The only 'instructions' for therapists in client-centered therapy are for them to be congruent, while *experiencing* unconditional positive regard (UPR) toward the client and *experiencing* empathic understanding (EU) of the client's internal frame of reference— these are the therapist conditions as delineated within the therapeutic process (Rogers, 1959: 213). Although unconditional positive regard and empathic understanding are theoretically part and parcel of being congruent, Rogers concluded that these two conditions had special import when perceived by the client.

The 'instructions' when applied to the theory of groups have most often referred to 'facilitators'. However, it appears more likely that the thrust of the therapeutic experience for an individual in a group is affected by her perception of the conditions existing in other participants, and not necessarily in the facilitators. Groups may or may not have designated facilitators, and anyone and everyone in a group is a potential facilitator in any moment as perceived by another participant. The therapeutic environment is created by individuals who are *congruent* in their relationship with any given person at a particular time. The psychological atmosphere is primarily created through the participant's experience of feeling free from introjected values of worth and unconditionally received by others in the group. Hence, certain individuals in the relationship of the moment are more empathic, more unconditionally accepting in the interactions with others. *Congruent individuals foster congruence in incongruent individuals.*

3. The occasion of the unstructured and non-directive person-centered group can foster the therapeutic psychological environment.

William Coulson (1970) suggested that the sole necessary and sufficient condition of the encounter group is the *occasion*. Allan Coulson (1999) independently makes a similar point. He suggests that the group might stimulate change through a *context* in which individuals are 'valued regardless of whether they meet the conditions of worth set out for them in their lives' (Coulson, 1999: 168). In short, the client's perception of a pervading, non-directive *psychological climate* in the group stimulates freedom. Bozarth (1998) emphasizes non-directivity as a core stimulant of the group atmosphere that allows the person's *struggle* to occur:

> The more non-directive, the more chaotic; the more chaotic, the more individuals struggle for their own direction and structure. The more individuals find their own structures and directions, the more they trust themselves and others. It may be in the struggle itself that is the greatest freeing factor. (Bozarth, 1998: 181)

The individual is psychologically free from conditions of worth. *Non-directivity is considered a natural consequence created by individuals who are congruent in the group.* At the same time, the individual is less inclined to try to direct the lives of others. That is, increased directivity of one's own life and non-directivity of others' lives are emergent qualities of congruence.

4. The psychological environment postulated in person-centered groups has social implications and relevance for such societal activities as education, organizational management, and conflict resolution.

As previously referenced (Aspy and Roebuck, 1974; Tausch, 1978), person-centered education has demonstrated success through specific examples and considerable cross-cultural research studies. Simply put, teachers who are more congruent (higher on the conditions of unconditional positive regard and empathic understanding of students) are more effective.

Rogers (1977) and others (Plas, 1996) offer evidence of successful results of psychological environment in multiple areas, including industrial organizations.

Rogers (1987c) wrote an article, 'On Reaching 85', shortly after his birthday and less than a month before his death. He expressed his appreciation at being able to see the international influence of his work. He was involved in three of the world's areas of greatest tension. These areas were: Northern Ireland, Central America, and South Africa.

In Northern Ireland, an ancient feud of militant Protestants and militant Catholics from Belfast was greatly softened in a brief intensive encounter group, and embers of the group made efforts to influence others when they returned to their country (Rogers, 1989).

Rogers and colleagues were able to meet with politicians, policymakers and shapers of public opinion from 17 countries to focus on 'the Central American challenge'. Rogers (1986a) describes the event as one that set a precedent for person-to-person workshops.

In 1986, Rogers and Ruth Sanford facilitated a group of black and white participants in South Africa. Rogers reports that he had never experienced 'such depths of rage, bitterness, and pain (on the part of the blacks), or such fear and guilt and prejudice (on the part of the whites)' (Rogers, 1989: 57).

Person-centered group postulates have an extended reach to societal groups. However, there is not wide acceptance by societal structures and the broad influence is not well publicized.

5. There is a transcendent awareness stimulated by group unity.

Rogers (1980) wrote 'a basic chapter' titled, 'The Foundations of a Person-Centered Approach' (pp. 113–36). He proposes a broader view of the actualizing tendency; i.e., 'The Formative Tendency'. He *tentatively* hypothesizes the following:

> There is a formative directional tendency in the universe, which can be traced and observed in stellar space, in crystals, in micro-organisms, in more complex organic life, and in human beings. This is an evolutionary tendency toward greater order, greater complexity, and greater interrelatedness. In humankind, this tendency exhibits itself as the individual moves from a single-cell origin to complex organic functioning, to knowing and sensing below the level of consciousness, to a conscious awareness of the organism and the external world, to a transcendent awareness of the harmony and unity of the cosmic system, including humankind. (Rogers, 1980: 133)

It was clear that this hypothesis was tentative but considered a formulation for a 'philosophical base for a person-centered approach' (Rogers, 1980: 134). This hypothesis developed, in part, from group experiences and led Rogers to say that 'perhaps we are touching the cutting edge of our ability to transcend ourselves, to create new and more spiritual directions in human evolution' (p. 134). This hypothesis relates closely to considerations of the group as a unit in and of itself (in addition to individual growth/ actualization). Various authors (Rogers, 1977: 143–85, 1980: 316–35; Wood, 1982; O'Hara and Wood, 1983; Spahn, 1992, 1984; Bozarth, 1998: 177–87; Kass, 1998; Wyatt, 2004) have speculated on such features as 'group wisdom', 'healing' and 'altered states' as related to group activities. The term, 'holonic shift' (Wyatt, 2004) signifies a shift of functioning from an individual level to a group level. Shared communal meanings emerge via the 'dialogue in the group'. Such observations and speculations are beyond the scope of this chapter except to note the frequent reference to this domain.

Van Belle (1980) aptly summarizes Rogers' theory as it extrapolates to 'separateness giving way to unity' (O'Hara and Wood, 1983; Spahn, 1992). Van Belle states that to live in this world is to experience yourself 'participating in a larger universal formative tendency' (1980: 128), that itself is 'up to something' (*ibid*.: 313). It shows a 'trend toward even greater complexity' (*ibid*.: 128). This is now no longer the impulse of life only but of the universe as a whole. All that exists, changes continually and participates in a kind of 'cosmic dance' (*ibid*.: 345).

Rogers (1980) refers to: 'the wisdom of the group' (pp. 182, 334); 'participation in a larger whole' (p. 128); being 'in a slightly altered state of consciousness' (p. 129); that the 'inner spirit seemed to reach and to touch the inner spirits of others' (p. 129); and that 'my presence is releasing and helpful to the other' (p. 129). Rogers (1980) verifies his view of the transcendent nature of the formative tendency. He states:

> The crucial point is that when a person is functioning fully, there are no barriers, no inhibitions, which prevent the full experiencing of whatever is organismically present. This person is moving in the direction of wholeness, integration, and a unified life. Consciousness is participating in this larger, creative, formative tendency. (p. 128)

Rogers' extrapolated his growth hypothesis 'to knowing and sensing below the level of consciousness, to a conscious awareness of the organism and the external world, to a transcendent awareness of the harmony and unity of the cosmic system including humankind' (Rogers, 1980: 133).

SUMMARY

Person-centered groups are inherently non-directive.

In a nutshell, the fundamental principles of person-centered groups, which range from family therapy to large community groups to organizations, are that individuals are in an event wherein personal freedom is facilitated. As a result, the individuals become increasingly congruent—moving toward greater harmony of their self-concept with their organismic tendencies and the ideal of the fully functioning person. Specifically, they both develop increased unconditional positive self-regard and unconditional positive regard for others, and are more empathic toward themselves and others. They have greater internal locus of evaluation and work more harmoniously with others. They are more efficient, less anxious and vulnerable, and more creative.

Facilitation in the group event occurs when an individual perceives congruence in those who are considered to be 'significant others' or when the individual perceives the psychological context for personal freedom. The non-directive nature of the person-centered group nurtures the trust of others to direct their own lives and results in non-interference, non-judgmental attitudes and unconditional reception of individuals.

Person-centered groups are events for the implementation of individual growth through freeing individuals to become more congruent. It is a non-directive approach that trusts the capacity of human beings and trusts the individual to direct his/her own life. As such, it is revolutionary and holds the promise that a more humane society can emerge. Rogers (1977) ponders the potential impact as follows:

> I believe that in our decaying culture we see the dim outlines of new growth, a new revolution ... I see that revolution as coming not in some great organized movement ... but through the emergence of a new kind of person ... (p. 124)

To Rogers, the person-centered approach was 'a way of being' and 'a basic philosophy' that when lived can empower individuals 'and when this personal power is sensed, experiences show that it tends to be used for personal and social transformation' (Rogers, 1977: 5).

Person-centered principles extend to the politics of social cooperation and natural processes of interpersonal interaction, and can facilitate personal and social transformation.

REFERENCES

Aspy DN & Roebuck FN (1974) From humane ideas to humane technology and back again many times. *Education*, *95*(2), 163–71.

Aspy DN & Roebuck FN (1975) Research Summary: Effects of training in interpersonal skills. Interim Report No. 4 for NIMH grant no. 5 P) IMH 19871 (Monroe, LA: Northeast Louisiana University, 1974; Abstracted in *Resources in Education* {October, 1975}, ERIC document ED106733).

Boy AV (1985) Mainstreaming the basic encounter group. *The Journal for Specialists in Group Work, 10*(4), 205–10.

Bozarth JD (1986) The basic encounter group: an alternative view. *The Journal for Specialists in Group Work*, 1, (4), 228–32.

Bozarth JD (1988) The person-centered large community group—Premise, axioms, and speculations. Paper presented at the Person-Centered Approach Workshop, Warm Springs, GA.

Bozarth JD (1992) The person-centered community group. Paper presented to the American Psychological Association symposium. 'Contributions of Client-centered therapy to American psychology's 100 years.' Washington, DC.

Bozarth JD (1995, May) Designated facilitators: Unnecessary and insufficient. Paper presented at the national conference for the Association of the Development of the Person-Centered Approach, Tampa, FL.

Bozarth JD (1998) *Person-Centered Therapy: A revolutionary paradigm*. Ross-on-Wye: PCCS Books.

Bozarth JD, Zimring F & Tausch R (2002) Client-centered therapy: Evolution of a revolution. In DJ Cain & J Seeman (Eds) *Handbook of Humanistic Psychotherapy: Research and practice*, Washington, DC: APA, pp. 147–88.

Coulson A (1999) Experiences of separateness and unity in person-centred groups. In C Lago & M MacMillan (Eds) *Experiences in Relatedness: Groupwork and the Person-Centred Approach*. Ross-on-Wye: PCCS Books, pp. 167–80.

Coulson WR (1970) Rejoinder. *The Counseling Psychologist, 2*(2), 56–60.

Coulson WR (1972) *Groups, Gimmicks, and Instant Gurus*. New York: Harper and Row.

Coulson WR (1987, November) The Californication of Carl Rogers. *Fidelity*, 20–31.

Coulson WR, Land D & Meador B (1977) *The La Jolla Experiment: Eight personal views*. La Jolla, CA: CSP.

Devonshire C (1991) The person-centered approach and cross-cultural communication. In E McIlduff & D Coghlan (Eds) *The Person-Centered Approach and Cross-Cultural Communication: An international review*, Vol. 1 Dublin: Centre for Cross-Cultural Communication, pp. 15–44.

Devonshire CM & Kremer JD (1980) *Toward a Person-Centered Resolution of Intercultural Conflicts*.

Dortmund: Pedagogische Arbeitsstelle.

Durkin HE (1939) Dr John Levy's relationship therapy applied to a play group. *American Journal of Orthopsychiatry*, 9, 583.

Frankel M (1988, May) The category error and the confounding of the therapeutic relationship. Paper presented at the Second Annual Meeting of the Association for the Development of the Person-Centered Approach, New York City.

Hobbs N (1951) Group-centered psychotherapy. In CR Rogers, *Client-Centered Therapy*. Boston: Houghton Mifflin.

Gordon T (1951) Group-centered leadership and administration. In CR Rogers, *Client-Centered Therapy*. Boston: Houghton Mifflin.

Kass J (1998, May) Research results from converging studies. Paper presented at the Twelfth meeting of the Association for the Development of the Person-Centered Approach, Wheaton, MA.

Kirschenbaum H (1979) *On Becoming Carl Rogers*. New York: Delacorte.

Hobbs N (1951) Group-centered psychotherapy. In CR Rogers *Client-Centered Therapy*. Boston: Houghton Mifflin, pp. 278–319.

Lago C & MacMillan M (Eds) (1999) *Experiences in Relatedness: Groupwork and the Person-Centred Approach*. Ross-on-Wye: PCCS Books.

MacMillan M & Lago C (1993) *Large Groups: Critical communication: An international review*, Vol. 11, Dublin: Centre for Cross-Cultural Communication, pp. 35–53.

MacMillan M & Lago C (1996) The facilitation of large groups: Participant's experiences of facilitative moments. In R Hutterer, G Pawlowsky, P Schmid & R Stipsits (Eds) *Client-Centered and Experiential Psychotherapy: A paradigm in motion*. Frankfurt: Peter Lang, pp. 599–610.

MacMillan M & Lago C (1999) PCA Groups: past, present, … and future? In C Lago & M MacMillan (Eds) *Experiences in Relatedness: Groupwork and the Person-Centred Approach*. Ross-on-Wye: PCCS Books, pp. 29–45.

McIlduff E & Coghlan D (Eds) (1991) *The Person-Centered Approach and Cross-Cultural Communication: An international review*, Vol. 1. Dublin: Centre for Cross-Cultural Communication, pp. 15–44.

Milton J (2002) *The Road to Malpsychia*. San Francisco: Encounter Books.

O'Hara M & Wood JK (1983) Patterns of awareness: Consciousness and the group mind. *The Gestalt Journal*, 6(2), 103–16.

Page RC, Weiss JF & Lietaer G (2002) Humanistic group psychotherapy. In DJ Cain & J Seeman (Eds) *Handbook of Humanistic Psychotherapies: Research and practice*. Washington, DC: American Psychological Association, pp. 339–68.

Plas JM (1996) *Person-Centered Leadership: An American approach to participatory management*. London: Sage.

Raskin NJ (1986a) Client-centered group psychotherapy, part 1: Development of client-centered groups. *Person-Centered Review*, 1(3), 272–90.

Raskin NJ (1986b) Client-centered group psychotherapy, part II: Research on client-centered groups. *Person-Centered Review*, 1(4), 389–408.

Raskin NJ (2004) *Contributions to Client-Centered Therapy and the Person-Centered Approach*. Ross-on-Wye: PCCS Books.

Rogers CR (1942) *Counseling and Psychotherapy*. Boston: Houghton Mifflin.

Rogers CR (1951) *Client-Centered Therapy: Its current practice, implications, and theory*. Boston:

Houghton Mifflin.

Rogers CR (1957) The necessary and sufficient conditions of therapeutic personality change. *Journal of Consulting Psychology*, *21*(2), 95–103.

Rogers CR (1959) A theory of therapy, personality, and interpersonal relationships as developed in the client-centered framework. In S Koch (Ed) *Psychology: Study of a science: Vol. 3. Formulation of the person and the social context.* New York: McGraw-Hill, pp. 184–256.

Rogers CR (1963) The actualizing tendency in relation to 'motives' and to consciousness. In M Jones (Ed) *Nebraska Symposium on Motivation.* Lincoln, NE: University of Nebraska Press.

Rogers CR (1969) *Freedom to Learn.* Columbus, OH: Charles Merrill.

Rogers CR (1970) *Encounter Groups.* Harmondsworth: Penguin.

Rogers CR (1975) Empathic: An unappreciated way of being. *The Counseling Psychologist* , *5*(2), 2–10 .

Rogers CR (1977) *Carl Rogers on Personal Power: Inner strength and its revolutionary impact.* New York: Delacorte.

Rogers CR (1978) The formative tendency. *Journal of Humanistic Psychology*, *18*, 23–6.

Rogers CR (1980) *A Way of Being.* Boston: Houghton Mifflin.

Rogers CR (1982) A psychologist looks at nuclear war. *Journal of Humanistic Psychology*, *22*(4), 9–20. Reprinted in H Kirschenbaum & VL Henderson (Eds) (1989) *The Carl Rogers Reader.* Boston: Houghton Mifflin, pp. 445–56.

Rogers CR (1983) *Freedom to Learn in the 80s.* Columbus, OH: Charles Merrill.

Rogers CR (1986a) The Rust Workshop. *Journal of Humanistic Psychology*, *26* (3), 23–45.

Rogers CR (1986b) The dilemmas of a South African white. *Person-Centered Review*, *1*, 15–35.

Rogers CR (1987a) Client-centered/person-centered? *Person-Centered Review*, *2*(1), 11–13.

Rogers CR (1987b) Inside the world of the Soviet professional. *Journal of Humanistic Psychology*, *27*(3), 277–304. Also in H Kirschenbaum & VL Henderson (Eds) (1989) *The Carl Rogers Reader.* Boston: Houghton Mifflin, pp. 478–501.

Rogers CR (1987c) On reaching 85. *Person-Centered Review*, *2*(2), 150–2.

Rogers CR (1989) On reaching 85. In H Kirschenbaum & VL Henderson (Eds) (1989) *The Carl Rogers Reader.* Boston: Houghton Mifflin, pp. 478–501.

Rogers CR & Freiberg J (1994*) Freedom to Learn* (3rd edn). New York: Macmillan College Publishing Company.

Rogers CR & Ryback D (1984) One alternative to nuclear interplanetary suicide. In RF Levant & JM Shlien (Eds) *Client-Centered Therapy and the Person-Centered Approach: New directions in theory, research, and practice.* New York: Praeger, pp. 400–22.

Shlien JM (2003) Theory as autobiography. In P Sanders (Ed) *To Lead an Honorable Life: Invitations to think about Client-Centered Therapy and the Person-Centered Approach. A collection of the work of John M. Shlien.* Ross-on-Wye: PCCS Books, pp. 212–16.

Spahn D (1992) Observations on healing and person-centered therapy. *The Person-Centered Journal*, *1*(1), 33–7.

Stubbs J-P (1992) Individual experiencing in person-centered community workshops: A cross-cultural study. Unpublished doctoral dissertation, University of Georgia.

Tausch R (1978) Facilitative dimensions in interpersonal relations: Verifying the theoretical assumptions of Carl Rogers in school, family, education, client-centered therapy, and encounter groups. *College Student Journal*, *12*, 2–11.

Thorne B (1988) The person-centred approach to large groups. In M Aveline & W Dryden (Eds) *Group Therapy in Britain.* Milton Keynes: Open University Press.

Van Belle HA (1980) *Basic Intent and Therapeutic Approach of Carl R Rogers.* Toronto: Wedge Publishing.

Wood JK (1982) Person-centered group therapy. In G Gazda (Ed) *Basic Approaches to Group Psychotherapy and Group Counseling.* Springfield, IL: Charles E Thomas.

Wood JK (1983) Communities for learning: A person-centered approach. Paper presented at the First International Forum on the person-centered approach. Quaxetec, Mexico.

Wood JK (1984) Communities for learning a person-centered approach. In RF Levant & JM Shlien (Eds) *Client-Centered Therapy and the Person-Centered Approach: New directions to theory, research, and practice.* New York: Praeger, pp. 297–336.

Wood JK (1994) A rehearsal for understanding the phenomenon of group. *The Person-Centered Journal, 1*(3), 18–32.

Wood JK (1997) Notes on studying large-group workshops. *The Person-Centered Journal, 4* (Fall), 65–77.

Wood JK (1999) Towards an understanding of large-group dialogue and its implications. In C Lago & M MacMillan (Eds) *Experiences in Relatedness: Groupwork and the Person-Centred Approach.* Ross-on-Wye: PCCS Books, pp. 137–66.

Wyatt GW (2004) An exploration of 'holonic shifts' in groups and its possible human ecological significance in transforming culture. Unpublished Masters thesis. Edinburgh: Centre for Human Ecology.

CHAPTER 17

CLIENT-CENTERED FAMILY AND COUPLE THERAPY: A RETROSPECTIVE AND A PRACTITIONER'S GUIDE[1]

JOHN K. MCPHERRIN

INTRODUCTION

Fifteen years ago it was very difficult finding information/articles on client-centered couple and family therapy if you wished to practice it. The articles that were available did an excellent job of outlining the fundamentals of the approach, but therapeutic dilemmas or challenges were not addressed because the approach was new. Since that time, more articles have been written about the subject, but they are still often hard to find or remain unpublished. This chapter presents a clear 'how to' for clinicians interested in doing non-directive couple and family therapy, and explores questions about the nature of directivity in this approach based on 15 years of experience and considerable trial and error. Before doing so, a brief history of the development of the approach will be outlined so as to provide a context for understanding the issues.

FOUNDATIONS OF CLIENT-CENTERED COUPLE/FAMILY THERAPY

As in individual client-centered therapy, client-centered family therapists base their approach on a belief in the actualizing tendency, as well as the formative tendency (Thayer, 1982; Bozarth and Shanks, 1989; Gaylin, 1990). The actualizing tendency is the innate tendency for persons to 'move in the direction of maintaining and enhancing themselves' and is the sole catalyst for all human motivation, expansion and enhancement (Bozarth and Brodley, 1991: 46). It is this tendency that allows client-centered therapists to have deep trust, not only in the individual, but in the family and couple as well. As a result, the therapist does not have to function in an authoritarian manner, diagnosing and restructuring the couple/family in ways that are believed to be healthier by the therapist. Rather, it is believed that a therapeutic relationship characterized by the attitudinal qualities of empathic understanding, unconditional acceptance, and genuineness, is enough to encourage the natural actualizing tendencies within each family member to help overcome the effects of

---

1. This chapter is based heavily on an unpublished dissertation by the author: McPherrin JK (1995) 'Client-Centered Couple and Family Therapy: When sexual abuse is an issue'. An unpublished dissertation submitted to the Illinois School of Professional Psychology in partial fulfillment of the requirements for the degree of doctor of psychology.

unfavorable or destructive circumstances that may have impacted individuals within a couple/family (Bozarth and Brodley, 1991: 47).

The formative tendency was a later development of Rogers' (1980), which he saw as 'a universal trend in all things toward increased order and interrelated complexity' (Thayer, 1982: 175). This concept accounts for the systemic aspect of a family, suggesting that when the proper therapeutic climate is provided, families and couples will work toward growth and orderliness. Bozarth and Shanks (1989) wrote that:

> ... the concept of the formative tendency combined with the phenomenological view can be used as a model for viewing family units as systems that will move toward growth when a facilitative psychological climate is provided. The model, in this case, is that of a family structure incorporating both the individual organismic model of actualization and the formative tendency. (p. 282)

ORIGINS OF CLIENT-CENTERED FAMILY THERAPY

Nathaniel Raskin and Ferdinand van der Veen (1970) were the first to address specifically the client-centered perspective on family therapy. They pointed out that working with families does not entail altering the basic therapeutic conditions as outlined by Rogers (1957), or the role and attitudes of the therapist. However, they did state that the emergence of therapist genuineness as the third therapist condition of client-centered therapy lent itself in particular to extending client-centered therapy beyond the individual. The condition of therapist genuineness, they asserted, allows the therapist a greater range of expressiveness than is typically seen in individual client-centered therapy. This greater freedom of therapist expression makes the client-centered approach all the more conducive to working with more than one person. They felt that in the family context, the therapist could interact more freely—making suggestions, or offering perceptions, but being led in turn by the family's reaction to them. The therapist as a participant in the process can follow his/her instincts and feelings, as long as these do not infringe upon the couple's, or a family's, freedom to determine what is best for themselves.

Another idea introduced by Raskin and van der Veen that is worth noting is the family concept. The family concept is essentially an outgrowth of the self-concept (Rogers, 1959), one of Rogers' basic principles for understanding human beings, which, briefly stated, is the awareness one has of oneself based on interactions with significant others in the environment. The family concept simply takes this a step further and takes into account the importance and impact of family and family life on one's development and overall psychological health.

Ronald Levant (1978, 1984), picked up where Raskin and van der Veen left off by expanding upon this approach to families and couples. He contrasted client-centered family therapy with systems and psychodynamic family approaches, both of which he viewed as potentially damaging to the individuals participating by being too directive and controlling. Such control, Levant (1978) stated, disregards what has been discovered to be associated with positive outcomes in therapy—namely, empathy, warmth, and genuineness (Bergin, 1967; Truax and Carkhuff, 1967; Truax and Mitchell, 1971)—and 'might lead to damaged self-esteem, reduced self-direction, and greater degrees of alienation of self from experience' (p. 36).

Levant was also very critical of the pessimistic attitudes that the psychodynamic and family systems approaches have regarding a family's capacity and willingness to change if left to members' own devices. The concepts of resistance and homeostasis, he said, are contradictory to a belief in a self-directed process, which Levant viewed as essential for true change to occur within a family. At the same time, he did not completely disregard the core elements of both approaches. In proposing a phenomenological view of the family, Levant attempted to bridge the intrapsychic beliefs of the psychodynamic practitioners and the systemic beliefs of the systems practitioners by stating that both internal and external influences direct how people relate, behave and feel within their families.

Levant further explained that the client-centered therapist is not interested in taking a detailed family history, diagnosing, creating treatment plans or implementing any therapeutic techniques. Instead, the role of the therapist involves understanding each family member and communicating this understanding to them, while facilitating an atmosphere of respect, honesty, trust and mutual understanding, thereby helping to release the family's natural abilities to change, restructure or act in ways that will promote change, growth and healing.

Louis Thayer (1982) offered a comprehensive summation of client-centered family therapy. Thayer pointed out two functions of the client-centered family therapist that are of particular significance and that tap into points that Raskin and van der Veen (1970) and Levant (1982) noted in their work. One is that the therapist be aware of personal experiencing within the session and relate such thoughts and feelings to the family with 'I' sentences. The other is for the therapist to trust and express intuitive hunches, and not to always rely on logic and intellect in understanding and communicating with the family. However, Thayer did not specify to what extent these sorts of personal communication can go.

THE COMPLICATION OF GENUINENESS/CONGRUENCE

Ned Gaylin (1989) pointed out that Rogers defined therapist congruence as when the therapist is 'freely and deeply himself' (p. 271). An 'openness to experience' (p. 271) or a lack of defensiveness on the part of the therapist allows the therapist to see both him/herself and the client distinctly and accurately. However, it is difficult to know how this then translates into family therapy, especially given the greater significance some therapists place on genuineness when doing family work (Levant, 1982; Raskin and van der Veen, 1970).

Some client-centered practitioners have articulated their beliefs about the importance of therapist genuineness in family sessions, but the implementation of what this attitude entails behaviorally is vague (Bozarth and Shanks, 1989; Gaylin, 1989; O'Leary, 1989; Rombauts and Devriendt, 1990). Gathering questionnaire responses from 15 client-centered therapists who practiced couple therapy, Jan Rombauts and Monica Devriendt (1990) stated that these client-centered therapists varied in the degree to which they expressed their subjective reactions in couple therapy. Most therapists agreed that it is important to avoid personal reactions, because it takes away energy that they should devote to understanding each member's experience. However, there was agreement that they experienced both positive and negative reactions during the process.

Bozarth and Shanks (1989) defined therapist genuineness as the therapist's being 'him/herself in the relationship, without putting up a professional or personal façade' (p. 283). In couple therapy, this translates, for them, into occasionally using personal experience to check understanding, and into feeling free to share personal metaphors or images that come to mind during sessions for aiding in and effectively communicating understanding.

Barbara Brodley, in her couple work, sometimes gave what she called 'spontaneous responses', responses that are not deliberate or well-thought-out but that communicate her own frame of reference (Topping, 1993). These included observations about communication and behavior patterns, and direct assertions about her ideas, beliefs, and past experiences. Though spontaneous responses were infrequent in Brodley's work, they came from a feeling within her that the clients will be interested in her input and perhaps be able to see their problem or issue as more 'normal' based on her personal communication. Spontaneous responses are also not always relevant to what the client is immediately expressing; according to Carol Topping (1993), they are not necessarily 'asked for or expected, but found to be insightful' (p. 115), and to hold them would result in incongruence within the therapist.

THERAPIST DIRECTIVENESS

While exploring the issue of how therapist genuineness is manifested in client-centered couple/family work, a natural question is raised regarding whether the approach loses its non-directive foundation by allowing too much leeway for therapist expression in the name of congruence/genuineness.

In describing his work with families, Wayne Anderson (1989) stated that he sometimes facilitated a 'frame shift' by listening to one person's perspective on an issue, empathically responding to it, and then asking for other perspectives on the same issue. He felt that this helped the family learn to communicate more directly in constructive ways.

Similarly, Barbara Brodley sometimes facilitated this type of shift in her couple work by asking a partner if he/she would like to respond to the other partner's communication (Topping, 1993). This type of facilitation has come out of Brodley's need to prevent couples from engaging in emotional violence during couple therapy and also to balance the use of time and discrepancy in power that exist between some partners. Additionally, Brodley facilitated communication by providing agenda responses during couple sessions (Topping, 1993). Brodley felt that it is important for both partners to agree on topics of discussion, because both people have to be willing to hear the other at any moment for the exchange to be worthwhile. If an agreement is not reached, the topic will not be brought up during that session.

Margaret Warner (1986) did what she called 'coaching communication' in her family work. Based on the communication work of Gordon (1972), Rosenberg (1976) and Guerney (1977), Warner invited clients to elaborate on missing aspects of their communication in order to 'increase the possibilities of empathy and constructive problem-solving in the relationship' (1986: 24). Ultimately, Warner felt that the experience of increased empathy and problem solving will lead to greater trust in the relationship, which will then facilitate further attempts at open communication.

Warner (1993) suggested that despite differences in psychotherapy styles, a very similar client–therapist relationship and therapeutic process will develop among therapists who share similar levels of authoritarianism and similar beliefs as to how much should be brought in from outside the client's frame of reference. In other words, very similar therapeutic phenomena occur when therapists work at similar levels of intrusiveness; i.e., to the same extent that they introduce things from outside the client's perspective. In Warner's opinion, client-centered therapists can introduce material into the therapeutic relationship from outside of the client's frame of reference without compromising the value of non-directiveness, as long as the therapist has a strong empathic relationship with the client, presents ideas in such a way that the client can easily choose not to pursue them, and maintains a belief that the client is in charge of the therapeutic process. However, she warned against creating conditions of worth for the client when introducing this material. If therapists approach their clients with an understanding that human beings have a natural tendency toward self-directed processing that moves in the direction of positive relationships, and they foster the conditions of empathy, unconditional positive regard, and genuineness/congruence, then client-centered therapy is being practiced, despite stylistic differences.

According to Brodley (1993), it is a misconception regarding the self-directive attitude that the therapist must make a conscious effort to avoid saying anything from within his/her own frame of reference. Quite to the contrary, Brodley suggested that 'the deepest expression of the non-directive attitude may be by providing responses from the counselor's frame of reference when asked, out of respect for the client's wishes' (p. 141). Brodley and Brody (1994) suggested that techniques can be used in client-centered therapy, as long as they are not approached from a diagnostic mindset. That is, a client-centered therapist cannot offer techniques from a position of knowing what is best for the client, i.e., identifying what is 'wrong' with the client and deciding what he/she needs to do to get better. However, a client-centered therapist can offer techniques in response to the client's requests or questions, as long as they do not impair the therapist's ability to maintain the essential therapeutic conditions of empathy, unconditional positive regard and genuineness when doing so.

Raskin (1988) appeared to agree with Brodley and Brody's (1994) position, feeling that the therapist should not be bound by rules during the course of therapy. However, he noted that it is a mistake in attitude once the therapist begins to have a preconceived notion of how to change the client, and works toward this goal in a systematic fashion. He explained that there is a range within which therapists can express the core conditions of client-centered therapy:

> The therapist may go further and, in a spontaneous and non-systematic way, offer reactions, suggestions, ask questions, try to help the client experience feelings, share aspects of his/her own life, etc., while maintaining a basic and continuing respect for the client as architect of the process. This may represent person-centered therapy at its optimal level, with a freely functioning therapist accepting the client as leading the way while not being bound by a set of rules. (p. 2)

Current psychotherapy research essentially affirms what was posited by client-centered therapists and researchers 50 years ago and is still practiced today—that the quality of the therapeutic relationship that is established between the therapist and client (characterized essentially by empathy, unconditional positive regard and genuineness) is the foundation for positive outcome in therapy, rather than any particular technique or expertise on the part of the therapist (Hubble, Duncan and Miller, 1999).

CLIENT-CENTERED FAMILY AND COUPLE THERAPY REDUX

The following is a set of guidelines on how to begin approaching and doing client-centered family and couple therapy, based on the historical developments presented in this article as well as the author's 15 years of experience doing couple and family work.

1. A prerequisite to doing non-directive couple and family work is having a deep conviction that as a therapist, you do not know what is best for the family and couple. You are not an expert on their problems, even though you may have experience dealing with others who share similar problems; and you do not hold a magic key to solving their problems, even though you may have thoughts or opinions on what could help a given situation if asked. At the same time, it is important to exude confidence in yourself that you offer something helpful in the way of an environment that will allow the family and couple to identify their issues, come up with solutions and grow in directions that are important to them. Do not be wishy-washy in explaining this to your clients, especially if they express concern that you are stating to not be an expert. Too often, client-centered therapists are apologetic about what they offer and this should not be the case. Tremendous work is done with couples and families using a non-directive approach and this should be acknowledged without being overly brash.

2. Once the family or couple comes to your office, you can give some instruction on office policy, the length of the session, fees, and generally how you work. Many families come to therapy not being sure what to expect and, more often than not,

expecting the therapist to take control of how the session proceeds. Remove this ambiguity by stating clearly that you are interested in hearing everyone's perspective on why they have come to therapy. Let the family know that you trust their wisdom as the basic guide for how the sessions will proceed. Once the couple or family knows that you are interested in hearing their unique perspectives, the sessions often naturally flow from here. If working with a family, it might be good to ask parents before beginning whether it is okay for their children to speak freely without fear of punishment should they bring up something controversial. This helps to set a tone of openness and safety for children who are prone to feeling powerless within a family. Conversely, I find that it is helpful to defer to parents when beginning the first session as a sign of respect. So after my introductory comments, I usually begin by saying something like, 'Mrs Smith, you called and informed me that you are having some difficulty with your youngest son, John. Do you wish to begin by telling me more about your concerns?'

3. Empathic understanding proceeds as it would in individual therapy from this perspective, but there are multiple frames of reference requiring attention. This can be very difficult for therapists who have not done couple or family work before. Keep in mind that you cannot attend to everyone or everything at the same time. Allow yourself to be human and attend to what seems to be most pressing in any given moment. For instance, once Mrs Smith elaborates on her concerns, make sure you understand those concerns accurately. This can be complicated by another family member verbally interrupting Mrs. Smith or showing a non-verbal reaction. As far as verbal interruptions go, I tend to permit more verbal interruption at the beginning of therapy, because I want to understand what is happening within the larger context of the couple/family. That is, how are people relating to each other and what reactions are they having? These spontaneous moments of interruption can aid your understanding of the family tremendously. However, it also interferes with your ability to attend to each participant and this may need to be controlled. With subsequent interruptions, you can say to 'John', the youngest son of the family who interrupted, 'I see you are having a strong reaction to your mother and I want to understand that, but let me first make sure I understand your mother's concerns.' This shows both John and Mrs. Smith the proper respect and allows all participants to know that you want to understand every perspective and that everyone will get his/her opportunity to speak. Despite trying to control for this, spontaneous reactions by family members are sometimes so strong that you will need to shift focus to the interrupter in that moment, while remembering to get back to the person who had been speaking.

It is also very important to attend to non-verbal reactions. Because they are non-verbal, it permits you time to first empathically respond to the speaker and then respond to the person exhibiting the non-verbal behavior. You may say, 'John, I noticed you had a strong bodily reaction to your mother's comments; do you wish to share what you are feeling?' Attending to non-verbal behavior is a tremendous form of empathy, especially for those clients who are more reluctant to speak and need to be understood in more subtle ways.

Some families will proceed from here quite naturally, spontaneously reacting to each other, uncovering problems and throwing out suggestions. This makes your job as the therapist easier. You simply need to attend to the various frames of reference and offer empathic understanding responses when necessary, while maintaining the other necessary therapeutic conditions. At times you may need to facilitate order by creating uninterrupted space for people to talk (e.g., 'Mary, I know you are eager to speak and I will get to you in just a moment.') or you may need to invite quieter members opportunities to speak (e.g., 'Tom, we have not heard from you yet and I am wondering if you care to share your perspective on the matter').

When families are more passive and reticent to speak I sometimes proceed a little differently. Allowing for silence is important, especially after you have stated some general guidelines of how you work, thereby eliminating ambiguity that might be at the core of their reticence. You can also comment on their reluctance to speak and quite often a participant decides to break the silence, especially when you show signs of being in tune with anxiety that might be present. Also, because you have the benefit of others present who might be the subject of discussion, it is appropriate to use what Thayer called a 'frameshift' when family members are being overly polite or not spontaneously responding, e.g., 'John, your mother has indicated that she is worried about you because you have been getting into fights recently—would you like to respond to her?' Or, 'John, your mother feels like you are intentionally trying to hurt her; what is your perspective on this matter?' This is an invitation to speak and a participant can certainly choose not to. Some people need an invitation to speak initially, and soon they realize that it is okay to spontaneously speak when they have the desire in the future.

4. Unconditional positive regard remains an attitudinal condition that is vital to effective family and couple work. Communicating an attitude of warmth and respect is critical to a family and couple feeling safe enough to reveal what is happening to them. This can come quite easily at times and can be very challenging at other times, especially when you do not necessarily have warm, respectful feelings toward a participant. As Rogers stated, unconditional positive regard is an attitude that is strived for, but often not achieved to its fullest capability. For instance, in dealing with couples where there is an issue of domestic violence, I have been plagued by feelings of disgust or dislike for someone. However, if I can acknowledge those feelings within myself (congruence) it usually allows me to put those feelings aside for the time being and focus on the couple/family. In doing so, I often discover some redeeming quality in the participant I had been judging that helps mediate my less desirable reactions.

5. Genuineness/congruence is a condition that has already been touched upon in this chapter, but I will elaborate a bit further. Genuineness is a condition that is rooted

within the therapist—it is a condition of being aware of your personal reactions and moment-to-moment feelings in therapy, without necessarily communicating them to the client(s). It is also about not hiding yourself from your clients or deceiving clients as to who you are as a person. It does not require you to share your feelings or history; it simply means that you are aware of and own your feelings internally and can speak to them if asked or compelled to do so. When this condition is met, it is much easier to control your personal reactions as the therapist. Additionally, if I feel the desire to put up a professional façade, I try to get in touch with what is going on within me in that moment. Usually it is some sort of fear or anxiety I am feeling in relation to my clients that I need to explore later in consultation with colleagues.

As discussed earlier in the chapter, there will be moments when your clients want more from you. They may pose direct questions to you regarding how to discipline their children, improve their marriage, negotiate conflict, increase passion, and compromise on all sorts of issues. When you feel as though you have a strong opinion, you can certainly offer it, as long as it is given in the spirit of not being an expert. Your opinion might be rooted in personal experience, experience with other couples/families or literature you have read, but it is not necessarily what will work for this couple/family—it is just your opinion.

More complicated moments come when your opinion has not been requested and yet you feel compelled to offer your perspective or a suggestion. In order to do this from a non-directive perspective, one must be firmly rooted in the non-directive attitude. That is, you cannot have a stake in the choices the family or couple makes— you have to really believe that what they decide is best for them. Assuming this attitude, sharing spontaneous, non-systematic reactions can be a very effective therapeutic tool.

Having worked extensively with persons sexually abused as children, as well as gay clients, I often find myself having reactions that I wish to share when working with couples/families who raise issues relevant to those areas. For example, a person in a couple might mention or allude to having been sexually traumatized as a child without expounding on the experience. If this couple is struggling with sexual issues that make no sense to them, and neither of the persons in the couple refers back to the sexual trauma, I would likely inquire into this experience and state some feelings as to why this might be relevant. Another scenario might involve working with a gay couple who find that they are unusually angry and frustrated with each other without apparent cause. In this case, the couple might look to you for some guidance. At this point, I might inquire into their history as a couple, i.e., whether they are 'out' to both sets of families, or whether they are dealing with discrimination or injustice related to a work situation, housing or the community in which they live. Perhaps you sense that one or both partners feels some internalized homophobia, leading to intense shame, guilt and frustration that they then take out on each other. These are all issues that can be tentatively explored if you are asked for your opinion or if you have a strong feeling that an issue might be present that has not been identified.

The important factor here is to not follow a formula for these situations, or any others in which you have a strong reaction or hunch. Remain rooted in the non-directive attitude and maintain your belief in the actualizing tendency. When this is the case, your advice, questions and suggestions will likely be applied properly and could be very helpful to your clients. For those not confident in a belief in the actualizing tendency and a non-directive attitude, take fewer risks in therapy until you are better grounded in the philosophy. Great work can still be done without having the experience under your belt that helps drive more advanced applications of the non-directive attitude when working with couples/families.

6. Lastly, allow the couple/family to decide when termination is best. Customarily it occurs once the presenting problem has been resolved or enough change has occurred. As the therapist, you can inquire into whether a couple/family has completed their work if it appears that they have. However, many couples/families like to continue therapy, on a less regular basis, for maintenance purposes. This can be an excellent idea if the couple/family feels vulnerable to losing their gains or if the couple/family is prone to crisis and needs to continue working on enhancing communication and problem-resolution skills.

Author's note: Comments on this chapter can be directed to him at <jmcpherr@uhs.bsd.uchicago.edu >.

REFERENCES

Anderson WJ (1989) Family therapy in the client-centered tradition: A legacy in the narrative mode. *Person-Centered Review, 4*(3), 295–307.

Bergin AE (1967) Some implications of psychotherapy research for therapeutic practice. *International Journal of Psychiatry, 3*, 136–50.

Bozarth JD & Brodley BT (1991) Actualization: A functional concept in client-centered therapy. In A Jones & R Crandall (Eds) Handbook of self-actualization. Special issue of *The Journal of Social Behavior and Personality, 6*(5), 45–59.

Bozarth JD & Shanks A (1989) Person-centered family therapy with couples. *Person-Centered Review, 4*(3), 280–94.

Brodley BT (1993) Response to Patterson's 'Winds of change for client-centered counseling'. *Journal of Humanistic Education and Development, 31*(3), 139–43.

Brodley B & Brody A (1994) Can one use techniques and still be client-centered? Paper presented at the International Client-Centered Conference in Vienna, Austria.

Gaylin NL (1989) The necessary and sufficient conditions for change: Individual versus family therapy. *Person-Centered Review, 4*(3), 263–79. Reprinted in NL Gaylin (2001) *Family, Self and Psychotherapy.* Ross-on-Wye: PCCS Books, pp. 106–14.

Gaylin NL (1990) Family-centered therapy. In G Lietaer, J Rombauts & R Van Balen (Eds)

Client-Centered and Experiential Psychotherapy in the Nineties. Leuven: Leuven University Press, pp. 813–28. Reprinted as 'Family Therapy Process' in NL Gaylin (2001) *Family, Self and Psychotherapy.* Ross-on-Wye: PCCS Books, pp. 115–29.

Gordon T (1972) *Parent-Effectiveness Training.* New York: Wyden.

Guerney BG (1977) *Relationship Enhancement.* San Francisco: Jossey-Bass.

Hubble M, Duncan B & Miller S (1999) *The Heart and Soul of Change: What works in therapy.* Washington, DC: American Psychological Association.

Levant RF (1978) Family therapy: A client-centered perspective. *Journal of Marriage and Family Counseling,* 4(b), 35–42.

Levant RF (1982) Client-centered family therapy. *American Journal of Family Therapy,* 10(2), 72–5.

Levant RF (1984) From person to system: Two perspectives. In RF Levant & JM Shlien (Eds) *Client-Centered Therapy and the Person-Centered Approach: New directions in theory, research, and practice.* New York: Praeger, pp. 243–60.

O'Leary CJ (1989) The person-centered approach and family therapy: A dialogue between two traditions. *Person-Centered Review,* 4(3), 308–23. Reprinted in DJ Cain (Ed) (2002) *Classics in the Person-Centered Approach.* Ross-on-Wye: PCCS Books, pp. 191–9.

Raskin NJ (1988) Responses to person-centered vs. client-centered. *Renaissance,* 5(3–4), 2–3.

Raskin NJ & van der Veen F (1970) Client-centered family therapy: Some clinical and research perspectives. In JT Hart & TM Tomlinson (Eds) *New Directions in Client-Centered Therapy.* Boston: Houghton Mifflin, pp. 387–406.

Rogers CR (1957) The necessary and sufficient conditions of therapeutic personality change. *Journal of Consulting Psychology,* 21, 95–103.

Rogers CR (1959) A theory of therapy, personality, and interpersonal relationships as developed in the client-centered framework. In S Koch (Ed) *Psychology: A study of science: Formulations of the person and the social context.* New York: McGraw-Hill, pp. 184–256.

Rogers CR (1980) *A Way of Being.* Boston: Houghton Mifflin.

Rombauts J & Devriendt M (1990) Conjoint couple therapy in client-centered practice. In G Lietaer, J Rombauts & R Van Balen (Eds) *Client-Centered and Experiential Psychotherapy in the Nineties.* Leuven: Leuven University Press, pp. 847–63.

Rosenberg MB (1976) *From Now On.* St. Louis, MO: Community Psychological Consultants.

Thayer L (1982) A person-centered approach to family therapy. In A Horne & M Olsen (Eds) *Family Counseling and Therapy.* Itasca, IL: FE Peacock, pp. 175–213.

Topping CJ (1993) An equal prizing: Couple therapy from a client-centered perspective. An unpublished dissertation submitted to the University of Georgia in partial fulfillment of the requirements for the degree of doctor of philosophy.

Truax CB & Carkhuff RR (1967) *Toward Effective Counseling and Psychotherapy: Training and practice.* Chicago: Aldine.

Truax CB & Mitchell KM (1971) Research on certain therapist interpersonal skills in relation to process and outcome. In AE Bergin & S Garfield (Eds) *Handbook of Psychotherapy and Behavior Change.* New York: Wiley, pp. 299–344.

Warner MS (1986) On coaching communication: Trust in the family system. Unpublished Draft.

Warner MS (1993) Levels of intrusiveness: A framework for considering the integration and differentiation of styles of psychotherapy. Unpublished Draft.

Chapter 18

TRUST BUILDS LEARNING:
THE CONTEXT AND EFFECTIVENESS OF
NON-DIRECTIVITY IN EDUCATION

Jeffrey H.D. Cornelius-White and
Cecily F. Cornelius-White

The non-directive approach to education (NE) developed in its incipient stages at nearly the same time as the non-directive approach to therapy, during the 1940s. While Rogers is often identified as the central figure for the person-centered approach, it is actually Aspy and Roebuck (and their colleagues, writing in English) and Tausch and Tausch (and their colleagues, writing in German) who are the primary researchers in the area of educational applications (Cornelius-White, 2005). The person-centered approach to education (PCAE) research reached its first peak in the late 1970s. Aspy and Roebuck's (1977) *Kids Don't Learn from People They Don't Like* is perhaps the best example of this peak. In the 1990s, McCombs and her colleagues developed the related learner-centered model, which continues to be highly influential (McCombs, 2004). The body of research in person-centered education is large and may be greater in size and significance than that in person-centered therapy.

Rogers' (1959) theory paper defines PCAE as an environment characterized by empathy, unconditional positive regard, congruence, and a growing reciprocity of these attitudes between teachers and students. While somewhat different in its theoretical base, the operational definitions of the more recent learner-centered model (American Psychological Association, 1997) are quite similar to those of the PCAE research tradition, and focus on positive relationships, honoring student voice, encouraging student thinking, adaptation to individual uniqueness, and teachers' beliefs about learners and learning (Cornelius-White, Hoey, Cornelius-White, Motschnig-Pitrik and Figl, 2004; Cornelius White, 2005). As in much of the therapy literature, the term 'non-directive' in the education literature gave way to the terms 'student-centered' or 'person-centered' during the 1950s. In the therapy literature the term non-directive began to be referenced more as an attitude than as a technique (Raskin, 1947/2005; Rogers, 1951).

As the publication of this book signifies, the non-directive attitude has recently regained popularity as a theoretical construct. Key to the non-directive attitude is that it is a natural extension of the central motivation hypothesis in the person-centered approach, the actualizing tendency, which involves a radical trust in persons' potential to maintain and enhance themselves. A related construct is the formative tendency, which is an aim towards maintenance and enhancement of systems, including other people beyond one's self. There are many manifestations and idiosyncratic interpretations of this central non-directive attitude, including responding to persons' requests, emergent modes of empathy involving self-disclosure, spontaneous behaviors, and principled integrations. The PCAE research tradition has not operationally included many of these subtle yet significant distinctions in relation to the non-directive attitude, with the possible exception of some of the earlier works of Tausch and Tausch (Cornelius-White, 2005).

CONTEXTUAL DIFFERENCES BETWEEN THERAPY AND EDUCATION

While the authors value the non-directive attitude, the manifestations of this attitude are necessarily different in education from those in therapy, as non-directive education presents different circumstances from non-directive therapy. First, there is typically much more extensive contact between teachers and students than there is between counselor and client. On average, teachers in elementary school spend 7 hours per day with children 180 days per year. A therapist today is often lucky to spend 7 hours in total with a client. This more extensive contact makes the likelihood of remaining congruent, and appearing non-directive in attitude throughout the entire duration of contact between teacher and child, unrealistically difficult. Teachers may have more requirements that they need to impose simply to remain available to students, such as silence or sitting behavior at various points during the extended contact.

Second, in education as compared to therapy, there is a requirement that more factual and concrete content be learned. Therapy is more often a subjective and abstract task. For example, to succeed students must learn to write letters and words, where clients (of the same age) may learn their feelings and wants in relation to letters and words. In educational settings a respect for the ambiguity of meaning (phenomena) must exist more frequently in a dialectic with objective material (noumena).

In many educational settings there is often a more pronounced power difference. Teachers typically, though not always, enjoy a higher social position than their students, based on several assumed discrepancies between the two. When teaching children, the first basic discrepancy is age. Children do not have the same rights or privileges as do adults. Prior to adolescence, they also do not have the intellectual capacities of an adult. Similarly to parenting or a hypothetical play therapy that lasts all day, five days a week, facilitators must take responsibility for the basic welfare of the children they engage. This may necessitate giving directions and advocacy for students, particularly at younger ages, which is less frequently necessary in play therapy lasting an hour or therapy with families and/or adults.

Within school systems there are generally more people involved in the relationship, in terms of number of students in a class versus numbers of clients in an individual, family or group session. Modal class sizes are probably more than 25 students each; modal therapy is with one client. Families and group sessions are rarely as high as 25. While there are exceptions, these general trends suggest a greater need for behavioral predictability in order to avoid chaos. Likewise, this need may indicate a different degree of stimulus and stress on teachers as opposed to the demands on therapists. Both the extent of contact and the number of people involved in the contact may allow more space for, and necessitate greater expression of, the teacher's subjective experience (including facts and requests that she or he may have). The typical level of expression of the non-directive facilitator's perspective may be described on a continuum, with individual counseling providing less space for the facilitator's perspective, group counseling more, and teaching more still.

Another issue that arises as a major difference between non-directive education and non-directive therapy is the demand in most educational systems for formalized evaluation. The type of evaluation present in non-directive educational systems need not be the standard, objective grading scale. There is, nonetheless, a social expectation that teachers, having accepted the task of imparting information to students, have likewise taken on the duty of ascertaining whether the students have successfully absorbed the information. Whatever form of measurement schools may use, it is nonetheless necessary that in order to comply with most local, state, and federal regulations, some formalized evaluation take place. This demand of evaluation further demarcates the already-present power hierarchy within classroom settings.

Furthermore, non-directive educational facilitation exists in more broadly defined and complex systems than non-directive therapy, involving both parents and schools. Structurally, teachers are more often accountable to principals, school boards and the public than they are to students. Even in inpatient or strictly managed care situations, the limitations on therapists' freedom and status rarely exceed those of teachers. Teachers also have the added task of negotiating with parents, larger numbers of colleagues with whom they have daily contact, and community members. While other differences exist, the above five differences—including more distinct power differentials, concretized learning agendas, more extensive contact between teachers and students, the need for formalized evaluation, and negotiation in systems—illustrate some of the crucial ways in which holding the non-directive attitude needs to be integrated with other goals, and may result in different manifestations in the educational context.

REVIEW OF RESEARCH

Based on a recent meta-analysis of person-centered education including 119 studies, written in English and German and involving 1450 findings with 355,000 students (Cornelius-White *et al.*, 2004; Cornelius-White, 2005), the authors parceled out the findings concerning non-directivity as a class of independent variables. The studies included persons from pre-K to grade 20, with a diverse geographic, ethnic and cognitive ability, and socioeconomic class array represented (Cornelius-White *et al.*, 2004; Cornelius-White, 2005). The person-centered literature was divided into three model categories: classical person-centered, based on Rogers' model (1940s–1980s); learner-centered, based on McCombs' model (1990s–present), and a third category comprised of parts of these models, mostly from the classical variables of empathy and warmth. A smaller sample on non-directivity involved 17 studies, with 131 findings and 7566 students. There was diversity in the operational definitions and perspectives used to measure the PCAE and non-directivity.

To orient the reader to an understanding of the research findings, the authors will briefly offer an explanation of the two main statistics used in meta-analysis: the correlation, r, and the effect size, d, as well as some benchmarks for interpreting. The r statistic refers to the degree of relationship between two variables and ranges from −1.00 to +1.00. A positive correlation between two variables shows that as one variable increases, for example educational level, so does a second variable, for example IQ. While interpretation varies widely depending on context, correlations are generally considered small if they are 0.10, medium if they are 0.25 and large if they are 0.40 or greater. The d statistic relates the degree of impact that one variable has on another. The d and r statistics may be converted back and forth, though the r does not imply causality where the d does. In keeping with the generic interpretation guidelines of r, an effect size d is considered small if 0.20, medium if 0.50, and large if 0.80 or larger. Small effect sizes are considered meaningful in the real world, but are often not perceivable to the naked eye. Large effect sizes are considered obvious to observation. For example, if a person walked by who was 5 feet 11 inches (1m 80) and another walked by a few minutes later who was 6 feet (1m 83), when asked after the fact an observer might have difficulty saying if one was taller than the other. In contrast, if a person walked by who was 5 feet 2 inches (1m 57) and a different person walked by afterwards who was 6 feet, such an obvious difference would allow an observer to state clearly which one was taller. This typifies the difference in a small versus large effect size. The authors will present all findings as r values for the reader's ease of interpretation.

From the meta-analysis of all PCAE, the overall study-level-weighted correlation between person-centered education and positive outcomes is 0.29. However, when only the classical person-centered findings are considered, the corrected correlation is 0.41. Teacher variables in PCAE research included nine categories of variables from the classical and learner-centered models, such as empathy, warmth, encouragement of higher-order thinking, adaptation to student differences, and composites of the variables. For cognitive outcomes in nine categories, including achievement, IQ and critical thinking variables, the overall finding-level-corrected correlation is 0.29. For affective/behavioral outcomes in nine categories, including motivation, mental health and attendance, the overall finding-level-corrected correlation is 0.32.

The findings concerned only with non-directivity yielded an overall corrected correlation of 0.35. Of the 131 findings, 101 came from controlled studies, while 30 came from studies that were correlational or involved uncontrolled comparison groups. Hence, the study quality for measures of non-directivity was relatively high. Non-directivity is measured in a variety of ways in these studies, including observer measures of the classical non-directive attitude, and inversions of measures of highly controlling teaching behavior from students' perspectives. The non-directivity findings from the three models (classical, learner-centered, isolated elements from the models) appear different. Non-directive findings from classical researchers (46 findings) show a mean corrected correlation of 0.45, learner-centered findings (4) show a 0.37 corrected

317

correlation, and findings which investigated only parts of the models without a clear orientation as classical or learner-centered show a corrected correlation of 0.22. Many potential reasons for this apparent difference exist, such as the biases of researcher allegiance, divergent operational definitions, or actual differences of the different models.

In terms of perspective used to measure non-directivity, relationships of positive educational outcomes with observer measures were 0.30, with teacher measures they were 0.25, with student measures they were 0.37, and with composites of these three different perspectives were 0.40. Hence, non-directivity in education appears to be a more valid concern when considered from the students' perspectives as compared to the teacher's. In terms of cognitive outcomes, non-directivity shows a corrected correlation of 0.18, while with affective/behavioral outcomes it shows a corrected correlation of 0.44. Affective/behavioral outcomes clearly appear to be more positively affected than cognitive outcomes. Measures of cognition are almost always from the student's perspective, while affective/behavioral outcomes are measured from varied perspectives. The corrected correlation for measures from the observer's perspective was 0.58, from the teacher's perspective 0.46 and from the students' perspective 0.41. Thus it appears that non-directivity in the classroom is strongly associated with beneficial affective and behavioral outcomes, with this finding most pronounced when measured from an observer's perspective. There were not affective/behavioral measures that were composites of these different perspectives.

Recall that the majority of findings (101) came from controlled studies, while the minority (30) did not. The controlled studies showed a lower corrected correlation: 0.29 compared with the uncontrolled studies at 0.58. It would appear that this signifies the presence of a non-causal or moderated relationship. That is, positive outcomes appear to be linked only partially to non-directivity as a causative factor. Positive outcomes might influence teachers to be more non-directive, or some uncontrolled third variable may account for this large difference. Almost none of the studies investigated the inverted causality possibility, where teachers are caused to be non-directive by students' levels of cognitive, affective and behavioral successes. This is, however, in keeping with Rogers' (1959) conceptualization of reciprocity in the PCAE, and remains a point of differentiation from his conceptualization of therapy.

Cognitive and affective/behavioral outcomes were broken down into nine categories each. In terms of affective/behavioral outcomes, Figure 1 (overleaf) shows the mean corrected correlations between non-directivity and the affective/behavioral sub-categories. Note that all categories show medium to large relationships, with student participation/ initiation and decreases in negative motivation showing the most extreme relationships to non-directivity. As all but one of the cognitive outcome categories had fewer than 10 findings and were more uniform than the affective/behavioral outcomes, no descriptive figure is provided.

To further ground the significance of the research in non-directive education, the authors offer a few examples of findings from therapy research, and several examples from educational literature. Therapy, regardless of the method of therapy used, appears to correlate near 0.40 with beneficial outcomes. Specific ingredients of therapy have

Figure 1. Mean corrected correlations of non-directivity with affective/behavioral outcomes (from Cornelius-White, 2005).

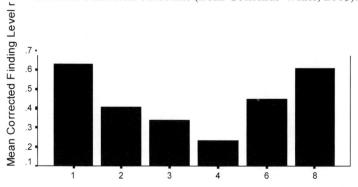

Affective/Behavioral Category

1=Participation, 2=Positive motivation, 3=Self-esteem/Mental health
4=Social skills/Support, 6=Student satisfaction, 8=Negative motivation

[Categories 5 (attendance), 7 (disruptive behavior) and 9 (drop-out) did not have non-directivity findings. Category 8 is inverted so that the high positive correlation shows that increases in non-directivity are related to decreases in negative motivation. This analysis is based on 131 findings from 17 studies with 7566 total students. All categories have 10 or more findings with the exception of category 8, which has only 5.]

been shown to correlate less with outcome. For example, efficacious individual interventions appear to correlate between 0.09 and 0.28 with positive outcome (Ahn and Wampold, 2001). Empathy, as an individual variable, appears more powerful than any specific intervention, correlating 0.32 with beneficial outcome (Greenberg, Elliott, Watson, and Bohart, 2001). Hence, classical person-centered education, at 0.41, shows a nearly identical size of relationship with beneficial outcomes to that of therapy. When all person-centered educational research, including classical, learner-centered and parts of these models are considered, person-centered education appears to have a smaller but still substantial relationship to beneficial outcome of 0.29. Non-directivity, as an individual variable correlating 0.35 with beneficial outcomes, is very similar in effectiveness to the individual variable of empathy. When non-directivity is viewed only with the classical studies, the corrected correlation is even larger at 0.53.

In terms of understanding the non-directive educational findings in the context of other research on educational innovations, two general principles and several examples are provided. Generally, educational innovations are more effective for achievement than for affective outcomes and are more effective the more proximal to the student they are (Fraser, Wahlberg, Welsch, and Hattie, 1987; Hattie, 1999). Person-centered education is concerned with proximal variables; that is, a student's internal experience and relationship to his or her teacher. Hence, it is understandable that its effects are large. What is somewhat different from other educational innovations is that person-centered education is more strongly related to positive affective/behavioral outcomes

319

rather than cognitive ones. This also makes sense, as it grew out of an approach to therapy and human relations, which does not have a focus on academic achievement.

In terms of specific examples, student maturation alone correlates 0.05 with academic achievement; having a teacher correlates 0.12; and innovative educational variables in general correlate about 0.19. Specific variables vary widely in their effectiveness for increasing academic achievement. For example, reinforcement correlates with academic achievement at a level of 0.49, students' prior cognitive learning at 0.47, cooperative learning at 0.33, questioning at 0.20, class size (inverted) at 0.04, desegregation at 0.01, physical attributes at -0.02, and retention (holding students back a year when they 'fail') at -0.22. Hence, person-centered education at 0.29 and non-directivity at 0.18, as individual variables, fare as above-average and average innovations for academic achievement, respectively.

In terms of the effectiveness of educational innovations on affective outcomes, the overall relationship is 0.11, while for class size (inverted) it is 0.24, student's prior cognitive learning is 0.22, teacher expectations is 0.15, and mass media exposure is -0.07 (Fraser *et al.*, 1987; Hattie, 1999). In this regard, person-centered education at 0.32 and non-directivity at 0.44 appear more potent than most other existing innovations (see Johnson and Johnson, 2001 for a humanistic, skills-oriented exception). This finding appears to be of profound significance to the educational literature, especially considering such serious problems as school violence, high drop-out rates, and teenage pregnancy.

INDIRECT EDUCATION'S CONTRIBUTIONS TO NON-DIRECTIVITY

While not considered to be part of the person-centered educational literature, or non-directivity as a construct, there is an innovation called indirect education (IE), which bears some relationship to non-directive education and may offer an important interpretive contribution to both the educational and therapy literature. Operational definitions changed for IE over time, but were basically characterized by the magnitude of the ratio of indirect teacher behaviors to direct teacher behaviors. Indirect behaviors usually included acceptance of students' feelings, elaboration of students' ideas, and asking students thinking and memory questions; while direct behaviors included lecturing, giving directions or justifying authority. Research in indirect education specifically discusses the merits of direct methods under certain conditions, valuing flexibility at times more than indirect behavior, unlike classical person-centered theory. Within IE, Flanders (Amidon, Casper and Flanders, 1985) may be viewed as the central originator, though a wider diversity of researchers exists in IE as compared to the PCAE tradition. In particular, there are many dissertations investigating Flanders' Interaction Analysis system, upon which indirect versus direct teaching comparisons are made. Interestingly, Aspy and Roebuck (1977) consistently utilized Flanders' system in their works, uniting the two traditions operationally. However, to the authors' knowledge there are few works that integrate the two traditions theoretically and historically.

The overall linear relationship of indirect teaching behaviors with student academic achievement is 0.17 (Fraser *et al.*, 1987), indicating that it is near average as an educational innovation and almost identical to the effectiveness on academic achievement of the non-directive research discussed above. More importantly, however, indirect behaviors have been shown to be more adequately described by a curvilinear correlation (Soar and Soar, 1978). While the optimal level of indirectness on academic achievement falls above that which typically occurs, it is not extreme. In other words, while more indirectness in teaching is generally better than less, extreme levels of indirectness are worse for academic achievement. Also, the cusp of optimal non-directive behavior varies with the concreteness of the outcome, where more concrete behaviors are better facilitated with less indirectness. In other words, learning to spell is better facilitated by less indirectness than learning to solve arithmetic problems, which in turn is better facilitated than analysis of literature or, further toward the extreme, expressing one's feelings to determine one's existential path.

IMPLICATIONS FOR THERAPY

The curvilinear relationship described above may exist in therapy as well, as exemplified in the relationship between the level of abstract task and the level of directivity. Some therapies, like cognitive-behavioral, are more 'educative' and concrete by definition, which yields a more directive style. In contrast, phenomenological approaches like person-centered therapy tend to be more exploratory and abstract, which yields a more non-directive style. Nevertheless, when clients are at less of a pre-contemplative or contemplative stage and more of an action stage, more observed directivity may be best (Prochaska and Norcross, 2001). This is also in keeping with Cornelius-White's (2003) findings, which suggested that very high levels of observed non-directivity may become less useful with clients who have significantly improved and are working on more concrete tasks.

To spell out an implication for therapy using the concept of 'resistance', a client who appears more resistant may tend to present more ambiguous and necessarily abstract tasks for the counselor–client relationship. The findings of Beutler, Rocco, Moleiro and Talebi (2001) that directive approaches work better with less resistant clients, while non-directive (not necessarily person-centered) approaches have been shown to work better with more resistant clients, also support this idea. Likewise, fragile (Warner, 1998) and pre-therapy (Prouty, 1998) processes may be helped more by higher levels of non-directivity because of the increased ambiguity of clients' experience. Because the lower functioning client is more concrete in perspective, abstract learning in the client represents more of a significant departure from their normal means of interpreting and interacting with the world, which may be best facilitated by greater non-directivity. In offering these speculations from the IE and general therapy literatures, the authors do not mean to imply the necessity for diagnostic or instrumental 'use' of non-directivity. These speculations are descriptive hypotheses open to further empirical investigation.

CONCLUSIONS

In conclusion, the authors recognize some of the crucial contextual differences between therapy and education, such as more distinct power differentials, concretized learning agendas, more extensive contact between teachers and students, the need for formalized evaluation, and negotiation in systems. These different contextual features imply a difference in manifestation of non-directivity in educational settings versus therapy settings. Because of the differing context, the parameters for non-directivity in education versus therapy may be more constrained or more mediated by external demands and expectations. A review of the findings of a recent meta-analysis by the first author shows the breadth and strength of person-centered educational research, as well as non-directivity as an isolated measured construct. It is clear that non-directive education has a positive effect on student outcomes in various areas of functioning, including academic achievement, cognitive performance and affective/behavioral functioning. The contribution of person-centered and non-directive variables to beneficial student affective/behavioral outcomes is especially profound. Finally, an examination of the indirect education literature reveals a curvilinear relationship that offers potential explanation for the role of optimal levels of non-directivity in concrete and abstract learning in educational and therapeutic settings. Although non-directivity most often brings positive results, extremes of non-directivity may not be beneficial in particular settings or with particular types of concrete task. It appears that more concrete tasks may necessitate more directivity, while more abstract learning tasks may be best served through more non-directivity. In general, just as trust in the client allows more space for the actualizing tendency to manifest itself in therapy, trust in the student's learning process does appear to increase learning potential in educational settings. Thus we may say definitively that people learn better from those who trust and believe in them.

REFERENCES

Ahn, H & Wampold B (2001) Where oh where are the specific ingredients? A meta-analysis of component studies in counseling and psychotherapy. *Journal of Counseling Psychology, 48*(3), 251–7.

American Psychological Association (1997) *Learner-Centered Psychological Principles: A framework for school redesign and reform.* Washington, DC: APA.

Amidon EJ, Casper IG, & Flanders NA (1985) *The Role of the Teachers in the Classroom: Interaction analysis for teachers.* St Paul, MN: Paul S Amidon & Associates.

Aspy DN & Roebuck FN (1977) *Kids Don't Learn from People They Don't Like.* Amherst, MA: Human Resource Development Press.

Beutler LE, Rocco F, Moleiro CM, & Talebi H (2001) Resistance. *Psychotherapy: Theory/Research/Practice/Training, 3,* 431–6.

Cornelius-White JHD (2003) The analyzed non-directiveness of a brief, effective person-centered practice. *Person-Centered Journal, 10,* 23–30.

Cornelius-White JHD (2005) Teachers who care are more effective: A meta-analysis of learner-centered relationships. Manuscript submitted for publication. Texas A&M International University, Laredo.

Cornelius-White JHD, Hoey A, Cornelius-White CF, Motschnig-Pitrik R & Figl K (2004) Person-centered edudcation: A meta-analysis of care in progress. *Journal of Border Educational Research, 3,* 81–96.

Fraser BJ, Wahlberg HJ, Welsch WW & Hattie JA (1987) Syntheses of educational productivity research. *International Journal of Educational Research, 11,* 145–252.

Greenberg LS, Elliott R, Watson JC & Bohart A (2001) Empathy. *Psychotherapy: Theory/Research/Practice/Training, 38,* 380–4.

Hattie JA (1999) Influences on student learning. Paper presented at the Inaugural Lecture, University of Auckland, New Zealand (August).

Johnson DW & Johnson RT (2001) Teaching students to be peacemakers: A meta-analysis. Paper presented at the Annual Meeting of the American Educational Research Association, Seattle, WA, April (ERIC Document Reproduction Service No. ED 460178)

McCombs BL (2004) The case for learner-centered practices: Introduction and rationale for session. Paper presented at the American Educational Research Association Annual meeting, San Diego, CA, April.

Prochaska JO & Norcross JC (2001) Stages of change. *Psychotherapy: Theory/Research/Practice/Training, 38,* 443–6.

Prouty GF (1998) Pre-therapy and pre-symbolic experiencing: Evolutions in person-centered/experiential approaches to psychotic experience. In L Greenberg & J Watson *Handbook of Experiential Psychotherapy.* New York: Guilford Press, pp. 368–87.

Raskin NJ (1947/2005) The nondirective attitude. In BE Levitt (Ed) *Embracing Non-directivity: Reassessing person-centered theory and practice in the 21st century.* Ross-on-Wye: PCCS Books, pp. 329–47.

Rogers CR (1951) *Client-Centered Therapy.* Boston: Houghton Mifflin.

Rogers CR (1959) A theory of therapy, personality, and interpersonal relationship as developed in the client-centered framework. In S Koch (Ed) *Psychology: A study of a science. Formulations of the person and the social context.* New York: McGraw-Hill, pp. 184–256.

Soar RS & Soar RM (1978) *Setting Variables, Classroom Interaction, and Multiple Pupil Outcomes.* Final Report. Florida University Gainesville: Institute for Development of Human Resources (ERIC Document Reproduction Service No. ED 225999).

Warner MS (1998) A client-centered approach to therapeutic work with dissociated and fragile process. In LS Greenberg & J Watson *Handbook of Experiential Psychotherapy.* New York: Guilford Press, pp. 368–87.

CHAPTER 19

SOME ESSENTIALS OF A CLIENT-CENTERED APPROACH TO ASSESSMENT

C. H. PATTERSON AND C. EDWARD WATKINS JR

Abstract

The process of client assessment is a counseling function in which most, if not all, professional counselors engage. The assessment enterprise, however, tends to be viewed differently by different counselors; thus the range of helping behaviors implemented in the process is often characterized by immense diversity and uniqueness. This commentary briefly summarizes some of the distinguishing features of a particular approach to assessment (i.e., the client-centered approach) and indicates some of its essential guiding tenets. More specifically, we will examine: (a) the therapeutic attitude in the assessment process, (b) the purpose of assessment, (c) test selection, and (d) test interpretation.

THE THERAPEUTIC ATTITUDE IN ASSESSMENT

The attitude of the counselor, characterized by the relationship conditions of empathy, respect and warmth, genuineness, and concreteness (Patterson, 1974, 1979), is a *sine qua non* in the practice of the assessment process. This attitude, which is basic to all counseling endeavors, provides clients with an atmosphere in which they can fully explore the intricacies of varied assessment data and understand the personal implications. Patterson (1958) indicated that there are two central elements of the client-centered counselor's attitude that seem to have special bearing on the assessment process:

1. Each person is a person of worth in himself [or herself] and is therefore to be respected as such.

2. Each individual has the right to self-direction, to choose or select his [or her] own values and goals, to make his [or her] own decisions. (p. 217)

The counselor's behavior, therefore, tends to be pervaded by a belief in the client's worth and self-direction; this belief provides the base from which the client-centered therapist operates.

The relationship conditions facilitate the construction of an open, nonthreatening,

First published in *Measurement and Evaluation in Guidance,* 1982, *15*, 103–6. Reprinted by permission of the publishers, American Counseling Association.

and receptive environment within which clients feel able to express and disclose themselves. When attending to clients' personal feelings and meanings, the client-centered counselor assists them to more adequately examine and synthesize assessment data. The conditions of empathy, respect and warmth, genuineness, and concreteness contribute to the process of client self-exploration and understanding and thereby aid in constructive development and change.

THE PURPOSE OF ASSESSMENT

Carkhuff (1969) stated that counseling is for the client. It can be added that assessment is for the benefit of client. The process is designed to assist clients in a better understanding of themselves and in using assessment data to learn about potentially desirable changes in their lives. The ultimate purpose of this process, therefore, is to facilitate clients' self-actualization.

The construct of self-actualization has many implications for the counselor and the procedures employed in gathering information about clients. Full and optimal development of one's self serves as an orienting focus, and the variety of counselor information collecting methods serves the ultimate goal and value of assessment; that is, client self-actualization. The client-centered counselor, recognizing that assessment is for the client, attempts to provide clients with programs that would be of the most personal benefit to them. Recognizing that assessment is a client-oriented process tends to bring a radical, refreshing view to the manner in which test selection and test interpretation are construed. We will examine these two procedures from a client-centered perspective and provide some indication of how a relationship therapist operates in the testing endeavor.

TEST SELECTION

Too often, the selection of tests is a function in which clients tend to have little input. In client-centered assessment, clients are given the opportunity to choose tests they consider best for their needs. Patterson (1971) states:

> The essential basis for the use of tests in counseling is that *they provide information which the client needs and wants* ... information concerning questions which the client raises in counseling ... Tests, then, are introduced ... when the client, either overtly or covertly, indicates a desire or need for the kind of information which tests can help to provide. The counselor indicates the kind of information which tests may provide and describes the appropriate tests in non-technical terms. The client decides whether or not he wants this information. (p. 144–5)

Throughout the test selection procedure clients are provided with the freedom of self-direction and the personal autonomy of thought and action. It is the client, therefore, not the counselor, who ultimately determines the usefulness and validity of the testing and assessment processes in the counseling relationship.

An essential aspect of test selection is that clients be provided with enough accurate and useful information about available tests so that they can choose those most appropriate for them. Watkins (in press), in his article on client-centered test interpretation, provides a brief description of how the California Test of Personality (CTP) can be introduced:

> The California Test of Personality is a personality test which can give some indication as to how you view your personal and social life. The test provides you with an opportunity to evaluate yourself and the results can indicate how you currently regard your life in several different areas. (in press)

Further elaboration on the CTF could provide clients with an understanding of the test's various scales and what they measure. For other ideas of how to introduce tests to clients, see Bixler and Bixler (1946), Bordin and Bixler (1946), Seeman (1948) and Stephenson (1963). More recent indications of the client-centered attitude can be found in Bradley (1978), Bradley and Snowman (1981) and Cummings (1981).

TEST INTERPRETATION

When using the client-centered approach to test interpretation, it is important that the locus of evaluation remain with the client. Patterson (1960) states: 'Tests can be used if this locus of evaluation is kept in the client and not transferred to the counselor' (p. 156).

The client-centered counselor should strive to facilitate clients' self-appraisal and assessment, thereby providing them the opportunity to interpret their own test results.

The reasons for allowing clients to engage in a self-interpretive process are multiple. Rogers (1946) seems to state the case well:

> For the counselor to interpret tests to the client is to say, 'I am the expert, I know more about you than you can know yourself, and I shall impart that superior knowledge'. (p. 141)

He continues:

> Tests which are initiated by the counselor are a hindrance ... [and] tend to increase defensiveness on the part of the client, to lessen ... acceptance of self, to decrease ... sense of responsibility, to create an attitude of dependence upon the expert. (p. 141)

Interpretation by the counselor is therefore avoided because it often arouses anxiety and threatens the client, thus preventing the test data from being fully used. If clients are to make adequate use of their test results, two elements are essential: the data must be (a) understandable and (b) acceptable (Patterson, 1971). Patterson (1971) stated:

> The results must be communicated objectively, that is, without judgments or evaluations by the counselor. The results must be allowed to speak for themselves, with the counselor providing only an explanation of the meaning of the scores. (p. 147)

Further, it is essential that counselors be honest when presenting test information (i.e., they should not conceal or withhold data from clients). Quite conceivably, some counselors may not divulge all of a client's scores for fear that unpleasant results will deeply hurt the client. Unfortunately, when clients are not fully informed, they must make decisions based on insufficient information, and difficulties that could arise from a decision based on inaccurate or incomplete data can be averted if counselors are accurate in their presentation of test results.

CONCLUSION

Traditional approaches to the assessment process have tended to focus on what the counselor can do to the client. The client-centered orientation, however, provides a radical and different view of assessment and how it should be conducted. We have attempted to highlight some of the essential elements of a client-centered approach to assessment and indicate four of the guiding tenets that orient the relationship therapist. We have specifically emphasized: (a) the function of empathy, respect and warmth, genuineness, and concreteness in the assessment endeavor; (b) the purpose of assessment; (c) test selection; and (d) test interpretation. It is our hope that these concepts will assist the reader to understand more fully how the client-centered approach can be implemented in the process of assessment.

REFERENCES

Bixler RH & Bixler VH (1946) Test interpretation in vocational counseling. *Educational and Psychological Measurement, 6*, 145–56.

Bordin ES & Bixler RH (1946) Test selection: A process of counseling. *Educational and Psychological Measurement, 6*, 361–73.

Bradley RW (1978) Person-referenced test interpretation: A learning process. *Measurement and Evaluation in Guidance, 10*, 201–10.

Bradley RW & Snowman J (1981) Modified access through interpretation: A third alternative to truth-in-testing. *Personnel and Guidance Journal, 59*, 439–43.

Carkhuff RR (1969) *Helping and Human Relations.* New York: Holt, Rinehart and Winston.

Cummings OW (1981) Student-centered test interpretation: An active technique. *School Counselor, 28*, 267–72.

Patterson CH (1958) The place of values in counseling and psychotherapy. *Journal of Counseling Psychology, 5*, 216–23.

Patterson CH (1960) Psychological testing and the counseling process. In CH Patterson (Ed) *Readings in Rehabilitation Counseling.* Champaign, Ill.: Stipes Publishing Co.

Patterson CH (1970) *An Introduction to Counseling in the School.* New York: Harper & Row.

Patterson CH (1974) *Relationship Counseling and Psychotherapy.* New York: Harper & Row.

Patterson CH (1979) Rogerian counseling. In JD Noshpitz (Ed) *Basic Handbook of Child Psychiatry.* New York: Basic Books, pp. 203–15.

Rogers CR (1946) Psychometric tests and client-centered counseling. *Educational and Psychological Measurement, 6,* 139–44.

Seeman J (1948) A study of client self-selection of tests in vocational counseling. *Educational and Psychological Measurement, 8,* 327–46.

Stephenson RR (1963) Client interpretation *Vocational Guidance Quarterly, 12,* 51–6.

Watkins CE Jr A client-centered approach to test interpretation with teacher education students. *Journal of College Student Personnel,* in press.

CHAPTER 20

THE NONDIRECTIVE ATTITUDE[1, 2]

NATHANIEL J. RASKIN

I. THE ATTITUDE

Nondirective therapists have for some time been aware of the fact that the attitude of the therapist is *the* important thing to consider in the evaluation of counselor participation in the therapeutic process. The 'recognition of feeling' response, first described in Rogers' (1942) *Counseling and Psychotherapy*, is the primary technique of the nondirective counselor, and for many people, has become the symbol of nondirective therapy. Too often, however, the appreciation of this school of therapy has been dulled, and its philosophy distorted, by an uncritical evaluation of the 'recognition of feeling' technique on a purely intellectual level, in strict separation from the counselor's attitude toward the client, which is the only thing that can give meaning to the technique.

One such uncritical evaluation has resulted in the belief that the nondirective counselor merely parrots the client's words back to him. Under this system, the following type of exchange would occur throughout the interview (we can be pretty certain that there would be no more than one):

> *Client: What do you think I ought to do—jump off a bridge, or look for another job to lose?*
>
> *Counselor: You wonder what I think you ought to do—whether to jump off a bridge, or look for another job to lose?*

A response more in keeping with the nondirective spirit would be:

> *Counselor: It's a pretty hopeless situation, isn't it? Your choice seems to lie between giving up entirely or facing further failure.*[3]

---

1. This essay also appears in the *Person-Centered Journal, 12* (1–2), 2005, accompanied by an interview with Nat Raskin.
2. Carl Rogers wrote notes in longhand in the margins of the original manuscript, referenced here as footnotes. He also attached a note to Nat Raskin, signed as 'C.R.' which reads, 'Raskin—I found this very stimulating. I disagree in spots and made some marginal notes. I think your idea of maladj. can be combined with mine into a definition better than either. I'd like this back, or a carbon, if I may. I also wish you would show it to Porter, Bowman & others at the C.C.' (Rogers is referring here to the Counseling Center in Chicago.)
3. Rogers' note: 'This doesn't quite catch cnslr's attitude.'

Occasionally, the counselor may feel that the most adequate way to represent the client's feeling is to repeat his expression verbatim, but this occurs only rarely, and it is certainly not a standard type of response in the nondirective method.

The 'parroting' criticism is made only on the basis of a highly superficial acquaintance with nondirective therapy, however, and need hardly concern us further.

There is another level of response which is more deserving of our attention because it represents the sincere efforts of many individuals who are trying to do nondirective counseling, and is one which can work with a certain degree of efficiency. This may be characterized as an attempt to catch the feelings expressed by the client, and in the main to give them back to him without going beyond them, but occasionally to comprehend relationships between attitudes expressed separately by the client, and to include these relationships in the counselor response, and at other times to go slightly beyond the client's expressed feeling so as to speed up the process of insight and therapy. This second level of response is based on an attitude which includes a high degree of respect for the client, while retaining the notion that because of the counselor's superior knowledge and experience, there are ways of subtly guiding the client to speedier and more satisfactory adjustment. This is a quite a popular form of therapy and is used by many of the modern psychoanalysts.

A third level of nondirective counselor response may be distinguished, in which the therapist has given up the goals of guidance and diagnosis and assumes the role of an observer of the client and his attitudes. At this level counseling becomes pretty much of an intellectual exercise, in which the counselor tries to catch the attitude being expressed, and reflects it back to the client. The counselor here feels quite ill at ease whenever the question of counselor responsibility for therapy arises; he feels the need frequently to structure (explain intellectually) the nature of the counseling relationship to the client, he is pretty much aware of the needs which the client is expressing in his statements, and he responds with unexpressed (verbally, that is) emotion to the client's ideas, on the basis of his own needs and predilections.

There is a fourth level of nondirective counselor response which to us represents the nondirective attitude. In a sense, it is a goal rather than one which is actually practiced by counselors. But, in the experience of some it is a highly attainable goal, which makes this level highly distinct from the third-level attitude we have just described, and changes the nature of the counseling process in a radical way. At this level, counselor participation becomes an active experiencing with the client of the feelings to which he gives expression:[4] the counselor makes a maximum effort to get under the skin of the person with whom he is communicating,[5] he tries to get *within* and to live the attitudes expressed instead of observing them,[6] to catch every nuance of their changing nature; in a word, to absorb himself completely in the attitudes of the other.[7] And in struggling to do this, there is

---

4. Rogers' note: '?'
5. Rogers' note: 'yes'
6. Rogers' note: '?'
7. Rogers' note: 'yes'

simply no room for any other type of counselor activity or attitude; if he is attempting to live the attitudes of the other, he cannot be diagnosing them, he cannot be worrying about their relationship to him, the therapist, he cannot be thinking of making the process go faster. Because he is another, and not the client, the understanding is not spontaneous but must be acquired, and this through the most intense, continuous and active attention to the feelings of the other, to the exclusion of any other type of attention.

Rank (1936: 5) was the first to stress the experiential as being the essential aspect of the therapeutic relationship, though with him the therapist was still largely an observer, making himself aware of the needs of the patient and responding to him on the basis of those needs.

Jessie Taft (1933) came much closer to the writer's conception of the nondirective attitude in her description of her role in play therapy:

> The contacts ... were carried through, as far as I was humanly able, in terms of the child as she actually was at the moment, and my recognition of her immediate will, feeling or meaning. Everything centered in her, was oriented with regard to her. This does not mean that there were no checks but that even when my response was a prohibition, it was also a seeing of her, never a denial of the nature of her impulse or her right to have it. Where my own curiosity as to her behavior symptoms or my interest in bringing out certain material got the better of me, as it did occasionally, I abandoned it, as soon as I became conscious of my folly ... Interpretation there was none, except a verbalization on my part of what the child seemed to be feeling and doing, a comparatively spontaneous response to her words or actions which should clarify or make more conscious the self of the moment whatever it might be. (pp. 27–8)

The present writer (Raskin, 1948) has shown, in an unpublished paper on 'The Development of Nondirective Therapy', how Taft at times departed from the present feelings of the child as the focal point of her interest in the therapeutic hour.

Rogers (1946), in discussing the client-centered nature of the therapeutic relationship, has given definitive meaning to the nondirective attitude:

> The third distinctive feature of this type of therapy is the character of the relationship between therapist and client. Unlike other therapies in which the skills of the therapist are to be exercised upon the client, in this approach the skills of the therapist are focused upon creating a psychological atmosphere in which the client can work. If the counselor can create a relationship permeated by warmth, understanding, safety from any type of attack, no matter how trivial, and basic acceptance of the person as he is, then the client will drop his natural defensiveness and use the situation. As we have puzzled over the characteristics of a successful therapeutic relationship, we have come to feel that the sense of communication is very important. If the client feels that he is actually communicating his present attitudes, superficial, confused, or conflicted as they may be, and that his communication is understood rather than evaluated in any way, then he is freed to communicate more deeply. A

relationship in which the client thus feels that he is communicating is almost certain to be fruitful.

All of this means a drastic reorganization in the counselor's thinking, particularly if he has previously utilized other approaches. He gradually learns that the statement that the time is to be 'the client's hour' means just that, and that his biggest task is to make it more and more deeply true.

Perhaps something of the characteristics of the relationship may be suggested by excerpts from a paper written by a young minister who has spent several months learning client-centered counseling procedures:

'Because the client-centered, nondirective counseling approach has been rather carefully defined and clearly illustrated, it gives the "Illusion of Simplicity." The technique seems deceptively easy to master. Then you begin to practice. A word is wrong here and there. You don't quite reflect feeling, but reflect content instead. It is difficult to handle questions; you are tempted to interpret. Nothing seems so serious that further practice won't correct it. Perhaps you are having trouble playing two roles—that of minister and that of counselor. Bring up the question in class and the matter is solved again with a deceptive ease. But these apparently minor errors and a certain woodenness of response seem exceedingly persistent.

'Only gradually does it dawn that if the technique is true it demands a feeling of warmth. You begin to feel that the attitude is the thing. Every little word is not so important if you have the correct accepting and permissive attitude toward the client. So you bear down on the permissiveness and acceptance. You **will** permit[8] and accept and reflect the client, if it kills him!

'But you still have those troublesome questions from the client. He simply doesn't know the next step. He asks you to give him a hint, some possibilities; after all you are expected to know something, else why is he here? As a minister, you ought to have some convictions about what people should believe, how they should act. As a counselor, you should know something about removing this obstacle—you ought to have the equivalent of the surgeon's knife and use it. Then you begin to wonder. The technique is good, but ... does it go far enough? Does it really work on clients? Is it **right** to leave a person helpless, when you might show him the way out?

'Here it seems to me is the crucial point. "Narrow is the gate" and hard the path from here on. No one else can give satisfying answers and even the instructors seem frustrating because they appear not to be helpful in your specific case. For here is demanded of you what no other person can do or point out—and that is to rigorously scrutinize yourself and your attitudes towards others. Do you believe that all people truly have a creative potential in them? That each person is a unique individual and that he alone can work out his own individuality? Or do you really believe that some persons are of "negative value" and others are weak and must be led and taught by "wiser," "stronger" people?

'You begin to see that there is nothing compartmentalized about this method of

---

8. Raskin indicates that although the original reads as 'permiss', Rogers intended to write the word 'permit,' accounting for the correction in this essay.

counseling. It is not just counseling, because it demands the most exhaustive, penetrating, and comprehensive consistency. In other methods you can shape tools, pick them up for use when you will. But when genuine acceptance and permissiveness are your tools it requires nothing less than the whole complete personality. And to grow oneself is the most demanding of all.'

He goes on to discuss the notion that the counselor must be restrained and 'self-denying'. He concludes that this is a mistaken notion:

'Instead of demanding less of the counselor's personality in the situation, client-centered counseling in some ways demands more. It demands discipline, not restraint. It calls for the utmost in sensitivity, appreciative awareness, channeled and disciplined. It demands that the counselor put all he has of these precious qualities into the situation, but in a disciplined, refined manner. It is restraint only in the sense that the counselor does not express himself in certain areas that he may use himself in others.

'Even this is deceptive, however. It is not so much restraint in any area as it is a focusing, sensitizing one's energies and personality in the direction of an appreciative and understanding attitude.'

As time has gone by we have come to put increasing stress upon the 'client-centeredness' of the relationship, because it is more effective the more completely the counselor concentrates upon trying to understand the client *as the client seems to himself.* As I look back upon some of our earlier published cases—the case of Herbert Bryan in my book, or Snyder's case of Mr. M.—I realize that we have gradually dropped the vestiges of subtle directiveness which are all too evident in those cases. We have come to recognize that if we can provide understanding of the way the client seems to himself at this moment, he can do the rest. The therapist must lay aside his preoccupation with diagnosis and his diagnostic shrewdness, must discard his tendency to make professional evaluations, must cease his endeavors to formulate an accurate prognosis, must give up the temptation subtly to guide the individual, and must concentrate on one purpose only; that of providing deep understanding and acceptance of the attitudes consciously held at this moment by the client as he explores step by step into the dangerous areas which he has been denying to consciousness.

I trust it is evident from this description that this type of relationship can exist only if the counselor is deeply and genuinely able to adopt these attitudes. Client-centered counseling, if it is to be effective, cannot be a trick or a tool. It is not a subtle way of guiding the client while pretending to let him guide himself. To be effective, it must be genuine. It is this sensitive and sincere 'client-centeredness' in the therapeutic relationship that I regard as the third characteristic of nondirective therapy which sets it distinctively apart from other approaches. (Rogers, 1946: 419–21)

Robert D. Quinn was one of the earliest to stress the importance of this 'experiencing' therapist within a Rogerian rather than Rankian frame of reference. In an unpublished paper in 1946, he wrote:

> it is important to differentiate experiencing from knowing ... Knowing involves the acquisition of meanings and can be exclusively an intellectual process, that is, need not involve the whole individual as an acting, feeling, expressive self. Experiencing, in contrast, involves active interplay of affect with imagery—it is a dramatic living or reliving of the situation wherein the feelings expressed give the intellectual content its vitalizing substrata. Experiencing is always temporally in the immediate present since it postulates some form of interaction between the expressive self and the milieu. Knowing, on the other hand, occurs in a historical frame of reference, is oriented temporally to the past, and these new meanings need not involve reorganization of the acting self as it impinges upon the milieu.

In another cogent passage, Quinn wrote:

> Here then, is the central issue for a constructive therapy: It must have at its point of origin the relationship between the client and the counselor, for this is the only social contact initially available, except that within the client's own self, which is inevitably in too chaotic a state to permit of much genuine experiencing. This relationship must be such that the client can will freely, can feel freely, and can eventually come to clarify his own self concept. Clearly, this must be a relationship in which the self organization of the therapist is consistently denied representation. His contribution must be solely a sympathetic largess, a rapt attention intent only upon understanding and reaffirming the experiences of the client as he sees and feels them, and always at the rate and to the depth that the client himself chooses to undergo them. Thus, the sessions are literally cleared of obstacles inhibiting the client's experiencing, so that, in Rank's terms, he may come to make himself what he is ... will it and do it himself without force or justification and without need to shift the responsibility for it.[9]

Bown has shown a profound appreciation for the importance of deep counselor participation in the client's expression of feelings. He has emphasized the

> *struggle* to understand the feelings which are being expressed. It is a struggle because the counselor is making his most sincere attempt to reflect feelings which are being expressed in confused and uncertain fashion, which are only at the periphery of consciousness.
>
> ... the literature would indicate that many counselors hesitate to reflect any feeling which has not been made obvious to them by the client. They are making every effort to be completely nondirective, but it seems to me that

---

9. Rogers' note: 'Here it is the *client* who is experiencing & this I think is entirely right.'

they are missing the most fruitful opportunities to offer real, deep understanding as well as to provide an area of concentration in which clarification and insight can be achieved most readily ...

If this kind of response is untainted with subtle directiveness, it conveys to the client the most complete acceptance; the counselor is not merely repeating what is already obvious to the client, but rather, he is showing his willingness to struggle with the client for the real meaning, the true attitudes

This is warmth and the most genuine interest. This is the kind of counselor effort which puts method so far in the background that it can no longer be noticed by either client or counselor ... (Quinn, 1946, unpublished paper)

Through these quotations and through the writer's own description of the nondirective attitude, it is hoped that the reader has been given some feeling for what it is. The question now arises, 'What is the justification, the rationale for the nondirective attitude? Why use such a method, verging on the mystical,[10] which is completely contrary to the traditional approach of science, of medicine? Where does the need for it arise?' In the succeeding sections of this paper, the writer will attempt to answer these questions, and to show the implications of the attitude, not only for psychotherapy, but for education and other areas of human relationships, and for the study of personality.

II. INTEGRO[11] AND THE SELF-CONCEPT

Every bit of matter in the universe is a dynamic system, an organization of forces. Living matter is distinguished by a capacity within itself to reorganize its system in order to effect a better relationship with its environment; it is adaptive. Living animal matter has the additional capacity of a conscious[12] perception of its environment, on the basis of which, largely, it makes its adaptation to it. In the human being we find, in addition to all of these capacities, the perception of self as separate from the environment, the consciousness of self as the adaptive force in coping with the environment, and a resulting value which is placed on this self, based largely on the satisfaction obtained for the individual in its interaction with the environment. The self has the capacity to achieve a continuously better self and a continuously better relationship with its environment and it is conscious of this capacity, so that when this capacity is not being well utilized— in other words, when an unsatisfying relationship with the environment exists, with a consequently low value placed on the self by the self—we have the condition of maladjustment.

The capacity of people to integrate their perceptions into insights which are creatively

10. Here, Rogers underlined the word 'mystical' and wrote, 'vague, subtle, etc., but hardly mystical is it?'
11. This is a term coined by Nat Raskin.
12. Here Rogers underlined the word 'conscious' and wrote, 'Not all animals are conscious.'

utilized towards the achievement of a more satisfying adjustment has been keenly recognized in the following statement of Rogers (1946) as a result of his experiences in psychotherapy. For purposes of convenience, we shall term this capacity, 'integro'. It is quite similar to Rank's 'will.'

> As we examine and try to evaluate our clinical experience with client-centered therapy, the phenomenon of the reorganization of attitudes and the redirection of behavior by the individual assumes greater and greater importance. This phenomenon seems to find inadequate explanation in terms of the determinism which is the predominant philosophical background of most psychological work. The capacity of the individual to reorganize his attitudes and behavior in ways not determined by external factors nor by previous elements in his own experience, but determined by his own insight into those factors, is an impressive capacity. It involves a basic spontaneity which we have been loath to admit into our scientific thinking.
>
> The clinical experience could be summarized by saying that the behavior of the human organism may be determined by the influences to which it has been exposed, *but it may also be determined by the creative and integrative insight of the organism itself.* This ability of the person to discover new meaning in the forces which impinge upon him and in the past experiences which have been controlling him, and the ability to alter consciously his behavior in the light of this new meaning, has a profound significance for our thinking which has not been fully realized. We need to revise the philosophical basis of our work to a point where it can admit that forces exist within the individual which can exercise a spontaneous and significant influence upon behavior which is not predictable through knowledge of prior influences and conditionings. The forces released through a catalytic process of therapy are not adequately accounted for by a knowledge of the individual's previous conditionings, but only if we grant the presence of a spontaneous force within the organism which has the capacity of integration and redirection. This capacity for volitional control is a force which we must take into account in any psychological equation. (pp. 421–2)

With these preliminary remarks serving as an orientation, the following propositions may be advanced:

1. The human organism, from the first, responds in an adaptive way to its environment.
2. Through the differential responses which it receives to different ways of behaving—because it is treated as an organism with the power of choice in its behavioral reactions, and because it learns that by exercising choice in its behavioral reactions, it can obtain desired responses from the environment—the organism gradually becomes conscious of its power to perceive and to react to its environment differentially, in order to achieve satisfaction (integro). This is concomitant with the growing consciousness of the self. At the same time, through being evaluated by

336

others and by learning itself to evaluate its integro capacity, a value is placed on the self.

3. This self-concept, which consists of the organism's evaluative impression of itself, becomes an important determining factor in its behavior, in that the organism wishes to achieve the maximum value for the self.

4. From the external frame of reference, the self tends to be viewed as the whole person—its physical appearance, personality characteristics, abilities, etc. From the internal frame of reference, the concept of self consists of an evaluation of all these characteristics as they relate to helping the organism to cope with its environment; thus, it may be said to consist of integro and the value which is placed on it—this is the self as perceived; the self as perceiver is also within the consciousness of the internal frame of reference, but this is a self which is not evaluated: it serves as a point of reference, as an identifying symbol. Thus, in the statement, 'I just don't think much of myself', a common attitude among people seeking help, 'I' is the reference point, the unevaluated self, the perceiver, while 'myself' is the evaluated integro.

Philosophers through the centuries have bandied the concept of 'self' about and never achieved much progress, chiefly because there was no common operational basis for their definitions. Verbatim recordings of treatment interviews provide a wealth of material on the self as viewed from an internal frame of reference (IFR). It is on the basis of such data and the consistent use of the IFR that it is hoped that some common principles about the self-concept may be attained.

III. MALADJUSTMENT[13]

A person cannot be said to be maladjusted simply on the basis of an observer's judgment of his efficiency in relating to his environment; this is a very relative matter. The writer's view is that maladjustment exists when the self-concept is viewed from the IFR as being unsatisfactory, i.e., the individual is not content with his own capacity to adjust to the environment in a manner which will give him satisfaction. It is necessary, if maladjustment is to exist, that this dissatisfaction be referred by the individual to his general capacity to adjust, to integro, to the self-concept. This becomes clear when it is considered that a well-adjusted individual may experience occasional frustrations without inferring that he is inferior in a general way.

It is also clear that in maladjustment, the self-concept will be the focus of the individual's attention and energies a considerable part of the time. We may say that in a condition of adjustment, the integro of the individual is focused on the outside world, while in maladjustment, it is focused on the self. This is the same as Rank's view that the

13. Rogers is referring to this discussion of maladjustment in his note to Raskin, referenced in footnote number 2.

neurotic is 'ego-bound' and that to be cured he must learn to will, to use his creative energies in the world about him.

If it was correct to say that from the IFR, the self-concept is largely identified with integro, the inference may now be made that in maladjustment we have a condition where integro is focused on integro, inadequately regarded capacities are grappling with inadequately regarded capacities, an unacceptable self is attempting to deal with an unacceptable self. This creates a 'going-around-in-circles' picture which corresponds with the feelings actually reported by maladjusted people.

With the psychotic personality, it may be said that this struggle has been given up, the self is so hard to face that all of the individual's difficulties have been projected on the world.

IV. FACTORS INVOLVED IN READJUSTMENT

When we wish to change even an inanimate organization, we must take into account what its present system of forces is. Any dynamic system can be changed only on its own terms; we must start with what it is and any changes must be based on the capacities of that present organization.

Anybody who wishes to change a maladjusted human being to a condition of adjustment must reckon with this factor. But in trying to change the attitudes of a human, an even more powerful force must be contended with. It derives from the fact that a person has within himself the capacity for change, for achieving a more satisfactory adjustment; he has his own integro. In other words, the individual himself holds the key to any change in himself.

Now even when the integro is weak, as is the case when a person is maladjusted, the person will seek jealously, so to speak, to utilize it—if only in a negative way—rather than accept the creative ideas of another in reference to himself. Thus, typically, a client will appear, asking for answers to his dilemmas. If answers are proposed, rather than accept them, he will utilize his creative energies in an effort to tear them down. This unwillingness to use another's integro is a fundamental fact which has too often been glossed over in the field of mental hygiene. 'He doesn't know what he wants' is a popular way for the interviewer to respond to such a situation, but this is obviously a superficial and inadequate explanation which ignores the client's IFR. In the terms of this paper, the explanation is not hard to find. The maladjustment *is* the dissatisfaction with integro; it is not simply the frustrations of many unsolved problems, but the pinning of the responsibility for the frustrations on a central factor, the self. Obviously then, satisfaction will not come with solutions to specific problems, but only with a different way of looking at the self which will result in satisfaction for the individual. This may come through an actually strengthened integro where in therapy the client comes to perceive his difficulties, grapples with them, and acquires confidence in himself through their successful solution. Or it may come through a re-evaluation of the self-concept, independent of the solution of any specific problem, in which the formerly unacceptable self becomes acceptable. But dissatisfaction with integro can never be converted to satisfaction through another's answers.

When the writer above cited the general fact of resistance to the use of another's integro, the question of the very dependent person will have occurred to many readers. It is true indeed that we can find people in this category who will not openly resist the solutions of another, but will actively seek and utilize them. But what of such a person's adjustment? Are we helping it any, or are we merely furthering his dependency, by providing him with answers? In the writer's terms, the dependent person is one with very weak integro, with such a weak concept of self that it will be very difficult for him to face it, but the only real help he can get *is* to face himself with his dependency and strive to overcome it, to strengthen his integro. We will find that dependent people can do this, with the integro they have; that their dependency has been accompanied all along by a deep hostility toward those who got in the way of their becoming people in their own right.

If integro, the growth force, or what have you, is such a widespread and powerful thing, it may be asked: why do we have clients coming in for help in the first place? Why do we have very dependent people who will accept the solutions of others? The answer is that to use integro, especially when one is maladjusted, is a painful process. It is painful to examine an inadequate self, to reconstruct it, to try out a new one.

Where does environmental treatment fit into this formulation? Cannot the independent capacities of the self be strengthened through placing the individual in the right kind of environment? Will not a good job, a good home placement, strengthen the maladjusted person? On first impulse, the answer to such questions is a simple affirmative. But on looking closer at what is involved, complicating issues emerge.

For one thing, a good job, a good home, a good environment, are not 'good' in the absolute sense. They are good as far as some of us are concerned, and good in ways which are different for each individual who lives in these environments. What we are getting at is that an individual who is dissatisfied with himself, and consequently with the world, is going to be very difficult to please with an environment provided by somebody else. We all look at the world through our own special brand of glasses, and the person who feels maladjusted will not have his rose-colored. We go at the problem in a much more basic way when we give the self an opportunity to change; then, instead of introducing certain specific environmental changes, the effects on the individual of which, are difficult to predict, we are providing an opportunity for a really sweeping environmental change, for the person who leaves therapy feeling satisfied with himself sees the whole world differently, and uses exactly the same (from the external frame of reference) conditions in a much more constructive way.

Another, perhaps less basic question connected with environmental treatment is the question of where the counselor stops helping. Recently the writer actively helped a person he was counseling—a very dependent one—to get a job. During the next interview, the client wished help on such problems as whether or not to take his own lunch to work with him, what to do if his supervisor asked him to do something he didn't know how, etc. And didn't he really have a right to get such help from the counselor because the latter had gotten him into the work situation? If you try to explain to such a client why you can help him with certain problems and not with others, you cannot, because you cannot give yourself a satisfactory answer to that question. The only answer for the writer to this problem is to let the person help himself from the very beginning; to the extent that he is helped by your specific solutions, to that extent you are hurting his chances for self-actualization.

V. OBJECT AND PROCESS

We are changing, developing organisms interacting with other changing, developing organisms in a changing, developing world. For some reason, through necessity or perhaps convenience, in interacting with different parts of this dynamic environment, we often tend to ignore their process aspects and treat them as static objects: we peg them, freeze them. The words we use are an example of our attempt to deal with our environment by 'freezing' the various processes of which it consists. Practically all organizations we set up—factories, schools, schedules—are examples of the same tendency.

What is so bad about identifying and organizing processes in this way? Well, whenever we treat something in a way which ignores its real characteristics, we are making an error, and sometimes the error is a very great one. It is not so bad when we call two things 'apple' when one is a Washington Winesap and the other is a Delicious. It is a little more serious when we identify the man who cleans our office as 'porter' and forget that he may have attitudes and a family and psychological needs just like ours. Or when we label a man 'psychopath' or 'paranoid schizophrenic' and forget that he has feelings which are just as real to him as ours are to us.

It is a convenient thing to set up plane schedules so that we can know at what time we can take off for Los Angeles; but it's not quite the same thing when we organize course schedules and decide that at 9 o'clock every Monday, Wednesday and Friday Professor Smith will lecture on Abnormal Psychology to the class in Psychology 111. The error there is that on many of these mornings, there will be many a student who will not be the least bit interested in hearing about Abnormal Psychology from Professor Smith, or from anyone else perhaps, and the learning which is supposed to take place will not occur. And it may be well to recognize that though it is very efficient to set up factories so that each of us who can afford it may have a smooth-running, six-cylinder automobile, the hundreds of thousands of fellows who are making the automobiles by doing the same job over and over again, year after year, are not developing their creative capacities.

In other words, our culture is shot through with examples of how we treat the people in it as objects, while in fact they are dynamic organisms with changing attitudes and with potentially improving abilities. The meaning of this for psychology and psychotherapy is obvious. If we are in the business of helping maladjusted people to become adjusted, let us not pigeonhole, peg, freeze, make objects out of them. We above all should be aware of the human being's feeling, changing, dynamic, adaptive, creative capacities.

This is not a straw man that the writer is setting up. This is no imagined danger. The standard way of treating human beings in mental hygiene practice today is as objects. He sits across the desk from us and we think, 'What has he got? What is his trouble? How did he get this way? Didn't that sound schizy? I feel sorry for his kids. There he goes, using me as a father figure,' etc. It is not our fault that we examine people in this way. We have been trained in the method of finding out what people are like in order that we may then help them. How can we treat intelligently unless we first diagnose? We have to find out what their symptoms are, what their needs are, what personality formation they have, how their present condition developed. But do we?

VI. THE NEED FOR THE NONDIRECTIVE ATTITUDE IN PSYCHOTHERAPY

When we take a diagnosing attitude toward our mental hygiene patients—when, in other words, we treat them as objects—we are doing more than misjudging what we are dealing with; we are doing more than making an object out of a dynamic process.

The effect we have is to change the nature of that process. When we look at a person as an object, we in fact help to make an object out of him. For when a person becomes aware that he is being examined he ceases to develop his own attitudes, but immediately takes a defending attitude. He strives to maintain what he is now. And so he tends actually to become an object.

This is even more true when, in therapy, we try to change the client in some way. If he does not submit, he resists, he maintains and defends his present system of attitudes. If he does change with the will of the therapist, his adjustment capacity and self-respect are weakened.

Thus, the effect of taking the diagnosing and changing attitudes towards our clients is to discredit their own capacities for change. For when we diagnose, we imply that we are going to do the changing, and when we try to do the changing, we are not giving the client a chance to do it.

In terms of the integro concept which was developed earlier in this paper, integro is stifled when the diagnosing or object attitude is adopted, and it ceases to operate in a positive way when the attempt is made to change the client, to influence him according to another's will. And if integro is not given an opportunity to operate in a positive way, if the client does not get a chance to perceive and act on his concept of self in an atmosphere free of threat, this concept of self is not going to change very much, and the individual will continue in a maladjusted state.

If we cannot diagnose, if we cannot advise our clients, what is there left for us to do? We return now to Quinn's distinction between knowing and experiencing which was quoted in the first section of this paper. The alternative to trying to know our client, which is equivalent to treating him as object, is to experience with him, to try to understand what it is that he is feeling at the moment, and to communicate that understanding to him. The alternative is to become part of the dynamic process which

341

our client represents and so to accept that process for whatever it is at the present time—weak, poor, inadequate, doubtful, confused, or whatever it happens to be.[14] And somehow,[15] the vicious circle of weak integro working on weak integro, of poorly regarded and unacceptable self grappling with poorly regarded and unacceptable self, is thus broken. The process, having been accepted in the unsatisfactory state, moves towards a more stable, comfortable condition in a manner which might be termed homeostatic.

To relate what has been said here with our description of the nondirective attitude is now a simple task. The nondirective attitude is *the* method of experiencing with the client, which allows no opportunity for trying to *know* him. Thus, integro is given the maximum opportunity to function and the self-concept is given the best chance of becoming a satisfactory part of an adjusted individual. The three levels of nondirection discussed in our introduction to the nondirective attitude represent various degrees of the 'knowing' approach, and so constitute various degrees of impediment to the integrative and creative capacities of the client in the reconstruction of his concept of self.

VII. PSYCHOTHERAPY AND GENERAL MEDICINE

The nondirective attitude constitutes for psychotherapy an approach quite at variance with that of the physician, whose standard method of procedure is to diagnose and then treat. Why should a psychotherapeutic approach be different?

The difference lies in the fact that in general medicine we deal with conditions of the human body which are subject to volitional control only in a very indirect way, while in psychotherapy we have to do with behavior and with attitudes, both of which are highly subject to the will. The hypothesis may be ventured that in any aspect of living which is governed by the will, the most efficient method of achieving a comfortable state is to accept the will or attitudes of the individual concerned; while in those areas that are relatively independent of volitional control, another's creative capacities may be utilized without difficulty.

Conditions formerly thought to be purely of a physical nature are coming more and more to be recognized as connected with psychological forces. The origins of these psychosomatic disturbances may well prove to be connected with disturbances of the concept of self. If this is true, the treatment of psychosomatic conditions should rely heavily on the nondirective attitude. At the same time it would seem to be necessary, in the case of any suggested organic disturbance, that a diagnostic study be made to evaluate the physical basis of the complaint. If a physical basis is established, the study will have justified itself. If a physical basis is not found, and the inference is made that the condition is of a psychological origin, then the study, with its total neglect of the patient's integro, with its implication that 'doctor will take care of things,' will have had a detrimental

---

14. Rogers' note: 'Very good.'

15. Rogers' note: 'How? And because we become temporarily a part of his process, from within, and accept his weakness, he too can bear to look at and accept it.'

effect on further treatment; but in our present state of knowledge, this would appear to be a cost which must be borne.

The attitudes of patients are important even in straight medical practices. Rogers (1946) has cited the changes made by one medical practitioner in recognition of the importance of the patient's point of view.

> The viewpoint appears to have implications for medicine. It has fascinated me to observe that when a prominent allergist began to use client-centered therapy for the treatment of non-specific allergies, he found not only very good therapeutic results, but the experience began to affect his whole medical practice. It has gradually meant the reorganization of his office procedure. He has given his nurses a new type of training in understanding the patient. He has decided to have all medical histories taken by a nonmedical person trained in nondirective techniques, in order to get a true picture of the client's feelings and attitudes toward himself and his health, uncluttered by the bias and diagnostic evaluation which is almost inevitable when a medical person takes the history and unintentionally distorts the material by his premature judgments. He has found these histories much more helpful to the physicians than those taken by physicians. (p. 422)

VIII. THE NONDIRECTIVE ATTITUDE AND EDUCATION

Psychological practices were introduced into education by Pestalozzi, Herbert, and others with the aim of making more efficient the task of teaching facts to individuals. Of more recent origin, the idea of educating people to become well-adjusted citizens who can function efficiently as individuals and as members of the community, as opposed to the notion of making them storehouses of facts, has been stressed by Dewey, Rugg, Prescott, and others. The nondirective attitude, with its stress on individuality and the ability of people to organize their perceptions in ways which are best for them, fits in well with this more modern aim, while it may, at the same time perhaps, have implications for efficiency in the teaching of facts.

Tentatively, it might be said that therapy is largely a matter of learning about oneself. Education, on the other hand, at least by the way it is generally organized today, deals with learning about the world. This distinction accounts for the fact that a large amount of material is learned under the prevailing system of education, despite the fact that most of this material originates with the teacher. A psychotherapist who tried to use the equivalent approach to teach a client about himself would not get far.

Does the fact that information which is not closely related to the concept of self can be absorbed without too much resistance mean that the present educational approach is satisfactory, even though it is at variance with our therapeutic philosophy? Before answering this question, let us examine the relation between the two fields of education and psychotherapy more closely.

In both cases we are dealing with a dynamic, creative, adaptive system engaged in an activity of acquiring new concepts. Can we not make the generalization that to be absorbed, any new concepts must have meaning for the system as it exists at present and must not be at variance with the creative and adaptive tendencies of the system? To learn Freud, for example, the student must be able to relate Freudian concepts to his present system of knowledge, and these concepts must not be too opposed to his present system of values, upon which is based his manner of behaving and the direction in which he is developing. Students of nondirective therapy who have extensive backgrounds in diagnostic techniques and in a diagnostic approach to treatment commonly experience difficulty in acquiring the nondirective method. Similarly, those who believe deeply in the nondirective philosophy sometimes find that learning new diagnostic methods such as the Rorschach test is no easy matter.

This fact—that in order for learning to take place, the new knowledge must be in accordance with the content and direction of the present dynamic system, which the learner represents—means that a good curriculum cannot be good in itself, but must be evaluated in relation to each individual learner.

A further fact of considerable importance is that learning takes place not simply over a period of time, but at a particular moment, which means that the learning system must jibe with the concepts to be acquired at the moment of impact.

If these principles are correct, it follows that present educational practice is highly inefficient. For in general, the matching of student knowledge and attitudes with curriculum takes place at a distance very far removed from the actual moment of learning. In general elementary-school practice, the attitudinal aspects are practically ignored, and a crude system of grade levels and of curricula which are based on a logical development of ideas, supposedly of general application, are the methods of matching present pupil knowledge with new ideas to be learned. In high school, the attitudinal aspects are dealt with largely by having the student choose the area of specialization and by allowing him a small number of elective courses. This system is continued and expanded at the college and university levels. But even the elective course, as it is usually taught, is still far removed in its organization from the conditions which have been described as necessary for learning. The typical moment in a typical hour will see the instructor trying to get across an idea which *he* may regard as important, an idea related to a course organization which *he* may have constructed, a course organization which may have real meaning for *him* in *his* scheme of living, or may be a relatively separate construct, divorced from his behavior goals. In this type of instruction, the number of students who will relate the concept being presented to *their* life activity, in any way other than to memorize it for an examination which they must pass, is going to be very small indeed.

Fact absorption under the present educational system, which emphasizes *teaching* rather than learning, which devotes more energy to building curricula than to studying the learning process, has been proved by follow-up studies, by public opinion polls, and by everyday observation of others and of ourselves, to be notoriously inefficient. The writer hopes that he has been able partially to account for this inefficiency.

But fact absorption is no longer the key goal of education, at least among the more advanced thinkers in the field. How may we evaluate the present system insofar as it produces independent, well-adjusted, useful, public-minded citizens? The answer becomes clear and the question farcical even as it is being stated. Most citizens do not meet this description very well. But why should they, having been brought up in an educational system in which they were taught to spend all of their time and energy doing homework *for* a teacher; in which a high value was placed on conformity to this pattern; in which individual creative thinking and the development of their individual system of attitudes and knowledge was given no encouragement but had to be subordinated to assigned work, to learning someone else's system of knowledge; in which their individual problems of learning and of general adjustment were buried in the mass process of outward conformity; in which as a result, they were forced to stew unproductively in their own juice and to utilize much of their energies in an unconstructive opposition to the patterns being imposed on them, leaving little inclination, time or energy for them to become active, interested members of the social groups of which they were a part?

Again, it must be asked, what is the alternative to present procedures? The answer would seem to lie in the direction of greater recognition of the creative, self-directive capacities of students, by revising classroom method and structure in a way which will provide an opportunity for individual students to express and develop their own attitudes and to clear up questions regarding factual material. We may proceed on the principle that both education and psychotherapy are processes of self-development which will function most efficiently when the present state of development, as viewed by the subject, is understood and accepted by the teacher or therapist. The nondirective attitude will therefore, by implication, belong in the classroom as well as in the therapeutic situation. It will not take exactly the same form in the educational environment because of the group situation, because the attitudes expressed will not be so consistently related to the individual's concept of self and will, therefore, not be as intense or deep, and because of the limits imposed by the institution in which the learning is taking place. Despite these conditions, the attitude is definitely practicable in the educational field, with Cantor (1946), Rogers (1946: 421), Blocksma and Porter (1947) and Shedlin (1947) all having utilized it to a very great extent, on the higher education level.

IX. IMPLICATIONS OF THE NONDIRECTIVE ATTITUDE FOR THE STUDY OF PERSONALITY

Rogers (1947) has pointed out the implications that experiences in nondirective therapy have for the study of personality. His main thesis is that behavior will be better understood and predicted if the point of reference used in our investigations is the subject's IFR.

The nondirective attitude is related to this point of view in the following ways:

1. Interviews in which the nondirective attitude is employed by the therapist yield material rich in depth and meaning for the client. Interviews of this nature have a minimum of counselor-originated ideas and counselor-influenced client concepts.

2. Nondirective interviews, because of the freedom provided for the positive operation of client integro, provide an unusual opportunity to observe the dynamic, adaptive, creative qualities of human personality, as the client is seen to deal with the self, and with problems which have the utmost of meaning for him.

3. If the assumption is granted that psychological reality for any individual consists of his feelings about, and his perceptions of, the world (including himself) at any given moment, the nondirective attitude provides the closest possible approach of another to psychological reality.

A corollary of this hypothesis would be that the most valid generalizations of a psychological nature would be those made on the basis of material obtained by employing the nondirective attitude with large numbers of people. If, further, it is granted that phenotypical data consisting of a subject's feelings and perceptions of the world at any given moment provide all the necessary data needed to predict his behavior at that moment, then it follows that data collected through the use of a nondirective attitude furnish the best means of predicting behavior.

In terms of general semantics, data provided by the nondirective attitude are at a low-order level of abstraction, close to reality, in contrast with high-order level of abstractions such as Rorschach 'C', 'M', 'affect', 'experience balance', 'shading shock', etc. It stands also in favorable contrast to the high-order level of abstractions provided by genotypical attempts to explain human behavior and personality, as, for example, the Freudian type of explanation.

X. THE NON-INTELLECTUAL NATURE OF THE NONDIRECTIVE ATTITUDE

Intellectually, the nondirective attitude can be explained in a matter of a few sentences. On the surface, it appears that nondirective therapy would be a very simple technique to learn. This is not the way it works out, even given very intelligent people who are well adjusted, eager to learn, and with fine backgrounds in psychological theory and in human relations experience. It has become clear that learning nondirective therapy is not a matter of acquiring technique, but of gradually gaining the conviction that people do not have to be guided into adjustment, but can do it themselves when accepted as they are. Blocksma and Porter (1947) have outlined some of the stages that counselors in training in the nondirective method can be observed to go through. These phases are similar to those observed in clients who are treated in nondirective therapy.

It is not surprising that learning this method and philosophy is a slow process. For acceptance is one principle of human relationships which does not run very deep in our culture. From the time we are born, others begin to determine our needs for us and, as we have seen, this continues through the school years, and many of us have the type of employment which sees the same pattern at work. In terms of other concepts that have been employed in this paper, it may be said that we have been taught to know, use or be used by other people, rather than experience with and accept them. This long-standing pattern of behavior, this deeply ingrained attitude, is not going to easily absorb a new idea which means new ways of behaving and looking at things.

REFERENCES

Blocksma DD & Porter EH Jr (1947) A short-term training program in client-centered counseling. *Journal of Consulting Psychology, 11*(2), 55–60.

Bown OH Unpublished paper.

Cantor N (1946) *The Dynamics of Learning.* Buffalo, NY: Foster and Stewart.

Quinn RD (1946) Unpublished paper.

Rank O (1936) *Will Therapy.* New York: Knopf.

Raskin NJ (1948/2004) The development of nondirective therapy. *Journal of Consulting Psychology, 12*, 92–110. In NJ Raskin (2004) *Contributions to Client-Centered Therapy and the Person-Centered Approach.* Ross-on-Wye: PCCS Books, pp. 1–27.

Rogers CR (1942) *Counseling and Psychotherapy: Newer concepts in practice.* Boston: Houghton Mifflin.

Rogers CR (1946) Significant aspects of Client-Centered Therapy. *American Psychologist, 1,* 415–22.

Rogers, CR (1947) Some observations on the organization of personality. *American Psychologist 2*(9), 357–68.

Shedlin, AJ (1947) A student-centered class. *Personal Counselor, 2*(2), 116–31.

Taft, J (1933) *The Dynamics of Therapy in a Controlled Relationship.* New York: Macmillan.

CONTRIBUTORS

THE EDITOR

Brian E. Levitt, PsyD, CPsych trained at the Chicago Counseling and Psychotherapy Center, the center that grew from Carl Rogers' work at the University of Chicago. After trees years of training at the Center, including a post-doctoral fellowship, he joined the staff as a therapist and trainer. He trained for two years at the Pre-Therapy Institute in Chicago, under the tutelage of Garry Prouty, earning certification in the practice of Pre-Therapy. Already licensed as a clinical psychologist in the United States, he underwent additional training after emigrating to Canada, respecializing as a rehabilitation psychologist. Currently, he maintains an independent practice in Toronto and Hamilton, Ontario. Contact Brian at brianlevitt@yahoo.com.

THE CONTRIBUTORS

Jerold D. Bozarth, PhD, is Professor Emeritus of the University of Georgia where his tenure included a decade as Chair of the Department of Counseling and Human Development and Counseling Psychology. He was also Director of the Person-Centered Studies Program and Director of Rehabilitation Counseling. He has been a consultant and advisor to a dozen international person-centered training programs including programs in England and Brazil. He has published over 350 articles and book chapters and is the author of *Person-Centered Therapy: A Revolutionary Paradigm* and co-editor of *Rogers' Therapeutic Conditions, Vol. 3: Unconditional Positive Regard.*

Barbara Temaner Brodley, PhD, is an adjunct professor at the Illinois School of Professional Psychology, Argosy University and has a private practice of client-centered therapy. She received her doctorate in clinical psychology at the University of Chicago where she was on the staff of the Counseling Center, founded by Carl Rogers. She has published many articles that express her interest in preserving recognition of non-directive client-centered therapy as a continuing form of effective psychotherapy.

Jeffrey H.D. Cornelius-White, PsyD, is an assistant professor of psychology at Missouri State University. He teaches primarily in a Masters of Counseling Psychology program and is an activist, cyclist, and husband. Jef is the managing editor of the *Person-Centered Journal* and an associate editor of the *Journal of Border Educational Research*. His scholarly and community work have been primarily concerned with person-centered and multicultural counseling, education, and social reform.

Cecily F. Cornelius-White has recently departed her position as an Assistant Professor of Psychology at Texas A&M International University in favor of more domestic pursuits. She currently teaches part-time at Missouri State University, and serves as a full-time mother to her baby daughter, Avery. Cecily is the book review editor for the *International Journal of Clinical and Experimental Hypnosis* and treasurer for the Society of Clinical and Experimental Hypnosis. Her interest areas include yoga, mind-body health, person-centered parenting, and changing diapers.

Françoise Ducroux-Biass After an eclectic journey through genetics, theology, linguistics and pedagogy, due to family circumstances, Françoise Ducroux-Biass finally trained at the Person-Centered Institute International founded by Carl Rogers, Charles Devonshire and Alberto Zucconi. She now is a practicing psychotherapist and supervisor in Geneva. She also is a trainer for a French Institute and a founding member of the European Association for Counselling. She co-authored and edited a multilingual glossary of Genetics and published a paper on interdisciplinary pedagogy.

Marvin Frankel received his PhD from the University of Chicago; completed his Clinical internship in client-centred therapy at the Counseling Center of the University of Chicago, and his Postdoctoral fellowship at the Educational Testing Service, Princeton, NJ. His special interest is in conflict, lying, self-deception and propaganda. He is the author and co-author of several articles including a chapter on Skinner's approach to personality, morality and psychotherapy and decision making, as well as a one-act play, *The Ventriloquist*. He is currently working on a book, 'Reflections on Teaching The Final Solution'. He has been a member of the Sarah Lawrence College since 1972.

Elizabeth Schmitt Freire is a Brazilian psychologist, with an MA in Clinical Psychology. She is currently completing a PhD in Developmental Psychology at the Universidade Federal do Rio Grande do Sul (Porto Alegre, Brazil) and developing part of her doctoral studies at the University of Strathclyde in Glasgow, UK. She is a person-centered therapist and one of the Directors of Delphos Institute, Brazil, where she coordinates the person-centered training program—the first person-centered program to be accredited by the professional body of Psychology in Brazil. She has published a book in Portuguese with Newton Tambara on theory and practice of client-centered therapy and other articles and chapters published in English. She has a fifteen-year-old daughter and loves to play the piano in her leisure time.

Barry Grant, PhD, is an Associate Professor and Chair of the Professional Counseling Program at the Texas School of Professional Psychology, Argosy University, Dallas. He has been thinking about the relationship between ethics and education and psychotherapy for twenty-five years. He can be reached at bag@runbox.com.

John K. McPherrin, PsyD, has been a staff psychologist at the University of Chicago Student Counseling and Resource Service since 2002. Concurrently, he has operated a private practice in downtown Chicago since 1998. John completed his degree at the Illinois School of Professional Psychology in 1995 and trained at the Chicago Counseling and Psychotherapy Research Center from 1990–1997. During that time he was influenced by Margaret Warner, Marge Witty, Anne Brody, Barbara Brodley & Hannah Frisch. John has practiced client-centered therapy with individuals, couples, families and groups in a variety of settings, and has had the joy of teaching it at both the Illinois and Chicago Schools of Professional Psychology.

Kathryn A. Moon is a therapist in the client-centered practice group that has devolved from the original Chicago Counseling Center. She has a passion for unfacilitated large group meetings and is intrigued by questions pertaining to family and couples therapy. She received her BA at the University of Chicago in 1973, MALS in Library Science in 1976, and her MA in Clinical Psychology at the Illinois School of Professional Psychology in 1989. She is involved in training programs for the Chicago Counseling and Psychotherapy Center and is an adjunct faculty member at the Illinois School of Professional Psychology.

C.H. (Pat) Patterson received his AB in sociology from the University of Chicago in 1938, his MA in child psychology in 1945 and his PhD in counseling psychology in 1955, both from the University of Minnesota. He is Professor Emeritus of the University of Illinois, where until 1978 he was chairman of the counseling psychology program and director of the rehabilitation program. He was president of the American Psychological Association, Division of Counseling Psychology (1972–73) which presented him with the Leona Tyler Award in 1994.

Dr Garry Prouty was trained in person-centered/experiential psychotherapy by Eugene Gendlin of the University of Chicago and developed his own therapeutic approach, 'Pre-Therapy', dealing with psychotic and retarded clients. He is the author of *Theoretical Evolutions in Person-Centered/ Experiential Therapy: Applications to schizophrenic and retarded psychoses* and co-author of the German text *Prä-Therapie*. He is the founder of the Pre-Therapy International Network, a European organization for working with psychotic persons. He has delivered the Frieda Fromm-Reichman Memorial Lecture at the Washington School of Psychiatry. In 2004 he was awarded a 'Lifetime Achievement Award for Pre-Therapy' by the Chicago Psychological Association. He was elected President of the Chicago International Society for the Psychological Study of Schizophrenia, and has been nominated as Scientific Associate to the American Academy of Psychoanalysis and Dynamic Psychiatry.

Nathaniel J. Raskin began graduate work with Carl Rogers at Ohio State University in 1940 and received his PhD at the University of Chicago in 1949. He taught at Hunter College, New York University and Columbia University Teachers College and was Director of Research Planning at the American Foundation for the Blind from 1952–57. He completed his academic career at Northwestern University Medical School and since 1991 has been Emeritus Professor of Psychiatry and Behavioral Sciences. He was Carl Rogers' student, associate and friend for 47 years until Rogers died in 1987.

Peter F. Schmid is Associate Professor at the University of Graz, Austria; Faculty Member of Saybrook Graduate School and Research Center, San Francisco; person-centred psychotherapist; practical theologian and pastoral psychologist; founder of person-centred training in Austria; director of the Academy for Counselling and Psychotherapy of the Austrian Institute for Person-Centred Studies and Board Member of both the World Association (WAPCEPC) and the European Network. He has authored and co-authored twelve books and numerous articles about the anthropology and further developments of the person-centred approach in German and English. He is co-editor of *Person-Centered and Experiential Psychotherapies*, the journal of WAPCEPC and of the international German language journal *PERSON*. Website www.pfs-online.at.

Lisbeth Sommerbeck, received her MSc from the University of Copenhagen and her accreditation as a specialist in psychotherapy and supervision by the Danish Psychological Association. She initiated the founding of the Danish Carl Rogers Forum in 2002. Since 1974, she has worked in a small psychiatric hospital, primarily occupied with individual therapy, supervision and teaching. Her special interest is in the application of the person-centred approach with staff and inmates in the 'backyards' of psychiatry. She is the author of articles on the non-directive attitude in client-centred therapy and on the 'Wisconsin Project', as well as *The Client-Centred Therapist in Psychiatric Contexts* (PCCS Books, 2003).

Sue Wilders writes: I first became interested in the person-centred approach in 1992 while working as an Outreach Worker with injecting drug users. Since then I have qualified as a client-centered therapist and continued, in various capacities, to work with drug and alcohol users as a person-centred practitioner. I currently manage a drug and alcohol service for a charity in London where I have begun to develop a wholly person-centred way of working and I am excited that the service may soon undertake a research project into the effectiveness of person-centred ways of working with this client group. In addition to the above I maintain a small private practice. Contact Sue at suewilders@yahoo.co.uk.

Marjorie Witty has been practicing client-centered therapy since 1974. She is an Associate Professor at the Illinois School of Professional Psychology and served on the staff of the Chicago Counseling and Psychotherapy Center.

INDEX

PCCS Books

The largest list of person-centred titles in the world

www.pccs-books.co.uk

• browse by subject and author •

• discounts on all orders •

• free p&p in the UK •

• low cost shipping worldwide •